AN
INTRODUCTORY
ENGLISH
GRAMMAR

AN INTRODUCTORY ENGLISH GRAMMAR

FOURTH EDITION

NORMAN C. STAGEBERG
University of Northern Iowa

Harcourt Brace Jovanovich College Publishers
Fort Worth   Philadelphia   San Diego
New York   Orlando   Austin   San Antonio
Toronto   Montreal   London   Sydney   Tokyo

Library of Congress Cataloging in Publication Data

Stageberg, Norman C.
  All introductory English grammar.

  Includes index.
  1. English Language—Grammar—1950-
I. Goodman, Ralph M. II. Title.
PE1112.S7   1981   425   80-29334
IBSN 0-03-049381-1

Printed in the United States of America
  5 6 7 8 9 0 059 20 19 18 17 16 15

to the Instructor

This is a college textbook of English grammar. It is essentially a structural grammar, with borrowings from transformational grammar and from European scholarly traditional grammar.

The limitations of a one-volume grammar must be acknowledged. No one has ever written a grammar describing completely the English language. The fullest grammars are those of Poutsma and Jespersen, running respectively to five and seven bound volumes; and these—admirable as they are and packed with fine material—do not cover the ground.* We must therefore expect that a single volume can at best present only the central features of English grammar and offer methods of description students can use in analyzing any further data they may collect. And we must expect to find rigorously curtailed or omitted altogether those refinements, exceptions, moot points, and extended developments that might be included in a comprehensive grammar. Thus this book does not pretend to completeness of coverage or to a set of inviolable grammatical statements. The fact is that for most if not all of the generalizations that you will meet here, or in any compact grammar, counterexamples are plentiful.

Let us illustrate counterexamples in the area of adjectives. If you point out to your class that one-syllable adjectives are compared with *-er* and *-est,* a dormant figure in the back row is likely to emerge from his or her cocoon long enough to inquire, "What about *mere* and *due?*" If you show that adjectives not compared with *-er* and *-est* will take *more* and *most* as substitutes, someone will call your attention to words like *dental* and *lunar.*

---

* H. Poutsma, *A Grammar of Late Modern English,* 5 vols. (Groningen, The Netherlands: P. Noordhoff, 1904–1926). Otto Jespersen, *A Modern English Grammar on Historical Principles,* 7 vols. (London: George Allen and Unwin, 1909–1949). A comprehensive grammar of 1120 pages has appeared in recent years: Randolph Quirk, Sidney Greenbaum, Geoffrey Leech, and Jan Svartik, *A Grammar of Contemporary English* (New York: Academic Press, Inc., 1972).

If you use the common frame sentence

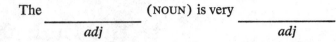

The _____ (NOUN) is very _____
        adj   *adj*

as a key to adjectives, you may have to face up to *alone* and *unable,* which do not occupy the first slot, and to *principal* and *olden,* which do not occur in the second one. If, following the usual rule, you say that the position for a single attributive adjective is before, not after, its noun head, the expressions *money necessary* and *something bad* may be cited. If you mention the well-known fact that adjectives are modified by qualifiers like *very,* an enterprising student may remind you of *daily* and *weekly.*

This kind of situation can and should be handled openly and honestly. Students must be made to realize early in the course that a grammatical generalization or rule is a descriptive statement of customary, not universal, usage. If the counterexamples are few, they can be listed as exceptions. If they are numerous and follow a pattern, the rule can be refined. If they are limited to a particular region, to a certain social group, to some trade or profession, or to an age or sex group, they can be assigned to the group that habitually uses them. Thus a class can, by its own observations, elaborate the basic grammar presented here. As a result those who go on to teach English grammar in the schools may be less dogmatic and more respectful of language data, however recalcitrant, than if counterexamples had been ignored or forced into a Procrustean bed.

Definitions also present a problem. A grammar is a closed system, a circle. Wherever one begins in this circle, say at X, it is necessary to use undefined terms. But if one goes back to W to cover these terms, there will be still other terms that need defining. And so one can go backward around the circle until X is reached again. Thus undefined terms are inevitable. In this book I have tried to devise an effective order of presentation with as few undefined terms as possible.

The exposition in this book advances by short-step progression, with an exercise after nearly every step. I have chosen this method because I believe that students must work actively with the language if they are to achieve a firm understanding of it. The exercises are self-corrective, providing students with immediate feedback.

A question may arise here. If the explanations are clear—and I have done my best to make them so—and if the exercises are provided with answers, what is there left for the instructor to do in the classroom? At the risk of expounding the obvious, permit me to mention a few classroom procedures that have been found useful.

1. **Preteach most lessons.** This will hold attention because the material is new. In preteaching it is sometimes valuable to proceed inductively: present examples of a principle to be learned, and by questioning, help your students to formulate the principle for themselves. When a class has successfully groped its way to the understanding of a grammatical principle,

that principle is likely to remain firmly fixed in mind. When your students study the lesson by themselves after preteaching, they will not be intimidated, because they are traversing known and friendly territory.

2. Ask for questions on the text and on the exercises. The answers to the exercises on the phonology in particular will evoke questions, for the student, when asked to write a given word in phonemic script, will sometimes record a pronunciation different from that shown in the answer. This is entirely normal because of the dialectal and idiolectal variations among speakers of English. For example, if you have your students pronounce in turn the word *wash,* they are very likely to produce at least these three pronunciations: /waš/, /wɔš/, and /wɔrš/. Students should be shown at the beginning that all persons do not pronounce English in exactly the same way.

3. During the first unit, on phonology, have daily transcription practice. This will sharpen auditory perception and develop a ready command of the phonemic symbols.

4. Have your class furnish original illustrations of the grammatical concepts presented in the text. The search for and discussion of such illustrations may help to strengthen understanding more than the performance of preshaped exercises.

5. Have your students justify their answers in those exercises which ask for the what but not the why. In this way you can find out which students really understand what they are doing.

6. Give the class short exercises, like those in the book, as a check on comprehension.

N. C. S.

Cedar Falls, Iowa
October 1980

Acknowledgments

Acknowledgments can never be made to all those who have nourished one's intellectual life. Chief among these, in my case, are the classroom teachers who have given me sustenance and have kindled the desire for more knowledge, and the linguists from whose books, articles, and monographs I have learned much.

For particular works I owe an especially heavy debt of gratitude to three linguists. Ilse Lehiste's *An Acoustic-Phonetic Study of Internal Open Juncture* furnished the information for my pages on internal open juncture. Archibald A. Hill's chapter on phonotactics in his *Introduction to Linguistic Structures* is the source of my treatment of the distribution of phonemes. James Sledd's *A Short Introduction to English Grammar* suggested the pattern for the double-track system of parts of speech that I have adopted.

In addition there are the professional meetings, conference discussions, correspondence and chats with colleagues—all these have furnished grist to the mill: a felicitous example, an apposite phrase, a new insight, a challenging position. These enter into one's intellectual bloodstream and become part of one's being; eventually their origin is lost. For all such, my thanks to the unknown benefactors.

Professor Andrew MacLeish of the University of Minnesota taught parts of the material in prepublication form and offered useful suggestions for improvement. Professor Ralph Goodman, my colleague at the University of Northern Iowa, brought the keen eye of a transformationist to bear on the text and offered valuable criticisms. Professor Frederick G. Cassidy of the University of Wisconsin read the final draft of the first edition with meticulous care and called attention to matters that needed correction or revision. Professors Harold B. Allen of the University of Minnesota and W. Nelson Francis of Brown University read the first draft of the phonology and made thoughtful suggestions that resulted in an improved treatment. Professor Valdon Johnson of the University of Northern Iowa pointed out typos and other errors that he discovered in classroom teaching of the third edition. The Committee on Research at the University of Northern Iowa, under the chairmanship of Professor Gordon Rhum, kindly gave financial assistance for the construction of teaching materials which, after classroom use, were incorporated into this book. To all these scholars I am deeply indebted for their friendly assistance.

I am also grateful to Professors Daniel Amneus, California State College of Los Angeles; Adolf Hieke, University of Northern Iowa; and Susan S. Yost, Methodist College of Fayetteville for their helpful suggestions and criticisms.

In addition eight professors who used the third edition sent critical comments to the publishers, who forwarded the letters to me while preserving the anonymity of the writers. Many of these comments were penetrating and relevant and have been incorporated in the present edition. Their names—though I do not know who said what—are as follows: Dorothy Sedley, West Virginia University; John Haskell, Northeastern Illinois University; Michael Haltresht, Corpus Christie State University; Alexandra Olsen, University of Colorado; Ann Johnson, Jacksonville University, Alabama; Janet Sawyer, Long Beach State College; Nancy Brilliant, Kean College; Robert O'Hara, University of South Florida.

Diagrams 6 and 7 have been reprinted with permission of the Regents of the University of Wisconsin from Professor R.-M. S. Heffner's *General Phonetics,* 1950, published by the University of Wisconsin Press. To them and to Professor Heffner I am obliged.

In stressful moments of struggle with a grammatical problem, both student and teacher may receive solace from these words of a great grammarian:

> In English the grammarian's path is strewn with scores of insoluble difficulties when he begins to put asunder what nature has joined together into one case; by 'nature' I mean the natural historical development of the English language.

Otto Jespersen,
SPE Tract No. xvi, *Logic and Grammar,* p. 16

Contents

PART II

THE SYNTAX OF ENGLISH 187

to the Student

At this very moment you have an excellent command of English grammar. This is an operational command that functions below the threshold of awareness. As you speak, you select—with little conscious thought or effort—the precise forms and arrangements of words that signal the meanings you wish to express. The process is almost automatic.

Now you are about to undertake a systematic study of the structure of this language that you handle so easily. Your situation is not unlike that of a skillful automobile driver who is about to begin a course in auto mechanics. But there is this difference: the English language is a machine vastly more complex than the finest car you could buy. And when you have completed this study of your language, you should have a good idea of what makes it go.

As you progress through this book, you will be given exercises at each step along the way. These are necessary and should be done with care, for they will enable you to get a firm grasp of matters that you might otherwise only half learn and quickly forget. The answers to these exercises are in the back of the book. As soon as you have finished each exercise, correct it. If you have made any mistakes, restudy the text to master the points that you did not learn on your first attempt.

There are two dangers for you in this procedure. An exercise may seem so easy that you will be tempted to do it orally instead of writing it out. This seems harmless enough, but it will exact its penalty later on. Research in programed learning reveals that students who work orally know as much at the time as those who do the writing; but several months later those who have faithfully written out their work show a higher retention rate.

The second danger is that you may merely use the answers instead of thinking through the exercises for yourself. But you cannot master the complexities of language by only reading about them any more than you can learn to swim by studying a textbook on swimming. You must work actively with the language itself, and this is what the exercises give you a chance to do.

Finally, the material in this course is cumulative. Each day you will build upon what you have previously learned. This means that you must work regularly, not by fits and starts. In the author's classes, to the best of his knowledge, every student who has done his work faithfully has earned a grade of C or better. And many have done exceedingly well. Why not you too?

PART I
THE PHONOLOGY OF ENGLISH

1
The Production and Inventory of English Phonemes

A descriptive structural grammar of English progresses upward through three levels of structure. The first or lowest level deals with the system of speech sounds employed by native speakers of English. The study of this level is called *phonology*. The next higher level is concerned with the meaningful forms made from the individual speech sounds. Generally speaking, we may say that it deals with words and their meaningful parts. This is the realm of *morphology*. The top level treats of the ways in which words are arranged to form sentences, and here we are in the area of *syntax*. Hence we begin our study of English grammar at the first level, with a consideration of the speech sounds of English.

At the outset, as we approach our study of English phonology, we must bear in mind two important facts.

First, language itself is ORAL—it lives on the lips and in the ears of its users—and writing is a visual symbolization of language itself. To realize that language is independent of writing, we have only to recall the many tribes, nations, and ethnic groups whose members possess no form of writing but whose LANGUAGES are being avidly studied today by linguistic scientists and anthropologists. When we study the grammar of a language through the medium of writing, as we shall do in this book, we must often supplement the writing with special marks to indicate the stresses, pitches, and breaks of oral speech; and sometimes we must replace writing with a different set of symbols to represent the sounds of the living voice.

Second, the English language as spoken in the United States is not uniform. It is made up of numerous dialects and subdialects, about which our knowledge is yet far from complete. In addition, each person has individual modes of expression that are unique. These modes comprise what we càll an *idiolect*. Thus every person speaks an idiolect that is not quite the same as the speech of any other individual. We have chosen to present here the phonology of what is called Inland Northern English.

The lack of uniformity of spoken English will soon become apparent as you do the exercises in which you represent your own pronunciation; for your pronunciation will differ in some respects from that of your classmates and from the author's Inland Northern, which is the form given in the answers. Do not be concerned about "correct" and "incorrect" pronunciation. Any pronunciation that is in normal use among the educated speakers in YOUR community is "correct."

A. The Speech-Producing Mechanism

Speech sounds are sound waves created in a moving stream of air. They are disturbances of the medium such as you would observe if you were to drop a stone on the quiet surface of a pool. The air is expelled from the lungs, passes between the two vocal cords in the larynx (Adam's apple), and proceeds upward. As you will note on diagram 1, this moving stream of air has two possible outlets. It can pass through the nasal cavity and emerge through the nose, or it can pass through the oral cavity and come out through the mouth. But why doesn't it go through both passages, which are shown to be open on the diagram? Because in speech one of them is ordinarily closed.

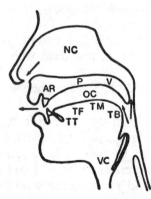

AR	Alveolar ridge
NC	Nasal cavity
OC	Oral cavity
P	Hard palate
V	Velum, or soft palate
TT	Tongue tip
TF	Tongue front
TM	Tongue middle
TB	Tongue back
VC	Vocal cords

Diagram 1　Speech-producing mechanism.

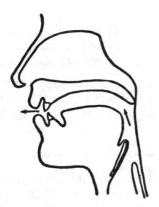

Diagram 2
Air passing through oral
cavity. Tongue position for /a/.

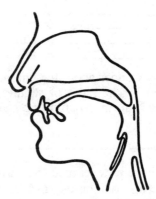

Diagram 3
Air passing through nasal
cavity. Lip position for /m/.

How does this happen? Let us consider the oral sounds first. On diagram 1 you will notice the velum, marked V. This is a movable curtain of flesh. If you run your finger back along the roof of your mouth, you will feel at first the bony structure of the hard palate, marked P. Just behind this hard palate you will feel the soft flesh of the velum. It ends in a pear-shaped pendant, called the uvula, which you can see hanging in your throat if you look in the mirror. Now, when you produce any oral sound, one that goes through the mouth—for example, *a-a-a-a-a-a-a*—you at the same time raise the velum until it touches the back of the throat, closing the nasal cavity. You can actually see this raising of the velum if you will open your mouth wide, flash a light into your mouth, look in the mirror, and say *a-a-a-a-a-a* several times in succession. The process is illustrated in diagram 2.

Now let us turn from the oral sounds to the nasals, those that pass through the nasal cavity. To make the three nasal sounds of English, you leave the velum in the position shown on diagram 1 and block off the oral cavity in one of three ways: with the lips (diagram 3), with the tongue tip (diagram 4), or with the tongue back (diagram 5). Thus, with the oral cavity blocked off, the sound can emerge only through the nasal cavity. It is evident now that every speech sound we utter is either an oral or a nasal sound. For illustration try exercise 1.

Exercise 1–1
As you pronounce the following words, hold the final sound for some time. As you hold the final sound, stop your nose with your fingers. If this action stops the sound, the sound is obviously a nasal. But if the sound continues, close your lips. The sound will thereupon be cut off, demonstrating that it

is an oral sound. After each word write "nasal" or "oral" to label the final sound.

1. rim _____ 4. see _____ 7. trim _____
2. saw _____ 5. sing _____ 8. pain _____
3. bin _____ 6. tall _____ 9. wrong _____

You may wonder about the "nasal twang" that you occasionally hear. This is caused by the habit of slightly lowering the velum for sounds that are normally oral, thus permitting some of the air to go out through the nasal cavity.

You have now learned the three nasals of English, which we symbolize in a special notation as /m/, /n/, and /ŋ/. The /m/ is a bilabial nasal, made by closing the two lips. The /n/ is an alveolar nasal, made by stopping the flow of air with the tongue tip against the alveolar ridge. The /ŋ/ is a velar nasal, made by stopping the flow of air with the back of the tongue against the velum. In all three the air moves through the nasal cavity. They are illustrated on diagrams 3, 4, and 5.

But one element is missing from our description of the three nasals. Where does the sound come from? To answer this question we must examine the vocal cords.

Inside the larynx (Adam's apple) are two short bands of flesh and muscle stretching from front to rear. In breathing and during the production of some speech sounds, like /f/ and /s/, these bands are held open, allowing free ingress and egress of air, as shown in diagram 6. But with many sounds they are pressed together, and the air passing between them causes them to vibrate, as shown in diagram 7. These vibrations are given reso-

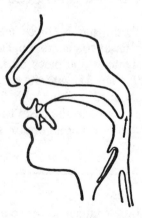

Diagram 4
Air passing through nasal
cavity. Tongue position for /n/.

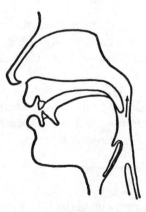

Diagram 5
Air passing through nasal
cavity. Tongue position for /ŋ/.

Rear

Rear

Diagram 6
Position of vocal cords
during exhalation.

Diagram 7
Position of vocal cords
when vibrating.

Reprinted with permission of the copyright owners, the Regents of the University of Wisconsin, from R.-M. S. Heffner, *General Phonetics*, 1950, the University of Wisconsin Press.

nance by the cavities of the mouth and nose, and the result is the phenomenon called voicing. In the making of every speech sound, then, these vocal cords are either vibrating or not vibrating. If they are vibrating, the sound is called voiced. If they are not vibrating, the sound is called voiceless. An exercise will illustrate.

Exercise 1–2
Hold your hands tightly over your ears and pronounce the last sound in each of the following words. Write "voiced" after those during the pronunciation of which you hear the vibration of your vocal cords, which will sound like a strong hum. Write "voiceless" after those during the pronunciation of which such vibration is absent.

1. less _____   4. pin   _____   7. mush _____
2. hum _____   5. sheath   8. fin   _____
                                    (noun) _____
3. if   _____   6. among _____   9. song _____

We see now that to our description of the three nasals we must add the fact that each one is voiced, that their sound comes from the vibration of the vocal cords.

Let us now turn for a moment to examine the voicing or voicelessness of speech sounds other than the nasals. As we pointed out above, every speech sound is either voiceless or voiced. The next two exercises will give you practice in distinguishing these two kinds.

Exercise 1–3
Pronounce the first sound in the following words with your hands over your ears. Write "voiced" after each word in which you hear the hum of your

vocal cords during the pronunciation of this first sound. Write "voiceless" after those that are pronounced without the hum.

1. fine _____	4. then _____	7. shock _____
2. vine __voiced__	5. seal __voiceless__	8. late __voiced__
3. thin __vo___	6. zeal _____	9. rate _____

Exercise 1–4

This is a little harder. Do the same as you did in exercise 1–3, but be very careful to keep the first sound in each word separate from the one that follows in the same word.

1. pin __voiceless__	3. time _____	5. coon __voiceless__
2. bin __voiced__	4. dime _____	6. goon _____

By this point, from the foregoing discussion of nasals, orals, and voicing, you should have acquired a working knowledge of these parts of the speech-producing mechanisms: nasal cavity, oral cavity, lips, alveolar ridge, hard palate, velum, tongue tip, tongue back, and the vocal cords. Test yourself by writing these terms in the appropriate places on diagram 8. Verify your answers by consulting diagram 1, and correct any errors.

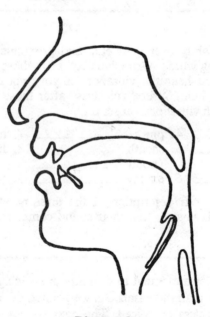

Diagram 8

B. The Phoneme

Before continuing with an inventory of English speech sounds and the ways of producing them, we must clearly understand one basic concept—the phoneme.

The phoneme is a speech sound that signals a difference in meaning. Consider, for example, the words *dime* and *dine*. They sound exactly alike except for the /m/ and the /n/, yet their meanings are different. Therefore it must be the /m/ and /n/ that made the difference in meaning, and these two nasals are thereby established as English phonemes. Likewise, if we compare the sounds of *sin* and *sing*, we find only one difference between them: *sin* ends in the alveolar nasal /n/ and *sing* in the velar nasal /ŋ/. (Don't be deceived by the spelling of *sing;* the letters *ng* represent a single sound /ŋ/, one that you can prolong as long as your breath holds out.) This contrast is evidence that /n/ and /ŋ/ are both phonemes. Pairs of words like those above which demonstrate a phonemic contrast are called minimal pairs.

Exercise 1–5

After each minimal pair write the phonemes that are established by the sound contrast between them. Be sure to contrast pronunciations, not letters. Since you have not yet learned most of the phonemic symbols, use letters to represent the phonemes.

1. pin ____	6. rattle ____	11. sad ____
bin ____	tattle ____	sat ____
2. big ____	7. fine ____	12. made ____
dig ____	vine ____	make ____
3. late ____	8. zoo ____	13. tool ____
rate ____	too ____	tomb ____
4. pill ____	9. hot ____	14. fate ____
kill ____	got ____	feign ____
5. go ____	10. sick ____	15. thin ____
so ____	wick ____	thing ____

A phoneme may be pronounced in different ways, depending on its position in the utterance, and still remain the same phoneme. As an example, let us take /l/. If you pronounce *lit* and *well* slowly and distinctly, you will hear two different [l]s. The second one seems to be preceded by an "uh" sound. With a little practice you can place your tongue tip on the alveolar ridge and change from the first to the second [l] without moving the tongue tip. Now, if you pronounce *well* with the [l] of *lit*, the word will sound different, a little unEnglish, but the meaning will not be changed. The use of one or the other of these two [l]s never makes a difference in meaning; hence they are not two phonemes but merely variants of the /l/ phoneme. You will sometimes hear still another [l] in words like *play* and *sled*. Here there may be a voiceless [l̥], whereas the [l]s of both *well* and *lit* were voiced. But whether you pronounce *play* and certain other words with a voiced or a voiceless [l], the meaning remains unchanged; so this third [l̥] is another variant of the /l/ phoneme.

Such variants of a phoneme are called allophones. (Allophones are enclosed in brackets with the occasional addition of diacritical marks to indicate the exact pronunciation. Phonemes are enclosed in slants.) Thus we may say that the /l/ phoneme has three allophones: [l] as in *lit*, [ɫ] as in *well*, and [l̥] as in *play*. A phoneme then is not an individual sound but a small family or class of similar sounds.

Let us consider one more case to illustrate the concept of phoneme and allophones. Pronounce *how* and *huge* slowly, prolonging the initial *h* in each word. You will probably discover that the *h* of *how* is breathy whereas the *h* of *huge* has a scraping, frictional, almost hissing sound.[1] But though these two *h*'s do not sound the same, the difference in sound never makes a difference in meaning. Each is heard as an *h*, and the difference in sound goes unnoticed. This is to say they are allophones of the /h/ phoneme.

In contrast let us look at two Dutch words, *heel*, meaning very, and *geel*, meaning yellow. The *h* of the Dutch *heel* is pronounced the same as the breathy *h* of the English *how;* the *g* of the Dutch *geel* is pronounced the same as the scraping *h* of the English *huge*. It is this difference in pronunciation between these two Dutch *h*'s that distinguishes between the two words of the minimal pair *heel–geel*.[2] Thus these two *h* sounds that were allophones in English are phonemes in Dutch.

With this introduction to the concept of the phoneme, we are now ready to examine the inventory of English phonemes.

C. The English Phonemic System: Vowels

The classification of English vowels is a complex and controversial matter; it is even difficult to define a vowel with precision. But we can make four statements about vowels that will help to show their nature:

1. Vowels are oral sounds. In some dialects and in certain contexts vowels may become partially nasal, but normally they are orals, not nasals.
2. Vowels are voiced.
3. Vowels are characterized by a free flow of air through the oral cavity.
4. The distinguishing features of the different vowels are determined largely by tongue position.

English may be said to have twelve vowels—five front, four back, and three central vowels—which we shall now take up systematically.

---

[1] This scraping *h* is the same as the last sound in German *ich*. It is possible that you may use the breathy *h* in both words, but many persons make the difference described here.

[2] These two Dutch words rhyme with the English *sale*.

FRONT VOWELS

If you pronounce the final sound of *be,* symbolized by /i/, and hold the /i/, you will find that the tongue front and middle are humped high in the mouth, leaving a narrow passage for the flow of air between the hard palate and the surface of the tongue. The tongue position of /i/ is the top one on diagram 9.

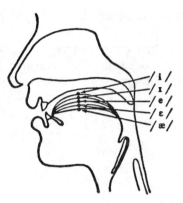

Diagram 9   Front vowels.

Next, say the same vowel /i/, holding your jaw in your hand, and then say the first sound of *add,* symbolized by /æ/. You will observe a considerable drop of the jaw and some flattening of the tongue. The tongue position of the vowel /æ/ is the bottom one on diagram 9. To fix these differences of position in your mind, hold your jaw and say /i/, /æ/ rapidly a number of times in succession.

Between the two extremes /i/ and /æ/ are three other vowels. To hear them in order from the top tongue position to the bottom one, pronounce the following words, noting the middle sound: *beat, bit, bait, bet, bat.* Now say just the vowels in the same order, holding your jaw, and observe how the jaw drops a little as each one is uttered. These five vowels are called the FRONT VOWELS, because they are formed in the front of the mouth by the position of the tongue front. For each front vowel the lips are spread, or unrounded. The tongue positions and the symbols for them are indicated on diagram 9.

English spelling cannot be used to represent accurately the speech sounds of English because of its inconsistencies. How, for example, would you symbolize the vowel of *bait* in English spelling? By *ai* as in *wait, eig* as in *reign, ey* as in *they, ay* as in *say, a* as in *late, ei* as in *vein, au* as in *gauge, ea* as in *steak?* So, to represent the sounds of words, we shall use a special alphabet in which one symbol always represents one and the same phoneme, and each phoneme is always represented by only one symbol. In this alphabet the five illustrative words in the preceding paragraph are written as follows:

beat = /bit/
bit = /bɪt/
bait = /bet/
bet = /bɛt/
bat = /bæt/

The symbols and words written in these symbols are enclosed in slants, like /bæt/.

In exercise 1–6 you are given transcription practice employing the five front vowels and six consonants. The phonemic symbols for these eleven sounds are written as follows:

/i/	m*eet*	/p/	*p*ie
/ɪ/	m*itt*	/b/	*b*y
/e/	m*ate*	/t/	*t*en
/ɛ/	m*et*	/d/	*d*en
/æ/	m*at*	/k/	*c*ob
		/g/	*g*ob

Exercise 1–6

In the second column transcribe the words in the first column as you normally pronounce them. The first two are done to show you how.

1. pack __pæk__	11. beak _____	21. get _____
2. cape __kep__	12. big _____	22. gate _____
3. Pete _____	13. date _____	23. gat _____
4. pit _____	14. debt _____	24. back _____
5. pate _____	15. kick _____	25. bake _____
6. pet _____	16. cap _____	26. tap _____
7. pat _____	17. peck _____	27. tape _____
8. keep _____	18. pick _____	28. tip _____
9. kid _____	19. peek _____	
10. cat _____	20. gad _____	

BACK VOWELS

Pronounce the final sound of *too,* symbolized by /u/. For this vowel, /u/, the lips are rounded and the back of the tongue is raised to a place near the velum, leaving a little space for the air to flow. The tongue position is the top one on diagram 10.

Now pronounce the sound you make when you say "aw," as in "Aw,

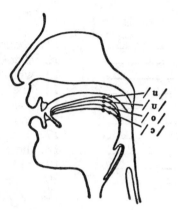

Diagram 10 Back vowels.

come on." For many Americans this is the vowel of *saw, raw,* and *jaw.*[3] It is symbolized by /ɔ/, like a backwards *c.* The tongue position is the bottom one on diagram 10 Next, utter the vowels /u/ and /ɔ/ in rapid succession, with your hand on your jaw. This will show you the upper and lower extremes of the range of the four vowels that are called back vowels. If you will look in the mirror while uttering the successive /u/s and /ɔ/s, you will see the close rounding of the lips for /u/ and the open rounding for /ɔ/.

As the back of the tongue is lowered from the /u/ position, it reaches in turn the positions for the three other back vowels: /ʊ/ as in *pull,* /o/ as in *note,* and /ɔ/ as in *ought, law,* and *ball.* And at each of these three positions the rounding of the lips is successively opened, as you can observe in the mirror. The four back vowels, from top to bottom, are illustrated by this series:

fool = /ful/
full = /fʊl/   also, cookie = /kʊki/
foal = /fol/
fall = /fɔl/

In exercise 1–7 you are given transcription practice in the four back vowels and are introduced to nine new consonants. The phonemic symbols for these thirteen sounds are written as follows:

/u/ as in b*oo*m /f/ as in *f*ine /z/ as in *z*eal
/ʊ/ as in b*oo*k /v/ as in *v*ine /š/ as in *sh*un
/o/ as in n*o*te /θ/ as in *th*in /ž/ as in a*z*ure
/ɔ/ as in *aw*e /ð/ as in *th*en /h/ as in *h*ow
        /s/ as in *s*eal

---

[3] This vowel /ɔ/ is not present in some American dialects.

Exercise 1–7

Transcribe the following words.

1. food	_____		11. voodoo	_____
2. foot	_____		12. shook	_____
3. foe	_____		13. who	_____
4. fought	_____		14. hoe	_____
5. shoe	_____		15. zone	_____
6. show	_____		16. zoo	_____
7. though	_____		17. thought	_____
8. thaw	_____		18. those	_____
9. soup	_____		19. oath	_____
10. ought	_____		20. vision	_____

(Use /ə/ for the second vowel.)

CENTRAL VOWELS

English has three central vowels. The first one is a mid-central vowel symbolized by /ər/. This vowel requires special consideration. If you pronounce *fur, sir, her,* you are uttering, as the final sound, a mid-central r-colored vowel, that is, if you belong to the majority of Americans who do not "drop their r's." But there are other Americans who use an /ə/ (the vowel of *up*) plus an r sound in words like *squirrel* /skwərəl/ and *hurry* /həri/, instead of using the single r-colored vowel. Thus we shall use the pair of symbols /ər/ to represent both pronunciations—the single r-colored vowel and the /ə/ plus an r-sound. It is the highest vowel in diagram 11.

The second central vowel may be illustrated by the first sound of *up* and *upon.* It is written /ə/, like an upside-down *e,* and its position is shown in

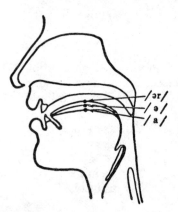

Diagram 11 Central vowels.

diagram 11. It is heard as the pronunciation of the italicized vowels in the following words:

Stressed: s*u*n, d*o*ne, fl*oo*d
Unstressed: sof*a*, *a*lone, kingd*o*m, c*o*nnect, s*u*ppose, hunt*e*d, ros*e*s, garb*a*ge

The /ə/ is a vowel of high frequency in English, especially in unstressed syllables, and is technically called *schwa*. Sometimes it approaches an /ɪ/ in pronunciation.

The third central vowel is the sound you make when the doctor says, "Open your mouth and say *a-a-a-a*." For most Americans this is the vowel of *not* and the first vowel of *father*. It is symbolized by /a/. In sounding this vowel you will note that the mouth is widely opened and that the tongue is nearly flat. The tongue position is the bottom one in diagram 11. The three central vowels, from top to bottom, are illustrated by this series:

nurse = /nərs/
nut   = /nət/
not   = /nat/

In exercise 1–8 three new consonant symbols are added to your repertoire. The phonemic symbols for these six sounds are written as follows:

/ər/ bird	/č/ churn /čərn/
/ə/ up	/ĵ/ judge /ĵəĵ/
/a/ pot	/r/ rap /ræp/
	hear /hɪr/
	part /part/

Exercise 1–8
Transcribe in phonemic symbols the following words as you normally pronounce them.

1. purr	pər	7. started	
2. murder		8. folded	
3. children		9. regard	
4. fear		10. herd	
5. churches		11. hurt	
6. rubs		12. hut	

Exercise 1–9
Transcribe in phonemic symbols the following words as you normally pronounce them.

1. urge		6. above	
2. stop		7. bird	
3. cut	kət	8. rust	
4. sofa	sofə	9. run	
5. rug		10. birch	bərč

11. leisure	_____	16. pocket	_____
12. urban	_____	17. today	_____
13. odd	_____	18. cupboard	_____
14. afféct (verb)	_____	19. journey	_____
15. efféct (noun)	_____	20. hot	_____

The twelve vowel phonemes of English can be seen in relation to one another on the vowel chart in diagram 12, a two-dimensional grid of tongue positions, the mouth being at the left and the throat at the right. Using this chart we can easily give to the twelve vowels descriptive names that will be useful in discussing them:

/i/   High-front   /ər/ Higher mid-central /u/ High-back rounded
/ɪ/   Lower high-front /ə/ Lower mid-central /ʊ/ Lower high-back
/e/   Higher mid-front /a/ Low-central   rounded
/ɛ/   Lower mid-front   /o/ Mid-back rounded
/æ/   Low-front   /ɔ/ Low-back rounded

This classification of vowels by tongue position is imprecise and generalized. Their relative positions, however, are correct. Also, there are further classifications—tense, lax; close, open; narrow, wide; long, short—that we are bypassing in the interest of a stringent simplicity. But by and large the above description and classification of vowel phonemes—though limited—will serve our purpose.

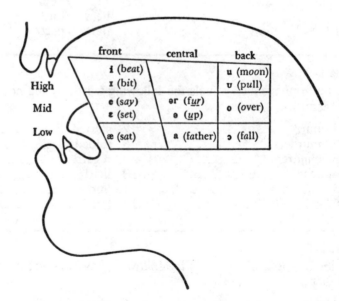

Diagram 12   Chart of English vowel phonemes.

THE SYLLABLE

Before moving ahead to the next group of phonemes, the diphthongs, **it** is necessary to examine the nature of the syllable.

When we speak, we can observe that certain sounds have a greater sonority or carrying power than others. For example, in *soap* /sop/, the /o/ has greater sonority than the /s/ or the /p/, even though all are spoken with equal force. If /sop/ is spoken at some distance, the listener may hear distinctly only the /o/. In *potato* /pəteto/, the /e/ and /o/ are more sonorous, more audible, than the /p/ and the /t/s. The sounds that have this greater inherent sonority or carrying power are mostly the vowels. Thus, as we utter connected discourse, we become aware of a peak-and-valley effect of sonority or audibility. The peaks of sonority are the vowels; the valleys of less distinctness are the consonants, as in *echo* /ɛko/, or the slight diminution of loudness, as in *create* /kri-et/. This brings us to the syllable. A syllable is a sound or a short sequence of sounds that contains one peak of sonority. This peak is usually a vowel, and the vowel is said to be the nucleus of the syllable. A segment of speech, then, contains as many syllables as there are peaks. Here are some examples of words with the peaks, or syllabic nuclei, underlined.

One syllable:	be	/bi/
	string	/strɪŋ/
Two syllables:	believe	/bəliv/
	being	/biɪŋ/
	stirring	/stərɪŋ/
Three syllables:	believing	/bəlivɪŋ/
Four syllables:	unbelieving	/ənbəlivɪŋ/
Five syllables:	unbelievingly	/ənbəlivɪŋli/

Exercise 1–10

Transcribe the following words in phonemic symbols, underline the peaks, and indicate how many syllables each word has.

Word	Transcription	No. of Syllables
Example: spoonful	/spunful/	2
1. seat	_____	_____
2. infect	_____	_____
3. paper	_____	_____
4. disenchant	_____	_____
5. unostentatious	_____	_____

We have seen that vowels are peaks of sonority and are therefore syllabic nuclei. But there are four consonants—/m/, /n/, /ŋ/, and /l/—that also have considerable sonority and that can be syllabic nuclei.

As our first example, let us take the two-syllable expression *stop 'em.* This can be uttered in two ways. The first is /stap əm/. After the lips are closed to make the /p/, they are opened for the /ə/ and closed again for the /m/. But there is a second way. Here the lips are closed for the /p/ and remain closed for the /m/. Try it and see for yourself. While you are making the /p/, no air can escape from the mouth. The closed lips shut off the mouth exit and the raised velum shuts off the nasal exit. Now, holding the lips closed, you open the velum by lowering it, and what happens? The air escapes with a slight explosion through the nasal cavity, producing an /m/. Here the /m/ is a peak of sonority and by itself constitutes a syllable. This /m/ is called a syllabic /m/.

Oral Exercise 1–A
Practice saying these expressions, using for the last syllable both (1) a schwa plus /m/ or /n/ and (2) a syllabic /m/.

      1. leap 'em
      2. rob 'em
      3. open

The syllabic /n/ is formed similarly. Consider, for example, *button*. You may pronounce it /bətən/ by dropping the tongue from the /t/ position on the alveolar ridge, uttering the /ə/, and then replacing the tongue for the /n/. But you can also pronounce *button* without removing the tongue. At the /t/ position the air is prevented from escaping by the tongue against the alveolar ridge and by the closed velum, which shuts off the nasal cavity. If you hold the tongue in the /t/ position and open the velum, you will get an /n/ as the air escapes through the nasal cavity. This is a syllabic /n/.

Oral Exercise 1–B
Practice saying these expressions, using for the last syllable both (1) a schwa plus an /n/ and (2) a syllabic /n/.

      1. beaten
      2. cotton
      3. sudden

The syllabic /ŋ/, which is less frequent, is heard in expressions like *Jack and Jill*, /jækŋjɪl/. At the /k/ position the air is held in by the back of the tongue against the velum and by the velum, which has been raised to cut off the nasal cavity. With a lowering of the velum, the nasal cavity is opened and the syllabic /ŋ/ is heard.

Oral Exercise 1–C
Practice saying these expressions in two ways. After the /k/ or /g/ position, use first the schwa plus an /n/, and then the syllabic /ŋ/.

1. back and forth
2. bag and baggage
3. rack and ruin

The syllabic /l/ is somewhat differently articulated. To make the common /l/, you place the tongue on the alveolar ridge, vibrate the vocal cords, and let the air flow over and off the tongue on one or both sides and escape through the mouth. To make the syllabic /l/, as in *rattle,* you first have the air completely closed off by the tongue in the /t/ position on the alveolar ridge and by a raised velum cutting off the nasal cavity. Then you open one or both sides of the tongue, without removing the tip from the alveolar ridge, activate the vocal cords, and let the air go around the tongue and out the mouth.

Oral Exercise 1–D
Pronounce the following words in two ways, using for the last syllable both (1) a schwa plus /l/ and (2) a syllabic /l/.

1. cattle
2. saddle
3. beetle

Although it is easy to locate the peaks of sonority that indicate syllabic nuclei, the vowels and syllabic consonants, it is sometimes impossible to find the boundary between syllables—that is, the point of minimum sonority. In the two-syllable *hushing* /həšɪŋ/, for example, where is the syllable boundary? After the /ə/? Before the /ɪ/? Or in the middle of /š/? It is like trying to establish in a valley the exact line separating the two hills on either side. For our purpose here we need not be much concerned with syllable division, and where the boundary is not audible, we can resort to an arbitrarily selected break.

DIPHTHONGS
A diphthong consists of a vowel plus a glide that occur in the same syllable, the tongue moving smoothly from one position to the other without hiatus, as in *sigh,* /say/, *sow* (female pig), /saw/, and *soy,* /sɔy/. The two sounds together represent the peak of sonority, though one always has greater prominence than the other. Many of our vowels are diphthongized

in various subareas of English, and four of them are normally diphthong-ized in Standard English: /i/, /e/, /u/, and /o/. For these, however, we shall use the symbols just given, since there is no phonemic difference be-tween the pure vowels and the diphthongized vowels.[4] According to the system we are using, the diphthongs are only three: /ay/ as in *by*, /aw/ as in *bough*, and /ɔy/ as in *boy*. All three are subject to considerable dia-lectal variation. For example, /ɔy/ is pronounced /oy/ by many speakers of Northern; /aw/ becomes /æw/ in the South and South Midland; /ay/ becomes /əy/, and /aw/ becomes /əw/, in parts of Canada.

Exercise 1–11

Transcribe the following words into phonemic symbols, using your own natural pronunciation.

1. my ___	6. joy ___	11. high ___	16. try ___
2. toy ___	7. chives ___	12. ouch ___	17. stripe ___
3. how ___	8. thou ___	13. mighty ___	18. rowdy ___
4. tie ___	9. shy ___	14. roil ___	19. Kilroy ___
5. cow ___	10. rye ___	15. coy ___	20. destroy ___

Under the heading of "diphthongs" we shall give attention to the knotty problem of the r sounds. You have already met the /r/ consonant, as in *race* /res/, and the higher mid-central r-colored vowel, as in *cur* /kər/. This leaves us to consider the r sound that occurs after vowels in the same syllable. Our practice here will be to consider these r's as consonantal and to transcribe them with the /r/ symbol, thus: *farm* /farm/; *pore* /por/; *poor* /pur/; *fair* /fɛr/; *fear* /fɪr/. The symbols /ər/ will be reserved for occasions when this sound is the center of a syllable, as in the two-syllable *stirring* /stərɪŋ/ contrasted with the one-syllable *string* /strɪŋ/.

Exercise 1–12

Transcribe the following words into phonemic symbols, following your own natural pronunciation.

1. we're ___	7. Mary ___	13. northern ___
2. beer ___	8. marry ___	14. floor ___
3. they're ___	9. barge ___	15. here ___
4. there ___	10. morning ___	16. tour ___
5. care ___	11. mourning ___	17. horse ___
6. merry ___	12. north ___	18. hoarse ___

---

[4] You may think that you are uttering single vowels in words like *cease* /sis/, *maim* /mem/, *noon* /nun/, and *moan* /mon/. But the vowel sounds you are actually making are diphthongized vowels something like these: 1. [ɪy], 2. [ey], 3. [ʊw], and 4. [ow]. If you can find a tape recorder which plays backward, you can easily hear them for yourself: simply record these four words and then play them backward.

19. pair	____	24. mayor	____	29. purr	____
20. payer	____	25. spurring	____	30. proud	____
21. stair	____	26. spring	____	31. burr	____
22. stayer	____	27. cur	____	32. bread	____
23. mare	____	28. crowd	____		

D. The English Phonemic System: Consonants

Vowels, you have learned, are characterized by a free flow of air. Consonants, on the other hand, except for the three nasals, are produced by stopping or obstructing this flow of air. The first six consonants presented here are those produced by a stoppage of air: /p b t d k g/.

Stops: /p/, /b/. If you hold your velum and lips closed and exert outward air pressure, nothing will happen except that your cheeks may puff out. Now if you suddenly open your lips, the air explodes outward and you have made a /p/. This consonant is called a voiceless bilabial stop because (1) the vocal cords do not vibrate, (2) two lips are used, and (3) a complete stop of the air flow is made. If during the same process you vibrate your vocal cords, you will produce a /b/, a voiced bilabial stop.

Stops: /t/, /d/. Instead of using the lips, you can stop the air flow by holding the tongue against the alveolar ridge, with the velum closed, and exerting outward air pressure. A sudden removal of the tongue will then produce a /t/, a voiceless alveolar stop. But if the vocal cords vibrate during the process, you will produce a /d/, a voiced alveolar stop.

Stops: /k/, /g/. The third pair of stops is produced by raising the tongue back against the velum, which is also raised to cut off the nasal cavity. When the tongue back is released, the outrushing air results in a /k/, a voiceless velar stop, or a /g/, a voiced velar stop, depending on whether or not the vocal cords are vibrating.

Oral Exercise 1–E

To increase your awareness of the three stop positions, pronounce slowly and in succession /p/, /t/, and /k/, and try to feel, tactually and kinesthetically, what is going on inside your mouth. Do this six times, and then repeat the process in reverse.

Exercise 1–13

Transcribe the following words into phonemic symbols.

1. pip	____	6. gag	____	11. fast	____
2. bib	____	7. stopped	____	12. fasten	____
3. tot	____	8. stopgap	____	13. oozed	____
4. deed	____	9. hiccough	____	14. hand	____
5. coke	____	10. subpoint	____	15. hands	____

16. liquor _____   18. guest _____   20. coop _____
17. six   _____   19. keep _____

Exercise 1–14

In *keep* and *coop* there are two different [k]s, which are allophones of /k/. In what way are they different? To answer this, try whispering the [k] of *keep* and that of *coop* alternately and note your tongue position and lip rounding. Furthermore, if you bear in mind the positions of the two vowels, you may be able to explain why the [k]s differ.

FRICATIVES

English contains nine consonants that are produced by an obstruction of the air stream causing audible friction. These nine fricatives are:

$$/f \quad v \quad \theta \quad ð \quad s \quad z \quad š \quad ž \quad h/$$

We shall discuss these in pairs, beginning with those in the front of the mouth and moving to the back.

The first pair, /f/ and /v/, are heard in *fail* and *vale*. They are produced when the outgoing air is obstructed by the lower lip touching the upper teeth. The /f/ is called a voiceless labiodental fricative, and /v/ a voiced labiodental fricative. They differ only in the fact that /v/ is voiced. You can feel the vibration of the vocal cords for /v/ if you press your fingers around the top of the larynx, sound a continuous /f/, and then change without stopping to a /v/. The next three pairs of fricatives can be tested in the same way for voicelessness and voicing.

The second pair, /θ/ and /ð/, are heard in *ether* and *either*. They are made with the tongue between the upper and lower teeth, obstructing the air stream between its tip and the upper teeth. The /θ/ is a voiceless interdental fricative, and /ð/ a voiced interdental fricative.

The third pair is /s/ and /z/, as in *face* and *faze*. These are pronounced by the tongue permitting a small stream of air to hiss over its surface at the alveolar ridge. The /s/ is a voiceless alveolar fricative, and /z/ a voiced alveolar fricative.

The fourth pair of fricatives is /š/, the third consonant in *dilution,* and /ž/, the third consonant in *delusion*. These are made by the friction of moving air between the tongue front and the palatal region just behind the alveolar ridge. The /š/ is a voiceless alveopalatal fricative, and /ž/ a voiced alveopalatal fricative. To get the feel of the voiceless alveolar and alveopalatal fricatives, take a deep breath and on a continuous stream of air repeat /s/ and /š/ in alternation, noting the movements of the tongue and the lips.

The last fricative is /h/, as in *hat* contrasted with *at*. This is produced by the breath rushing through the vocal cords closing to a position for vibrating, and through the oral cavity. Its tongue and lip position is that of the following sound. You can see this easily by preparing your mouth to say *ha, he, who*. It is called the voiceless glottal fricative, the glottis being the space between the vocal cords.

Exercise 1–15
Transcribe the following words in phonemic symbols:

1. enough _____	8. scent _____	15. luxury _____
2. wife _____	9. close _____	16. luxurious _____
	(adjective	
3. wives _____	10. clothes _____	17. measure _____
	(noun)	
4. fifth _____	11. news _____	18. humble _____
5. south _____	12. newspaper _____	19. honest _____
6. southern _____	13. house _____	20. homage _____
7. with _____	14. husband _____	

Exercise 1–16
For each word below, find a word that, with it, forms a minimal pair demonstrating the phonemic status of the fricative. Write this word in phonemic notation.

Examples: *n*ick/θɪk/, sta*p*le /stebəl/, bar*ge* /bark/

1. *f*ind _____	4. *th*us _____	7. *sh*irk _____
2. *v*ase _____	5. *s*eem _____	8. a*z*ure _____
3. bo*th* _____	6. *j*azz _____	9. *h*ang _____

AFFRICATES

English has two affricates—the voiceless /č/, as in *chill,* and the voiced /ǰ/, as in *Jill.* The /č/ begins with the voiceless stop /t/, which is exploded as a voiceless fricative /š/. Thus it is sometimes written /tš/. It is known as the voiceless alveopalatal affricative. The /ǰ/ consists of a voiced stop /d/, which is exploded as a voiced fricative /ž/, and is sometimes writen /dž/. It is called the voiced alveopalatal affricate.

NASALS

The three nasals—/m/, /n/, and /ŋ/—have already been described on pages 7–8.

LATERAL

The lateral /l/, as in *louse,* is made by placing the tongue tip on the alveolar ridge and vibrating the vocal cords as the air passes out on one or both sides of the tongue. To feel the tongue position, hold the tongue firmly at the alveolar ridge and make a series of /l/s and /n/s, noting how the sides of the tongue open and close as you alternate sounds.

GLIDES

The three glides—/y/, /r/, and /w/—are signalized by a moving, not a stationary, tongue position. They are all voiced.

With /y/, as in *yoke* contrasted with *oak,* the tongue begins in the /i/ region and moves toward the position for the following vowel. It is called the high front glide. In the case of /r/, as in *rate* contrasted with *ate,* the tongue begins in the position of the r-colored vowel of *purr,* /ər/, and moves toward the following vowel. It is known as the retroflex alveolar glide, though this name is not descriptive of some /r/s. The third glide is /w/, as in *will* versus *ill.* Here the tongue takes an /u/ position and then moves into the following vowel. It is called the high back glide.

These glides also follow vowels to form diphthongs, as in *my* /may/, *cow* /kaw/, and *coy* /koy/.

Exercise 1–17

Transcribe the following words into phonemic notation:

1. food	_____	11. stronger	_____
2. feud	_____	12. illusion	_____
3. eon	_____	13. folk	_____
4. yon	_____	14. milk	_____
5. judge	_____	15. use (verb)	_____
6. solemn	_____	16. opinion	_____
7. each	_____	17. try	_____
8. singer	_____	18. wear	_____
9. linger	_____	19. where	_____
10. strong	_____	20. berate	_____

We have now covered briefly the twelve vowels and twenty-four consonant phonemes of English. These are charted on the diagrams on page 18 and below. You will find that memorizing these charts is an excellent way to keep in mind the basic facts about each sound.

Note that the consonant chart, like the vowel chart, is arranged from the front of the mouth at the left to the throat at the right.

	Bilabial	Labio-dental	Inter-dental	Alveolar	Alveo-palatal	Velar	Glottal
Stops vl	p			t		k	
vd	b			d		g	
Fricatives vl		f	θ	s	š		h
vd		v	ð	z	ž		
Affricates vl					č		
vd					ǰ		
Nasals	m			n		ŋ	
Lateral				l			
Glides				r	y	w	

Diagram 13   Chart of English consonant phonemes.

Exercise 1–18

As a review of the vowel, consonant, and diphthong symbols, write in phonemic notation one illustrative word for each phoneme given below.

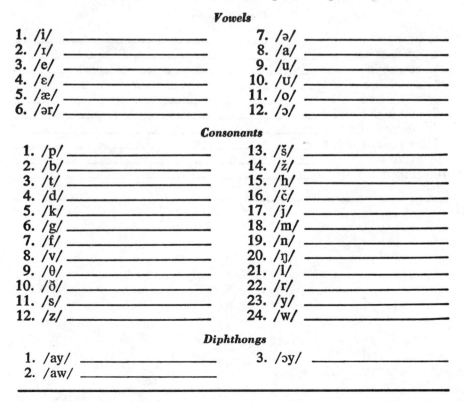

Vowels

1. /i/ _____
2. /ɪ/ _____
3. /e/ _____
4. /ɛ/ _____
5. /æ/ _____
6. /ər/ _____

7. /ə/ _____
8. /a/ _____
9. /u/ _____
10. /ʊ/ _____
11. /o/ _____
12. /ɔ/ _____

Consonants

1. /p/ _____
2. /b/ _____
3. /t/ _____
4. /d/ _____
5. /k/ _____
6. /g/ _____
7. /f/ _____
8. /v/ _____
9. /θ/ _____
10. /ð/ _____
11. /s/ _____
12. /z/ _____

13. /š/ _____
14. /ž/ _____
15. /h/ _____
16. /č/ _____
17. /ǰ/ _____
18. /m/ _____
19. /n/ _____
20. /ŋ/ _____
21. /l/ _____
22. /r/ _____
23. /y/ _____
24. /w/ _____

Diphthongs

1. /ay/ _____
2. /aw/ _____

3. /ɔy/ _____

Exercise 1–19

Read aloud the following words and word groups. Watch out for this danger: You may recognize a word and pronounce it as you ordinarily do instead of following the notation. A stress mark /′/ has been added to show the syllable of greatest emphasis. In the blanks write out in ordinary spelling the word or word group. These are all real pronunciations made by native American speakers.

Single Words

1. frag	13. paunz
2. sári	14. əkrɔ́st
3. hway	15. əfɛ́kt
4. rum	16. waš
5. rʊm	17. wɔš
6. príti	18. wɔrš
7. wúmən	19. hɔrs
8. wímɪn	20. hors
9. čifs	21. səmpθɪŋ
10. layvz	22. lǽŋgwəǰ
11. sɛnz	23. kántækt
12. sɛnts	24. kəntǽkt

25. tyuzdi

Word Groups

1. lɛmi gó
2. am gɔnə kráy
3. hu æst yu
4. ay tóld ɪm
5. wi tól ðəm
6. ayšt θɪŋk i wúd
7. šiz pərdi číki
8. ðe kʊdəv bɔt ðəm
9. ayl míšu
10. al tríču

2
Assimilation and Other Phonetic Processes

A. Assimilation

Up to this point we have been dealing mainly with words in isolation. The pronunciation of such words is called the citation form. But the citation form of words is often not the pronunciation heard in everyday speech. For words are compounded with other words to make new ones; they take on prefixes and suffixes; and usually they are met as part of a continuous stream of speech. Thus the sounds with which a word begins and ends are frequently in contact with adjoining sounds. When two sounds occur cheek by jowl, a change is likely to occur in one (or both) of them: it becomes more like its neighbor in some respect. A few examples will make this tendency clear.

The citation form of *news* is /nuz/ or /nɪuz/. Let us take *news*, with its final /z/, and add *paper* to it. Now the voiced /z/ of *news* is juxtaposed to the voiceless /p/ of *paper*. Do the two sounds remain the same? In the speech of many persons the voiced /z/ changes to a voiceless /s/—/nuspepər/. The change can also work the other way, from voicelessness to voicing. The citation form of *north,* /nɔrθ/, ends in a voiceless /θ/, but when the voiced suffix *-ern* /ərn/ is added, the /θ/ becomes /ð/, thus *northern* /nɔrðərn/.

The process we have just illustrated is called assimilation. Assimilation may be defined as the phonetic process by which one speech sound comes to resemble or become identical with a neighboring sound between words or within a word. In the cases above we were concerned with voice assimilation, a very common kind. In many two-syllable words like *matter, butter, dirty,* where the voiceless /t/ is surrounded by voiced sounds, there is a tendency to voice the /t/, making it a kind of /d/. In cases like *sit down* /sɪdawn/ the /t/ becomes identical with the /d/; that is to say, it disappears.

Exercise 2–1

Transcribe the following. Use double underlining to show voice assimilation to neighboring sounds. Be able to explain each assimilation.

1. letter _____
   bottle _____
   forty _____
2. south _____
   southern _____
3. it _____
   it is _____
4. worth _____
   worthy _____
5. got _____
   I've got it _____
6. cup _____
   cupboard _____

7. goose _____
   gooseberry _____
8. shut _____
   shut up _____
9. have _____
   I have to fish _____
   I have two fish _____
10. How many guests will you have to feed?
    a. _____
    b. _____
11. used _____
    He used to dance _____
    He used two eggs _____

Voice assimilation plays a role in the formation of English s plurals. In spelling, the s plural consists of the addition of an *s* or *es* to the singular form of the noun. But in the spoken language, there are three s plurals. You can readily discover these by means of the next exercise.

Exercise 2–2

Transcribe the following words in both their singular and plural forms. When you have finished, compare the plural suffix you added with the final sound of the singular to see what relationship the two have. Then answer these two questions:

1. What are the three forms of the s plural?
2. What principle governs the choice of the plural suffix?

	Singular	Plural		Singular	Plural
1. stop	_____	_____	5. breath	_____	_____
2. right	_____	_____	6. mob	_____	_____
3. cake	_____	_____	7. ride	_____	_____
4. muff	_____	_____	8. frog	_____	_____

	Singular	Plural			Singular	Plural
9. wave	_____	_____	15. glass	_____	_____
10. sum	_____	_____	16. rose	_____	_____
11. son	_____	_____	17. dish	_____	_____
12. song	_____	_____	18. mirage	_____	_____
13. doll	_____	_____	19. ditch	_____	_____
14. fear	_____	_____	20. edge	_____	_____

There are apparent exceptions to the principle governing the choice of the s plural suffix—for example, pairs like *life, lives* and *wreath, wreaths*—which can be explained historically. The principle is also operative with two other grammatical suffixes—the noun possessive, as in *Jack's, John's, George's,* and the *s* ending of the verb in the present tense, third person singular, as in *bakes, begs, itches.* All this we shall take up later in the study of English morphology.

A case of assimilation similar to that of the s plural exists with the past-tense suffix *-ed.* Here again we shall proceed inductively with an exercise.

Exercise 2–3

Transcribe each word both in the present-tense form given and in the past-tense form. Then study your results and answer two questions:
   1. How many phonemic forms does the *-ed* suffix have?
   2. What principle governs the choice of suffix?

	Present	Past			Present	Past
1. pass	_____	_____	11. hug	_____	_____
2. laugh	_____	_____	12. rave	_____	_____
3. mop	_____	_____	13. mill	_____	_____
4. back	_____	_____	14. stir	_____	_____
5. rush	_____	_____	15. rot	_____	_____
6. wrench	_____	_____	16. load	_____	_____
7. rob	_____	_____	17. seat	_____	_____
8. seem	_____	_____	18. sod	_____	_____
9. loan	_____	_____	19. need	_____	_____
10. wrong	_____	_____	20. repeat	_____	_____

Assimilation may stem not only from the action or inaction of the vocal cords but also from the action of other parts of the speech-producing apparatus. As two adjoining speech sounds are uttered, the set of movements producing one of these sounds may accommodate itself to the movements that produce the other sound. In brief, the production of the two sounds is short-cut, resulting in economy of effort and a change in the sounds themselves. An example will clarify this point. Consider the last two sounds of *length* /lɛŋθ/. This is sometimes heard in the assimilated form of /lɛnθ/, in which the velar nasal /ŋ/ has become the alveolar nasal /n/. In the first form, /lɛŋθ/, the tongue back is raised to the velum for /ŋ/; then the tongue tip is placed at the bottom of the upper teeth for /θ/. Two tongue movements are needed. But in /lɛnθ/ the two tongue movements are reduced to one. The tongue tip goes immediately to the bottom of the upper teeth to produce a dental instead of an alveolar /n/, and then remains in exactly the same position for /θ/. Thus production is short-cut with a consequent alteration of sound. The phonetician describes this by saying that the /ŋ/ has been assimilated to (= made like) the /θ/, becoming /n/. This kind of assimilation is called place assimilation.

In the preceding example of *length*, one sound was made to resemble another: the /n/ became partially like the dental /θ/ in that it changed from an alveolar to a dental. In the next example of place assimilation, one sound becomes identical with the second. If we utter *horse* and *shoe* individually, we find that *horse* ends in /s/ and *shoe* begins with /š/. But if we utter them as one word, *horseshoe,* the final /s/ of *horse* is assimilated to the initial /š/ of *shoe,* becoming identical with it in /hɔršu/. In short, the /s/ disappears. The assimilative disappearance of sounds in spoken discourse is not uncommon. When /t/, for instance, becomes part of a consonant cluster, usually enclosed by consonants, as in *softness,* it tends to disappear.

Exercise 2–4

Transcribe the following expressions and be able to explain in class, in terms of the vocal apparatus, just what assimilation is likely to occur at the places in boldface type.

1. stren**gth**	_____	6. con**qu**er	_____
		(cf. con**t**act)	
2. thi**s s**ugar	_____	7. wa**s y**our	_____
3. gran**dp**a	_____	8. He lef**t th**e town.	_____
4. gran**dm**a	_____	9. Jus**t th**ink.	_____
5. han**dk**erchief	_____	10. Di**d y**ou?	_____

Exercise 2–5

Answer the following questions:

1. In the sixteenth century the two forms *unpossible* and *impossible* existed side by side. Why do you think *impossible* survived as the standard form?
2. In *Webster's Third New International Dictionary* we find the variant verb forms *enplane* and *emplane.* Which do you believe will survive? Why?
3. The Latin *cum,* meaning "with," became *con-* in many words. The *n* of *con-* represents either /n/ or /ŋ/. Which is it in these words: *condemn, congress.* Why?
4. A sentence like "She was writing this morning" is sometimes misunderstood as "She was riding this morning." Explain.

5. Chinese *san pan*, meaning "three planks," appears in English as *sampan*. Explain the *m*.
6. Explain the assimilations in the following historical cases:
   a. Vulgar Latin *patre* (= father) developed into Italian *padre*.
   b. Vulgar Latin *domna* (= mistress of household) developed into *donna* in Italy and into *damme*, later *dame*, in France.
   c. Vulgar Latin *debta* (= sum owed) developed into French *dette*.
   d. Vulgar Latin *armata* (= armed, army) developed into Spanish *armada* (= armed fleet).
   e. Vulgar Latin *amta* (= father's sister) developed into Old French *ante* (= aunt).
   f. Vulgar Latin *salata* (= salted) developed into Portuguese *salada* (= salad).
   g. Vulgar Latin *securo* (= secure, safe) developed into Portuguese *seguro* (= secure).
   h. Old English *hæfde* (= had) developed into Middle English *hadde*.

B. Metathesis

Metathesis is the transposition of speech sounds. The person who says *tradegy* for *tragedy* or *revelant* for *relevant* is metathesizing. The dialect form *axe* /æks/ for *ask* /æsk/ is another case, going back a thousand years to Old English. The most commonly heard metatheses occur in the phonetic situation of /r/ plus a vowel. Take *pretty* for example. In the sentence "She's a pretty girl," we are likely to say /prɪti/. But when *pretty* is given minimal stress, as in "That's pretty good," the word tends to become /pərti/. If you listen carefully to the pronunciation of *hundred, apron, pronounce,* and similar words with /r/ plus vowel in an unstressed position, you will notice many metathesized /ər/s in the speech of educated people.

Exercise 2–6

In word history, metathesis has been occasionally responsible for changing pronunciations and spellings. As examples, look up the etymology of these words and write the early unmetathesized forms in the blanks.

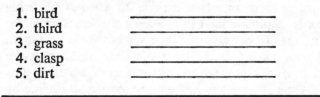

1. bird   _____
2. third   _____
3. grass   _____
4. clasp   _____
5. dirt   _____

C. Epenthesis

Epenthesis is the insertion of an extra consonant within a word, such as the /p/ you may hear in *something* or the /t/ in *sense*. The extra sound is termed excrescent. Of the various epenthetic situations we shall discuss one that is rather common.

After an /m/ an excrescent /p/ may occur before these voiceless consonants: /t/, /k/, /f/, /θ/, /s/, and /š/. The /p/ occurs because of a slight lack of coordination in the speech-making mechanism, which can be illustrated with *something*. To pronounce *something* as /səmθɪŋ/ requires a precise functioning of the speech apparatus at the critical point of /-mθ-/. For /m/ the lips are closed, the velum is lowered, and the vocal cords vibrate as the /m/ hums through the nose. Now, in shifting to the /θ/, four actions must take place at exactly the same time: the vocal cords must cease vibrating, the tongue tip take an interdental position, the velum rise to close off the nasal passage, and the lips open. However, if the velum closes off the nasal passage a fraction of a second before the lips open, then air pressure builds up behind the lips, and when they are opened, the air bursts out in a /p/.

In other words in which /m/ is followed by a voiceless consonant, the reason for the excrescent /p/ is fundamentally the same: the velum closes the nasal passage before the lips open.

Exercise 2–7
Answer the following questions:

1. Is the *p* in *glimpse* and *empty* the result of epenthesis? To find out, look up etymologies of these words.
2. What variant spellings do *Samson* and *Thomson* have? Explain.
3. Which of these words may be heard with an excrescent /p/: *comfort, combat, warmth, warmly, Tomkins, Tomlin, dreamt.*

D. Epithesis

Epithesis is the addition of an extra consonant to the end of a word. It occurs after a final /n/ or /s/. Consider the word *sound*. In Middle English this was *soun* /sun/. First, we must note that /n/ and /d/ are homorganic; this means that both are made at the same position of the speech organs—the tongue tip at the alveolar ridge. If, when /n/ is being sounded, the vocal cords stop vibrating as the tongue is released from the alveolar ridge, the /n/ merely ceases. But if the velum should be raised, closing off the nasal passage, before the tongue is lowered, air pressure builds up behind the tongue. Upon release of the tongue a /d/ is produced. It was doubtless the latter set of articulatory movements, made by many people in early England, that gave *sound* its /d/, which later appeared in the spelling. The same /d/ can be heard today in /draund/, a nonstandard pronunciation of *drown*.

After final /s/ an epithetic /t/ occasionally appears. It is caused by the fact that the tongue, instead of being lowered to end the /s/ sound, is pressed against the alveolar ridge while the breath is moving outward; then, when the tongue is lowered, the release of air pressure produces a /t/. You will now and then hear this /t/ at the end of *once, across,* and *wisht* (= wish).

Exercise 2–8

Look up the etymology of the following words to determine the source of the final sound: *lend, bound* (adjective), *against, midst, amongst.*

3

Spelling and Pronunciation

A. Relations Between Spelling and Pronunciation

Languages are reduced to writing by means of three kinds of writing systems. Some systems, like Cherokee, use one symbol for each syllable. Others, like Chinese, use one symbol for each morpheme, the smallest segment of an utterance that carries meaning. But most languages, including English, use an alphabetic, that is to say, a phonemic system. This means that the letters stand for phonemes. An ideal alphabetic writing system would be one in which each letter always stood for the same phoneme and each phoneme was always represented by the same letter. Such a two-way one-for-one correspondence between letters and phonemes does not exist in any standard alphabet now in general use. Of course you have been using such a phonemic system in this book, but systems like this are used only by the relatively few who are students of language.

English is far from the ideal writing system, as anyone with spelling difficulties is well aware. In fact, English does not contain a single instance of a two-way one-to-one correspondence—letter to sound and sound to letter. Small wonder. Our language has twelve vowel phonemes and twenty-four consonant phonemes—thirty-six in all. And to represent these thirty-six it has only twenty-six letters, of which three are superfluous. A few illustra-

tions will reveal this inadequacy of letter-sound and sound-letter corre-
spondences. The first letter of the alphabet, *a,* represents at least eight
phonemes, as shown by this series: *dame* /e/, *any* /ɛ/, *pan* /æ/, *father*
/a/, *ball* /ɔ/, *pillage* /ɪ/, *lunar* /ər/, *opera* /ə/. If we go the other way,
from sound to letter, we find that nearly all phonemes have from two to
over a dozen spellings. In this respect the vowel phonemes are worse of-
fenders than the consonants. Here are some ways in which the phoneme
/i/ is spelled: *ee,* feet; *e,* me; *ae,* Caesar; *eo,* people; *ea,* beat; *ei,* deceive;
oe, amoeba; *ie,* relieve; *i,* ravine; *ey,* key; *ay,* quay.

Exercise 3–1 (from letter to sound)
Write in each blank the phonemic symbol for the boldface letter:

a. 1. such _____   8. delicious _____
   2. devise _____   9. cello _____
   3. sure _____   c. 10. be _____
   4. treasure _____   11. met _____
   5. aisle _____   12. English _____
b. 6. cite _____   13. silent _____
   7. copper _____   14. sergeant _____

Exercise 3–2 (from sound to letter)
a. Write one word illustrating each of the spellings of the phoneme /š/
listed below:

1. sh _____   8. se _____
2. ch _____   9. si _____
3. ce _____   10. ti _____
4. ci _____   11. ss _____
5. sch _____   12. ssi _____
6. sci _____   13. xi _____
7. s _____   14. x _____

b. Write one word illustrating each of the spellings of the phoneme /o/
listed below:

1. o _____   6. ow _____
2. oh _____   7. eo _____
3. oa _____   8. au _____
4. oe _____   9. ew _____
5. ou _____   10. eau _____
            11. ough _____

Illustrations like the foregoing, which could be multiplied, suggest that
English spelling is unpredictably capricious. But remember that we have
been selective, choosing examples that demonstrate this one aspect of spell-

ing, its irregularity. If all English spelling were like this, it would be virtually useless as a writing system. Yet we do succeed in representing the spoken language with our spelling; witness the fact that most persons can read aloud with little trouble. Furthermore, when we meet new words in our reading, we seldom have trouble in pronouncing them. An exercise in nonsense words will illustrate this point:

Exercise 3–3

a. *Spelling to sound.* Write the following nonsense words in phonemic notation to show your pronunciation of them:

1. lete _____   6. theet _____
2. vake _____   7. noot _____
3. zite _____   8. deat _____
4. noke _____   9. poat _____
5. fube _____   10. boe _____

b. *Sound to spelling.* The following words are given in phonemic notation. Write them out in conventional spelling.

1. /dɪt/ _____   6. /zel/ _____
2. /tɛt/ _____   7. /omɛkt/ _____
3. /ǰæt/ _____   8. /bæmθəm/ _____
4. /zat/ _____   9. /sayl/ _____
5. /čət/ _____   10. /θut/ _____

Up to this point we have seen that English spelling contains both regularities and irregularities. Professor Robert A. Hall, Jr., in his excellent *Sound and Spelling in English,* divides English spellings into three groups— the regular, the semiregular, and the downright irregular. He offers a list of forty-seven phonemes and combinations of phonemes which have regular letter equivalents and concludes, "English orthography does afford to each phoneme of the language at least one regular, clear and consistent alphabetic representation." The semiregular spellings, he points out, are irregular only in the way they symbolize one or two phonemes of a word; furthermore, these spellings fall into subsets which are consistent within themselves. The downright irregular are relatively few. As examples of the last, Hall lists such words as *quay, busy, schism, who, debt, choir.*

Here is an exercise which will give you instances of some of the simpler regularities in English spelling.

Exercise 3–4

Begin with the syllable /ɪn/. Go through the chart of English consonant phonemes, diagram 13, and list all the words you can make by placing single consonants at the beginning of /ɪn/. Write each word in both phonemic notation and in conventional spelling. Then do the same for /æt/ and /at/. What correspondence do you find between the consonant phonemes and the letters representing them?

	/ɪn/		/æt/		/at/	
	Phon. Not.	*Spelling*	*Phon. Not.*	*Spelling*	*Phon. Not.*	*Spelling*
1.						
2.						
3.						
4.						
5.						
6.						
7.						
8.						
9.						
10.						
11.						
12.						
13.						
14.						
15.						
16.						
17.						
18.						

Exercise 3–4 suggests, within its limited data, that English consonant phonemes have one spelling that may be considered regular and stable. In addition to one regular spelling nearly all consonant phonemes have others. The number of spellings varies considerably. At one end of the scale is /θ/, which is always spelled *th*. At the other end are /k/, which has eleven spellings, and /š/, which has fourteen. Within all this irregularity, however, are subsets of words which tend to be regular and consistent within each set. The phoneme /f/ will serve to illustrate these subsets. In initial position its regular spelling is *f*, as thousands of words will attest. But a large subset spell this initial /f/ as *ph*, words like *physics, phenomenon, philosophy, pheasant, pharmacy*. In final position the /f/ phoneme has its regular spelling in words like *if, loaf, serf, spoof, beef*. But the subsets give us more possibilities.

   ff as in *biff, miff, off, scoff, buff*
   gh as in *laugh, cough, tough, rough, enough*

And there are the less frequent final spellings of *fe* as in *knife*, *ph* as in *epitaph*, and *ffe* as in *giraffe*.

Subsets like these are manifold. They are the basis of the spelling "rules" that you learned in school—for example, "*i* before *e* except after *c*"—which were often accompanied by lists of exceptions. The presence of such subsets, which lead a random existence in our minds, both aids and misleads us in our spelling. They aid us in that they limit spelling choices. If a word begins with the phoneme /f/, we know automatically that it begins with *f* or *ph* and that it does not begin with *ff* or *gh*. Or if we wish to spell a word containing the sounds /ayt/, we are reasonably sure that the spelling will be either *-ight*, following the subset *might, night, light, right, sight, fight, delight*—or *-ite*, following *mite, kite, site, recite, bite*. But such dual sets mislead us, too, for the sounds do not tell exactly which spelling to choose; and also there are exceptions to harass us, like *height*.

Exercise 3–5

English has numerous subsets involving the addition of a suffix. In subsets *a* and *b* below state the principle that governs the spelling of a word when the suffix *-ed, -ing,* or *-er* is added.

a.			b.		
1.	hope	hoped hoping	1.	hop	hopped hopping
2.	dine	diner dining dined	2.	din	dinned dinning
3.	ride	rider riding	3.	rid	ridder ridding
4.	cite	cited citing	4.	sit	sitter sitting
5.	dote	doting doted	5.	dot	dotting dotted

a. _____

_____

b. _____

_____

Exercise 3–6

This is a continuation of exercise 3–5. Study the words below ending in silent *e* and state the spelling principle governing the addition of suffixes.

1. care	+ ed	= cared	+ ful	= careful
2. love	+ ing	= loving	+ ly	= lovely
3. blame	+ able	= blamable	+ less	= blameless
4. fine	+ ed	= fined	+ ness	= fineness
5. game	+ est	= gamest	+ ly	= gamely
6. disgrace	+ er	= disgracer	+ ful	= disgraceful

_____

_____

_____

We may conclude that English spelling is far removed from an ideal pho-nemic system with a two-way one-to-one correspondence between sounds and letters, but despite the uncertain and insecure relations between spell-ing and pronunciation, it does have many regularities that are available to the alert writer.

B. Spelling Pronunciation

In the act of reading we sometimes meet words that we have never heard sounded, that are familiar to our eyes but not to our ears. In such cases we do the natural thing—we give them the most plausible pronunciation sug-gested by the spelling. If, for instance, a plains dweller, in reading a sea story, comes across the words *boatswain* and *gunwale,* he is likely to pro-nounce them /botswen/ and /gənwel/; whereas one reared in a boating en-vironment would have learned by ear the traditional pronunciations of /bosən/ and /gənəl/. This contrast affords an illustration of spelling pro-nunciation, which is simply a pronunciation that departs from the tradi-tional pronunciation and conforms closely to the spelling.

The words we acquire in childhood, before learning to read, are those that are resistant to spelling pronunciation. The word *cupboard* is a good example. This is normally spoken as /kəbərd/, and few persons notice how far this traditional pronunciation has moved away, by assimilation and weakening of stress on the last syllable, from an aural combination of *cup* and *board.* Now let us compare *cupboard* with *clapboard,* which has gone through exactly the same processes of change and has the traditional pro-nunciation of /klæbərd/. Many Americans have never heard this word, certainly not in childhood, and others have seen it only in print. Thus it is only to be expected that it should be given the spelling pronunciation of /klæpbɔrd/.

Place names, which may endure for centuries, tend to develop vagaries of pronunciation known only to those in intimate association with the places. It is not surprising that strangers to these places, with only the spelling to guide them, will mispronounce the names. Countless Americans pronounce *Edinburgh* as /ɛdɪnbərg/, not realizing that in Scotland the city is known as /ɛdɪnbəro/. Personal names too tend to change through the influence of spelling. A well-known instance is *Theobald.* When Pope slan-dered "piddling Theobald" some two centuries ago, he created in the word combination an especially effective collocation of sounds, for *Theobald* still had at that time its traditional pronunciation of /tɪbəld/. Today it is gen-erally known by the spelling pronunciation of /θiəbɔld/.

It is not uncommon for spelling pronunciations to be generally adopted by all speakers of English, thus becoming the standard pronunciation. A special class of such words deserves mention. English contains hundreds of words borrowed from Latin and French with a *th* spelling. In these words the *th* was pronounced /t/ in Latin and French, and it was with this voice-less stop /t/ that they came into English. Two examples are *theme* and *theater,* both first recorded in English in the fourteenth century. In that century they were spelled in English with either *th* or *t,* the latter reflecting the actual pronunciation. The spelling *th* eventually prevailed, and with it came the spelling pronunciation /θ/ that we use today. In personal first names with *th* an interesting situation exists that can be made clear by an exercise.

Exercise 3–7

After each name in the first column write in phonemic notation your pronunciation of it. In the second column spell out your nickname for each personal name. In the third column write in phonemic notation your pronunciation of the nickname.

1. Anthony _____ _____ _____
2. Theodore _____ _____ _____
3. Dorothy _____ _____ _____
4. Arthur _____ _____ _____
5. Elizabeth _____ _____ _____
6. Matthew _____ _____ _____
7. Nathaniel _____ _____ _____

Explain the /θ/—/t/ disparity in these names. What two Biblical names with *th* have resisted spelling pronunciation and are still pronounced with a /t/?

_____ _____

Exercise 3–8

After each word write in phonemic notation your pronunciation of it. Then look it up in your desk dictionary to see whether you have used a spelling pronunciation. If your dictionary records two or more pronunciations, try to decide whether one is a spelling pronunciation which has become acceptable. Sometimes the Middle English form of the word will give you a clue to the traditional pronunciation. After your notation write SP (spelling pronunciation) or TP (traditional pronunciation) to show which pronunciation you used.

1. breeches _____ _____
2. blackguard _____ _____
3. comptroller _____ _____
4. almond _____ _____
5. nephew _____ _____
6. coxswain _____ _____
7. Greenwich _____ _____
8. falcon _____ _____
9. Pall Mall _____ _____
10. arctic _____ _____

That the spelling of words has at times wrought changes in their pronunciation does not at all mean that spelling is an infallible guide to pronunciation. Yet you will frequently hear people justify a pronunciation by an appeal to spelling. They may insist, for example, that *often* should be pronounced /ɔftɪn/, because it is spelled with a /t/, though they do not remember to apply this argument to *soften*. Or they may wish to pronounce the *h* in *vehicle*, the *b* in *subtle*, or the *l* in *calm* or *salmon* because their eyes have seen these letters in the printed word. Such a principle is rendered impossible of application by the irregularities of English spelling, as we have already seen. The answer to those who appeal to spelling to justify pronunciation is to ask them to apply this principle to words like those in the next exercise.

Exercise 3–9

Write in phonemic notation your pronunciation of the following words:

1. come _____
   home _____
2. move _____
   shove _____
3. friend _____
   fiend _____
   sieve _____
4. swore _____
   sword _____
5. hornet _____
   hour _____

6. house
   (noun) _____
   carouse _____
   famous _____
7. corps _____
   island _____
   debt _____
   sovereign _____
   pneumatic _____
8. colonel _____

4
Stress

A. Stress Phonemes

In our discussion of phonemes up to now we have been concerned with the thirty-six phonemes of English. These are called segmental phonemes because each is a segment of the continuous flow of speech. But this is only part of the phonemic story. We utter phonemes with varying degrees of prominence or stress; we sound voiced phonemes on different pitch levels; and we employ breaks or disjunctures to break up the whole utterance into groupings. The consequence of these three oral practices is that three more language elements require scrutiny—stress, pitch, and juncture (the common term for disjuncture). All three are phonemic, and as they accompany, and are said to be superposed on, the segmental phonemes, they are called suprasegmental phonemes. In this chapter we shall investigate the first of these three suprasegmental phonemes, that of stress.

Stress refers to the degree of prominence a syllable has. In *agree,* for example, the *gree* sounds more prominent than the *a.* In any utterance there may be as many degrees of stress as there are syllables, but many of the differences will be slight and even imperceptible. We are concerned here only with those differences of stress that have the power to distinguish meanings, namely the stress phonemes. Of these there are three, when we limit our analysis to individual words. Going from the most prominent to the weakest, we distinguish them by the following diacritics and names:

- ′ Primary stress
- ‵ Mid stress
- ˘ Weak stress (usually not indicated)

They are all illustrated in the word *légĕndàrў*.

To demonstrate that stress is phonemic in words we shall again employ a minimal pair. If we contrast /pàrmít/ with /pə́rmìt/, we see that the segmental phonemes are identical and that the two words differ only in the position of their primary and mid stresses. So it must be these stresses that distinguish them as signifying a verb and a noun respectively, and the stresses must therefore be phonemes.

Since some students have difficulty in differentiating various degrees of stress, a few graduated exercises may be useful.

Exercise 4-1

Place a primary stress mark over the syllable that has the greatest prominence.

1. defer
2. differ
3. pervert (verb)
4. pervert (noun)
5. conflict (verb)
6. conflict (noun)
7. evil
8. superb
9. romance
10. detail
11. research
12. defense

Exercise 4-2

Place a mid-stress mark over the syllable that has the next-to-the-greatest prominence. The primary stress marks are supplied.

1. díctionary
2. sécretary
3. separátion
4. íntellect
5. fundaméntal
6. aviátion
7. perpendícular
8. académic
9. univérsity
10. absolútely

Exercise 4-3

Mark the primary and mid stresses on the following words:

1. accent (noun)
2. austere
3. ambush
4. humane
5. blackbird
6. forgive
7. irate
8. pathos
9. diphthong
10. phoneme

Exercise 4–4
Mark all three degrees of stresses that you hear in the following words.

1. intellectual
2. designate
3. education
4. busybody
5. interruption

6. humanitarian
7. socialized
8. ceremony
9. military
10. uninspired

In the preceding exercises you have been putting stress marks of three degrees on isolated words, the citation forms. When we turn our attention to word groups and sentences, we shall need four degrees of stress. These are indicated as follows:

′ Primary stress
⌃ Secondary stress
ˋ Third stress (same as mid stress on words)
˅ Weak stress

The word *ìntelléctual* has all three degrees of word stress; but when it occurs in a phrase, *ìntellêctual cùriósity*, its primary stress is demoted to second, as the markings show, and four degrees of stress are needed to describe the stress patterning. An exercise will furnish more illustrations.

Exercise 4–5
Place a primary stress mark on the single words, and both the primary and the secondary stress marks, /′/ and /⌃/, on the longer expressions. Omit the third and the weak stress marks.

1. remarkable
2. remarkable invention
3. tiresome
4. tiresome job
5. contract (noun)
6. contract bridge

7. praiseworthy
8. praiseworthy remark
9. academic
10. academic procession
11. blooming
12. blooming plant

Note, however, that the secondary stress, as in *remârkable invéntion,* is still the strongest stress in the individual word, even though it has been demoted.

The reason for the demotion of stress we saw in exercise 4–5 lies in the nature of English phrase stress. Only one primary stress can occur in a phrase, and the strongest stress in a phrase (construction or word group) is normally near or at the end, as in these examples: *a tall búilding, an iron tóol, in the pántry, very háppy, delightfully ígnorant, way óut, often wálks, goes for béer, the day before yésterday, joyful as a lárk, get up éarly, wants to léave, ladies and géntlemen, up and dówn, walk or ríde.* Exceptions to this principle occur, especially with phrases containing personal pronouns.

Exercise 4–6   **EXERCISE 43**

Place a primary stress mark on the most strongly stressed syllable in each phrase.

1. a wooden gate
2. a gate of wood
3. completely gone
4. gone completely
5. run for the practice
6. practice for the run

7. Jack and Jill
8. tea or coffee
9. not at all
10. all at once
11. call the thief a liar
12. call the liar a thief

The phonemic status of stress in individual words has been mentioned above, just before exercise 4–1. But stress can also be phonemic in word groups. As illustration let us look at a minimal pair, *Òld Glóry* (= the flag) and *óld glóry* (= a glory that is old). The difference between the two lies in the secondary and third stresses. A newspaper story telling of the discovery of a very old American flag juxtaposed these two *old*'s in a way that highlights the difference in stress: *ôld Òld Glóry*.

B. Shifting Stress

Many words in English have what is called shifting stress; the position of stress may shift with a change of context. In isolation, before a pause, or before weakly stressed syllables, these words have a primary stress on the last syllable, like *unknówn* and *downtówn*. But when the primary stress in such a word occurs directly before another syllable with primary stress, two things happen, as is illustrated in *an ûnknòwn thíef* and *the dôwntòwn bákery*. First, the stronger stress is shifted toward the front of the word, because English tends to avoid consecutive primary stresses. English is an iambic language and favors an alternation of weaker with stronger stresses. Second, the primary stress is demoted to secondary, because an English phrase can have only one primary stress, and that is near or at the end, as we learned above in exercise 4–6.

Exercise 4–7

Place primary /'/, secondary /ˆ/, and third /ˋ/ stress marks on the words in italics.

1. His job was *inside*.
2. He had an *inside job*.
3. Our *overnight guests* did not stay *overnight*.
4. The *cut-glass bowl* was not really *cut-glass*.
5. *Inlaid tiles* are always *inlaid*.
6. Wasn't he *almost killed? Almost*.
7. She went *overseas* for her *overseas job*.

8. The soldiers are *Chinese* in the *Chinese army*.
9. He waited to be *fourteen* for *fourteen years*.
10. A *left-handed pitcher* doesn't always bat *left-handed*.

C. Grammatical Stress Patterns

Grammatical patterns are accompanied by regular stress patterns. Sometimes such stress patterns are the sole means of differentiating one grammatical pattern, with its concomitant meaning, from another. At other times the stress patterns just ride along. Of those in English we shall take up only four.

Pattern 1. A compound noun is usually accompanied by the stress pattern of ' `. It is exemplified by *blúebìrd, hígh schòol, díning ròom*. A compound may be spelled as two words, as one, or as a hyphenated word. Both *sidewalk* and *shoe store* are compounds, because of their stress pattern, regardless of the fact that one is written as a single word and the other as two.

Exercise 4–8
Place the compound noun stresses over the following words.

1. blackboard
2. hotbed
3. paleface
4. mailman
5. shortcake

6. roundhouse
7. paperback
8. rocking chair
9. spinning wheel
10. flying teacher

Pattern 2. The modifier + noun pattern is signaled by the stress pattern of ^ ', as in *sîck núrse, pôor hóuse, wôrking mán*.

Exercise 4–9
Place the modifier + noun stresses over the following words.

1. hot house
2. dark room
3. black bird
4. tender foot
5. handy man

6. red skin
7. funny bone
8. dancing teacher
9. mowing machine
10. moving van

Exercise 4–10
Here are twelve pairs of compound nouns and modified nouns distinguished by stress. The items in column 1 have modifier + noun stress; those

in column 2 have compound-noun stress. Write a brief statement of the meaning of each.

1a. hîgh cháir	1b. hígh chàir
2a. gâme físh	2b. gáme fìsh
3a. blûe bóok	3b. blúebòok
4a. grêen hóuse	4b. gréenhòuse
5a. dôuble ú	5b. dóuble ù
6a. râcing hórse	6b. rácing hòrse
7a. smôking róom	7b. smóking ròom
8a. trâveling mán	8b. tráveling màn
9a. dâncing gírl	9b. dáncing gìrl
10a. côoling lótion	10b. cóoling lòtion
11a. Frênch téacher	11b. Frénch tèacher
12a. lông hánd	12b. lónghànd[1]

---

[1] The distinction between compound noun {ˊ ˋ} and modifier-plus-noun {ˆ ˊ} cannot be consistently maintained in English. Here are a few of the complications:
1. Compare *his pêrsonal ínterests* with *his párty ìnterests*. By our rules the first is a modifier-plus-noun and the second a compound noun. Now let's make a sentence out of them:
He has both *pêrsonal* and *párty* interests.
Here *personal* and *party* are coordinated by *and*, so that *party* must be a modifier and not part of a compound noun. You can repeat this coordination test with pairs like *mîlitary clóthes—búsiness clòthes*.
2. Apart from the stress patterns, there seems to be no structural difference between *Fîrst Strèet* and *Fîrst Ávenue*, *páperbàck* and *pâper dóll*, *bóy frìend* and *bôy scíentist*, *flŷing machìne* and *flŷing sáucer*, and similar pairs. Thus it does not appear sensible to call the first member of each pair a compound noun and the second a modifier-plus-noun.
3. English contains expressions like *grêat grándfather*, *sprîng féver*, and *grând júry*, which have modifier-plus-noun stress but whose meanings are certainly not the additive total of those of their components. Furthermore, when the first member is an adjective, we cannot add a second modifier after the first without destroying the meaning, e.g., *great old grandfather*. Hence these seem to be compound nouns with a secondary-primary stress pattern.
Despite such limitations we shall maintain the distinction because it is so widely operative.

Pattern 3. The verb + noun-object grammatical pattern has a stress pattern of ˆ ', as in *They lôve bírds* and *They are bâking ápples*. This pattern occasionally contrasts with the compound noun stresses ' ', as you will see in the next exercise.

Exercise 4–11

Restate the following sentences so as to explain the meaning of the word combinations that have stress marks.

1. They are râcing hórses. _____

2. They are rácing hòrses. _____

3. Rûnning gréyhounds is his favorite sport. _____

4. He raises rúnning grèyhounds. _____

5. They are côoking ápples. _____

6. They are cóoking àpples. _____

7. Sally has a drîving ambítion: she wants to become a doctor. _____

8. Sally has a dríving ambìtion: she wants to use the family car as soon as she can get a driving license. _____

We have seen that the stress pattern ˆ ' is used for both a modifier plus a noun and for a verb plus a noun-object. This situation results in ambiguity when we do not know which of the two grammatical patterns is intended by the ˆ'. For example, in "Flŷing plánes can be dangerous," the first two words can mean either "planes that are flying" or "the act of piloting planes."

Exercise 4–12

State briefly the two meanings of the italicized phrases.

1. She abhors *scrâtching dógs.*

_____

2. *Môving bóoks* always disturbed him.

_____

3. We enjoy *entertâining vísitors.*

_____

4. They are *encôuraging repórts.*

_____

5. *Bûrning óil* frightened him.

_____

_____

Exercise 4–13

Place stress marks over the words to indicate the verb + noun-object and the compound-noun patterns.

1. *Jump ropes* are used by boxers.
2. They *jump ropes* for exercise.
3. He has to *wash rags* after cleaning his gun.
4. *Washrags* are hard to get.
5. She likes to *map routes* for travel.
6. We never follow *map routes.*
7. The guards *flash lights* into the dark corners.
8. They all carry *flashlights.*
9. We *watch dogs* with great interest during the hunting season.
10. There are three *watchdogs* on their farm.

Pattern 4. The verb + adverbial grammatical pattern also has a ˆ ' stress pattern, as in *You must lôok óut* and *The tent had been pûshed óver.* The compound noun derived from such verb + adverbial combinations has the usual ' ` pattern, as in The *lóokòut had a long vigil* and *This problem is no púshòver.*

Exercise 4–14

Place stress marks over the italicized words to indicate the verb-adverbial and the compound-noun combinations.

1. George is always *cutting up.*
2. He is an inveterate *cutup.*
3. This information is not to be *handed out.*
4. These *handouts* will give you the necessary information.
5. The movie was *held over.*
6. This movie is a *holdover* from last week.
7. She doesn't want to *come down.*
8. What a *comedown* she had.
9. She gave Jack the *comeon,* and he *came on.*

D. Gradation

Let us approach gradation through examples. The vowel of the word *and* is pronounced /æ/ when it is uttered with any of the three upper degrees of stress, as in

Not Tom ór I but Tom ánd /ænd/ I.

But when *and* is spoken with weak stress, as is customary, its vowel is likely to change to schwa /ə/, as in

Tom ănd /ən/ I have been appointed.

Or consider *to*. With primary, secondary, or third stress the vowel is /u/, as in

The party he cáme tò. /tu/

But under weak stress the vowel will probably become a schwa, that is, the lower mid-central vowel /ə/, as in

He came tŏ /tə/ the party.

As a third example let us take *-ate*. Here the vowel is /e/ when it has one of the stronger stresses, as in

to graduate /græ̆juèt/

Now if the stress is reduced to the weakest, the vowel tends to change to the lower mid-central vowel /ə/, as in

a graduate /græjuət/

A final example will complete our case. Some words with a vowel plus /r/, like *for* and *are*, also have a change of vowel quality under weak stress. The vowel of *for* is /ɔ/ under strong stress, as in

What is it fór? /fɔr/

Under weak stress, however, the combination /ɔr/ may become the higher mid-central r-colored vowel /ər/, sometimes spelled "fer" in dialect stories and comic strips. You will hear this frequently in expressions like

This is fŏr /fər/ you.

With these examples in mind we are ready to define gradation. Gradation is a change in vowel quality, when stress is reduced to weak stress, to one of the central vowels /ə/ or /ər/. As spoken discourse contains many weakly stressed syllables, it is obvious that occurrences of these vowels are very frequent in daily speech. This frequency is disguised by the fact that there are many spellings for these vowels.

Exercise 4–15

Write the following items in phonemic notation as you say them in natural speech.

1. instáll _____
2. installátion _____
3. áre _____
4. They ăre gone. _____
5. depóse _____
6. depŏsition _____
7. háve _____
8. He must hăve left. _____
9. ór _____
10. Will it be wind ŏr rain? _____
11. He cán but he won't. _____
12. He căn do it. _____
13. thé _____
14. Thĕ best one _____
15. Ás you see _____
16. Just ăs good _____
17. mán _____
18. postmăn _____

5
Pitch Levels and Terminals

A. Intonation Contours

Because vowels and many consonants are voiced, they possess the tonal quality of pitch, for pitch is a necessary concomitant of the vibration of the vocal cords. In English we make use of this pitch as a part of our signaling system. Although we employ many degrees of pitch in speaking, we use only four levels of relative pitch as phonemes, that is, to make distinctions in meaning. These four are as follows:

4. extra-high
3. high
2. normal
1. low

This is to say, the normal pitch of your speaking voice, whatever its actual height, is called level 2; and from this you make departures upward and downward. Take these two sentences:

2   3   1
I'm going hóme.

2   3 1
Her dog found the bone there in the back yárd.

You begin on level 2, your natural and normal level, and remain there until you reach the last primary stress. Here your voice rises one level and then drops to level 1. This 2 3 1 pattern is the pitch signal for statements. The extra-high level, 4, is reserved as a substitute for level 3 when you wish to express special emphasis or excitement. It is rather sparingly used.

Pitches combine into patterns to make meaningful melodies over the whole phrase or sentence—like the 2 3 1, meaning that a statement or proposition is being uttered. These melodies have three methods of closure, which are called terminal junctures or merely terminals.

The first terminal, which occurs at the end of a sentence, is the fading terminal. It is characterized by a rapid fadeaway of the voice into silence and by a considerable prolongation of the preceding word with pitch level 3. It is symbolized by / ↓ /. This symbol should be used to indicate the closure of our last example sentence:

2   3   1
I'm going hóme ↓

To sense the prolongation of *home,* the pitch 3 word, compare it with the length of *home* in the next sentence:

2   3   1
I'm going home Thúrsday ↓

The second terminal is the rising terminal. It is a short, slight rise in pitch from the last level heard, but it does not go all the way up to the next level. The preceding pitch 3 word is somewhat prolonged, but less so than for the fading terminal. It is symbolized by / ↑ / and commonly occurs at the end of yes-or-no questions:

2   3   3
Are you thére ↑

The third terminal is the sustained terminal. One recognizes this terminal by a slight lengthening of the preceding pitch 3 word, less than before the second terminal, and by a sustaining of the last-heard pitch. The following word, however, may be at a different pitch level. Its symbol is / → /, and it may be heard at the end of a long sentence-subject:

2   3 2 2   3   1
All the occupants of the cár → seemed dazed by the shóck ↓

To hear this terminal more sharply, compare what happens at *car* with what you hear in this sentence:

2   3   1
The car is réady ↓

Note that of the two preceding examples the first has two intonation contours and the second only one.

Patterns of pitch, with their accompanying terminals, like the three above—2 3 1 ↓, 2 3 3 ↑, and 2 3 2 →—are called intonation contours.

All sentences, as well as some grammatical word-group units within a sentence, have an intonation contour. In symbolizing contours you should indicate the pitch levels at three places: the beginning of the grammatical unit, the beginning of the syllable bearing the primary stress, and the end of unit before the terminal. There will be a primary stress somewhere between every two terminals. Primary stress usually accompanies pitch level 3.

There are two exceptions to this requirement of three pitch indications for every contour, as you will note in the pages to follow. First, the initial syllable of a contour may be given primary stress for emphasis, as in

3   1
Jósephine got the reward ↓ (not Harry)

In such cases a beginning 2 pitch need not be shown. Second, a single word may take an intonation contour, as in

2   3   1 1   2
Come hóme ↓ Tómmy ↑

In these cases only the beginning and end pitches are shown.

We are now ready to examine some of the more commonly used intonation contours in American English and the kinds of grammatical units they accompany. But first a word of caution. The contours described below are widely employed, but not to the total exclusion of variant ones. For instance, instead of the 2 3 1 pattern for "I'm going home," some speakers will use a 2 2 1 pattern. So, when you do the exercises, don't try to slavishly follow the contours described in the text; just put down exactly what you hear yourself say.

1. **2 3 1 ↓ (or 2 2 1 ↓).** These contours occur in three kinds of sentences.

a. Statement or declarative sentence:

2   3 1
We drove to the láke ↓

b. Command:

2   3 1
Go to your róom ↓

c. QW question (this means a question that begins with a question word, like *who, what, which, when, where, why, how*):

2   3   1
Who is your fríend ↓

It is interesting to note that the ordinary statement contour can be used for this kind of question because the sentence already contains a sure signal that a question is coming: the question word at the beginning.

Although the 2 3 1 ↓ contour accompanies the three types of sentences just described, it also is used randomly, especially in long sentences. If you listen carefully to serious TV speeches, you may hear it in unexpected places.

2. 2 3 3 ↑ (or 2 2 3 ↑). This contour is used in three common situations.

a. Yes-or-no question in statement form:

> 2   3   3
> He's góne ↑

Here a special contour is needed to signal a question, for without it the sentence would be a statement.

b. Yes-or-no question in question form:

> 2   3   3
> Are you thére ↑

c. Initial grammatical unit (phrase or clause or sentence segment)

> 2 3   3
> In shórt ↑
> 2   3   3
> If you'll wáit ↑

Exercise 5–1

For each sentence or grammatical unit supply the marks of the intonation contour—the pitch levels and terminal junctures. It will help you to put in the primary stress first.

1. He walked to the lab.
2. Get out of my sight!
3. Where is my necktie?
4. She won't be home till twelve?
5. Are you going to the game early?
6. To tell the truth, I haven't learned to dance.
7. Unless you take the car, I won't go.

---

3. 2 3 2 → . This contour signals incompleteness. In the first situation below it is an alternate for the 2 3 3 ↑ of 2c.

a. Initial grammatical unit (phrase or clause):

> 2 3   2
> In shórt →
> 2   3   2
> If you'll wáit →

b. Statement, to indicate that the speaker has more to say; often the word following this contour is *but*:

> 2   3 2
> She's a nice gírl →

4. 3 2 ↓ or (2 2 3 ↑). This is a call, such as you hear from neighborhood mothers. The handful of English names which are stressed on the last syllable—for example; *Marie, Eugene, Bernice, Monroe*—may take the **2 2 3** ↑ intonation pattern:

> **2 2 3**
> Maríe ↑ .

Others take either pattern:

> **3 2 2 3**
> Hárry ↓ or Hárry ↑

If neither of these patterns brings results, the mother may change to the threatening

> **3 1**
> Hárry ↓

which is more likely to bring the culprit scampering home.

5. 2 3 ↑. On an individual question word this contour signals a request for repetition of some part of the preceding message:

> **2 3 1 2 3**
> Jane has a new piáno teacher ↓ Whó ↑

6. 3 1 ↓. On an individual question word this contour constitutes a request for further information:

> **2 3 1 3 1**
> Jane has a new piáno teacher ↓ Whó ↓

Exercise 5–2

For each sentence or grammatical unit supply the primary stress and the marks of the intonation contour—the pitch levels and terminal junctures.

1. When do we eat?
2. If you'll come,
3. For the most part,
4. He's very handsome, (but)
5. George, (come home at once).
6. We're going to eat in Chicago. Where? (= In what city did you say?)
7. We're going to eat in Chicago. Where? (= In which restaurant?)

---

7. 2 2 3 ↑ or (2 3 ↑). This contour is used on a stressed word, phrase, or clause in a series, with the exception of the last item. Note that in each example there are three contours because there are three primary stresses:

> **2 2 3 2 3 2 3 1**
> She prefers óranges ↑ ápples ↑ and chérries ↓

> **2 2 3 2 2 3 2 3 1**
> She looked under the béd ↑ in the dráwers ↑ and in the clóset ↓

8. Repetition of Previous Pitch. This is used for a quoter clause of the "he said" kind in medial or final position:

```
2       3    3 3 3    3
Are you góing ↑ he ásked ↑
2 3       1  1 1  1
I'm thróugh ↓ he sáid ↓
```

9. 1 2 ↑ or (3 3 ↑). The name of the person whom you are addressing is accompanied by various contours, of which these are quite common:

```
2          3    1  1 2
Why are you wáshing → Jóhn ↑
2                  3  1  1   2
What did you put on the táble ↓ Méllon ↑
2    3     3 3   3
Are you cóming ↑ Géorge ↑
```

10. 2 3 3 ↑ 2 3 1 ↓. In this and the following section two contours combine to make a distinction in meaning. This one signals a choice of two possibilities:

```
2        3 3  2 3   1
Do you want téa ↑ or cóffee ↓
```

This means, "Which of the two do you want, tea or coffee?"

11. 2 3 3 ↑ 2 3 3 ↑. This contour proposes a yes-or-no question:

```
2        3 3  2 3  3
Do you want téa ↑ or cóffee ↑
```

The meaning is "Do you want tea or coffee in preference to something else?"

Exercise 5–3

For each sentence or grammatical unit, supply primary stress, pitches, and terminals.

1. Will you have hot chocolate or milk? (one or the other)
2. Will you have hot chocolate or milk? (or something different)
3. I'm taking physics, chemistry, German, and American history.
4. "When are you driving home?" she asked.
5. Give me a lift, Gertrude.

B. Variations for Emphasis

The contours described above are modified when we single out certain words for emphasis. One way to get special emphasis is to give primary stress and a higher pitch level to the word we wish to emphasize.

<pre>
                 2   3   1
Normal: He wants to eat all the tíme ↓
                 2   3 2 2   3   1
Emphatic: He wants to éat → all the tíme ↓
</pre>

Such a primary stress on the emphasized word abrogates the primary stress that would normally come later in the same contour:

<pre>
                 2   3   1
Normal: He fell into the pónd ↓
                 2 3   1
Emphatic: He féll into the pond ↓ (He didn't jump.)
</pre>

In sentences like the foregoing the pitch slopes gradually down from level 3 to level 1. If the emphasized word has more than one syllable, it is the syllable with the highest word-stress that is given the primary stress and the higher pitch level.

<pre>
                 2   3   1
Normal: Spike does not enjoy intellectual gámes ↓
                 2   3   1
Emphatic: Spike does not enjoy intelléctual games ↓
</pre>

   (He prefers other kinds.)

Another mode of emphasis is found in yes-or-no questions. The word to be emphasized takes a primary stress and higher pitch level, just as in the previous examples, but the pitch remains at this higher level for the duration of the question. The next illustrative sentences show the contours used when the emphasis is placed on different words.

<pre>
                 2   3   3
Normal: Are you walking to the párty this evening ↑
                 2 3   3
Emphatic: Are yóu walking to the party this evening ↑
                 2   3   3
Emphatic: Are you wálking to the party this evening ↑
                 2   3   3
Emphatic: Are you walking to the party this évening ↑
</pre>

Exercise 5–4

You are given below two groups of sentences. For the first sentence in each group indicate the normal intonation contour and primary stress. For the others indicate the contours and primary stresses that take into account the emphasized (italicized) word.

   1a. Did his sister make him a cake?
    b. Did his *sister* make him a cake? (not his mother)
    c. Did his sister *make* him a cake? (not buy)
    d. Did his sister make *him* a cake? (not his brother)
   2a. Is the library in your college quite large?

   b. Is the *library* in your college quite large? (not the gym)
   c. Is the library in *your* college quite large? (not Jim's)

C. Review Exercises on Stress, Pitch Levels, and Terminals

Oral Exercise 5–A

Practice reading these sentences aloud, following the signs of stress, pitch, and juncture. Be prepared to restate the meaning of each.

      2   3   1
  1. What are you going to find óut there ↓
      2   3 3 2   1
  2. What are you going to fínd → out thére ↓
      2   3   1
  3. We have ladies ready-to-wear clóthes ↓
      2   3   2 2   3   1
  4. We have ládies → ready to wear clóthes ↓
      2   3   1
  5. Give poor food instead of tíckets ↓ (headline)
      2   3 2 3   1
  6. Give póor → fóod instead of tickets ↓
      2   3 2 2 3   1
  7. I had to gó → on Súnday ↓
      2   3 2 3   1
  8. I had to go ón → Súnday ↓
      2   2 3 2 3 2 3 3 23 2 3   1
  9. State your náme ↑ áge ↑ addréss ↑ séx ↑ and résidence requirements ↓
      2   2 3 2 3 23 3 2   3   1
 10. State your náme ↑ áge ↑ addréss ↑ sex and résidence requirements ↓
      2   3   1
 11. Hope you are both wêll and wárm ↓
      2   3 3 2   3   1
 12. Hope you are bóth → wêll and wárm ↓
      2   3   1
 13. Harris is a black cóunselor ↓
      2   3   1
 14. Harris is a bláck counselor ↓
      2   3 3 2   3 1
 15. They work oút → in the fíeld ↓
      2   3 3 2   3 1
 16. They wórk → out in the fíeld ↓
      2   2 3 2   2 3 2   3   1
 17. He lives with his wífe ↑ a former módel ↑ and his dáughter ↓
      2   3 2 2   3 2 2   3   1
 18. He lives with his wífe → a former módel → and his dáughter ↓
      2   3 1
 19. Some teenagers are home léss ↓

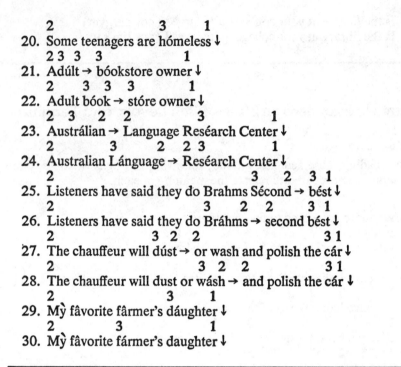

```
                2                 3        1
20. Some teenagers are hómeless ↓
    2 3 3   3                 1
21. Adúlt → bóokstore owner ↓
    2      3   3   3          1
22. Adult bóok → stóre owner ↓
    2 3   2 2              3            1
23. Austrálian → Language Reséarch Center ↓
    2           3         2  2 3        1
24. Australian Lánguage → Reséarch Center ↓
    2                            3    2  3 1
25. Listeners have said they do Brahms Sécond → bést ↓
    2                            3    2  2   3 1
26. Listeners have said they do Bráhms → second bést ↓
    2                         3 2  2              3 1
27. The chauffeur will dúst → or wash and polish the cár ↓
    2                         3 2  2              3 1
28. The chauffeur will dust or wásh → and polish the cár ↓
    2              3       1
29. Mỳ fâvorite fârmer's dáughter ↓
    2              3        1
30. Mỳ fâvorite fármer's daughter ↓
```

Exercise 5–5

In these pairs of sentences the segmental phonemes are identical, but the intonation contours and the positions of the primary stresses are different. Explain briefly the difference of meaning in each pair.

```
      2                                  3            1
1a. He took pictures of the Salvation Army cóoking students ↓
```

```
      2              ·              3    2  2   3    1
 b. He took pictures of the Salvation Ármy → côoking stúdents ↓
```

```
      2          3      1
2a. I called Bill an ámateur ↓
```

```
      2     3  1 2 3      1
 b. I called Bíll ↓ an ámateur ↓
```

```
      2                  3 1
3a. Why are you scratching Béss ↓
```

```
      2            3        1 1 2
 b. Why are you scrátching ↓ Béss ↑
```

```
      2          3  1
4a. Have some hóney ↓
```

<pre>
      3   1 1   2
b. Háve some ↓ hóney ↑
</pre>

<pre>
   2   3   1   1 2
5a. What are we having for súpper → Hám ↑
</pre>

<pre>
   2   3   1 2 3
b. What are we having for súpper ↓ Hám ↑
</pre>

<pre>
   2   3   1
6a. I have instrúctions to leave ↓
</pre>

<pre>
   2   3 1
b. I have instructions to léave ↓
</pre>

<pre>
   2   3 1
7a. I suspect that you were right thére ↓
</pre>

<pre>
   2   3   1
b. I suspect that you were ríght there ↓
</pre>

<pre>
   2   3   2 2 3   1
8a. People who drink Old Stúmp → don't knów any better ↓
</pre>

<pre>
   2   3 2 2   3 1
b. People who drink Old Stúmp → don't know âny bétter ↓
</pre>

<pre>
   2   3 1
9a. I believe thăt man is idealístic ↓
</pre>

<pre>
   2   3 2   3 1
b. I believe thât mân is idealístic ↓
</pre>

<pre>
   2   3 1
10a. It's âll right here in the bóok ↓
</pre>

<pre>
   2   3   1 2   3 1
b. It's all ríght ↓ here in the bóok ↓
</pre>

Exercise 5–6

On each expression place the stress marks that will result in the meaning stated.

1a. fair crowd	a. a medium-sized crowd
b. fair crowd	b. a crowd at the fair
2a. wet suit	a. a special suit for divers and surfers
b. wet suit	b. a suit that is wet

3a. a record sale	a. a sale of records
b. a record sale	b. a sale that breaks the record
4a. a secondary road program	a. a program for secondary roads
b. a secondary road program	b. a road program that is secondary
5a. They're wading pools	a. They are pools for wading
b. They're wading pools	b. They are wading through pools

Exercise 5–7

Supply sustained junctures /→/ where needed to make, or help make, the differentiation in meaning. Some of the stresses are supplied. Remember that sustained juncture is a matter of the lengthening of the preceding pitch-3 word.

  1a. Every dáy passengers enjoy a meal like thís.
      = Passengers enjoy the meal every day.
  b. Everyday pássengers enjoy a meal like thís.
      = Ordinary passengers enjoy a meal like this.
  2a. The blue dréss particularly ínterested her.
      = interested her particularly.
  b. The blue dress partícularly ínterested her.
      = particularly the blue dress.
  3a. French pláne with twenty-four cráshes
      = the plane which has had twenty-four crashes
  b. French plane with twenty-fóur cráshes.
      = Plane crashes with twenty-four aboard.
  4a. I consider thése érrors.
      = I consider these things to be errors.
  b. I consider these érrors.
      = I think about these errors.
  5a. The sóns raise méat.
  b. The sun's ráys méet.

Exercise 5–8

Indicate any primary stress, pitch, and juncture that occur on the italicized words. Use your own natural pronunciation as your guide.

  1. He was looking for a *lake that* always offered good fishing.
  2. Every Saturday Sam drove to Clear *Lake, which* was about thirty miles away.
  3. The *freshmen who* make a B average will be given a picnic by the national honorary society.
  4. The incoming *freshmen, who* will arrive during the weekend, will take their examinations on Monday and Tuesday.
  5. He chose the *canoe that* seemed the most durable.
  6. May I present Michael *Smith, who* is from Seattle?
  7. There will be a meeting of *students who* are from California.
  8. The neighbors did not approve of the *shrubs which* we had planted.
  9. The hedge was composed of French *lilacs, which* flowered in May.
  10. Dr. *Bloom, who* specializes in bone surgery, built a new clinic.

Exercise 5–9

Indicate any primary stress, pitch, and juncture that occur on the italicized words. Use your own natural pronunciation as a guide.

1. That young woman is Harriet *Boulder, a promising junior.*
2. *Hoskins, a first-string quarterback,* was on the bench with an injured ankle.
3. *Typhoon, a well-known novel,* is famous for its descriptive writing.
4. She was reading the *novel Typhoon.*
5. For Christmas she gave him a silk *necktie, a hand-painted beauty.*
6. My *sister Karen* is trying out for a national merit scholarship.
7. We all hoped that *Karen, my younger sister,* would win a scholarship.
8. He lives in Elk *Valley, a county seat.*
9. Her favorite opera was *Carmen, a work by Bizet.*
10. The *opera Carmen* was her favorite.

Exercise 5–10

State the meaning of each expression.

    2   3 1
1a. Còmic strîp àrtist díes ↓
_____

    2   3 1
  b. Cômic strìp àrtist díes ↓
_____

    2   3 1
2a. He àccidêntally drôwns a wânted mán ↓
_____

    2   3   1 2   3 1
  b. He àccidêntally drówns ↓ a wânted mán ↓
_____

3a. Automâtic brídge tòll collèctors
_____

  b. Automâtic brîdge tóll collèctors
_____

4a. Mentally retárded teachers ↓
_____

  b. Mentally retarded téachers ↓
_____

    2 3 1
5a. Ôh bóy ↓
_____

    2 3 3
  b. Ôh bóy ↑
_____

6a. Gêorge's bódy wòrks
_____

      2   3   1
  b. Gêorge's bôdy wórks ↓

---

      2   3   1
7a. I am an oútdòor lòver ↓

---

      2   3 1
  b. I am an ôutdôor lóver ↓

8a. Some wôrk in the líbrary

---

      3   2   2   3   1
  b. Sóme → work in the líbrary ↓

---

      2   3   1
9a. Hè gâve the líbrary bòoks ↓

---

      2   3   1
  b. Hè gâve the líbrary bóoks ↓

---

      2   3   1
10a. More and more doctors are spécializing ↓

---

      2   3   2   2   3   1
  b. More and móre → doctors are spécializing ↓

6

Internal Open Juncture

In the preceding chapter we studied the three terminal junctures and noted that they occur at the end of grammatical units or sentences. The fourth juncture of English differs from the others in that it occurs within grammatical units or sentences. It is found between words and between parts of words, and is called *internal open juncture*. Like the other three it is phonemic, as this minimal pair will show:

keep sticking
keeps ticking

Internal open juncture is indicated by a plus sign /+/ and is sometimes called plus juncture. Here it is with a complete phonemic notation of the pair above:

2   3 1
kîp + stíkɪŋ ↓
2   3 1
kîps + tíkɪŋ ↓

By means of internal open juncture we are able to make distinctions between pairs like these: *an itch, a niche; its praise, it sprays; Grade A, gray day; see Mabel, seem able*. But although most native speakers have little difficulty in perceiving internal juncture, they have trouble in explain-

67

ing just what gives them a sense of break or separation at the junctural point. It is only through the combined efforts of sharp-eared linguists and spectograph analysts that we have been able to learn the conditions under which internal juncture occurs. In general, it is the nature of the sounds surrounding the juncture that serves to locate it. The details are numerous and complex and vary with the kinds and positions of the sounds involved. All we can do here is to examine a few examples of the sound characteristics that define internal open junctures. You will find it good ear training to try to detect for yourself the differences in sounds between the members of each pair before you read the explanation that follows each.

1a. kêep stícking
b. kêeps tícking

There are three differences here between *a* and *b* in the sounds around the junctures. First, the /p/ of *keep* is longer than the /p/ of *keeps;* that is to say, the lips remain closed for a longer time. Second, the /s/ of *sticking* is longer than the /s/ of *keeps.* Initial (postjunctural) consonants are usually longer than those in other positions. Third, the /t/ of *ticking* has more aspiration than that of *sticking.* This means merely that there is more air following the explosion. See for yourself. Hold the palm of your hand an inch from your mouth, say *stick* and *tick,* and notice which /t/ is followed by the stronger blast of air. The same difference is true of all three voiceless stops /p t k/. In initial position before a stressed vowel they have heavy aspiration, but after an /s/ (with no juncture intervening), only slight aspiration. Such are the differences in sound that cue the listener to differentiate between *keep sticking* and *keeps ticking.*

2a. a + níce màn (with emphatic stress)·
b. an + íce màn

In 2*a* the /n/ of *nice* is about twice as long as the /n/ of *an.* This is the clue that it belongs in initial position with *nice.*

3a. it + swings
b. its + wings

Here we find two sound differences that determine internal juncture. The first you already know—the initial /s/ of *swings* is longer than the final /s/ of *its.* The second is a kind of assimilation. In *wings* the /w/ is voiced, as it normally is in initial position, but in *swings* the /w/ is wholly or partly devoiced because of the preceding voiceless /s/. This kind of devoicing is common; a voiceless consonant tends to make voiceless a following /w/, /l/, /r/, /m/, /n/. A few examples of this devoicing are *twist, flee, cream, smoke, snow.*

4a. why + choose
b. white + shoes

In this pair the /ay/ is longer in *why* than it is in *white.* In general, final (prejunctural) vowels and diphthongs are longer than those in other positions. The /š/ of *shoes,* being initial, is longer than the /š/ that is the second component of /č/ in *choose.* (Remember that /č/ consists of /t/ plus /š/ uttered as a single speech sound).

The foregoing examples illustrate a few of our speech habits that enable us to distinguish internal open junctures between words. Now let us recapitulate those that you will find helpful in doing exercise 63.

1. Initial (postjunctural) consonants are longer than those in other positions. For example, the /m/ in *may* is longer than the /m/ in *seam.*

2. Final (prejunctural) consonants are longer than internal consonants. The /p/ in *keep* is longer than that in *keeps.*

3. Initial voiceless stops /p t k/ are strongly aspirated. Examples are *pot, tot, cot.* If, however, these are preceded by /s/, the aspiration is greatly reduced. Compare the aspiration of these pairs: *pan, span; top, stop; kill, skill.* But when there is a juncture between the /s/ and the /p/, /t/, or /k/, there is no reduction of aspiration. For example, you can feel on your hand the aspiration after the /p/ in *this + pot* but not in *this + spot.*

4. In initial position the consonants /w l r m n/ are voiced, as in *way, led, ray, might,* and *nag.* But after a voiceless consonant they tend to become devoiced, as in *sway, fled, pray, smite,* and *snag.*

5. Final (prejunctural) vowels and diphthongs are longer than those in other positions. For example, the /u/ is longer in *new* /nu/ than in *nude* /nud/, and the /ɔ/ is longer in *I saw + Ted* than in *I sought + Ed.*

Exercise 6–1

Write the following expressions in phonemic notation with segmental phonemes and internal junctures. After each pair, explain what characteristics of the surrounding sounds identify the position of the internal junctures. All the information you need for these cases has been included in the foregoing discussion.

1a. I scream _____
b. ice cream _____

2a. night-rate _____
b. nitrate _____

3a. that stuff _____
b. that's tough _____

4a. seem able _____
 b. see Mabel _____

_____

5a. its lid _____
 b. it slid _____

_____

6a. new dart _____
 b. nude art _____

_____

7a. it sprays _____
 b. its praise _____

_____

Exercise 6–2

Can you distinguish by ear between *a name* and *an aim?* Many persons
find this difficult because there may be no internal juncture between a
weakly stressed and a strongly stressed syllable. In the history of English
such difficulty had led to some changes in spelling, as this exercise will
reveal.

Look up the etymology of each of the following words in your desk
dictionary, write down its ME (Middle English) original, and show how
each received a new spelling through incorrect division.

	Present Form	*ME Form*	*Process*
Example:	newt	an ewte	became "a newt"
1.	adder	_____	_____
2.	apron	_____	_____
3.	auger	_____	_____
4.	nickname	_____	_____
5.	umpire	_____	_____

An accurate and exceptionless statement about the distribution of internal junctures cannot be made because the habits of speakers vary too
much. It can be said that in running discourse many words are separated
from one another by /+/. But also, there are cases where words run together in close transition without the /+/, like the unstressed *tŏ thĕ abóve.*
Contrariwise, internal juncture may occur within words, as in *sly + ness*
compared with *minus.* We can at best offer just a few principles that will
help guide your ear to the presence of internal junctures, with the warning
that they are not inviolable.

1. If two vowels in successive syllables carry primary or secondary
stresses, there will be a /+/ somewhere between them.

lĭkes + méat   blûe + dréss

But if two such vowels carry primary and third stresses, there may or may not be a /+/ between them.

bóathoùse   bóot + blàck

2. Two adjoining vowels are usually separated by /+/.

ăn ópĕră + of   thĕ + ĭdéă + ămúses

3. A vowel with weak stress followed by a consonant is often in close transition with the consonant, and there is no /+/.

ăbóve   ă bág   thĕ bést

4. A consonant followed by a vowel with weak stress is in close transition, with no intervening /+/.

móst ŏf   fóund ĭn

5. Between successive syllables with weak stress there is no /+/.

ŏf thĕ wátər

Exercise 6–3

Put in internal junctures where they belong, following the five principles given above. Then read these expressions aloud, following the markings, and try to hear the difference between internal juncture and close transition.

1. fîne   jób
2. môst   of   the   tíme
3. the   párty
4. thât   párty
5. tâlk   wísely
6. sòme   of   the   inspîred   ártists
7. Jâne   lôves   cándy
8. stône   fénce
9. bîrd   in   the   búsh
10. óutlòok

Internal open juncture is the last phoneme in our enumeration of the suprasegmentals. Now we shall revert to the segmental phonemes and see how they pattern in English words.

7
Phonotactics

The English language, we have seen, has thirty-six segmental phonemes. These phonemes are peculiar to English in that no other language has exactly the same inventory. The *th* phonemes that seem so natural to us, /θ/ and /ð/, are not found in most European languages; and the high front rounded vowel of French, German, and Chinese does not exist in English.

When phonemes are joined together in syllables and words, it becomes apparent that there are limitations to the positions they may occupy and to the ways in which they may be arranged in sequences. For example, an English word never begins with /ŋ/ or ends with /h/. An English word may begin with /st/ but not with /ts/. Spanish words, on the other hand, do not begin with /st/ and German words do begin with /ts/. Thus languages vary not only in their stock of phonemes, but also in the ways they permit these phonemes to associate together. The totality of the positions in which any language element may occur is called its distribution, and it will now be our task to examine in part the distribution of English phonemes, known as phonotactics. We shall begin with the consonants.

First, however, we must be clear about the meaning of two terms that will be used frequently in this chapter—"initial position" and "final position." "Initial position" means a position that begins a syllable. Thus a group of consonants in initial position, like /str/, will occur not only at

72

the beginning of words but also within a word, at the beginning of a syllable, as in *restress* /ri + strɛs/. The second term, "final position," means a position that follows a vowel and ends a syllable. It ordinarily means the position at the end of words.

English consonant phonemes occur singly or in groups, and in the word, they occupy three positions—initial, medial, and final. This descriptive statement is not as trite as it appears, for it is not necessarily true of other languages. In Japanese, for instance, consonants occur only singly, not in groups, and in Mandarin Chinese consonants do not appear in final position, except for nasals. Our immediate concern now will be with consonants in groups in the initial positions. A group of two or more consonants which adjoin each other in the same syllable is called a consonant cluster; and a cluster after a juncture, an initial consonant cluster.

A preliminary exercise with nonsense words will perhaps reveal that you, as a native speaker, are already aware of which initial consonant clusters are permitted and which are not permitted in English, even though you have given the matter no thought.

Exercise 7–1

Write E after each nonsense word that sounds English to you, and NE after each one that sounds non-English.

1. /ŋwa/	_____	6. /frun/	_____
2. /spro/	_____	7. /kpadi/	_____
3. /pfunt/	_____	8. /twab/	_____
4. /glɪŋ/	_____	9. /psalmist/	_____
5. /šči/	_____	10. /plon/	_____

It is the odd-numbered words above that contain the non-English initial consonant clusters. They are real words taken from these languages: 1. ancient Chinese, 3. German, 5. Russian, 7. Loma (Liberian), and 9. French.

In English initial consonant clusters the maximum number of phonemes is three. These clusters of three have the following positional characteristics:

1. Only /s/ can occupy first position.
2. Only the voiceless stops /p t k/ appear in second position.
3. Only /l r y w/ appear in third position.

But all possible combinations do not occur, and we actually have only the nine of the following exercise.

Exercise 7–2

Give in conventional writing one word beginning with each of the following three-consonant clusters. Note carefully here and in the following exercises that /y/ at the end of a cluster is always followed by /u/. In words like *student, duty, tune, suit, chew, juice,* and *lute* the pronunciation may vary between /u/ and /yu/.

1. /spl-/ _____	6. /skl-/ _____
2. /spr-/ _____	(in learned words only)
3. /spy-/ _____	7. /skr-/ _____
4. /str-/ _____	8. /sky-/ _____
5. /sty-/ _____	9. /skw-/ _____

From the three-consonant initial clusters we derive four classes of two-consonant clusters. Each class has one consonant position vacant, and the two remaining consonants retain the same order as that of the three-consonant cluster. All clusters in these derived classes are listed in the next exercise.

Exercise 7–3

Give in conventional writing one word beginning with each of the following two-consonant clusters. (Numbers refer to the three positions listed above exercise 7–2.)

    a. Derived 1–2 class
        1. /sp-/ _____
        2. /st-/ _____
        3. /sk-/ _____
    b. Derived 2–3 class
        1. /pl-/ _____
        2. /pr-/ _____
        3. /py-/ _____
        4. /tr-/ _____
        5. /kl-/ _____
        6. /kr-/ _____
        7. /ky-/ _____
        8. /kw-/ _____
        9. /tr-/ _____
      10. /tw-/ _____
      11. /ty-/ _____
    c. Derived 1–3 class
        1. /sl-/ _____
        2. /sw-/ _____
        3. /sy-/ _____
    d. Derived 3–3 class (first two positions vacant)
        1. /ly-/ _____

In addition to the three-consonant and the two-consonant derived clusters in initial position there is also a sizable group of nonderived two-consonant clusters. Each of these contains only one consonant found in the three-consonant clusters. Therefore it is not a derived but a nonderived cluster.

Exercise 7–4

Give in conventional writing one word to exemplify each of the following nonderived two-consonant initial clusters.

1. /sn-/ _____
2. /sm-/ _____
3. /bl-/ _____
4. /br-/ _____
5. /by-/ _____
6. /dr-/ _____
7. /dy-/ _____
8. /dw-/ _____
9. /gl-/ _____
10. /gr-/ _____
11. /gy-/ _____
12. /sf-/ _____
13. /my-/ _____
14. /ny-/ _____
15. /fl-/ _____
16. /fr-/ _____
17. /fy-/ _____
18. /θr-/ _____
19. /θy-/ _____
20. /θw-/ _____
21. /šr-/ _____
22. /vy-/ _____
23. /hw-/ _____
24. /hy-/ _____
25. /čy-/ _____
26. /ǰy-/ _____

A useful generalization can be made about the initial two-consonant clusters. It is the principle that the louder of the two consonants occurs next to the vowel. The order of loudness of English speech sounds, from least to most loud, is as follows: **obstruent** (stops, fricatives, affricates, in that order), **sonorant** (nasals, laterals, glides, in that order), and **vowel.** Thus we can say that initial two-consonant clusters follow the order of O–S before a vowel. Here are a few examples, employing all the sonorants except /ŋ/, which does not follow another consonant: *shriek* /šrik/, *play* /ple/, *beauty* /byuti/, *quite* /kwayt/, *smoke* /smok/, and *snake* /snek/. An exception to this generalization is the derived 1-2 class, *sp-, st-,* and *sk-,* because among obstruents fricatives are louder than stops.

In two-consonant clusters after the vowel the sonorant occurs next to the vowel and is followed by the obstruent. Some examples are *hand* /hænd/, *self* /sɛlf/, *ramp* /ræmp/, and *fort* /fort/. Thus the formula for two-consonant clusters before and after the vowel can be expressed as OSVSO. To this we might add two refinements. In final two-consonant clusters in which two obstruents occur the fricative precedes the stop, as in *last, risk, deft,* and *clasp.* These follow the principle that the louder consonant is next to the vowel because fricatives and affricates are louder than stops. Also, when the final cluster consists of a glide plus nasal, as in *harm* and *horn,* or of the lateral plus nasal, as in *elm* and *kiln,* the principle is observed. Exceptions are words ending in /r/ plus /l/, as in *snarl* and *whorl.*

Exercise 7–5

Classify the first three sounds of each word by writing over each the abbrevation V (vowel), O (obstruent), or S (sonorant)

1. tree   4. cute (second consonant is not shown)
2. class   5. smell
3. swig   6. sneeze

Exercise 7–6

Classify the last three sounds of each word by the abbreviations V, O, or S.

1. clump   5. sink
2. hint   6. barn
3. help   7. task
4. hard

The two-consonant clusters you have seen in exercises 7–5 and 7–6 are the ones that are thoroughly English. Besides these there are some which exist in a sort of twilight zone. They belong to foreign words which have come into English retaining something of their foreign pronunciation, like *moire* and *pueblo,* and especially to foreign personal and place names, like *Buena Vista, Schmidt,* and *Vladivostok.* It is difficult to say whether or not such consonant clusters belong in the inventory of initial English consonant clusters. If you'd like to try your hand at them, do the next exercise.

Exercise 7–7

Give in conventional writing one word exemplifying each of the following two-consonant clusters. For some you may have to resort to names of persons or places. An unabridged dictionary will help you with the more resistant ones. If some baffle you, don't waste time but look at the answers.

1. /pw-/ _____   11. /šm-/ _____
2. /bw-/ _____   12. /šn-/ _____
3. /gw-/ _____   13. /šw-/ _____
4. /mw-/ _____   14. /ts-/ _____
5. /nw-/ _____   15. /vl-/ _____
6. /sv-/ _____   16. /vr-/ _____
7. /šp-/ _____   17. /vw-/ _____
8. /št-/ _____   18. /zl-/ _____
9. /šk-/ _____   19. /zw-/ _____
10. /šl-/ _____   20. /žw-/ _____

Exercise 7–8

When we turn to the single-consonant phonemes that may occupy initial position, we find that all but two may begin a word. Go through the chart of English consonant phonemes, diagram 13 (page 27), find these two, and list them:

1. _____ 2. _____

So much for initial consonants and consonant clusters. The clusters that remain, those in medial and final positions, are numerous. We shall deal with them scantly, however, since our look at initial clusters will be sufficient to illustrate this area of language patterning known as phonotactics.

In final position—that is, after a vowel and ending a syllable—the maximum number of consonants that can cluster together is five, though it is doubtful whether clusters of five are ever sounded in normal speech.

Exercise 7–9

In the first column write in phonemic notation your pronunciation of the final consonant or consonant clusters in each of the following words. In the second column write down the number of consonantal phonemes sounded in the final clusters.

1. pass	_____	_____		9. strength	_____	_____
2. ask	_____	_____		10. text	_____	_____
3. asked	_____	_____		11. first	_____	_____
4. health	_____	_____		12. sixth	_____	_____
5. eighth	_____	_____		13. twelfth	_____	_____
6. attempt	_____	_____		14. texts	_____	_____
7. chintz	_____	_____		15. sixths	_____	_____
8. mince	_____	_____		16. twelfths	_____	_____

The answer-key to this exercise will give the greatest number of consonants that might possibly be heard in deliberate speech. But you will probably, like many speakers, assimilate and take shortcuts through the prickly maze of consonant sounds. For instance, in number 3 one can easily say /æskt/, but more often the /k/ is assimilated to the /t/, giving /æst/. And in *sixths,* instead of the full /sɪkstθs/, one is likely to produce a shortened form, like /sɪks:/. The [:] here is a diacritic standing for greater length.

Vowels do not cluster. When two or more of them occur successively, one of two things happens: (1) one glides effortlessly into the other, as in /tray/ and /kɔy/, producing a diphthong; or (2) they are separated by juncture, as in *naïve* /na + iv/. So, in the distribution of English vowels, one has only position to consider.

Now we shall examine three propositions in regard to vowel positions.

1. Every vowel can begin an English word.

Exercise 7–10

To see if every English vowel can be used at the beginnings of words, write in phonemic notation one word beginning with each of the twelve vowels.

1. /i/ _____	7. /ə/ _____
2. /ɪ/ _____	8. /a/ _____
3. /e/ _____	9. /u/ _____
4. /ɛ/ _____	10. /ʊ/ _____
5. /æ/ _____	11. /o/ _____
6. /ər/ _____	12. /ɔ/ _____

Exercise 7–11

The vowels /u/ and /ʊ/ have a low frequency in initial position. List in phonemic notation all the words you can think of in ten minutes that begin with /u/ and /ʊ/.

/u/	/ʊ/
_____	_____
_____	_____
_____	_____
_____	_____
_____	_____

---

2. Every vowel can be preceded and followed by a single consonant, as in /bɛd/ and /sup/.

Exercise 7–12

To test this proposition, give one example for each vowel of the pattern CVC, that is, consonant-vowel-consonant.

1. /i/ _____	7. /ə/ _____
2. /ɪ/ _____	8. /a/ _____
3. /e/ _____	9. /u/ _____
4. /ɛ/ _____	10. /ʊ/ _____
5. /æ/ _____	11. /o/ _____
6. /ər/ _____	12. /ɔ/ _____

3a. Not all vowels can end a word or morpheme. Here we must make a distinction between checked vowels and free vowels. Checked vowels are those that cannot end a morpheme or word. The checked vowels are /ɪ/, /ɛ/, /æ/, /a/, and /ʊ/.

Exercise 7–13

See if you can find any exceptions to the statement above about the non-occurrence of checked vowels at the end of words. (If you live in an "r-dropping" region, you will have words like *far* that end in /a/.) Use phonemic notation.

1. /ɪ/ _____
2. /ɛ/ _____
3. /æ/ _____

4. /a/ _____
5. /ʊ/ _____

3b. Free vowels are those that can occur at the end of morphemes and words. The free vowels are /i/, /e/, /ər/, /ə/, /u/, /o/, and /ɔ/.

Exercise 7–14

Give an example of each free vowel occurring at the end of a word. Use phonemic notation.

1. /i/ _____
2. /e/ _____
3. /ər/ _____
4. /ə/ _____

5. /u/ _____
6. /o/ _____
7. /ɔ/ _____

The phonotactic patterns of a language have a compulsive effect upon its speakers in that these speakers find it hard to break the patterns of their native tongue and habituate themselves to the use of new ones. If, for example, you try to teach a Spaniard to pronounce *student*, he is likely to persist in saying /ɛstudɛnt/ for some time because /st-/ is not an initial consonant cluster in Spanish, whereas /ɛst-/ is common. Likewise, an American in India has great difficulty in pronouncing the native term for washerman, *dhobi* /dʰobi/, because /dʰ-/, an aspirated /d/, does not occur initially in English. Instead, he will say /dobi/. Yet this same American can say *Toby* /tʰobi/ with perfect ease because initial /tʰ-/, an aspirated /t/, is a normal word-beginning in English.

The general tendency is for a speaker to pronounce words borrowed from another tongue with the phonotactic patterns of his own language, even when he can utter the foreign clusters. For instance, it is easy for us to say /šn-/ at the beginning of a word, as in the German *Schnorchel*, but we normally change the word to /snɔrkəl/ to conform to our own English initial cluster /sn-/.

Optional Exercise 7–15

Here are eleven words, each beginning with a consonant or consonant cluster that is not native to English in initial position. Assume that you see each one in print and wish to pronounce it. Write down in phonemic symbols your probable pronunciation. Some will be easy; others may be difficult and require the substitution of English initial sounds.

1. German *Pfund* /pfunt/, pound _____
2. German *Zeit* /tsait/, time _____

3. French *Psyché* /psiše/, Psyche _____
4. Mazahua (an unwritten Mexican
   language) /ndišu/, woman _____
5. African *Mboya* /mbɔya/, = a proper name _____
6. Norwegian *sving* /sviŋ/, curve _____
7. Chamorro *nganga* /ŋanga/ duck _____
8. Dutch *wrak* /vrak/, wreck _____

The next three are not transliterated but are given only in phonemic symbols. Can you pronounce them as given or would you make substitutions?

9. Modern Greek /dzikas/, grasshopper _____
10. Modern Greek /ksilo/, wood _____
11. Russian /ščɛpka/, sliver _____

With this chapter on phonotactics we conclude the description of basic English phonology, that is, of that phonological information that you willl need in the later sections on morphology and syntax.

PART II
THE MORPHOLOGY OF ENGLISH

8
Morphemes

We now turn our attention to the study of the internal structure of words, which is known as morphology. We shall use the term *word* loosely, in its familiar sense, since a strict definition will not be necessary till later.

A. Definition of Morpheme

Before we can examine the structure of words, we must become acquainted with an entity known as the morpheme. A morpheme is a short segment of language that meets three criteria:

1. It is a word or a part of a word that has meaning.
2. It cannot be divided into smaller meaningful parts without violation of its meaning or without meaningless remainders.
3. It recurs in differing verbal environments with a relatively stable meaning.

Let us examine the word *straight* /stret/ in the light of these criteria. First of all, we recognize it as a word and can find it listed as such in any dictionary. Second, it cannot be divided without violation of meaning. For example, we can, by dividing straight /stret/, get the smaller meaningful forms of *trait* /tret/, *rate* /ret/, and *ate* /et/, but the meanings of these violate the meaning of *straight*. Furthermore, when we divide it in these ways we get the meaningless remainders of /s-/, /st-/, and /str-/. Third, *straight* recurs with a relatively stable meaning in such environments as *straightedge, straighten,* and *a straight line.* Thus *straight* meets all the criteria of a morpheme.

As a second example let us compare the morpheme bright (= light) with the word *brighten* (= make light). In sound the only difference between the two words is the added /-ən/ of *brighten*, and in meaning the difference is the added sense of "make" in *brighten*. This leads us to conclude that /-ən/ means "make." Thus we see that /-ən/ is a part of a word that has meaning. We also know that it cannot be divided into smaller meaningful units and that it recurs with a stable meaning in words like *cheapen, darken, deepen, soften,* and *stiffen.* It is therefore obvious that /-ən/ must be considered a morpheme.

Exercise 8-1

After each word write a number showing how many morphemes it contains.

1. play	_____	11. keeper	_____
2. replay	_____	12. able	_____
3. date	_____	13. unable	_____
4. antedate	_____	14. miniskirt	_____
5. hygiene	_____	15. rain	_____
6. weak	_____	16. rainy	_____
7. weaken	_____	17. cheap	_____
8. man	_____	18. cheaply	_____
9. manly	_____	19. cheaper	_____
10. keep	_____	20. cover	_____

Exercise 8-2

Write the meaning of the italicized morphemes.

1. *ante*date _____
2. *re*play _____
3. man*ly* _____
4. keep*er* _____
5. *un*able _____
6. rain*y* _____
7. cheap*est* _____
8. *in*active _____
9. *im*possible _____
10. *mal*function (noun) _____

B. Free and Bound Morphemes

Morphemes are of two kinds, free and bound. A free morpheme is one that can be uttered alone with meaning. For instance, in reply to "What are you going to do now?" you might answer "Eat." This is a free morpheme. A bound morpheme, unlike the free, cannot be uttered alone with meaning. It is always annexed to one or more morphemes to form a word. The italicized morphemes in exercise 8-2 are all bound, for one would not utter in isolation forms like *ante-*, *re-*, *-ly*, *-er*, and *un-*. Here are a few more examples: *pre*view, play*ed*, activ*ity*, super*vise*, *inter-*, *-vene*.

Exercise 8–3

Underline the bound morphemes It is possible for a word to consist entirely of bound morphemes.

1. speaker
2. kingdom
3. petrodollar
4. idolize
5. selective

6. biomass
7. intervene
8. remake
9. dreamed
10. undo

C. Bases

Another classification of morphemes puts them into two classes: bases and affixes. A base morpheme is the part of a word that has the principal meaning.[1] The italicized morphemes in these words are bases: *deni*al, *lov*able, *annoy*ance, re-*enter*. Bases are very numerous, and most of them in English are free morphemes; but some are bound, like *-sent* in con*sent*, dis*sent*, and as*sent*. A word may contain one base and several affixes.

[1] This *ad hoc* definition will do for our present purpose. A more exact definition, which requires terms that you will not meet until later, would go something like this: A base is a linguistic form that meets one or more of these requirements:

1. It can occur as an immediate constituent of a word whose only other immediate constituent is a prefix or suffix.

   Examples: re*act*, *active*, *fertil*ize

2. It is an allomorph of a morpheme which has another allomorph that is a free form.

   Examples: *dep*th (*deep*), *wolv*es (*wolf*)

3. It is a borrowing from another language in which it is a free form or a base.

   Examples: *bio*metrics, *micro*cosm, phrase*ology*

The third point is open to the theoretical objection that it imports diachronic lore to clarify a synchronic description.

Readability, for example, contains the free base *read* and the two affixes *-abil-* and *-ity;* and *unmistakable* has the free base *take* and the affixes **un-**, **mis-**, and *-able.*

Exercise 8–4
Underline the bases in these words.

1. womanly	6. lighten	11. unlikely
2. endear	7. enlighten	12. prewar
3. failure	8. friendship	13. subway
4. famous	9. befriend	14. falsify
5. infamous	10. Bostonian	15. unenlivened

All the bases in the preceding exercise are free bases. Now we shall look at bound bases, to which it is sometimes hard to attach a precise meaning. A good number of bound bases in English come from the Latin and Greek, like the *-sent-* in *sentiment, sentient, consent, assent, dissent, resent.* The standard way to pin down the meaning is to search for the meaning common to all the words that contain the base (in these words, *-sent-* means "feel"). A base may have more than one phonemic form. In the above list it has these forms: /sɛntɪ-/, /sɛnš-/, /-sɛnt/, and /-zɛnt/. Here is an exercise in this method.

Exercise 8–5
Write in the blanks the meaning of the italicized bound bases. To be exact, we should write these words below in phonemic script to show the various forms of the base, but this would involve a complication that will be explained later. So here we must be content to indicate the base in a loose way with spelling.

1. *audi*ence, *audi*ble, *audi*tion, *audi*tory   _____
2. sui*cide,* patri*cide,* matri*cide,* infanti*cide*   _____
3. *or*al, *or*ation, *or*acle, *or*atory   _____
4. *aqua*plane, *aqua*tic, *aqua*rium, *aqua*naut   _____
5. photo*graphy,* xero*graphy,* bio*graphy,* calli*graphy*   _____
6. *corps, corpse, corpor*ation, *corpor*eal   _____
7. *ten*able, *ten*ant, *ten*ure, *ten*acious   _____
8. *pend*ulum, *pend*ant, sus*pend*ers, im*pend*ing   _____
9. *manu*al, *mani*cure, *manu*script   _____
10. e*ject,* in*ject,* pro*ject,* re*ject*   _____

This method can be difficult and baffling. An easier way that often works is to look up in your dictionary the word in question, like *consent,* and in the etymology find out the Latin or Greek meaning of the base. Under *consent* you will find that *-sent* means "feel" in Latin, and this area of meaning seems to have been retained for the base of all the words in the *-sent* list. Also, you will find some of the more common base morphemes listed as separate entries. The following, for example, are all separately entered in *Webster's New Collegiate Dictionary*: *phot-, photo-* (light); *xer-, xero-* (dry); *bi-, bio-* (life); *mis-, miso-* (hate); *ge-, geo-* (earth); *biblio-* (book); *-meter* (measure); *tele-, tel-* (distant); *-phil, -phile* (lover); *-logy* (science or study of).

Exercise 8–6
Look up in your desk dictionary the meanings of the bound bases italicized in the words below. Write the meanings of these bound bases in the first column. In the second column write another English word that contains the same base.

1. *geo* graphy _____ _____
2. *bio* logy _____ _____
3. *biblio* phile _____ _____
4. inter*vene* _____ _____
5. compre*hend* _____ _____
6. re*cur* _____ _____
7. in*spect* _____ _____
8. op*pose* _____ _____
9. in*spire* _____ _____
10. *rod*ent _____ _____
11. *port*able _____ _____
12. *rup*ture _____ _____
13. *ann*ual _____ _____
14. *carn*al _____ _____
15. big*amy* _____ _____

D. Difficulties in Morphemic Analysis

Let us now digress long enough to point out that the identification of morphemes is not as tidy a business as may appear in these exercises and that there are serious, perhaps insoluble, difficulties in morphemic analysis.

The first difficulty is that you have your own individual stock of morphemes just as you have a vocabulary that is peculiarly your own. An example will make this clear. Tom may think of *automobile* as one morpheme meaning "car," whereas Dick may know the morphemes *auto-* (self) and *mobile* (moving), and recognize them in other words like *autograph* and *mobilize*. Dick, on the other hand, may consider *chronometer* to be a single morpheme, a fancy term for "watch," but Harry sees in this word two morphemes, *chrono-* (time) and *meter* (measure), which he also finds in *chronology* and *photometer,* and Sadie finds a third morpheme *-er* in it, as in *heater;* thus, *mete* (verb) to measure, + − *er,* one who, or that which.

The second difficulty is that persons may know a given morpheme but differ in the degree to which they are aware of its presence in various words. It is likely, for instance, that most speakers of English know the agentive suffix /-ər/ (spelled *-er, -or, -ar*) meaning "one who, that which," and recognize it in countless words like *singer* and *actor.* But many may only dimly sense this morpheme in *professor* and completely overlook it in *voucher, cracker,* and *tumbler.* Thus, can we say that *sweater* has enough pulse in its *-er* to be considered a two-morpheme word? This will vary with the awareness of different individuals. A less simple case is seen in this group: *nose, noseful, nosey, nasal, nuzzle, nozzle, nostril, nasturtium.* Only a linguistically knowledgeable person would see the morpheme *nose* in each of these words. Others will show considerable differences in awareness.

Thus, we conclude that one individual's morphemes are not those of another. This is no cause for deep concern, though it may be a source of controversy in the classroom, for we are dealing with the morphemes of the ENGLISH LANGUAGE, not merely with the individual morpheme inventories of Tom, Dick, Harry, and Sadie.

But in the language itself there are problems of morphemic analysis because the language is constantly changing. One problem is that of obsolescence.

Morphemes may slowly fade away into disuse as the decades and centuries roll by, affecting our view of their morphemehood. For instance, we can be sure that *troublesome, burdensome, lonesome,* and *cuddlesome* are two-morpheme words consisting of a base morpheme plus the suffixal morpheme *-some. Winsome,* however, has an obsolete base (Old English *wynn,* pleasure, joy), so that the word is now monomorphemic. Between these two extremes are words like *ungainly.* This means of course "not gainly," but what does *gainly* mean? Certainly it is not in common use. In current dictionaries it is called "rare" or "obsolete" or "dialectal," or is unlabeled. Then should we call *ungainly* a word of one or two or even three morphemes?

Another problem results from the fact that metaphors die as language changes. Let us take the morpheme *-prehend-* (seize) as an example. In *apprehend* (= to arrest or seize) and *prehensile* it clearly retains its meaning, but in *comprehend* the metaphor (seize mentally) seems to be dead, and the meaning of the word today is merely "understand." Does it then still contain the morpheme *-prehend-*? Another case is seen in *bankrupt* (bench broken). The morpheme *bank,* in the sense of a bench, may be obsolete, but *-rupt* is alive today in *rupture* and *interrupt.* The original metaphor is dead, however, and the meaning of these two morphemes does not add up at all to the current meaning of *bankrupt.* Is the word then a single morpheme?

This last matter, additive meanings, is a problem in itself. Meaning is very elusive, and when morphemes combine in a word, their meanings tend to be unstable and evanescent; they may even disappear altogether. Consider, for example, the morpheme *pose* (place). In "pose a question" the meaning is clear, and it is probably retained in *interpose* (place between). But in *suppose* and *repose* the meaning appears to have evaporated. Between these extremes are words like *compose, depose, impose, propose,* and *transpose,* in which the sense of *pose* seems to acquire special nuances in combination. Which of all these words, then, may be said to contain the morpheme *pose* (place)? Such are some of the problems in morphemic analysis that have plagued linguists.

Optional Exercise 8–7

This exercise is an excursus into dead metaphor, simply to show you a fascinating aspect of words that many people are unaware of. Look up the etymology of the following words in your desk dictionary and note the original meaning that underlies the words. A little thought will show you the connection between the original meaning and the present sense.

1. daisy   _____   6. hazard   _____
2. muscle   _____   7. calculate _____
3. supercilious _____   8. spurn   _____
4. window   _____   9. stimulate _____
5. easel   _____   10. stagnate _____

E. Affixes

An affix is a bound morpheme that occurs before or within or after a base. There are three kinds, prefixes, infixes, and suffixes, two of which you have already met in passing. Now we shall deal with them in greater detail.

Prefixes are those bound morphemes that occur before a base, as in *im*port, *pre*fix, *re*consider. Prefixes in English are a small class of morphemes, numbering about seventy-five. Their meanings are often those of English prepositions and adverbials.

Exercise 8–8

Look up in your desk dictionary each italicized prefix. (Be careful here. If you are looking up the prefix *in-* in the *American College Dictionary,* you will find eight entries for *in.* The first is the word *in* itself, which you don't want. The next three are prefixes, indicated as such by a hyphen after the morpheme; thus, *in-*. One of these is what you are looking for. Sometimes, when you have located the exact entry you want, you will find several meanings for it, as is the case with *de-*.) From the meanings given for the prefix, choose the one that fits the word and write it in the first column. In the second column write another word containing the same prefix with the same meaning. Numbers 3, 7, 8, and 11 contain variants of a prefixal morpheme.

1. *anti*freeze
2. *circum*vent
3. *co*pilot
   *col*lapse
   *com*pact
   *con*vene
   *cor*rode
4. *contra*dict
5. *de*vitalize
6. *dis*agreeable
7. *in*secure
   *im*perfect
   *il*legible
   *ir*reverent
8. *in*spire
   *im*bibe
9. *inter*vene
10. *intra*mural
11. *ob*struct
    *op*pose
12. *pre*war
13. *post*war
14. *pro*ceed
15. *retro*active
16. *semi*professional
17. *sub*way
18. *super*abundant
19. *un*likely[2]
20. *un*dress

---

[2] In the New York *Times* Russell Baker wrote: "Congress passes a bill. The President unpasses it. Then Congress disunpasses it."

Infixes are bound morphemes that have been inserted within a word. In English these are rare. Occasionally they are additions within a word, as in *un get at able,* where the preposition *at* of *get at* is kept as an infix in the *-able* adjective, though the preposition is usually dropped in similar words, like *reliable* (from *rely on*) and *accountable* (from *account for*). But infixes in English are most commonly replacements, not additions. They occur in a few noun plurals, like the *-ee-* in *geese,* replacing the *-oo-* of *goose,* and more often in the past tense and past participles of verbs, like the *-o-* of *chose* and *chosen* replacing the *-oo-* of *choose.* When we meet such infixes at the end of this chapter, we shall call them by the more precise term of "replacive allomorphs."

Exercise 8–9

In the following groups of words, underline each infix. In the case of verbs, the stem (= dictionary-entry form) is the form into which the infix is inserted. Thus, in *freeze, froze, frozen* the stem is *freeze*, and into this the infix *o* is inserted in the past tense *froze* and the past participle *frozen*.

1. foot, feet
2. mouse, mice
3. take, took, taken
4. grow, grew, grown
5. spin, spun, spun

6. shake, shook, shaken
7. ring, rang, rung
8. tear, tore, torn
9. ride, rode, ridden
10. find, found, found

Suffixes are bound morphemes that occur after a base, like shrink*age*, fail*ure*, nois*y*, real*ize*, nail*s*, dream*ed*. Suffixes may pile up to the number of three or four, whereas prefixes are commonly single, except for the negative *un-* before another prefix. In *normalizers* we perhaps reach the limit with four: the base *norm* plus the four suffixes *-al, -ize, -er, -s*. When suffixes multiply like this, their order is fixed: there is one and only one order in which they occur.

Exercise 8–10

In these words the base is italicized. After each word write the number of suffixes it contains.

1. *organ*ists _____
2. *person*alities _____
3. *flirt*atiously _____
4. *atom*izers _____
5. *friend*liest _____

6. *contradict*orily _____
7. *trust*eeship _____
8. *greas*ier _____
9. *countri*fied _____
10. *respons*ibilities _____

Exercise 8–11

Each group contains a base and suffixes. Make each into a word. In each case see if more than one order of suffixes is possible.

1. -ed, live, -en _____
2. -ing, -ate, termin _____
3. -er, -s, mor, -al, -ize _____
4. provinc, -s, -ism, -ial _____
5. -ly, -some, grue _____
6. -ity, work, -able _____
7. in, -most, -er _____
8. marry, -age, -ity, -abil _____
9. -dom, -ster, gang _____
10. -ly, -ion, -ate, affect _____

F. Inflectional Affixes

The inflectional affixes can be schematized as follows:

Inflectional Affix	*Examples*	*Name*
1. {-s pl.}	dog*s*, ox*en*, m*i*ce	noun plural
2. {-s sg ps}	boy'*s*	noun singular possessive
3. {-s pl ps}	boys', men'*s*	noun plural possessive
4. {-s 3d}	vacate*s*	present third-person singular
5. {-ING vb}	discuss*ing*	present participle
6. {-D pt}	chew*ed*, r*o*de	past tense
7. {-D pp}	chew*ed*, eat*en*, sw*u*m	past participle
8. {-ER cp}	bold*er*, soon*er*, near*er*	comparative
9. {-EST sp}	bold*est*, soon*est*, near*est*	superlative

The words to which these affixes (suffixes and infixes) are attached are called stems. The stem includes the base or bases and all the derivational affixes. Thus, the stem of *playboys* is *playboy* and that of *beautified* is *beautify*.

The inflectional suffixes differ from the derivational suffixes in the following ways, to which there are few exceptions.

1. They do not change the part of speech.

> **Examples:** sled, sled*s* (both nouns)
> cough, cough*ed* (both verbs)
> cold, cold*er* (both adjectives)

2. They come last in a word.

> **Examples:** shorten*ed*, villaini*es*, industrializ*ing*

3. They go with all stems of a given part of speech.

> **Examples:** He eat*s*, drink*s*, dream*s*, entertain*s*, motivate*s*.

4. They do not pile up; only one ends a word.

> **Examples:** flake*s*, work*ing*, high*er*, writt*en*

The exception here is {s pl ps}, the plural possessive of the noun, as in "The student*s'* worries."

Exercise 8–12

Write the morphemic symbol and name for each inflectional affix in bold-face type. The term *affix* here includes both suffixes, like dream*ed,* and infixes, like sw*u*m, r*o*de, r*a*ng.

1. The flagpole sto**od** in front of Main Hall.
   _____

2. Four pledg**es** were initiated.
   _____

3. Shirley pledg**es** to do her best.
   _____

4. The pledge**'s** shirt was torn.
   _____

5. The pledges**'** shirts were torn.
   _____

6. We were discuss**ing** the editorial.
   _____

7. The novel was short**er** than I had expected.
   _____

8. They wait**ed** at the dock.
   _____

9. Which is the long**est** route?
   _____

10. Have you tak**en** calculus yet?
    _____

11. Chris play**ed** well in the second set.
    _____

12. The dealer weigh**ed** the poultry.
    _____

13. Would you mind repeat**ing** the question?
    _____

14. The sheets were soon iron**ed.**
    _____

15. He never lock**s** the door.
    _____

G. Derivational Suffixes

In addition to a short list of inflectional suffixes English has a large supply of another kind of suffix, called derivational suffixes. These consist of all the suffixes that are not inflectional. Among the characteristics of derivational suffixes there are three that will be our immediate concern.

1. The words with which derivational suffixes combine is an arbitrary matter. To make a noun from the verb *adorn* we must add *-ment*—no other suffix will do—whereas the verb *fail* combines only with *-ure* to make a noun, *failure.*

Exercise 8–13

The left-hand column contains ten words. The right-hand column contains thirteen derivational suffixes used to make nouns and having the general meanings of "state, condition, quality, or act of." By combining these suffixes with the words listed, make as many nouns as you can.

1. happy	1. -hood	11. -ance
2. friend	2. -acy	12. -th
3. girl	3. -ism	13. -ure
4. compose	4. -ness	
5. shrink	5. -ment	
6. active	6. -age	
7. supreme	7. -y	
8. true	8. -ation	
9. pagan	9. -ship	
10. discover	10. -ity	

Nouns: _____ _____ _____

_____ _____ _____

_____ _____ _____

_____ _____ _____

_____ _____ _____

---

2. In many cases, but not all, a derivational suffix changes the part of speech of the word to which it is added. The noun *act* becomes an adjective by the addition of *-ive*, and to the adjective *active* we can add *-ate*, making it a verb, *activate.* Although we have not yet taken up the parts of speech, you probably know enough about them to distinguish between nouns, verbs, adjectives, and adverbs, as you are asked to do in the next exercise.

Exercise 8–14

The words in the second column are formed by the addition of a derivational suffix to those in the first column. After every word in both columns indicate its part-of-speech classification by N (noun), V (verb), Aj (adjective), or Av (adverb).

1. break	_____	breakage	_____
2. desire	_____	desirable	_____
3. conspire	_____	conspiracy	_____
4. rehearse	_____	rehearsal	_____
5. ideal	_____	idealize	_____
6. false	_____	falsify	_____
7. sweet	_____	sweetly	_____
8. doubt	_____	doubtful	_____
9. mouth	_____	mouthful	_____
10. sing	_____	singer	_____
11. familiarize	_____	familiarization	_____
12. passion	_____	passionate	_____
13. host	_____	hostess	_____
14. gloom	_____	gloomy	_____
15. martyr	_____	martyrdom	_____
16. novel	_____	novelist	_____
17. day	_____	daily	_____
18. prohibit	_____	prohibitory	_____
19. excel	_____	excellent	_____
20. create	_____	creative	_____
21. vision	_____	visionary	_____
22. cube	_____	cubic	_____
23. ripe	_____	ripen	_____
24. real	_____	realism	_____
25. accept	_____	acceptance	_____

3. Derivational suffixes usually do not close off a word; that is, after a derivational suffix one can sometimes add another derivational suffix and can frequently add an inflectional suffix. For example, to the word *fertilize,* which ends in a derivational suffix, one can add another one, *-er,* and to *fertilizer* one can add the inflectional suffix *-s,* closing off the word.

Exercise 8–15

Add a derivational suffix to each of these words, which already end in a derivational suffix.

1. reasonable _____
2. formal _____
3. organize _____
4. purify _____
5. purist _____

Exercise 8–16
Add an inflectional suffix, one of those listed on page 92, to each of these words, which end in derivational suffixes. In the third column put any words you can think of that are formed by a suffix following the inflectional suffix you added in the second column.

1. kindness _____ _____
2. beautify _____ _____
3. quarterly _____ _____
4. popularize _____ _____
5. depth _____ _____
6. pressure _____ _____
7. arrival _____ _____
8. orientate _____ _____
9. friendly _____ _____
10. funny _____ _____

A glance in the dictionary will reveal that many words have relatives, close and distant, and in grammatical study it is often necessary to examine families of related words. To label such families we employ the word *paradigm*. There are two kinds of paradigms, inflectional and derivational. The inflectional will be explained later. The derivational paradigm is a set of related words composed of the same base morpheme and all the derivational affixes that can go with this base. Here is an example: *man, manly, mannish, manful, manhood, manikin, unman, manliness, manward, manfully, mannishly.*

Exercise 8–17
You are given here five bases, or words with their bases italicized. Give all the words in the derivational paradigm of each. Do not include words with two bases, like *manhunt* or *manpower*. (Use other paper for this exercise.)

1. sin
2. kind
3. live /laiv/
4. trans*port* (-port = carry)
5. *aud*ible (aud- = hear)

H. Suffixal Homophones

Some suffixes, both inflectional and derivational, have homophonous forms.
The inflectional morpheme {-ER cp} has two homophones. The first is the derivational suffix {-ER n}, which is attached to verbs to form nouns. This is a highly productive suffix, that is, it is used to produce hundreds

of English nouns like *hunter, fisher, camper, golfer, lover*. It is often called the agent *-er* and conveys a meaning of "that which performs the action of the verb stem," as in *thriller* and *teacher*. It may also be attached to non-verbal stems, e.g., *probationer, New Yorker, teen-ager, freighter*. The *-er* on such words could be said to convey a more general meaning of "that which is related to"; and since this meaning is inclusive of the previous one, both these *-er* suffixes can be considered to belong to {-ER n}.

The second derivational *-er* morpheme appears at the end of words like *chatter, mutter, flicker, glitter, patter*. This {-ER rp} conveys the meaning of repetition. The acceptance of this {-ER rp}, however, is problematic and raises questions about the analysis of the remainders in words of this class. For example, if the *-er* in *glitter* is a morpheme meaning repetition, we are left with the remainder *glitt-*, whose morphemic status is dubious.

Exercise 8–18
Identify the italicized *-er* as

1. {-ER cp} inflectional suffix, as in *bigger*
2. {-ER n} derivational suffix, as in *singer*
3. {-ER rp} derivational suffix, as in *flutter*

1. This is a heavi*er* tennis racket than I want. _____
2. We watched the shimm*er* of the evening light on the waves. _____
3. The fight*er* weighed in at 180 pounds. _____
4. He was tough*er* than he looked. _____
5. The jabb*er* of voices came through the open door. _____

The verbal inflectional suffix {-ING vb} has two homophones in *-ing*. The first one is the nominal derivational suffix {-ING nm}, which is found in words like *meetings, weddings, readings*. This nominal {-ING nm} is obviously derivational since it permits the addition of an inflectional suffix to close it off, the noun plural {-s pl}. When such a word occurs alone without the inflectional suffix, e.g., *meeting*, the *-ing* is ambiguous, for it could be either {-ING vb}, as in "He was mee*ting* the train" or {-ING nm}, as in "He attended the meet*ing*."

The second homophone of {-ING vb} is the adjectival morpheme {-ING aj}, as in *a charming woman*. There are two tests by which the verbal {-ING vb} can be distinguished from the adjectival {-ING aj}.

The verbal {-ING vb} can usually occur after as well as before the noun it modifies, e.g.,

I saw a burning house.
I saw a house burning.

The adjectival {ING aj} can be preceded by a qualifier like *very, rather, quite,* or by the comparative and superlative words *more* and *most,* as in

It is a very comforting thought.
This is a more exciting movie.

but not

*I saw a rather burning house.

Also, compare

that interesting snake
that crawling snake.

The adjectival {-ING aj} can occur after *seems:*

That snake seems interesting,

whereas the verbal {-ING vb} cannot:

*That snake seems crawling.

Exercise 8–19
Identify the -*ing*'s of the italicized words by these symbols:

V-al = verbal {-ING vb}
N-al = nominal {-ING nm}
Aj-al = adjectival {-ING aj}

1. It was a *charming* spot. _____
2. Jim lost both *fillings* from his tooth. _____
3. It was located by a sweetly *babbling* brook. _____
4. It was *exciting* to watch the flight. _____
5. Old *sayings* are often half-true. _____
6. From the bridge we watched the *running* water. _____
7. That *barking* dog keeps everyone awake. _____
8. He told a *convincing* tale. _____
9. The *shining* sun gilded the forest floor. _____
10. Matisse's *drawings* are magnificently simple. _____
11. A *refreshing* shower poured down. _____
12. The attorney made a *moving* appeal. _____
13. A *moving* elephant is a picture of grace. _____
14. What an *obliging* fellow he is! _____
15. That was a *touching* scene. _____

The verbal inflectional {-D pp} has a homophone in the adjectival derivational {-D aj}, as in

Helen was *excited* about her new job.
She was a *devoted* mother.[3]

The adjectival {-D aj} is characterized by its capacity for modification by qualifiers like *very, rather, quite,* and by *more* and *most.*

---

[3] {-D aj} is considered derivational because it often can be followed by another suffix, e.g., *excitedly, devotedness.*

Example: A *rather faded* tapestry hung over the fireplace.

The verbal {-D pp}, on the other hand, does not accept such modifiers. We would not, for example, say

*The *very departed* guests had forgotten their dog.

The *seems* test for adjectival {-ING aj} is applicable to adjectival {-D aj}; for example, "The tapestry seems faded" but not "The guests seem departed."

Exercise 8–20

Identify the suffixes of the italicized words with these symbols: V-al = {-D pp}; Aj-al = {-D aj}.

1. You should read the *printed* statement.   _____
2. Merle was a *neglected* child.   _____
3. This is a *complicated* question.   _____
4. His *chosen* bride had lived in India.   _____
5. He bought a *stolen* picture.   _____
6. The *invited* guests all came.   _____
7. We had a *reserved* seat.   _____
8. The skipper was a *reserved* (= quiet) man.   _____
9. A *celebrated* painter visited the campus.   _____
10. A *worried* look crossed his face.   _____

Exercise 8–21

Ambiguity occurs when the *-ed* suffix can be interpreted as either {-D pp} or {-D aj}. This exercise will illustrate. For each sentence below write two meanings.

1. It was a finished job.
   a. _____
   b. _____
2. Our new surgeon is reserved.
   a. _____
   b. _____

The adverbial derivational suffix {-LY av} is added to most adjectives to form adverbs of manner, as in *rich, richly; kind, kindly; formal, formally; happy, happily*. A small group of adjectives does not take this {-LY av}, among them *big, small, little, tall, long, fast*.

This adverbial {-LY av} has as a homophone the derivational suffix {-LY aj}, an adjectival morpheme that is distributed as follows:

1. It is added to monosyllabic nouns to form adjectives that are inflected with *-er, -est*.

Examples: love, lovely; friend, friendly; man, manly

2. It is added to nouns to form adjectives that are not inflected with *-er, -est.*

Examples: king, kingly; beast, beastly; scholar, scholarly; mother, motherly; leisure, leisurely

3. It is added to a few adjectives, giving alternate adjectival forms that are also inflected with *-er, -est.*

Examples: dead, deadly; live, lively; kind, kindly; sick, sickly

Here the adjectives *kindly* and *lively* are homophonous with the adverbs *kindly* and *lively,* which end in {-LY av}. For example, we see the adverb in "She spoke kindly to the children," and the adjective in "She was the kindliest woman in the village."

4. It is added to a short list of "time" nouns to form adjectives.

Examples: day, daily; hour, hourly; month, monthly

These are not inflected with *-er, -est,* and some of them undergo functional shift to become nouns, e.g., "He subscribes to two dailies and three quarterlies."

Exercise 8–22

Identify the italicized *-ly* as either (1) {-LY av} adverbial derivational suffix, as in *glumly;* or (2) {-LY aj} adjectival derivational suffix, as in *fatherly.*

1. The witness testified false*ly*. _____
2. Grace has a dead*ly* wit. _____
3. Janet always behaved with a maiden*ly* demeanor. _____
4. He tiptoes soft*ly* into the room. _____
5. Jimmy receives a week*ly* allowance. _____
6. The dear old lady has a heaven*ly* disposition. _____
7. She spoke quiet*ly* to her grandson. _____
8. What a time*ly* suggestion! _____
9. What a manner*ly* child! _____
10. It was a coward*ly* act. _____

Exercise 8–23

This is an exercise reviewing the inflectional and derivational suffixes. Label the italicized suffixes as DS (derivational suffix), IS (inflectional suffix), or Amb (ambiguous).

1. prince*s* _____
2. princ*ess* _____
3. find*ings* _____
4. friendli*er* _____
5. show*s* _____
6. weav*er* _____
7. lean*er* _____
8. satir*ize* _____
9. sput*ter* _____
10. bright*en* _____

11. quick*ly*	_____		16. hear*ing*	_____
12. recti*fy*	_____		17. dri*er*	_____
13. brother*ly*	_____		18. griev*ance*	_____
14. respect*able*	_____		19. dropp*ings*	_____
15. young*er*	_____		20. sunny	_____

I. Noun Feminine Forms

English has a small clutch of nouns with feminine derivational suffixes. All but one of these feminizing suffixes (*-ster*) are of foreign origin. They have been added to a masculine form or to a base morpheme. Here is a list of most of them, with examples of the feminine nouns to which they have been attached and the corresponding masculine forms.

Suffix	*Masculine*	*Feminine*
1. -e	fiancé	fiancée
2. -enne	comedian	comedienne
3. -ess	patron	patroness
4. -etta	Henry	Henrietta
5. -ette	farmer	farmerette[4]
6. -euse	masseur	masseuse
7. -ina	George	Georgina
8. -ine	hero	heroine
9. -ster	spinner	spinster
10. -stress	seamster	seamstress (= -ster + -ess)
11. -ix	aviator	aviatrix[5]

These suffixes vary in vitality from *-ess,* the most productive, to *-stress,* which is completely dead. Two of them, *-enne* and *-euse,* occur only in words borrowed from French. The *-e,* also from French, is merely orthographic and is not heard in the spoken word. The *-ster* is no longer a feminizing suffix but now indicates any person, usually male: *gangster, oldster, prankster.*

English also has about fifty pairs of words with separate forms for the masculine and the feminine, e.g., *bull, cow; uncle, aunt; gander, goose.* But these are a matter of lexicography rather than morphology, and we shall pass them by.

---

[4] The suffix *-ette* can also be a diminutive, as in *kitchenette.*

[5] Some feminine forms have gone out of fashion. Today, for example, we say *pilot* and *poet* instead of *aviatrix* and *poetess.* The current tendency in English is to avoid feminine forms.

Exercise 8–24

Write the feminine form (or erstwhile feminine form) of these words.

1. Paul	_____	9. Carol	_____
2. chanteur	_____	10. emperor	_____
3. protégé	_____	11. launderer	_____
4. czar	_____	12. proprietor	_____
5. songster	_____	13. waiter	_____
6. major	_____	14. tricker	_____
7. heir	_____	15. executor	_____
8. equestrian	_____		

J. Noun Diminutive Forms

In English six diminutive suffixes can be found. These are morphemes which convey a meaning of smallness or endearment or both. They are the following:

1. -ie, -i, -y	as in *auntie, Betty, sweetie, Willy*
2. -ette	as in *dinette, towelette*
3. -kin, -ikin, -kins	as in *lambkin, manikin*
4. -ling	as in *duckling, darling* (= little dear)
5. -et	as in *circlet*
6. -let	as in *booklet, starlet*

The vowels of these diminutive suffixes are three front vowels: /i/, /ɪ/, and /ɛ/.

The first suffix, pronounced /i/ and spelled -ie, -i, and -y, is highly productive. It is frequently attached to one-syllable first names to suggest endearment and intimacy, or smallness, as in *Johnny, Janey, Jackie,* and *Geri.* Similarly, it is attached to common nouns, as in *doggie, sweetie, birdie.*[6]

The second suffix is also in active use, generally to indicate smallness. Thus, a *dinette* is a small dining area, and a *roomette* is a small room.

The other four diminutive suffixes exist in the language as diminutives but are rarely if ever added to new nouns. In short, they are unproductive, inactive. Furthermore, in some words, like *cabinet* and *toilet,* the meaning of the diminutive suffix has faded away to little or no significance.

---

[6] Warning to students: Some of these diminutive suffixes have homophones that can be a source of confusion. Here, for instance, are four of them:

1. -y, an adjective-forming suffix added to a noun, as in *cloudy*
2. -ie, a noun-forming suffix added to an adjective, as in *smartie, toughie*
3. -ette, a feminine suffix, as in *majorette*
4. -ling, a noun suffix denoting animals, as in *yearling, shearling, fledgling, nestling, weanling*

Exercise 8–25
Give a noun diminutive form for each of the following words.

1. Bob _____
2. goose _____
3. statue _____
4. lock _____
5. dear _____

6. baby _____
7. pack _____
8. pup _____
9. table _____
10. Ann _____

11. lord _____
12. drop _____
13. lad _____
14. man _____
15. cigar _____

In addition to these six diminutives, many others have come into English as a part of borrowed words. These were diminutives in their own or parent language but are non-morphemic in English. For illustration, here is a handful of them.

mosqu*ito*
bamb*ino*
armad*illo*

peccad*illo*
flot*illa*
Prisc*illa*
cook*ie*
colon*el*
citad*el*

nov*el* (noun)

pan*el*
mors*el*
dams*el*

scalp*el*
satch*el*
mus*cle*
part*icle*
pup*il*
viol*in*
violon*cello*
pupp*et*

Venezu*ela*
quart*et*
bull*etin* (two successive
          diminutives here)
fals*etto*
stil*etto*
Maur*een*
loch*an*
form*ula*
caps*ule*

calcu*lus*

Most of these borrowed diminutive endings, you will observe, contain the vowels /i/, /ɪ/, and /ɛ/, though these vowels have often been reduced to /ə/ in English because of lack of stress. Only the last four do not have a front vowel or /ə/ in the diminutive suffix. Furthermore, nearly all these suffixes have lost the diminutive sense that was once alive in them.

Exercise 8–26
Diminutive suffixes occur in many languages. Here are a few samples. Underline the diminutive suffixes. Then list the three vowels that occurred in these suffixes.

1. French *fillette* /fijét/, little girl
           sonnette /sɔnét/, little bell
2. Spanish *casita* /kasíta/, little house
           maquinilla /makiníya/, little machine
3. Italian *stanzina* /stantsína/, little room
4. Romanian *fetiţa* /fetítsa/, little girl
5. Hawaiian *puliki* /pulíki/, vest
6. German *Hündchen* /hçntçɛn/, puppy
7. Portuguese *casinha* /kasíña/, little house
8. Dutch *huisje* /hüisjə/, little house

K. Immediate Constituents

Up to this point we have scrutinized the four sorts of morphemes—bases, prefixes, infixes, and suffixes—of which words are composed. Now we shall see how these are put together to build the structure that we call a word.

A word of one morpheme, like *blaze,* has, of course, just one unitary part. A word of two morphemes, like *cheerful,* is obviously composed of two parts, with the division between them:

cheer | ful

But a word of three or more morphemes is not made up of a string of individual parts; it is built with a hierarchy of twosomes. As an illustration let us examine the formation of *gentlemanly,* a word of three morphemes. We might say that *man* and *-ly* were combined to form *manly* and that *gentle* and *manly* were then put together to produce the form *gentlemanly.* But the total meaning of *gentlemanly* does not seem to be composed of the meanings of its two parts *gentle* and *manly,* so we reject this possibility. Let's try again. This time we'll say that *gentle* and *man* were put together to give *gentleman.* And if we remember that *gentle* has the meanings of "distinguished," "belonging to a high social station," we see that the meaning of *gentleman* is a composite of those of its two constituents. Now we add *-ly,* meaning "like," and get *gentlemanly,* like a gentleman. This manner of forming *gentlemanly* seems to make sense.

Now when we analyze a word we show this process but in reverse. We usually divide a word into two parts of which it seems to have been composed. Thus

gentleman | ly

We continue in this way, cutting every part into two more until we have reduced the word to its ultimate constituents, that is, to the unit morphemes of which it is composed. Our analysis of *gentlemanly* would look like this:

gentle | man | ly

Next, let us suppose that the word to be analyzed is *ungentlemanly.* If we make the same first cut as before, cutting off the *-ly,* we get *ungentleman* plus *-ly.* But as English contains no such word as *ungentleman,* our word could not be composed of the two parts *ungentleman* and *-ly.* Instead, let's cut after the *un-.* This gives *un-* plus *gentlemanly,* a common English negative prefix plus a recognizable English word. This seems to be the right way to begin, and as we continue we get this analysis.

un | gentle | man | ly

We have now shown the layers of structure by which the word has been composed, down to the ultimate constituents—*un-, gentle, man,* and *-ly.*

In doing word diagrams like those above to show layers of structure, we

make successive divisions into two parts, each of which is called an immediate constituent, abbreviated IC. The process is continued until all component morphemes of a word, the ultimate constituents, have been isolated.

Here are three recommendations on IC division that will assist you in
the exercise to follow:

1. If a word ends in an inflectional suffix, the first cut is between this
suffix and the rest of the word. So:

pre conceiv | ed   mal formation | s

2. One of the IC's should be, if possible, a free form. A free form is one
that can be uttered alone with meaning, e.g., *enlarge, dependent, support-
able*. Here are examples of wrong and right first cuts:

Wrong: en | large ment   **Right:** en large | ment
        in depend | ent   in | depend ent
        in support | able   in | support able

3. The meanings of the IC's should be related to the meaning of the
word. It would be wrong to cut *restrain* like this:

rest | rain

because neither *rest* nor *rain* has a semantic connection with *restrain*. Nor
would a division of *starchy* as

star | chy

be right because this would give an unrelated morpheme and a meaningless fragment. The two examples are properly cut in this way:

re | strain   starch | y

The ultimate constituents are the morphemes of which the word is composed.

Exercise 8–27

One of the following IC diagrams showing the layers of structure is wrong.
Which one is it and why?

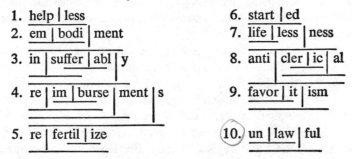

1. help | less
2. em | bodi | ment
3. in | suffer | abl | y
4. re | im | burse | ment | s
5. re | fertil | ize

6. start | ed
7. life | less | ness
8. anti | cler | ic | al
9. favor | it | ism
10. un | law | ful

Exercise 8–28
Diagram these words to show the layers of structure.

1. item ize d

2. pre pro fess ion al

3. news paper dom

4. counter de clar ation

5. mal con struc tion

6. contra dict ory

7. dis en throne

8. mid after noon

9. Ice land ic

10. super natur al

11. un com fort able

12. fest iv al

13. en gag ing

14. ex press ion ism

15. mis judg ment

L. Allomorphs

It is now time to sharpen and extend our understanding of the morpheme. So far we have been treating the morpheme as if it were invariable in phonemic form, that is, in the way it is pronounced. But in the preceding exercises you may have noticed occasional variations in phonemic form. In exercise 8–16 (page 96), for instance, the morpheme {press} of *pressure* ends in an /š/, whereas the same morpheme standing alone as the word *press* ends in /s/. Likewise, the first morpheme in *depth* is pronounced /dɛp/, but the same morpheme occurring as the word *deep* has the phonemic form of /dip/. So we see that a morpheme may have more than one phonemic form.

Next we'll go back to the past-tense ending, the morpheme {-D pt}. We learned in exercise 2–3 of the phonology section that this morpheme has three phonemic forms, the choice depending on the preceding sound. After an alveolar stop, /t/ or /d/, the sound is /əd/, as in *parted* /partəd/ and *faded* /fedəd/. After a voiceless consonant other than /t/ it is /t/, as in *passed* /pæst/ and *laughed* /læft/. After a voiced sound other than /d/ it is /d/, as in *seemed* /simd/ and *begged* /bɛgd/. Furthermore, these three phonemic forms of {-D pt} are not interchangeable. The occurrence of one or another of them depends on its phonological environment, in this case, the preceding sound. This pattern of occurrence of related forms, according to which each form occupies its own territory and does not trespass on the domain of another, is called complementary distribution, abbreviated CD. When the related forms of a set, like the three forms of {-D pt}, have the same meaning and are in complementary distribution, they are called allomorphs, or positional variants, and belong to the same morpheme. So we say that the morpheme {-D pt} has three allomorphs: /-əd/, /-t/, and /-d/. This is expressed in the formula:

$$\{\text{-D pt}\} = /\text{-əd}/ \sim /\text{-t}/ \sim /\text{-d}/$$

Braces are used for morphemes and slants for allomorphs; a tilde (~) means "in alternation with." It must be emphasized that many morphemes in English have only one phonemic form, that is, one allomorph—for example, the morphemes {boy} and {-hood} each have one allomorph—/bɔy/ and /-hʊd/—as in *boyhood.*

Now we are in a position to refine our understanding of free and bound morphemes (page 85). It is really not the morpheme but the allomorph that is free or bound. Consider, for example, the morpheme {louse}. This has two allomorphs: the free allomorph /laws/ as a singular noun and the bound allomorph /lawz-/ in the adjective *lousy.*

Exercise 8-29
Each pair of words here contains one free and one bound allomorph of the same morpheme. Indicate the morpheme in braces and write each allomorph between slants in phonemic script.

	Morpheme	Free allomorph	Bound allomorph
Example: long, length	{long}	/lɔŋ/	/lɛŋ-/
1. strong, strength	_____	_____	_____
2. chaste, chastity	_____	_____	_____
3. courage, courageous	_____	_____	_____
4. Bible, Biblical	_____	_____	_____
5. wife, wives	_____	_____	_____

Exercise 8-30
Explain why *a/an* are allomorphs of one morpheme.

Exercise 8–31

Write the base morpheme and its allomorphs for each group. Supply primary stresses in answers.

Examples: steal, stealth {steal} = /stil/ ~ /stɛl-/

1. wide, width
2. broad, breadth
3. wolf, wolves
4. áble, abílity
5. supreme, supremacy
6. divine, divinity
7. fame, fámous, ínfamy, ínfamous
8. vision, televise, revise
9. sun, sunny, sunward
10. átom, atómic

Exercise 8–32

This exercise, related to exercise 2–2, concerns the plural morpheme {-s pl}, which (we'll say for the moment) has three allomorphs. Write out each plural word in phonemic script. Then, using these as evidence, list the allomorphs of {-s pl} and describe their complementary distribution.

1. sons _____
2. naps _____
3. passes _____
4. hogs _____
5. sacks _____

6. fizzes _____
7. dishes _____
8. garages _____
9. hoes _____
10. staffs _____

11. churches _____
12. gorges _____
13. sums _____
14. heaths _____
15. gongs _____

Allomorphs and CD:

_____

_____

_____

_____

_____

M. Conditioning: Phonological and Morphological

In examining the past-tense morpheme {-D pt}, we saw that the three allomorphs /-əd ~ -d ~ -t/ were in CD and that this distribution was determined by the phonological environment, in this case by the nature of the preceding sound. The same was true of the plural morpheme {-s pl}, where the addition of /-əz/, /-z/, or /-s/ was also determined by the kind of sound immediately preceding the suffix. In these and similar cases, when the phonological environment determines which allomorph is used, we say that the selection of allomorphs is phonologically conditioned.

But the plural morpheme {-s pl} has further allomorphs, as shown by the /-ən/ of *ox-oxen* and by the /ø/ (zero) suffix of *sheep-sheep*. These two, /-ən/ and /ø/, are in CD with all the others in that they stay in their own territory, associate only with specific words, and do not overlap in positions where /-əz/, /-z/, and /-s/ are found. But the positions in which they occur—that is, the words they attach themselves to—have nothing to do with their phonological environment. Instead the use of /-ən/ as the plural of *ox* is determined by the specific morpheme *ox;* in other words, *ox* simply takes /-ən/ and that's that. Likewise, the occurrence of the plural ø allomorph in a few words—*swine, deer, sheep, trout, pike, quail, grouse,* and others—is determined by the fact that these special morphemes require a ø plural. In such cases, when we can describe the environment that requires a certain allomorph only by identifying specific morphemes, we say that the selection of allomorphs is morphologically conditioned.

To describe by formula these five allomorphs of {-s pl} we write

$$\{\text{-s pl}\} = /\text{-əz}/ \sim /\text{-z}/ \sim /\text{-s}/ \infty /\text{-ən}/ \infty /\text{ø}/$$

The ~ refers to a phonologically conditioned alternation and the ∞ to a morphologically conditioned alternation.

Exercise 8–33
Write the formula to express the fact that the past-tense morpheme {-D pt} has, in the verb *be,* the two morphologically conditioned allomorphs *was* and *were.*

N. Replacive Allomorphs

Most of the allomorphs we have been dealing with have been additive; that is, we have been forming words by adding prefixes and suffixes to bases. Now we must look at an allomorph of a different kind, the replacive, which can be illustrated by going back to the past-tense {-D pt}. We noted that this morpheme has three allomorphs, /-əd ~ -t ~ -d/. But if this is all, how do we account for forms like *sang?* It would appear to contain an allomorph of {-D pt} since it is a parallel formation with regular past-tense forms:

Yesterday we *parted* /partəd/
Yesterday we *laughed* /læft/
Yesterday we *played* /pled/
Yesterday we *sang* /sæŋ/

What happens is that there is a replacement here instead of an additive.

The /ɪ/ of *sing* is replaced by the /æ/ of *sang* to signal the past tense. This is symbolized as follows:

$$/sæŋ/ = /sɪŋ/ + /ɪ > æ/^7$$

Here the /ɪ > æ/ is another allomorph of {-D pt}, and you can readily see how it is in CD with the others. Sometimes replacive allomorphs are called "infixes," because they are positioned *within* a word, as opposed to prefixes and suffixes, as in *sang* and *rode*.

Exercise 8–34

Write the allomorphic formula for each of the following past-tense forms.

Examples: spin, *spun*   /spən/ = /spɪn/ + /ɪ > ə/

1. see, *saw*   _____
2. begin, *began*   _____
3. bite, *bit*   _____
4. give, *gave*   _____
5. grow, *grew*   _____
6. ride, *rode*   _____
7. grind, *ground*   _____
8. take, *took*   _____
9. tear, *tore*   _____
10. speak, *spoke*   _____

O. Homophones

You are acquainted with many pairs, trios, and even foursomes of words in English which sound alike but differ in meaning: *heir, air; pare, pair, pear.* Such words are called homophones. In morphology it must be remembered that words like these are different morphemes.

Examples: Did you like the *meet?*   /mit/ (track meet)
     Did you like the *meat?*   /mit/ (roast beef)

The same is true of bound forms. Compare

Verbal inflectional suffix: It feels /-z/ good
Noun plural inflectional suffix: Those frogs /-z/
Noun possessive inflectional suffix: John's /-z/ book

These three homophonous /-z/s are three different morphemes.

---

[7] The symbol > means "becomes."

Exercise 8–35
Write the morphemes to which each of these homophonous allomorphs belongs.

Examples: /et/ = {ate}
              /et/ = {eight}

1. /mit/   _____   4. /pɛr/   _____
   /mit/   _____   /pɛr/   _____
   /mit/   _____   /pɛr/   _____
2. /mayt/   _____   5. /ɪts/   _____
   /mayt/   _____   /ɪts/   _____
   /mayt/   _____   6. /tu/   _____
3. /yu/   _____   /tu/   _____
   /yu/   _____   /tu/   _____
   /yu/   _____   /tu/   _____

P. Phonesthemes

Phonesthemes are speech sounds that in themselves express, elicit, or suggest meaning. For instance, let us consider a minimal pair, the Chinese words *ch'ing* /čɪŋ/ and *ch'ung* /čuŋ/. One of these means "heavy," the other "light,." The question for you is "Which meaning goes with which word?" If you, like most respondents, say that *ch'ing* means "light" and *ch'ung* means "heavy," you are correct. And since the two words differ only in their vowels, it must be these vowels that elicit the two meanings. These vowels, then, are phonesthemes.

Two of the most common phonesthemes in English are the pair of high front vowels, /i/ and /ɪ/, suggesting smallness. These appear in many words that have smallness as a part of their meaning. Here are a few: *wee, peep, squeak, seep, bit, jiffy, clink, tipple, giggle, dwindle, whimper, chink.* They are also two of the three diminutive vowels in English, as exemplified in *birdie* and *manikin*.

The presence of the "small" phonesthemes /i/ and /ɪ/ in English is not only known by language students but sensed by the average person. Witness two cases. A recent cartoon employed these two vowels to make its point. It showed an auto mechanic in a garage talking with an unhappy car owner whose engine had been malfunctioning. The mechanic pointed out, "In car language 'clunk, rattle, thump' means 'too bad you didn't listen when I said "ping, ping, squeak" '!" And a radio comedian presented a large public with this gag: "What do you call a large pipsqueak?" "A poopsquawk."

Another common English phonestheme is the vowel /ə/, as in *dung, slut, flunk.* Professor F. W. Householder, in a study of over six hundred

English monosyllables, found that the vowel /ə/ has, in a large majority of cases, the general meaning of "undesirable."[8] These monosyllables will illustrate: *muck, gunk, dump, slum, grunt, dud, klutz, glum, grudge.* And in words of more than one syllable the meaning of "undesirable" seems to be present in terms like these: *grumpy, grumble, blunder, clumsy, humdrum, muddle, slovenly, puddle, lunkhead.*

At the beginnings of words, a number of consonant clusters appear to have phonesthematic value. Among them are these:

/gl-/ = light.   Examples: *glow, glare, glint, gleam, glisten*
/fl-/ = moving light.   Examples: *flame, flash, flare, flambeau*
/sp-/ = point.   Examples: *spire, spark, spot, spout, spade*
/sl-/ = movement.   Examples: *slide, slink, slosh, slither, slouch, slump*

At the ends of one-syllable words, the voiceless stops /p/, /t/, and /k/ are expressive of an abrupt stoppage of movement. Examples of these are *slap, pat, flick, tap, hit, crack.* In contrast with these, a final voiceless fricative /š/ suggests an unabrupt stoppage of movement, as in *mash* and *squash.* The expressiveness of these sounds becomes especially noticeable when we observe contrasts like these: *clap* vs. *clash*; *bat* vs. *bash*; *smack* vs. *smash*; *crack* vs. *crash.*

At the ends of two-syllable words, we find the phonesthemes /-əl/ and /-ər/, each having the meaning of "repetition." The repetition may be of auditory or visual details. Examples:

/-ər/ *chatter, clatter, gibber, patter, sputter, mutter, jabber, twitter,*
litter, shatter, clatter, flutter, shimmer, stammer
/-əl/ *babble, giggle, twinkle, waggle, freckle, dribble, juggle, crackle,*
chuckle, rattle, sparkle, stipple, prattle, wriggle, drizzle

A speech sound is a phonestheme only when its imputed sense is related to the sense of the word of which it is a part. Thus, as the sense of /i/ and /ɪ/ is related to the sense of *wee* and *drizzle,* these two vowels are phonesthemes in these words. But in words whose meaning does not include smallness, the /i/ and /ɪ/ are merely meaningless vowels. Thus *seat* and *sit* and countless others with /i/ and /ɪ/ do not contain phonesthemes. Some words are doubtful cases. For example, does *whisper* really contain the phonesthemes /ɪ/ for smallness and /-ər/ for repetition?

Whether or not phonesthemes should be considered morphemes is problematic. But since their existence is now generally accepted and since numerous linguists do acknowledge their morphemic status, we shall label them morphemes.

[8] "On the Problem of Sound Meaning, an English Phonestheme," *Word,* 2:83–84, 1946.

Exercise 8–36

The phonesthemes in the following words are underlined. Give the meaning of each.

1. spike	_point_	11. glossy	
2. flicker	_moving light_	12. spatter	
3. glimmer		13. shrink	
4. nibble		14. warble	
5. crud		15. ugly	
6. sulky		16. kid	
7. snap		17. tack	
8. splash		18. sniffle	
9. sip		19. slit	
10. señorita		20. jangle	

Oral Exercise 8–A

The Romanian word *mic* /mɪk/ has one of these meanings: sad, small, dark, slow, tall. Which one is it? How do you know?

Oral Exercise 8–B

The eminent grammarian Otto Jespersen recounts this incident: "One summer, when there was a great drought in Fredriksstad (Norway), the following words were posted in a W.C. [= toilet]: 'Don't pull the string for bimmelin, only for bummelum.' This was immediately understood."[9]

Explain *why* this was immediately understood.

[9] "Symbolic Value of the Vowel I" (1922) in *Linguistica* (Copenhagen: Levin and Munksgard, 1933), p. 284.

9
Words

A. Definition of "Word"

That the word is a genuine linguistic unit is scarcely questioned, and everyone seems to know what it is. Teachers have no difficulty in making up spelling lists, which consist of words. Lexicographers produce dictionaries, whose entries are mainly words. When we read, we recognize words by the white spaces between them. Occasionally, however, we are puzzled by printed forms of words that are inconsistent one with another. Here are several examples from one page of a scholarly desk dictionary, *Webster's New Collegiate Dictionary* (eighth edition). This book on the same page lists *woodchuck* and *woodcock* as one word and *wood duck* and *wood louse* each as two words. All four words have the same stress pattern, and no formal criteria are evident for differences in the printed form. Such moot cases apart, however, we commonly have no doubt about the identity of words.

But all these instances are concerned with written words, whereas in linguistic analysis our main interest is in the spoken word. Here again the isolation of the unit called a word appears easy. If one asks "What does _____ mean?" or "How do you pronounce _____?" the blank usually represents a word. And there is a high correlation between the written and the spoken forms of words. Yet the task of devising an exact definition of *word* is a prickly one that has engendered much controversy.[1]

Let us begin with the act of speech. When people are speaking, they often pause—formulating their thoughts, getting the sentence structure in order, and groping for the right word. Such pauses do not occur within words, but between words. This is our cue, and it leads us to a useful definition of *word*, that of Professor Charles F. Hockett: "A word is ... any segment of a sentence bounded by successive points *at which pausing is possible*." [2] This pausing can be either silent or vocalized by "u-u-u-h." The following sentence will illustrate:

<pre>
p   p p   p p   p p   p   p p   p[3]
Since the streetlamp is out, I must call up our councilman.
</pre>

In this sentence the positions of possible pauses are marked by *p*'s, and every segment between two *p*'s is a word. Note that *call up* is considered a word. *Call up* belongs to a special class of two-part verbs—like *keep on* (continue), *take off* (depart), *butt in* (interrupt), and *show up* (appear) —that speakers of English seem to sense as single words. Hence there would normally be no pause between the two parts.

Exercise 9–1

In this exercise let us apply the foregoing definition to ascertain the number of words in the following sentences. In the first blank write the numbered position or positions where a pause would NOT be possible, or likely. In the second blank write the number of words in the sentence.

<pre>
              1   2   3   4 5   6 7
</pre>
Example: Cohen gave his brother a power-of-attorney.   <u>6,7</u>   <u>6</u>

<pre>
        1   2   3   4 5 6   7
1. Little Jimmy plays with a big soft ball.   ___   ___
      1   2   3   4 5   6 7
2. His older brother likes to play softball.   ___   ___
      1   2   3   4 5
3. Will you look up the address?   ___   ___
      1   2   3 4   5 6   7 8
4. He has always been a Johnny-on-the-spot.   ___   ___
      1   2   3 4   5 6
5. A dark room is conducive to sleep.   ___   ___
      1   2   3 4 5   6   7
6. He develops films in the darkroom upstairs.   ___   ___
</pre>

---

[1] This definition of a word is useful for many words: "A word is the smallest segment of speech that can be used alone." But it hardly accounts for words like *not, the, a, if,* and *with.*

[2] *A Course in Modern Linguistics* (New York: Macmillan, 1958), p. 167.

[3] Each "p" marks not only a point where pausing is possible, but also positions where the insertion of other words is possible.

B. Simple and Complex Words

English words may be classified on the basis of the kinds and combinations of morphemes of which they are composed. We shall adopt a classification of three main classes: simple, complex, and compound words.

1. Simple words consist of a single free morpheme.

    Examples: slay, flea, long, spirit

2. Complex words contain, as their immediate constituents, either two bound forms or a bound and a free form.

Examples of two bound forms as IC's:

matri	cide	tele	vise
ex	clude	cosmo	naut

Examples of bound and free forms as IC's:

dipso	mania	lion	ess
tele	phone	eras	er

Exercise 9–2

Make the first IC cut in the words below which permit such cutting. Then classify each word, using S for simple and Cx for complex.

1. knave	_____	8. purist	_____	15. enable	_____
2. knavish	_____	9. oyster	_____	16. mete	_____
3. graph	_____	10. misanthrope	_____	17. meter	_____
4. telegraph	_____	11. philosophy	_____	18. hydrometer	_____
5. aquanaut	_____	12. cannibal	_____	19. discography	_____
6. bicycle	_____	13. refusal	_____	20. skinik	_____
7. pure	_____	14. dental	_____	(cf. *sputnik*)	

C. Compound Words

The third class of words is compound words. These have free forms, usually two, as their immediate constituents.

Examples:

green	house	out	side	no	show
under	go	over	ripe	attorney	general

A small number of compound words have three or four free forms as coordinate IC's.

Examples:

happy	-go	-lucky	spic	and	span

Compound words resemble grammatical structures in that they imply, though they do not state, a grammatical relationship. Here are a few of the structures implied:

Implied Grammatical Structures	*Examples*
1. subject + verb	éarthquake (... earth quakes)
	crýbaby (... baby cries)
2. verb + object	kílljoy (... kills joy)
3. verb + adverbial	stópover (... stops over)
	dównpour (... pours down)
	stáy-at-home (... stays at home)
	underéstimate (... estimates under)
4. subject + *be* + adjectival	hígh chair (... chair is high)
5. subject + *be* + nominal	gírl friend (... friend is a girl)
6. subject + *be* + adverbial	íngroup (... group is in)
7. prepositional phrase	extrasénsory (beyond the senses)
8. adjective modified by prepositional phrase	treetop (... top of tree)
9. coordination	give-and-take

Exercise 9–3

Using the nine numbers given above, indicate the number of the grammatical structure implied by each compound word.

1. workman　　_____
2. afternoon　_____
3. pickpocket　_____
4. quicksand　_____
5. knockdown　_____
6. airtight　　_____

7. praiseworthy _____
8. outgo　　_____
9. fly-by-night _____
10. booster shot _____
11. overheat　_____
12. rough-and-ready _____

Compound words can be distinguished from grammatical structures in three ways.

1. Compound words cannot be divided by the insertion of intervening material between the two parts, but grammatical structures can be so divided. As illustration, let us compare two sentences:

a. She is a sweetheart.
b. She has a sweet heart.

In the first the compound word *sweetheart* is indivisible: you cannot insert anything between *sweet* and *heart*. But in the second sentence you could say

> She has a sweet*er* heart than her sister.
> She has a sweet, *kind* heart.
> She has a sweet, *sweet* heart.

thereby dividing the components *sweet* and *heart*. Thus sentence *b* contains a grammatical structure, not a compound word. Following this principle of divisibility, we find that the next sentence is ambiguous:

She loves sweet potatoes.

When *sweet potatoes* means the yellow kind, the expression cannot be divided and is therefore a compound word. But when the words refer to white potatoes that are sweet, then division is possible, as in

She loves sweet, fresh potatoes,

and we have a grammatical structure.

2. A member of a compound word cannot participate in a grammatical structure. Compare *hârd báll* and *básebàll*. *Hârd báll* is a grammatical structure of modifier plus noun, and its first member, *hard*, can participate in the structure *very hard*:

It was a very hard ball.

But one cannot say

*It was a very baseball,

as *baseball* is a compound word. Ambiguous cases can occur in sentences like

He is fond of sparkling water.

When *sparkling water* refers to ordinary water that sparkles, the first member, *sparkling*, can participate in a grammatical structure, e.g., *brightly sparkling water*. So *sparkling water* with this meaning is a grammatical structure. But when the expression refers to carbonated water, such participation cannot occur and we have a compound word.

3. Some compound nouns, you may recall, have the stress pattern {′ `}, as in *blúebìrd*, that distinguishes them from a modifier plus a noun, as in *blûe bírd*, which structure carried the stress pattern {^ ′}. For the same reason a *swîmming tèacher* is different from a *swîmming téacher*. You should also remember that you cannot depend on the printed form of words to reveal this distinction. For example, the compound noun *hígh chàir* (a chair for children) and the modifier plus noun *hîgh cháir* (a chair that is high) are both written as two words.

---

* An asterisk *before* a sentence or a phrase means that the sentence or phrase is ungrammatical.

Exercise 9–4

Indicate whether each italicized expression is a compound word (Cd) or a grammatical structure (Gs). Pay no attention to hyphens or spaces, for these are deceptive.

1. Jim's new car is a *hardtop*. _____
2. This jar has a rather *hard top*. _____
3. It was a *jack-in-the-box*. _____
4. There was a *plant in the box*. _____
5. A *hót dòg* is not a *hôt dóg*. _____ _____
6. He has a *dog in the manger* attitude. _____
7. She has a *strong hold* on him. _____
8. She has a *stronghold* in the Women's Club. _____
9. George found his *father-in-law*. _____
10. George found his *father in trouble*. _____
11. They bought it on the *black market*. _____
12. The electricity went off, and we were caught in a *black,* completely lightless, *market*. _____
13. Henry is a *desígning teàcher*. _____
14. Henry is a *desîgning téacher*. _____

Exercise 9–5

For a review of the three classes of words, identify the following items with these symbols:

S Simple word	**Cd** Compound word
Cx Complex word	**Gs** Grammatical structure

Make the IC cuts for Cx and Cd.

1. shárpshòoter _____
2. shârp shóoter _____
3. act _____
4. react _____
5. rattlesnake _____
6. passbook _____
7. apparatus _____
8. glowworm _____
9. import _____
10. ripcord _____
11. unearth _____
12. rat-a-tat _____
13. beauty _____
14. beautify _____
15. geometry _____
16. búll's èye (of target) _____
17. bûll's éye (of bull) _____
18. outlast _____
19. biochemical _____
20. inaccessible _____

10
Processes of Word Formation

It has been estimated that the English language contains more than a million words, of which fewer than half are included in unabridged dictionaries. It is natural to wonder where all these words came from. The answer is not difficult to find.

First of all, our language contains a core of words that have been a part of it as far back as we can trace its history, 5000-plus years. A few examples are these words: *sun, man, foot, father, eat, fire, I, he, with, of.*

Second, English has been a prodigious borrower of words from other languages throughout its history, and a vast number of borrowed words are now in our language. This has come about through invasions, immigration, exploration, trade, and other avenues of contact between English and some foreign language. Below are a few examples of these borrowings. In many cases a word may pass, by borrowing, through one or more languages before it enters English. A case in point is the Arabic plural noun *hashshashin,* hashish eaters, which entered French in the form *assassin,* and from French was borrowed into English.

1. chauffeur   French   stoker of train engine, driver

English Word	Source Language	Meaning in Source Language
2. campus	Latin	field, plain
3. guru	Hindi	spiritual leader
4. sheikh	Arabic	old man, chief
5. alligator	Spanish	the lizard
6. window	Old Norse	wind eye
7. agnostic	Greek	unknowable
8. bazaar	Persian	market
9. chow mein	Chinese	fried noodles
10. sake	Japanese	rice wine
11. macho	Spanish	male

A look at the etymologies in your desk dictionary—they are the part of each entry enclosed in brackets—will give you an idea of the amount of borrowing that has taken place in English and of the many languages that have contributed to make the English word-stock rich and full.

Apart from borrowing, English gets new words by means of easily definable processes employed by users of English. It is to these that we shall now turn our attention.

A. Compounding

Compounding is simply the joining of two or more words into a single words, as in *hang glider, airstrip, cornflakes, busybody, downpour, cutoff, skywarn, alongside, breakfast, long-haired, devil-may-care, high school.* As the foregoing examples show, compounds may be written as one word, as a hyphenated word, or as two words. Occasionally it is hard to say whether or not a word is a compound; compare, for instance, *despite* with *in spite of* and *instead of* with *in place of.*

B. Derivation

Derivation is the forming of new words by combining derivational affixes or bound bases with existing words, as in *disadvise, emplane, deplane, teleplay, ecosystem, coachdom, counselorship, re-ask.* Words like these, some of which you have never heard before, are often formed in the heat of speaking or writing. You will note that they are immediately understandable because you know the meaning of the parts.

C. Invention

Now and then new words are totally invented, like *kodak, nylon, dingbat, floosy, goof, quark,* and *blurb,* but few of these find their way into the common vocabulary.

D. Echoism

Echoism is the formation of words whose sound suggests their meaning, like *hiss* and *peewee*. The meaning is usually a sound, either natural like the *roar* of a waterfall or artificial like the *clang* of a bell. But the meaning may also be the creature that produces the sound, like *bobwhite*. Examples: *moan, click, murmur, quack, thunder, whisper, lisp, chickadee, bobolink*. The vulgar "four-letter" words of English are largely echoic; and at the other end of the cultural scale are the echoic words called onomatopoetic in literary studies, which are frequent in poetry.

Exercise 10–1

Indicate by the first letter the process of formation represented by each of the words below.

	Compounding Derivation			Invention Echoism	
1. roughneck	___		6. pop	___
2. codgerhood	___		7. cream puff	___
3. clink (of glasses)	___		8. wheeze	___
4. doodad	___		9. weirdoism	___
5. dacron	___		10. exflux	___

E. Clipping

Clipping means cutting off the beginning or the end of a word, or both, leaving a part to stand for the whole. The resultant form is called a clipped word. The jargon of the campus is filled with clipped words: *lab, dorm, prof, exam, gym, prom, math, psych, mike,* and countless others. As these examples suggest, the clipping of the end of a word is the most common, and it is mostly nouns that undergo this process. Clipping results in new free forms in the language and sometimes in the creation of new morphemes, like *prof* and *mike*.

Exercise 10–2

Give the original words from which these clipped words were formed.

1. porno	_____		9. curio	_____
2. disco	_____		10. memo	_____
3. taxi	_____		11. Fred	_____
4. cab	_____		12. Al	_____
5. deli	_____		13. Tom	_____
6. vibes	_____		14. Joe	_____
7. gin	_____		15. Phil	_____
8. hype	_____			

Less common than the back-clipped words, like the foregoing, are those words that lose their forepart, like *plane* and *phone*.

Exercise 10-3

Give the original words from which these clipped words were formed.

1. sport (game) _____
2. pike (road) _____
3. bus _____
4. van _____
5. chute _____

6. wig _____
7. cute _____
8. Gene _____
9. Beth _____
10. Tony _____

Only a very few words have been formed by both fore and aft clipping. Four common ones are *flu, Liz, still* (apparatus for distilling hard liquor), and *fridge*.

Clipped words are formed not only from individual words but from grammatical units, such as modifier plus noun. *Paratrooper,* for example, is a clipped form of *parachutist trooper*. In cases like this it is often the first part that is shortened while the second part remains intact. Also, two successive words may be clipped to form one new word, as in *sitcom* (= situation comedy).

Exercise 10-4

Give the originals of these clipped words.

1. Amerindian _____
2. maître d' /metər di/ _____
3. contrail _____
4. taxicab _____
5. moped _____
6. agitprop _____
7. comsat _____
8. agribusiness _____

F. Acronymy

Acronymy is the process whereby a word is formed from the initials or beginning segments of a succession of words. In some cases the initials are pronounced, as in *MP* (military police, or Member of Parliament). In others the initials and/or beginning segments are pronounced as the spelled word would be. For example, *NATO* (North Atlantic Treaty Organization) is pronounced as /neto/ and *radar* (radio detecting and ranging) as /redar/.

Exercise 10–5

Pronounce these acronyms and give their originals.

1. RV _____
2. NOW _____
3. UNESCO _____
4. OK _____
5. scuba _____
6. OPEC _____
7. WASP _____
8. ICBM _____
9. jeep _____
10. laser _____

In the last forty years there has been a great increase in the use of acronyms. They tend to abound in large organizations—for instance, in the army, in government, and in big business—where they offer neat ways of expressing long and cumbersome terms. The very names of some businesses have been acronymized, like *Nabisco, Texaco,* and *Alcoa.* Many acronyms are used and understood only by initiates in a given field, like the military *CQ, TDY,* and *BOQ,* whereas others gain general currency, like *GI, CO,* and *PX.* It is likely that you employ some campus acronyms that would not be understood elsewhere.

G. Blending

Blending is the fusion of two words into one, usually the first part of one word with the last part of another, as in *gasohol,* from *gasoline* and *alcohol.* The resultant blend partakes of both original meanings. Many blends are nonce words, here today and gone tomorrow, and relatively few become part of the standard lexicon. The two classes, blends and clipped words, are not sharply separated, and some words may be put into either class.

Exercise 10–6

Give the originals of these blends:

1. flunk _____
2. happenstance _____
3. stagflation _____
4. simulcast _____
5. gelignite _____
6. smog _____
7. dumbfound _____
8. telecast _____
9. dandle _____
10. splatter _____

Exercise 10–7
Give the blends that result from fusing these words.

1. transfer   + resistor = _____
2. automobile   + omnibus = _____
3. escalade   + elevator = _____
4. blare or blow + spurt   = _____
5. squall   + squeak = _____

H. Back-formation

If someone should ask you, "What does a *feeper* do?" you would probably answer, "He feeps, of course." You would answer thus because there exist in your mind such word-pairs as *tell-teller, reap-reaper, write-writer, sing-singer;* and you would reason, perhaps unconsciously, that on the analogy of these forms the word *feeper* must have a parallel verb *feep.* Likewise, centuries ago, after the introduction of the nouns *peddler, beggar, swindler,* and *editor* into our language, speakers followed the same analogy and created the verbs *peddle, beg, swindle,* and *edit.* This process is just the reverse of our customary method of word formation, whereby we begin with a verb like *speak* and, by adding the agent morpheme {ER n}, form the noun *speaker.* The process is called back-formation. It may be defined as the formation of a word from one that looks like its derivative. An example is *hedgehop,* from the noun *hedgehopper.* Back-formation is an active source of new words today.

Exercise 10–8

1. The noun *greed* is a back-formation from the adjective *greedy.* Write four pairs of words that constitute an analogy for the creation of *greed.*

   _____   _____
   _____   _____
   _____   _____
   _____   _____

2. The pairs *revise-revision* and *supervise-supervision* are in common use in English. From this analogy what verb is back-formed from *television?* _____

3. English has many pairs on the pattern of *create-creation, separate-separation,* and *deviate-deviation.* On this analogy what back-formations would you expect from *donation* and *oration?* _____ and _____

Exercise 10–9

These verbs are back-formations. Write the words from which they are back-formed.

1. housekeep	_____	9. escalate	_____
2. typewrite	_____	10. reminisce	_____
3. administrate	_____	11. snap-judge	_____
4. resurrect	_____	12. deficit-spend	_____
5. baby-sit	_____	13. emote	_____
6. advance-register	_____	14. reluct	_____
	_____	15. party-poop	_____
7. laze	_____	16. back-seat-drive	_____
8. sidle	_____	17. hang glide	_____

I. Folk Etymology

The tennis term *let ball* affords a good illustration. In this context *let* has retained the obsolete meaning of "prevented," common in the language of Shakespeare.[1] A let ball is one which has been prevented from taking its true course by touching the top of the net. It is an entirely different word from the *let* that means "allow." But a neophyte, hearing the word on the tennis court, may understand it as *net,* because /l/ and /n/ are not far apart in sound and *net* makes sense to him whereas *let* does not. Thus he may use the term *net ball* until corrected by a more knowledgeable player.

Such a process—changing a word, in part or in whole, to make it more understandable and more like familiar words—is known as folk etymology.

Exercise 10–10

Look up in your desk dictionary the following examples of folk etymology and write the source of each in the blanks. Usually the reason for the change will be apparent.

1. female	_____	5. Welsh rarebit	_____
2. carryall	_____	6. coleslaw	_____
3. cockroach	_____	7. bridegroom	_____
4. hangnail	_____	8. helpmate	_____

---

[1] In *Hamlet,* Act I, scene 4, Hamlet says to his two friends who are holding him back from following his father's ghost:

Unhand me, gentlemen.

By heaven I'll make a ghost of him that lets me."

Here *lets* means "prevents." A modern reader, understanding *lets* as "allows," would get exactly the opposite meaning from that which Shakespeare intended.

The obsolete meaning of *let* survives also in the legal phrase "without let or hindrance."

J. Antonomasia

Antonomasia means the formation of a common noun, a verb, or an adjective from the name of a person or place. For example, the word *frisbee* comes from the Frisbie Bakery in Bridgewater, Connecticut, whose pie tins were used for a throwing game. The term *vandal* derives from the Vandals, a Germanic people who overran southern Europe 1500 years ago and sacked and looted Rome in the fifth century.

Names from history and literature have given us many common nouns. A lover, for instance, may be called a *romeo,* a *don juan,* a *casanova,* or a gay *lothario.* If he is too *quixotic,* he may meet his *waterloo* at the hands of some *sheba* or *jezebel.*

Exercise 10–11

Look up in your desk dictionary the following instances of antonomasia and write the original of each in the blanks.

1. sandwich	_____	6. denim	_____
2. hamburger	_____	7. cashmere	_____
3. frankfurter	_____	8. jeans	_____
4. wiener	_____	9. leotard	_____
5. baloney, bologna	_____	10. guy	_____

K. Reduplication

Reduplication is the process of forming a new word by doubling a morpheme, usually with a change of vowel or initial consonant, as in *pooh-pooh, tiptop,* and *hanky-panky.* The basic, originating morpheme is most frequently the second half, like *dilly-dally,* but it may be the first half, like *ticktock,* or both halves, like *singsong,* or neither half, like *boogie-woogie.*

Since the word *reduplication* has three meanings relevant to our discussion—the process, the result of the process (that is, the new word), and the element repeated—let us avoid confusion by calling these words "twin-words."

Exercise 10–12

Underline the originating morpheme in each of these twin-words:

1. wiggle-waggle
2. pitter-patter
3. nitwit

4. super-duper
5. hugger-mugger
6. lovey-dovey

Twin-words can be divided into three classes, leaving only a small residue of irregular forms.

1. The base morpheme is repeated without change.

Examples: clop-clop, tick-tick

This is the smallest class. The twin-words in this group are often onomatopoetic—that is, they represent sounds, like *gobble-gobble* and *chug-chug*.

2. The base morpheme is repeated with a change of initial consonant.

Examples: fuddy-duddy, tootsie-wootsie, razzle-dazzle, roly-poly, teeny-weeny, heebie-jeebies, hootchy-kootchy.

3. The base morpheme is repeated with a change of vowel.

Examples: chitchat, tiptop, criss-cross.

The first vowel is usually the high front lax vowel /ɪ/, and the second is a low vowel /æ/, /a/, or /ɔ/.

Examples: zigzag, ticktock, pingpong

Exercise 10–13

Identify the class of twin-word by one of these numbers:

1. Repetition without change
2. Repetition with change of initial consonant
3. Repetition with change of vowel

___ 1. knick-knack   ___ 6. hotsy-totsy
___ 2. ding-dong   ___ 7. hocus-pocus
___ 3. wishy-washy   ___ 8. flipflop
___ 4. quack-quack   ___ 9. humdrum
___ 5. rowdy-dowdy   ___ 10. nitty-gritty

11
Inflectional Paradigms

A paradigm is a set of related forms having the same stem but different affixes. As a reminder, here is a derivational paradigm with the stem *head:* *ahead, behead, header, headlong, headship, heady, subhead.*

Paradigms are also formed by the words to which the inflectional affixes are attached. These are called inflectional paradigms. There are only four of them.

NOUN PARADIGM

Forms: Inflectional suffixes:	Stem	Plural {-s pl}	Possessive {-s ps}	Plural + Possessive {-s pl ps}
Models:	woman	women	woman's	women's
	doctor	doctors	doctor's	doctors'

PRONOUN PARADIGM

		Singular		
	Subject	Object	Prenominal Possessive	Substitutional Possessive
1st	I	me	my	mine
2nd	you	you	your	yours
3rd M	he	him	his	his
F	she	her	her	hers
N	it	it	its	its

Plural

1st	we	us	our	ours
2nd	you	you	your	yours
3rd	they	them	their	theirs
Interr. } Relative }	who	whom	whose	whose

The pronoun paradigm differs from the other three in that it is not a stem-and-affix group but a small and closed set of words of fixed form. Such a closed set of words is called a structure class. We shall take up the personal pronouns in Chapter 13, together with the other structure classes.

VERB PARADIGM

Forms:	Stem	Present Third-Person Singular	Present Participle	Past Tense	Past Participle
Inflectional suffixes:		{s 3d}	{-ING vb}	{-D pt}	{-D pp}
Models:	show	shows	showing	showed	showed (also: shown)
	ring	rings	ringing	rang	rung
	cut	cuts	cutting	cut	cut

COMPARABLE PARADIGM

Forms:	Stem	Comparative	Superlative
Inflectional suffixes:		{-ER cp}	{-EST sp}
Models:	sweet	sweeter	sweetest
	lively	livelier	liveliest
	friendly	friendlier	friendliest
	soon	sooner	soonest
	near	nearer	nearest

In paradigms the meaning of the stem remains constant; the suffixes produce the differences in meaning among the forms of each paradigm. Membership in one of these inflectional paradigms is one of the signals that enable us to group words into three of the four major parts of speech —nouns, verbs, adjectives, and adverbs. We shall take up this matter in Chapter 12. Now we shall examine the paradigms one by one.

A. The Noun Paradigm

The noun paradigm is as follows:

Forms:	Stem	Plural	Possessive	Plural + Possessive
Inflectional suffixes:		{-s pl}	{-s ps}	{-s pl ps}
Models:	man	men	man's	men's
	doctor	doctors	doctor's	doctors'

This four-form paradigm is maximal, and not all nouns have all the four forms. Many nouns do not take the possessive forms, since an *of* structure often takes the place of the {-s ps} morpheme. For example, one is more likely to say "the ceiling of the room" than "the room's ceiling." In the spoken language we cannot always be sure which s morpheme we are hearing, because the possessive and the plural have identical forms—/-s/, /-z/, and /-əz/—except in the case of irregular plurals. If, for instance, you were to hear /ðə daktərz semɪnar/, it could mean "the doctor's seminar," "the doctors' seminar," or "the doctors seminar."

A few groups of so-called nouns have only one form of this paradigm. The words in one group—like *tennis, courage,* and *haste*—have the form of the stem. Another group does not have a singular form but only that of the -s plural: *clothes, environs, trousers,* and others. These take *they/them* as a pronoun substitute and go with the plural form of the verb, e.g., "My clothes [they] are clean." Still another group ends in an -s, words like *economics, linguistics, mathematics, physics,* but these take *it* as a pronoun substitute and go with a singular form of the verb, e.g., "*Linguistics* [it] is an exacting discipline." Words in a certain ill-defined group end in -s, like *ethics, oats, pliers, suds, measles,* but may be either singular or plural, depending on the context in which they occur or on the meaning expressed.

Examples:
Singular: *Measles* (= a malady) is a contagious disease.
Plural: Have you ever had them, the *measles?* (= a malady)
Singular: *Ethics* (= a philosophic discipline) is a challenging subject.
Plural: I don't approve of his personal *ethics* (= beliefs and actions).

For the time being we shall treat all such irregular forms as nouns.

Exercise 11–1

Write the paradigmatic forms of these nouns. For some slots you may have two forms or none.

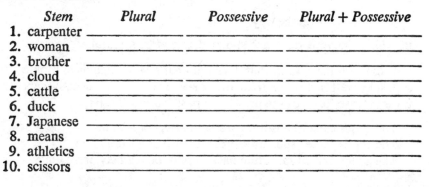

	Stem	Plural	Possessive	Plural + Possessive
1.	carpenter			
2.	woman			
3.	brother			
4.	cloud			
5.	cattle			
6.	duck			
7.	Japanese			
8.	means			
9.	athletics			
10.	scissors			

1. NOUN PLURALS

At this point it is convenient to set forth the ways of distinguishing singular from plural nouns. For many nouns the long-used meaning test will do: a noun is singular if it means one and plural if it means more than one. But meaning does not always work as a test of number. Take for instance this sentence: "I like your *hair*." Is hair singular or plural, assuming it means not a single strand but the coiffure or thatch on someone's head? Nor will form always do, since some nouns ending in an -s seem to be singular, e.g., *physics*, and others without an -s plural seem to be plural, e.g., *several salmon*.

There remain three useful tests for number in the noun.

1. A noun is singular if it can take one of these substitutes: *he/him, she/her, it, this,* or *that*. It is plural if it can take as a substitute *they/them, these,* or *those*.

> **Examples:** The beach was covered with *white* sand. (= it)
> Have you studied *phonetics?* (= it)
> Where did you hang *my trousers?* (= them)

2. The number of a noun may be signaled by a modifier like *several, many, this, that, these, those, fifteen,* or by a pronoun reference like *his/ her/its, their*.

> **Examples:** We saw *many fish* swimming under the bridge.
> In returning to the fold, the *sheep* changed *its* direction.
> In returning to the fold, the *sheep* changed *their* direction.

3. When a noun functions as subject of a verb, its number is sometimes shown by the form of the verb. It is the singular noun that goes with the {-s 3d} form of the verb, as in

Measles *is* a contagious disease.

Contrast this with

The goods *are* on the way

in which the verb form *are* shows that *goods* is plural.

If the verb has a form that does not change for singular and plural (e.g., a past tense form other than *was* or *were*) one can usually substitute a present tense form, or the present or past tense of *be*, e.g.,

The goods came (substitute present tense, *come*) late.
The goods came (substitute present tense of *be, are*) late
The goods came (substitute past tense of *be,* namely, *were*) late.

Each of these substitutions shows that *goods* is plural.

Exercise 11-2

In the blanks of the first column write a word that you would substitute for the italicized word—*he/him, she/her, it, this, that, they/them, these, those.* In the blanks of the second column write Sg (singular) or Pl (plural) to show the number of the italicized noun.

1. Miss Shen is wearing *hose* today. _____ __
2. What did they do with the *molasses?* _____ __
3. The *summons* came in the mail. _____ __
4. Why doesn't she call the *police?* _____ __
5. Jack likes to fish for *pike.* _____ __
6. The firm transported the *goods to* Australia. _____ __
7. The jar is filled with *sugar.* _____ __
8. Have you ever had the *mumps?* _____ __
9. She became fond of *mathematics.* _____ __
10. Does your brother eat *soap?* _____ __

Exercise 11-3

Encircle the noun modifier or pronoun reference that reveals the number of the italicized noun.

1. The hunting party saw few *deer* this season.
2. That *news* delighted her.
3. He studied *poetics* in all its complications.
4. My *scissors* lost their sharpness.
5. She shot both *quail* on the wing.

Exercise 11-4

Encircle the verb that reveals the number of the italicized noun.

1. The *Chinese* was preparing the dinner.
2. The *Chinese* were preparing the dinner.
3. *Oats* is his best crop.
4. The *bass* are biting today.
5. The *species* has become extinct.

One group of nouns known as collective nouns may be either singular or plural in meaning when they are singular in form. These are nouns that represent a collection or unit of individuals, like *tribe, family, team, committee, faculty, choir.* A speaker is likely to use singular forms (verbs, pronouns, determiners) in connection with such nouns when he is thinking of the unit as a single whole, but he will use plural forms when he has uppermost in mind the separate individuals within the unit.

Examples: Singular: The family (= it, the unit) *is* sitting at the dinner table.

Plural: The family (= they, the individuals) *have* gathered from many parts of the country.

Exercise 11–5

Indicate in the blanks by Sg or Pl whether the italicized collective nouns are singular or plural. Decide by using the tests for number that you have learned.

1. The *band* is playing well today. _____
2. The *band* are playing well today. _____
3. The *choir* became dissatisfied with their robes. _____
4. The *choir* became dissatisfied with its singing. _____
5. The *staff* of the college paper was a high-quality group. _____
6. The *staff* of the college paper were assembled to discuss their _____ last edition.
7. The *tribe* were on the warpath. _____
8. The *tribe* was the owner of the river bottom. _____
9. The *congregation* rose to its feet. _____
10. The *congregation* have all helped with the fund-raising drive. _____

The plural form of the noun signals the meaning of more than one. The most frequently employed plural forms are the three allomorphs of {-s pl}, such as we hear in *hats* /-s/, *fads* /-z/, and *kisses* /-əz/. These -s plurals are customarily considered the regular forms, not only because of their numerical preponderance but also because new nouns, either from other languages (*pizzeria*) or composed from existing morphemes (*astronaut*), tend to follow the -s plural.

In addition to the regular -s plural there are several small groups of irregular plurals.

1. Three nouns still retain an -en plural—*oxen, children,* and *brethren* —the last two having in addition a replacive stem vowel and a suffixal -*r*.

2. This group has a ø (zero) suffixal plural. This is a convenient way of saying that the plural is the same as the singular. It is shown in this way:

deer /dir/ (pl.) = /dir/ + /ø/

The ø plural allomorph refers to a significant absence of suffix. The words in this group are the names of edible animals, game animals, fish, and birds. Among them are *deer, sheep, swine, bear, antelope, bass, pike, carp, perch, pickerel, quail, grouse.* Beside these we may set similar words with a regular plural: *pigs, goats, suckers, muskies, bullheads, pheasants, ducks.* Some have both forms; a farmer, for example, who has *ducks* on his pond may go out hunting *duck.*

3. Seven common nouns form their plural by a replacive allomorph; for instance,

/gis/ = /gus/ + /u > i/

These are *man, woman, goose, tooth, foot, louse,* and *mouse.* In *women* there are two replacives:

/wɪmɪn/ = /wʊmən/ + /ʊ > ɪ/ + /ə > ɪ/

4. One set of nouns has as the stem of the plural an allomorph that is different from the stem of the singular. The morpheme {calf}, for example, has /kæf/ as the singular allomorph but /kæv-/ as the plural allomorph, and the plural suffix /-z/ conforms to the voiced sound /v/. Changes in the phonemic form of allomorphs as they are grouped into words, or as they appear in different forms of a word, are called morphophonemic changes. Among the morphophonemic changes we have already noted for the plural are these:

calf > calves /kæf/ > /kæv-/
child > children /čayld/ > /čɪld-/

Each of these changes in an allomorph is an example of a morphophonemic change. Nouns in this group end in /-s/, /-f/, or /-θ/. Here are three examples:

house > houses /hawzəz/ = /haus/ + /s > z/ + /-əz/
knife > knives /nayvz/ = /naif/ + /f > v/ + /-z/
mouth > mouths /mawðz/ = /mauθ/ + /θ > ð/ + /-z/

Of the words in this group only *house* ends in /s/. Examples of the others are *half, loaf, self, wife, bath, path, oath.* Some nouns ending in /-f/ or /-θ/ do not make a morphophonemic change, like *chiefs;* others have two forms of the plural, like /yuθs/ or /yuðz/.

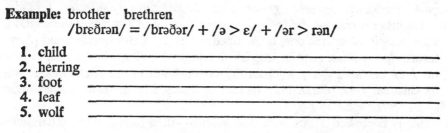

Exercise 11–6

Write in phonemic script the allomorphic formula for the formation of the plural of these words.

Example: brother brethren
/brɛðrən/ = /brəðər/ + /ə > ɛ/ + /ər > rən/

1. child _____
2. herring _____
3. foot _____
4. leaf _____
5. wolf _____

Exercise 11–7
Divide these words into two groups: (1) those that undergo no change
of the base allomorph in the plural, e.g., "those two toughs"; (2) those that
have two forms of the plural, e.g., *hoofs, hooves*. The words are *grief,
scarf, chief, truth, wharf, sheath, belief, wreath, waif, staff.*

One Allomorph	*Two Allomorphs*
_____ _____	_____ _____
_____ _____	_____ _____
_____ _____	_____ _____

Every language has its own ways of signaling plurality in nouns. In the
Germanic tongues the suffixal consonants /-s/, /-n/, and /-r/ are common for this purpose. In Italian, on the other hand, the suffixal vowels /-i/
and /-e/ are employed. Chinese, an exception, does not signal plurality at
all, save in the personal pronouns.

When foreign words are borrowed into English, their pronunciation becomes assimilated more or less to the phonemic system of English. This
means that we follow our own native pronunciation habits as we utter these
foreign words. Take, for example, the Italian noun *soprano* /soprano/.
This is pronounced /səprӕno/ by most Americans. We replace the first
Italian /o/ by /ə/ because this accords with our way of pronouncing
countless three-syllable words that have a primary stress on the medial
syllable: /pəteto/, /bətӕnɪk/, /səfɪstɪk/, /məlɪgnənt/. And the Italian /a/
becomes /ӕ/ because it is our habit to pronounce *an* as /ӕn/ in many
words like *abandon, mechanic, outlandish, pedantic, titanic.*

Now, what happens to the pluralizing morpheme of foreign nouns that
are imported into English? Frequently this pluralizer is completely aban-
doned, and the adopted noun is made to conform to the allomorphic pattern of the English plural {-s pl}. An instance is the Italian *soprano*, which
has lost its native plural of /soprani/ and is pluralized like any English
word ending in a vowel /səprӕnoz/. And this has been the fate of many
such Italian imports in *-o: piano, cello, solo, rondo, casino, studio, canto.*
Spanish plurals—/-s/ after a vowel and /-ɛs/ after a consonant—are so
similar to the English that they seem to assimilate to English plural pattern
without exception. Witness such borrowings from Spanish as *patio, mos-
quito, barbecue, cafeteria, guitar, cigar, lariat, canyon, alligator, tornado.*

On other occasions the foreign spelling is retained but the pronunciation,
with occasional exceptions, is modified. Thus the Latin singular and plural
forms, *datum-data*, keep in English the original spelling, but the Latin plural /-a/ becomes /-ə/, whereas the Greek-Latin plural *phenomena*, with
its classical /-a/ plural, may remain unchanged in English, though some
speakers change it to /-ə/.

Many borrowed nouns have both plurals—their foreign ones, often modified, and the English plural, like *concerti* and *concertos, curricula* and

curriculums, syllabi and *syllabuses*. The tendency is for such words to adopt the English {-s pl}, but some have proved resistant to change, like *agenda* and *alumni*.

Exercise 11–8

Look up the plurals of these words in your desk dictionary. Then write in phonemic script the pluralizing allomorph of each. If there are two pluralizers, write both.

Examples: criterion   **1.** /-z/   **2.** /-ən > ə/
         thesis   /-ɪs/ > /-iz/

1. alumna _____
2. formula _____
3. opus _____
4. appendix _____
5. stratum _____
6. hypothesis _____
7. kibbutz _____
8. apparatus _____
9. medium _____
10. stimulus _____
11. memorandum _____
12. graffito _____
13. nucleus _____
14. analysis _____
15. fedayee _____

---

2. NOUN POSSESSIVE

The noun possessive morpheme {-s ps} has the same phonologically conditioned allomorphs as the plural: /-s/, /-z/, and /-əz/, plus a zero allomorph as in *students'*. The term *possessive* is not a satisfactory label for this morpheme because a variety of different semantic relationships can exist between the possessive noun and the one that follows. The following cases will illustrate.

Relationship	*Example*
1. Possession or belongingness	John's hat
	Judy's home
2. Characterization or description	a cowboy's walk
	men's coats
3. Origin	Raphael's paintings
	Cary's novels
4. Measure (time, value, space)	an hour's wait
	a dollar's worth
	a stone's throw
5. Subject of act	John's flight (John flew)
	the judge's decision (the judge decided)

6. Object of act   Jane's punishment was deserved.
(Someone punished Jane.)

Eliot's critics were many. (They criticized Eliot.)

Exercise 11-9

Using the numbers above, indicate the relation shown between the italicized possessive and its following noun.

1. We missed the other car by a *hair's breadth*. _____
2. A *wren's song* floated through the window. _____
3. They were playing *children's games*. _____
4. The police provided for *Richard's protection*. _____
5. The *boy's jump* saved his life. _____
6. The *moon's beams* were brilliant that night. _____
7. *Willard's arrival* was a surprise. _____
8. He has never done a *day's work*. _____
9. She met *Dickie's father*. _____
10. He was happy about *Jane's winning*. _____

A noun possessive is ambiguous when it expresses more than one of the above relationships at the same time. For example, "His son's loss grieved him" has two meanings: (1) He lost his son (object of underlying verb), and this grieved him; or (2) His son (subject of underlying verb) lost something, perhaps a family heirloom, and this grieved him.

Exercise 11-10

Using the numbers 1 to 6 on page 137, indicate the relationships expressed by each ambiguous possessive.

1. Dr. McCoy's examination was a long one. _____
2. That is my father's photograph. _____
3. He was carrying a woman's coat on his arm. _____
4. We bought one of Rutherford's paintings. _____
5. The case was about his wife's fatal shooting. _____

In making a choice between the possessive (*student's*) and the *of* structure (*of the student*), there is no hard-and-fast guideline, and often the form chosen depends on personal taste. The tendency, however, is to use the possessive with animate nouns and the *of* structure with inanimate nouns; thus, *the dog's leg,* but *the leg of the table.*

Exercise 11–11
This is an exercise to investigate the usage of the class in regard to the possessive {-s ps} in contrast to the *of* structure. You will be given pairs of sentences like this:

   a. The *garage's* cement floor is cracking.
   b. The cement floor *of the garage* is cracking.

If you would use only one of these forms, write *only* after the sentence containing that one. If you would use either without any particular preference, write *both* in both blanks. If you would give preference to one but might also use the other, write *pref* in the proper blank.

   1a. The *building's roof* was blown off by the wind.   _____
   b. The roof *of the building* was blown off by the wind.   _____
   2a. The *soldier's* rifle had been thoroughly cleaned.   _____
   b. The rifle *of the soldier* had been thoroughly cleaned.   _____
   3a. The *lawn's* color had become brown.   _____
   b. The color *of the lawn* had become brown.   _____
   4a. We admired the *dog's* silky coat.   _____
   b. We admired the silky coat *of the dog.*   _____
   5a. The *hat's* brim was torn.   _____
   b. The brim *of the hat* was torn.   _____

A quick tabulation on the board will show the extent to which the members of the class make a distinction between animate nouns (*soldier* and *dog*) and inanimate nouns (*building, lawn,* and *hat*) in their use of {-s ps} and the *of* structure.

This concludes our look at the forms of the noun paradigm. We shall return to them again in our study of syntax. There our knowledge of the noun paradigm will help us to single out nouns in this simple way: If a word has two or more forms of the paradigm, we shall label it a noun, e.g.,

   daughter   daughter's   daughters   daughters'

But if it has only one form, like *bravery,* it is not a noun by this paradigmatic test, although it may be shown to be a noun by other tests.

Exercise 11–12
Write N after every word that is a noun *according to the paradigmatic test* described above.

1. player ___	**6.** nation ___	**11.** chess ___
2. pray ___	**7.** uncle ___	**12.** field ___
3. sidewalk ___	**8.** discovery ___	**13.** pocket ___
4. chaos ___	**9.** together ___	**14.** game ___
		(in playground context)
5. relax ___	**10.** shears ___	**15.** game ___
		(in hunting context)

B. The Verb Paradigm

The next set of forms to come under our scrutiny is the verb paradigm. Verbs have three, four, or five forms. Those with four, like *learn* below, are the most common. The verb paradigm goes as follows:

Forms:	Stem	Present Third-Person Singular	Present Participle	Past Tense	Past Participle
Inflectional suffixes:		{-s 3d}	{-ING vb}	{-D pt}	{-D pp}
Models:	learn	learns	learning	learned	learned
	choose	chooses	choosing	chose	chosen
	set	sets	setting	set	set

Each of these five forms has its own uses, which we shall now run through.

1. The first form is the stem. This occurs after *to,* after auxiliaries such as *can* and *will,* and in the present tense, except for the third-person singular.

Examples: to *sit,* can *go,* we *eat*

2. The present third-person singular is the form used with singular nouns, with *he, she, it,* and words for which these pronouns will substitute, and with word groups.

Examples: That *freshman* cuts his class every Wednesday.
He cuts his class every Wednesday.
Each is expected to do his duty.
Somebody has left a note for you.
Winning the championship cuts no ice with me.

The morpheme {-s 3d} has the same allomorphs in the same distribution as the plural and possessive forms of the noun: /-s/, /-z/, and /-əz/, as in *cuts, begs,* and *buzzes.*

3. The present participle is the {-ING vb} form. It combines with seven of the eight forms of *be—am, is, are, was, were, be, been—*to make verb phrases.

Examples: They *were writing* letters.
She must have *been sleeping.*

It is also used as a subjectless verbal, that is, when it is not the main verb and does not have a subject, as in

His passion used to be *playing* golf.

A few verbs—mostly referring to mental activities—are seldom heard in the {-ING vb} form as main verbs in the sentence. These verbs include *own, need, prefer, know, hear, like, remember,* and *understand.* The following sentences, for instance, are ungrammatical:

*Jake is *owning* a cabin in the north woods.
*She was not *knowing* what to say.

But they are in common use as subjectless verbals, as in

Owning a cabin in the north woods, Jake was very popular during the summer vacation period.
Not *knowing* what to say, Marilyn maintained a discreet silence.

This present-participle verbal {-ING vb} morpheme should not be confused with the nominal {-ING nm} morpheme or the adjectival {-ING aj} morpheme, both of which are described on page 97. You will study it in more detail in "Syntax," pages 225–226.

4. The past tense takes on numerous forms, e.g., *shrunk, kept, led, began, rode, built, found, knew, swore, shook.* The most usual ones end in the allomorphs /-t/, /-d/, and /-əd/, as in *passed, pleased,* and *parted.*

5. The past participle also has numerous forms. Those most frequently occurring end in the same three sounds mentioned above, but here they are allomorphs of {-D pp}. The past participle is used with *have, has, had, having* to form verbal phrases.

Examples: She *has selected* a stunning gown.
He *had* never *flown* in a helicopter.

It is also used with the forms of *be* to form the passive.

Examples: The orchestra *was selected* by the committee.
By night the missing lad *had been found.*

This past-participle verbal {-D pp} morpheme should not be confused with the adjectival {-D aj} morpheme, described on page 98.

Exercise 11–13
Fill out the following verb paradigms. Then indicate by a 3, 4, or 5 whether the verbs are three-form, four-form, or five-form.

	Stem	Pres. 3d Sg.	Pres. P.	Past T.	Past P.	Number
1.	bid					
2.	bite					
3.	keep					
4.	freeze					
5.	set					
6.	sell					
7.	put					
8.	rise					
9.	tease					
10.	sleep					

Most verbs follow faithfully the first three forms—the stem, the present third-person singular, and the present participle—with occasional exceptions like *does* and *says*, which have replacive allomorphs in the stem:

/dəz/ = /du/ + /u > ə/ + /-z/
/sɛz/ = /se/ + /e > ɛ/ + /-z/

And in the past tense and past participle most verbs have identical forms, as in *learned, have learned; batted, have batted; cried, have cried.* Such are commonly known as regular verbs. It is because of the influence of this large number of verbs having this same pattern in the past tense and past participle that children utter such forms as *knowed, runned, drinked.* The child is simply following the pattern he knows best and in so doing he creates what we call an analogical form.[1]

There still remain, however, numerous verbs, many of them of high frequency, that form their past tense and past participle in various ways. If we should classify all English verbs according to the phonemic changes and patterns of change in the past tense and past participle, the total would amount to about fifty classes. This is hardly worth our time; an exercise in such classification will show you four of these classes as samples of the patterns of change in the past tense and past participle.

Exercise 11–14

Write in phonemic symbols the past tense and past participle of each verb. Then classify the verbs into four classes according to the phonemic forms they have in common.

		Past Tense	*Past Participle*
Examples:	1. blow	*blu*	*blon*
	2. freeze	*froz*	*frozən*
	3. grow	*gru*	*gron*
	4. speak	*spok*	*spokən*

[1] In language, analogy is the process by which a new form or pattern is created on the basis of existing forms or patterns. For example, the pattern *ring, rang* and *sing, sang* is the basis for *bring, brang.* And other nonstandard forms in the past tense are created analogically from other patterns. Pairs like *fling, flung* and *sting, stung* are responsible for *bring, brung,* whereas the widespread use of the allomorph /-d/ following a voiced sound to signal past tense, as in *wing, winged, long, longed, seem, seemed, mow, mowed, rob, robbed,* results in *bring, bringed,* heard in children's speech. The suffixal morpheme /-ize/ added to adjectives to form verbs like *legalize* and *rationalize* has brought about the analogical *finalize.* With nouns the child or foreign speaker who knows *years, fears, peers,* and *beers* is likely to use the analogical plural *deers.* Both standard and nonstandard forms are brought into being by analogy.

New grammatical patterns as well as new forms are also created by analogy. The foreign learner of English who has heard "I want to tell you something" is likely to say "I want to explain you something." Among native speakers the high frequency of object pronouns like *me* after the verb, as in "The man saw me," "The man found me," and "The man met me," has produced the analogical pattern "The right man for the job is me" and "It is me."

Analogy is an important and widely operative process in language growth.

Class 1:   *blow* and *grow*. {-D pt} = /o > u/
                                {-D pp} = /-n/
Class 2:   *freeze* and *speak*. {-D pt} = /i > o/
                                {-D pp} = /i > o/ + /ən/

1. sting   _____   _____
2. creep   _____   _____
3. drive   _____   _____
4. sing   _____   _____
5. ride   _____   _____
6. write   _____   _____
7. cling   _____   _____
8. ring   _____   _____
9. keep   _____   _____
10. deal   _____   _____
11. swim   _____   _____
12. spin   _____   _____
13. win   _____   _____
14. spring _____   _____

Class 1: _____

Class 2: _____

Class 3: _____

Class 4: _____

---

1. SUPPLETION

The next kind of verb form change we are going to examine, suppletion, had best be introduced by example. Let's look at the five-part verb *go*.

go   goes   going   went   gone

In this paradigm one form, *went*, seems out of place. It ought to be **goed*, or at least a word that begins with /g/. But the entire stem /go-/ has been replaced by a wholly different stem /wɛn-/. Such a total change within a paradigm is called suppletion, and the new form is a suppletive form. The suppletion here can be simply expressed by this diagram:

/wɛnt/ = /go > wɛn/ + /t/

One English verb, *be*, is unique in that it has eight paradigmatic forms:

be   am/is/are   being   was/were   been

The stem is obviously *be*, and the alien forms that have intruded themselves into the paradigm—*am, is, are, was, were*—are suppletive forms.

Knowledge of the verb paradigm is helpful in determining whether or not a given word should be classified as a verb. If a word can fit into three or more slots of the paradigm, we classify it as a verb. The word *begin* fits into all five positions

    begin   begins   beginning   began   begun

and therefore is given the classification of verb.

With *cut,* however, the case is different. It does have three of the five possible forms:

    cut   cuts   cutting   cut   cut

But it also fits partially into the noun paradigm

    cut (singular)   cuts (plural)

So we are faced with two homophonous *cut*'s, one a verb and the other a noun, and we cannot classify the isolated word. When it occurs in context, however, the matter is simple: "She is *cutting* the bread." *Cutting* is one verb form, and we can make substitutions showing the other verb forms:

    She *cuts* the bread
    She *cut* the bread yesterday

Obviously *cut* in this context is a verb. Likewise, in "He has a cut on his finger," we can substitute a plural form

    He has several *cuts* on his finger

showing that *cut* here is a noun.

Exercise 11–15

Take a quick look again at the noun and verb paradigms. Then, using membership in a paradigm as a criterion, classify these words as N (noun), V (verb), or NV (both noun and verb).

1. driver	_____	11. bird	_____
2. compliment	_____	12. join	_____
3. appear	_____	13. end	_____
4. world	_____	14. morning	_____
5. agency	_____	15. variety	_____
6. agonize	_____	16. mother	_____
7. truck	_____	17. grammar	_____
8. decide	_____	18. melt	_____
9. emotion	_____	19. note	_____
10. book	_____	20. carve	_____

---

2. ASPECT IN THE VERB PHRASE

Aspect is the expression of meanings concerned with the continuity or distribution of events in time. Here are a few such MEANINGS, expressed in various ways in English:

    1. Beginning of event
      He began to sweat.

2. End of event
   He stopped sweating.
3. Frequency of event
   She sang often.
4. Repetition of event
   Jim pounded on the door.
5. Habitual performance of event (called habitual aspect)
   They used to eat dinner early.
6. Single occurrence of event in time (called indefinite aspect)
   I ate my lunch.
   He stepped down.
7. Progression or duration of event in time (called progressive or durative aspect)
   I was eating my lunch.
   He walked to the library.
8. Completion of event (called completive aspect)
   I have eaten my lunch.

In many languages such meanings are expressed by the form of the verb and are therefore a part of the grammar. In Russian, for example, if one adds to the verb /pisal/ (= wrote) the prefix /na/, the meaning becomes "has finished writing," the completive aspect, number 8 above. In standard French, which has three past tenses, one can choose a form which signals both past time and either of two aspects simultaneously. An example is

Il travaillait.

Here the suffix *-ait* enables the verb to be translated in either of two ways:

He *was working*. (progressive aspect, number 7 above)
He *used to work*. (habitual aspect, number 5 above)

In English, aspectual meanings are expressed in many different ways. For instance, aspectual meaning may be implicit in the meaning of the verb itself, as in *strike* (single event in time, indefinite aspect, number 6) and in *beat* (progressive aspect, number 7; or repetitive aspect, number 4). Or the aspectual meaning may be determined by the context in which the verb is embedded. Examples:

He *wrote* a letter this morning. (single event, indefinite aspect, number 6)
As a young man, he *wrote* for a living. (habitual aspect, number 5)
He *wrote* all morning to finish his report. (progressive aspect, number 7)

Although English expresses aspectual meanings in many various ways - as part of its verb system, English may be said to have only three aspects: indefinite, progressive, and completive.

1. Indefinite aspect

The form of the indefinite aspect is the verb alone, without auxiliaries, like *write, writes, wrote*. The event is thought of as a single event in time, as in She *wrote* a letter this morning.

But it must be remembered that the verb alone may signal other aspects instead, as we saw above, according to the meaning provided by the context.

With the verb alone, one often finds an adverbial of definite time (answering the question "When?") or an adverbial of duration ,(answering the question "How long?"). When the adverbial of duration is used, the verb with it is, of course, progressive or durative. Examples:

I *overslept* yesterday morning. (adverbial of definite time, indefinite aspect)

They *talked* for two hours. (adverbial of duration in time, progressive aspect)

2. Progressive or durative aspect, as in

She *was writing* a letter.

The form of the progressive is *be* + verb + *ing*. The *be* may occur in any of its forms, for example:

They may *be* sleeping.
She *is* driving the car.
She has *been* practicing law.

In the progressive aspect the event is thought of as progressing, going on, without any indication of an end. This aspect may show something going on over a period in which other events happen, as in

She was writing a letter when I entered.

The progressive aspect is generally employed with verbs whose meaning is capable of noticeable extension in time; these are verbs of activity and process, such as *walk, throw, grow, change.* It tends not to be used with verbs of mental activity and feeling, like *know, understand, remember, prefer, want, need, like,* or with verbs of non-action, like *own, consist of, seem, include.*

3. Completive aspect, as in

He has written a letter.

The form is *have* (in any of its forms) + past participle. The completive aspect presents us with two ways of interpreting the continuity of time. First, the event began in the past and has been completed, as in

Jane has attended college.

Second, the event continues up to the present, as in

Jane has attended college since last September.

In a sentence like this, with the present-tense *has* or *have* before the verb, the time adverbial is one of duration—*since last Sunday, for two months, the whole evening*—answering the question "How long?" But an adverbial of definite time (answering the question "When?") is not commonly used with the completive aspect. For example, this sentence is ungrammatical:

*Jane has attended college last year.

Exercise 11–16

Cross out the adverbials that are improperly used.

1. I have practiced my piano lesson yesterday afternoon.
2. I practiced my piano lesson yesterday afternoon.
3. Her roommate received an award last Wednesday.
4. Her roommate has received an award last Wednesday.
5. Two years ago I have visited Spain.
6. She stayed in the hospital fifteen days.
7. She has stayed in the hospital fifteen days.
8. It has rained since one o'clock.
9. She has played tennis last night.
10. I have worked in the garden for three days.

Thus far we have discussed the completive aspect only in its *has/have* form (traditionally called the present perfect tense). It also has a past form

They *had studied.*

and a seldom-heard future form

They *will have studied.*

Each of these bears a sense of completion, as in

They *had studied* hard before the exam was canceled.
They *will have read* eleven novels by the end of the semester.

The completive aspect combines with the progressive in verb phrases like

George *has been working.*

This verb phrase is completive for three reasons. First, it has the form of *have* + past participle—in this case, *been.* Second, it cannot take an adverbial of definite time, like *yesterday.* And finally, it can take an adverbial of duration, as in

George has been working all week.

On the other hand it is progressive because the form includes *be* + verb + *-ing, been working,* and in meaning it expresses the going-on of an event. So we can say that such verb phrases carry a compound aspect, completive-progressive.

Exercise 11–17

Indicate by initial letters the aspect of the underlined verb phrases.

Indefinite	Completive
Progressive	Completive-Progressive

_____ 1. Jorge played in the band last night.

_____ 2. Hans was building a doghouse.

_____ 3. Charlotte had been sick.

_____ 4. Miss Garcia had been lecturing on water pollution.

_____ 5. We saw the movie last night.

_____ 6. She was preparing for an exam.

_____ 7. They have been practicing the whole day.

_____ 8. He shaved at seven o'clock.

_____ 9. Have you done your homework?

_____ 10. Geraldine noticed an error in the minutes.

C. The Comparable Paradigm

The comparable paradigm is as follows:

Forms:	Stem	Comparative	Superlative
Inflectional suffixes:		{-ER cp}	{-EST sp}
Models:	sweet	sweeter	sweetest
	deadly	deadlier	deadliest
	friendly	friendlier	friendliest
	soon	sooner	soonest

This paradigm furnishes the pattern for these groups:

1. Nearly all one-syllable adjectives, e.g., *hot, small, proud*.

2. Some two-syllable adjectives, especially those ending in *-ly* and *-y*, such as, *lovely, funny, polite*.

3. A few adverbials of one or two syllables, e.g., *fast, early*.

4. One preposition, *near*, as in "She sat nearest the door."

Other adjectives and adverbs usually take a preceding *more* or *most* in lieu of the inflectional *-er* and *-est*.

Exercise 11–18

Here is a list of two-syllable adjectives. Write the comparative and superlative forms, *-er* and **-est,** of those that you would inflect in this way.

1. angry	_____ _____		11. quiet	_____ _____
2. healthy	_____ _____		12. remote	_____ _____
3. bitter	_____ _____		13. severe	_____ _____
4. common	_____ _____		14. solid	_____ _____
5. cruel	_____ _____		15. stupid	_____ _____
6. foolish	_____ _____		16. noble	_____ _____
7. handsome	_____ _____		17. dusty	_____ _____
8. honest	_____ _____		18. dirty	_____ _____
9. mellow	_____ _____		19. lively	_____ _____
10. pleasant	_____ _____		20. gentle	_____ _____

Exercise 11-19

Here is a list of adverbials of one and two syllables. Write out the comparative and superlative forms of those that you would inflect with -er and est. Write *no* after the adverbials that you would not use with these inflectional endings.

1. often	_____ _____	11. under	_____ _____
2. seldom	_____ _____	12. near	_____ _____
3. already	_____ _____	13. upward	_____ _____
4. gently	_____ _____	14. far	_____ _____
5. late	_____ _____	15. quick	_____ _____
6. ahead	_____ _____	16. above	_____ _____
7. weekly	_____ _____	17. loud	_____ _____
8. perhaps	_____ _____	18. quickly	_____ _____
9. sidewise	_____ _____	19. high	_____ _____
10. slow	_____ _____	20. low	_____ _____

A few adjectives have suppletive and irregular forms in the comparative and superlative, like *good*:

good   better   best

Thus the morpheme {good} has three allomorphs: /gʊd/, /bɛt-/, and /bɛ-/. The allomorphic diagrams of *better* and *best* go like this:

/bɛtər/ = /gʊd > bɛt-/ + /-ər/
/bɛst/ = /gʊd > bɛ-/ + /-st/

In the last one the /-st/ is an allomorph of {-est}, spelled -*est*.

Exercise 11-20

Write the forms of the comparative and superlative of these words.

1. well	_____ _____	4. little	_____ _____
2. bad, ill, badly	_____ _____	5. much, many	_____ _____
3. old	_____ _____	6. few	_____ _____

The capacity to take the inflectional suffixes -*er* and -*est* is one of the signals that enables us to distinguish adjectives from nouns in the position of modifier preceding a noun. In the cluster *a stone fence* the *stone* is not an adjective because we would never say *a stoner fence* or *the stonest fence*.

Exercise 11–21

In the blanks write Aj (adjective) or NA (nonadjective) to label the italicized words.

1. the *light* plane _____
2. the *night* plane _____
3. a *strange* idea _____
4. a *glass* vase _____
5. his *steel* file _____

6. that *clay* pot _____
7. her *red* davenport _____
8. a *dull* volume _____
9. a *bound* volume _____
10. my *close* friend _____

12
Parts of Speech: Form-Classes

As the parts of speech are a central and controversial area of English grammar, a brief historical introduction may prove apropos and shed light on some sticky problems.

Early in the 1500s a Renaissance Latinist, William Lyly, aided by Colet and Erasmus, prepared materials for the teaching of Latin at St. Paul's School, London. These materials were later published and became known as *Lyly's Grammar*. This was the first Latin grammar written in English. In 1540 it was "authorized" by Henry VIII, to the exclusion of competitors, and remained in wide use for three centuries. Most English schoolboys, as well as many in America, learned Latin from its pages. Its users included Shakespeare, Spenser, Jonson, Milton, Dryden, Pope, Samuel Johnson, and other famous men of letters. Because the explanation of Latin grammar was written in English, as the quotation below will show, this Latin grammar became a handy model for those writers who were later to write English grammars:

A noune is the name of a thinge, that may be seene, felte, hearde, or understande: As the name of my hande in Latin is Manus: the name of an house is Domus: the name of goodnes is Bonitas.

The heading of the first section (in the 1567 edition) is of interest to anyone studying the parts of speech in English:

An Introduction of the eyght parts of Latin speache. In Speache be these eight partes followinge:

Noune ⎫
Pronoune ⎪ declined
Verbe ⎬
Participle ⎭

Adverbe ⎫
Coniunction ⎪ undeclined
Preposition ⎬
Interiection ⎭

In the text the adjective is a subclass of noun.

In 1640 Ben Jonson, who had cut his teeth on Lyly, brought out his little *English Grammar*. In this he wrote concerning the parts of speech:

In our English speech we number the same parts with the Latines.

Noune,   Adverbe,
Pronoune,   Conjunction,
Verbe,   Præposition,
Participle,   Interjection.

Only, we adde a ninth, which is the article. . . .

The English grammarians who followed Jonson continued to use the Latin parts of speech, but these writers varied in the number of parts of speech they employed, from two to nine. By the 1760s the participle had been dropped for the most part, and eminent grammarians like the scientist Joseph Priestley and Bishop Robert Lowth chose these eight parts of speech: noun, adjective, pronoun, verb, adverb, preposition, conjunction, and interjection.

The question of which parts of speech would be used to classify English words was settled for many decades to come by Lindley Murray, whose *English Grammar* in 1795 was the first of a host of original grammars, revised grammars, and abridged grammars that appeared under his name. The estimated number of Murray grammars sold on both sides of the Atlantic is between 1,500,000 and 2,000,000, a world record. His influence was enormous, and he had many competitors. Murray espoused the eight parts of speech of Lowth, to which he added the article, and most of his competitors followed this lead.

In America about thirty English grammars appeared before 1800, and 265 more grammars came into print between 1800 and 1850. In general these adopted Murray's parts of speech. So the use of Latin-derived parts of speech to sort out our English vocabulary has had a long tradition, one that is still alive today. For you will find these same parts of speech—article, noun, adjective, pronoun, verb, adverb, preposition, conjuction, and interjection—in current dictionaries and grammars. These parts of speech can be satisfactorily employed to classify the words of English if we make some additions and refinements and if we define anew each part of speech.

The latter condition is necessary because the conventional definitions are faulty. Let us test a few of them. For a starter try this sentence:

The motionless boy stared at the flames.

A verb, we are told in conventional grammars, is a word that shows action or state of being. In the sentence above we note that the only word showing action is *flames,* which must therefore be a verb. We also find a word showing state of being, namely *motionless,* so this too must be a verb, according to the definition. How much easier it would be for both student and teacher to conclude, with more exact definitions, that *flames* is a noun because it changes form to show plurality, that *motionless* is an adjective because it is composed of the noun *motion* plus the suffix *-less,* and that *stared* is the verb because it changes its form to show past time.

We are also told in conventional, or traditional, grammars that an adjective is a word that modifies a noun. This statement is true. But it obscures that fact that any, or almost any, part of speech can modify a noun.[1] Here are some instances where we should perhaps be unwilling to call the italicized words adjectives:

The *evening* train
The *waiting* train
The *stolen* box
Our friend
The *upstairs* room
The *in* group
The *above* statement
An *if* clause

Next, the adverb. This is traditionally defined as a word that modifies a verb, adjective, or another adverb. This definition produces these alleged adverbs:

It can't be *that* good.
Ice-cold lemonade
Boiling hot water
That tree is *fifty feet* high.

The italicized words above modify adjectives. Should they be called adverbs?

Now let us compare two sentences:

He ran swiftly.
She was very sick.

In the first sentence *swiftly* modifies the verb *ran,* and in the second *very* modifies the adjective *sick.* But can *very* modify verbs, as in "He ran *very*"? It seems as if words like *very, quite,* and *rather,* which do not modify verbs, ought to be in a class by themselves.

[1] That is to say, learners may turn it around mentally to "a word that modifies a noun is an adjective," which is false.

Another difficulty with the definitions of the traditional parts of speech is that they are based on two different criteria. The definitions of noun and verb are based on meaning; the rest are based on function or their use in the sentence. The result of this double standard can be seen in a phrase like

a red shirt.

The word *red* is the name of a particular color and hence is a noun. But *red* modifies the noun *shirt* and hence is an adjective. Likewise, in

the fighting dog

fighting means an action and is therefore a verb. But it modifies the noun *dog* and is therefore an adjective.

In view of complications like these it appears that the Latin-derived parts of speech, as traditionally defined, do not offer an effective instrument of language analysis. Instead of using them we shall set up a more elaborate but more workable set of word classes (that is, parts of speech).

For convenience in a brisk overview let us split these new word classes into three groups.

The first group, which you will study in this section on morphology, consists of the form-classes. There are five of these: nouns, verbs, adjectives, adverbs, and uninflected words. The term form-class is used because membership in a class is determined by the form of a word. For example, if the form of a word can take an inflectional morpheme, such as {-s ps}, or if the form ends in a noun-forming derivational suffix, such as *-ness* or *-ism,* it will therefore be labeled a noun. These form-classes are large and open; they readily admit new members, that is, new words coming into the language from other tongues, as well as new words formed within English, like *workaholic* and *minibus.*

The second group of word classes is positional classes. You will study these later in Chapter 16. There are four main positional classes: nominal, verbal, adjectival, and adverbial. Membership in these classes is determined by position or word order. Take, for example, the sentence "We enjoyed the _____." The blank is a noun position, and any item that occupies this slot is labeled a nominal. Here are a few slot-fillers for this blank: *concert, singing, wine, peace, art.* Each is a nominal though not necessarily a noun.

The third group of word classes consists of the structure-classes, like prepositions and auxiliaries. Each structure-class is very small, and the membership is fixed and closed. The structure-classes will be taken up in Chapter 13.

A. Nouns

Nouns are identified as nouns by two aspects of form, their inflectional morphemes and their derivational morphemes. The inflectional morphemes, you remember, are the noun plural {-s pl} and the noun possessive {-s ps}. Any word that has the possessive {-s ps} is a noun, except for phrases,

like "the Queen of England's dress." Any word that has the plural {-s pl}
is also a noun. And if it does not have the {-s pl} but can take it in the
same position, sometimes with a readjustment of context to allow for a
plural form, it is a noun. Thus in

The author seems tired,

author is a noun because it can be changed to the plural in the same position, with the readjustment of *seems* to its plural form *seem:*

The *authors* seem tired.

But in the sentence

Her brother may author a new biography

author cannot be made plural in this position and hence is not a noun.

Exercise 12–1

Underline the words that are nouns according to the inflectional criteria
just above. After each, explain your choice with these numbers:

1. Has possessive morpheme.
2. Has plural morpheme.
3. Can take plural morpheme in same position, with or without a read-
   justed context to allow for a plural form.

The first column is for the first noun and the second column for the second
noun, if there is one.

1. Our president has a new plan.   _____   _____
2. The janitors had not seen the umbrella. _____   _____
3. The counselor may plan a different approach. _____   _____
4. My aunt always mothers her youngest son. _____   _____
5. Mother's cake never tasted so good.   _____   _____

In addition we shall consider as nouns those words that have only a
plural form, words like *clothes, goods, vitals, glasses* (spectacles), *oats,
pants, pliers, scissors,* and *thanks.*

Nouns are identified not only by inflectional morphemes but also by
noun-forming derivational suffixes added to verbs, adjectives, nouns, adverbs, and bound forms. Compare these sentences:

The quality is pure.
The quality is purity.

It is the form of *purity,* with its *-ity* added to an adjective, which signifies
that it is a noun. In general the suffix itself, together with our consciousness of the part of speech to which it has been attached, provides the signal

of nounness. Here is a partial list of word pairs, the second word in each containing one of the suffixes that enable us to classify a word as a noun.

Source Verb[2]	Derived Noun
accept	acceptance
achieve	achievement
advise /z/	advice /s/
arrive	arrival
assist	assistant
block	blockade
break	breakage
complain	complaint
contemplate	contemplation
deceive	deceit
deceive	deception
decide	decision
defend	defense
deform	deformity
deform	deformation
deliver	delivery
depart	departure
draft	draftee
help	helper[3]
liberate	liberator
lie	liar[3]
paint	painting
purify	purification
save	savior[3]

Source Adjective	Derived Noun
big	bigness
brave	bravery
ideal	idealist
ideal	idealism
important	importance
pure	purity
supreme	supremacy
true	truth
violent	violence
wise	wisdom
wise	wizard

Source Noun	Derived Noun
advocate (or source verb)	advocacy
Asia	Asian (-n, -an)
book	booklet

[2] In this list and those to follow the words labeled "source" usually provide the source in the sense that they take an affix to form the derived word. However, in a few cases—like *bath* and *bathe, associate* /et/ and *associate* /ət/—we have significantly contrastive forms but with no discernible source-result relationship.

[3] The suffixes *-er, -or, -ar* are the same in spoken English.

Source Noun	*Derived Noun*
cartoon	cartoonist
coward	cowardice
dog	doggie
friend	friendship
gang	gangster
king	kingdom
labor	laborite
lemon	lemonade
mathematics	mathematician
mile	mileage
monarch	monarchy
murder	murderess
novel	novelette
pagan	paganism
priest	priesthood
pulpit	pulpiteer
slave	slavery
Vietnam	Vietnamese

These same noun-forming suffixes are sometimes attached to bound stems, as in *dentist* and *tailor*.

Optional Exercise 12–2

You will find it rewarding to try to locate a matching set for each pair of words. This is an excellent way to become well acquainted with these noun-forming derivational suffixes.

Exercise 12–3

Underline each noun that can be identified by its derivational suffix. In the first blank write the source verb, adjective, or noun. In the second blank write the noun-forming suffix.

1. Jim was distressed by his failure. _____ _____
2. The payment was not large. _____ _____
3. What did the assistant say? _____ _____
4. He was a clever sailor. _____ _____
5. The catcher missed the ball. _____ _____
6. A collision was narrowly averted. _____ _____
7. There is a leakage under the sink. _____ _____
8. The history class was studying the Reformation. _____ _____
9. Who made the discovery? _____ _____
10. The amusement proved dull. _____ _____
11. She is often troubled by sickness. _____ _____

12. His refusal was polite. _____ _____
13. He swam the width of the river. _____ _____
14. Can you doubt his sincerity? _____ _____
15. Who does not enjoy freedom from want? _____ _____
16. Childhood is an unhappy time. _____ _____
17. Jane became a lawyer. _____ _____
18. You might improve your scholarship. _____ _____
19. The fragrance was overwhelming. _____ _____
20. The intimacy of the occasion was marred. _____ _____

During the discussion just above two questions may have occurred to you. First, since inflectional endings follow derivational suffixes and are used to identify nouns, why should we bother at all about the derivational suffixes? The reason is that in practice some words with such suffixes are seldom or never inflected. Here are a few examples: *derision, drainage, fertility, iciness, manhood,* and *nourishment.* Thus it seems best not to short-cut this mode of noun recognition. Second, why aren't the personal pronouns included among the form-classes? The personal pronouns resemble nouns in that they are inflected for the plural and the possessive and they occupy most noun positions in the basic patterns. They differ from nouns in that they have object forms and do not pattern in some ways like nouns. For instance, you can say, "Those happy girls" but not "Those happy them." Furthermore, the personal pronouns are a small closed structure class, whereas nouns are a large open class. Our practice here will be to consider them as a structure class with the label of "personal pronouns." They will be taken up in Chapter 13, "Structure Classes."

B. Verbs

Verbs have a maximum of five different inflectional forms, as you have already learned. All five are shown in the forms of *rise:*

Stem	Present Third-Person Singular	Present Participle	Past Tense	Past Participle
rise	rises	rising	rose	risen

Any word that has three or more of these inflectional forms is said to belong to the form-class called the verb. For example, *cut* has the minimum of three forms—*cut, cuts, cutting.* One form, *cut,* does quadruple duty for the stem, the present tense (except the third-person singular), the past tense, and the past participle. *Depart* has four forms *(depart, departs, departing,* and *departed),* and *break* has five *(break, breaks, breaking, broke, broken).* Therefore, *cut, depart,* and *break* belong to the form-class *verb.* Remember that a verb is always a single word and never a word group.

Exercise 12–4

Each verb is italicized. Indicate in the first column how many of the five inflected forms it has. In the second column identify the form used in the sentence.

Example: Jim *lost* his slide rule.　　　　　　__4__　　　__past tense__

1. The President *met* the leaders of the parade.　　　　　　　　　　___　　　_____
2. The mines had been *swept* away.　　___　　　_____
3. The bridge players would not *leave* the table.　　　　　　　　　　　　___　　　_____
4. The water is *spreading* into the meadow.　___　　　_____
5. The canary might have been *eaten* by the cat.　　　　　　　　　　　　___　　　_____
6. Theodore always *eats* between meals.　___　　　_____
7. June *set* the table.　　　　　　　___　　　_____
8. The ruler is *lying* on the table.　　___　　　_____
9. Have you *bought* the refreshments?　___　　　_____
10. The ball *sank* into the pond.　　　___　　　_____

The derivational suffixes by which a verb is identified are few. This list contains verbs with such suffixes and the source parts of speech from which the verbs are derived.

Source Noun	*Derived Verb*
bath	bathe
beauty	beautify
colony	colonize
length	lengthen
strife	strive

Source Adjective	*Derived Verb*
ripe	ripen
safe	save
solemn	solemnize
solid	solidify

These verb-forming suffixes are occasionally found combined with bound stems, as in *sanctify*.

Exercise 12–5

Underline each verb that can be identified by its derivational suffix. In the first blank write the source noun or adjective. In the second, write the verb-forming suffix.

1. He amplified his statement.　　　_____　　____
2. The judge personifies justice itself.　_____　　____

3. Can you prove your contention? _____ _____
4. This paragraph will weaken your paper. _____ _____
5. Those dorm rules should be liberalized. _____ _____
6. Mann's novel may strengthen your
   intellectual life. _____ _____
7. Why do you idolize that boob? _____ _____
8. That tale must have terrorized you. _____ _____
9. I can't soften it. _____ _____
10. Dylan was frightened by the spectacle. _____ _____

C. Adjectives

You may recall from the previous chapter the comparable paradigm (p. 148), with its compared words having the *-er* and *-est* inflectional suffixes. These suffixes enable us to set up a class of words called "comparables," but they do not permit us by themselves to separate into two classes the words traditionally called adjectives (e.g., *rich, kind*) and adverbs (e.g., *soon, often*). We can, however, dip into the reservoir of derivational suffixes and define adjectives by a combined test in this way: A word that is inflected with *-er* and *-est* and that is capable of forming adverbs with *-ly* and/or nouns with *-ness* is called an adjective.

Exercise 12–6

Fill in the blanks as follows: first column, *-er* form; second column, *-est* form; third column, *-ly* adverb form; fourth column, *-ness* noun form. Underline those words that are not adjectives by this test.

	-er	-est	-ly	-ness
1. close	_____	_____	_____	_____
2. icy	_____	_____	_____	_____
3. sweet	_____	_____	_____	_____
4. sad	_____	_____	_____	_____
5. high	_____	_____	_____	_____
6. sunny	_____	_____	_____	_____
7. gentle	_____	_____	_____	_____
8. small	_____	_____	_____	_____
9. little	_____	_____	_____	_____
10. fast	_____	_____	_____	_____
11. holy	_____	_____	_____	_____
12. long	_____	_____	_____	_____
13. friendly	_____	_____	_____	_____
14. ill	_____	_____	_____	_____
15. natural	_____	_____	_____	_____

In addition to the adjective test just described we can usually identify adjectives by derivational suffixes alone. With most of these words the degrees of comparison are expressed by *more* and *most* rather than by *-er* and *-est*. The adjective-forming suffixes are illustrated in this list.

Source Noun	*Derived Adjective*
age	agèd
child	childish
cloud	cloudy
consul	consular
crystal	crystalline
culture	cultural
economy	economic
economy	economical
fortune	fortunate
friend	friendly
moment	momentary
peace	peaceable
penny	penniless
picture	picturesque
pomp	pompous
power	powerful
science	scientific
sense	sensible
suburb	suburban
wood	wooden

Source Verb	*Derived Adjective*
associate /et/	associate /ət/
collect	collective
continue	continual
exist	existent[4]
expect	expectant
prohibit	prohibitory
prosper	prosperous
read	readable[5]
restore	restorative
shake	shaky

Source Adjective	*Derived Adjective*
dead	deadly
red	reddish

These adjective-forming suffixes and others are frequently added to bound forms; e.g.,

pens- + ive > pensive
cred- + ible > credible
loc- + al > local

---

[4] Also -ant, as in *observant*.

[5] *-ible* is a variant spelling of *-able*. The source word is commonly a verb, as in *discernible* and *corruptible,* or a bound base, as in *visible* and *credible*.

splend- + id > splendid
frag- + ile > fragile
cert- + ain > certain
domest- + ic > domestic
curi- + ous > curious
terri- + fic > terrific

Exercise 12–7

Here is a list of adjectives formed by derivational suffixes. In the first blank write the source noun, verb, adjective, or bound form. In the second write the adjective-forming suffix.

1. golden _____ _____
2. helpless _____ _____
3. lovely _____ _____
4. messy _____ _____
5. peaceful _____ _____
6. insular _____ _____
7. nervous _____ _____
8. fragmentary _____ _____
9. repentant _____ _____
10. affectionate _____ _____
11. foolish _____ _____
12. rhythmic _____ _____
13. regional _____ _____
14. tired _____ _____
15. separate /ət/ _____ _____
16. recurrent _____ _____
17. instructive _____ _____
18. perishable _____ _____
19. meddlesome _____ _____
20. congratulatory _____ _____
21. pleasant _____ _____
22. goodly _____ _____
23. lively _____ _____

D. Adverbs

The adverb has four suffixes to set it apart from other form classes—the derivational suffixes -*ly*, -*wise*, -*ward*, and -*s*—and the free form *like*.

1. Source Adjective   *Derived Adverb*

fortunate   fortunately

2. Source Noun   *Derived Adverb*

student   studentwise

This -*wise* suffix, about five centuries old in English, has taken on renewed vitality in recent years and today may be heard attached to almost any noun to form an adverb.

3. *Source Noun*   *Derived Adverb*

north   northward

Words consisting of a source noun + -*ward* are at home in the positions of both adjectives and adverbs, as in

1. The *earthward* drop of the parachutist was spectacular.
   (adjective position)
2. As she stepped out the plane door and parachuted *earthward,* she momentarily lost consciousness.
   (adverb position)
3. A population movement *cityward* has been observed.
   (adjective position)
4. He looked *cityward* for a sign of the train.
   (adverb position)

Here we shall label such words as adverbs because -*ward* has a directional meaning that is usually considered adverbial (see entry "adverb" in *Webster's Third NID*). This applies to words like *shoreward, skyward, landward, churchward, deathward, manward, riverward,* and *heavenward.* It does not apply to words like *forward, inward, downward.* These are not formed on a source noun and are termed uninflected words (UW's).

In examples 1 and 3 above, *earthward* and *cityward* are adverbs in form. Later you will learn that they are adjectivals in position and modifiers by function.

4. *Source Noun*   *Derived Adverb*

night   nights

This -*s* suffix is a remnant of the Old English genitive singular suffix -*es*. It is attached to words denoting a time period, like

He works *days.*
He is busy *mealtimes.*
She plays golf *Saturdays.*

The italicized words here are classified as adverbs. They could, with equal justification, be considered plural nouns, adverbial in position, and modifiers by function. In addition, -*s* is suffixed to words in the -*ward* series, resulting in two forms of each word. For example,

Jeanne stepped *backward/backwards.*
They looked *toward/towards* the speaker.

Finally, this same -*s* closes some adverbs, like *always, unawares,* and the adverb suffix -*wise* (formerly, the genitive of *way*). It is sometimes called the adverbial -*s*.

5. *Source Noun*	*Derived Adverb*
student	studentlike

6. *Source Adjective*	*Derived Adverb*
casual	casual-like

Exercise 12–8

Classify the italicized words according to the form-class to which they belong: Av (adverb) or Aj (adjective).

1. Your ideas seem *sensible.*   _____
2. They are playing *happily.*   _____
3. He turned the hands *clockwise.*   _____
4. Be *careful.*   _____
5. Have you seen the paper *lately?*   _____
6. It's fragile. Lift it *easylike.*   _____
7. She walked *homeward.*   _____
8. *Luckily,* the brake was set.   _____
9. Jack looked *glum.*   _____
10. It smells *sweet.*   _____
11. You *richly* deserve the prize.   _____
12. Tharp is *professor-wise* pretty knowledgeable.   _____
13. Annie is a waitress *evenings.*   _____
14. A Gothic spire pointed *heavenward.*   _____
15. *Mondays* she sleeps late.   _____

E. Uninflected Words

Words that cannot be kenneled in one of the four form-classes—noun, verb, adjective, or adverb—are known as uninflected words, UW's. There are a good many of these leftovers. Here are examples:

1. Words that are traditionally called nouns:
   pathos, advice, tennis, evidence, botany, charisma.
2. Words traditionally called adverbs:
   often, seldom, also, never, perhaps.
3. Words traditionally known as adjectives:
   antic, menial, only, tired.
4. Most of the words in the structure classes:
   the, must, quite, from, and, since, which, all.

Since these leftovers, and numerous others, do not meet the criteria for any of the form-classes, we must toss them in the UW basket. But this is no cause for concern. Today's grammarian employs the dual criteria of form and position (often termed word order) to sort out the parts of speech, and so far we have employed only form for this purpose.

Later, in the section on syntax, we shall classify words by the second criterion, position, using the parallel parts-of-speech classes of nominal, verbal, adjectival, and adverbial; and then the recalcitrant words above will fall into place. Even then, there may remain a few outcasts, for no part-of-speech system has ever been devised for English that neatly and fully classifies all the words of English.

An especially refractory class of words is a group of about seventy-five, mostly of two syllables, which begin with the prefix *a-*. Their formation is like this:

Prefix	Stem	Word
a- + noun	-foot	afoot
	-ground	aground
	-kin	akin
a- + verb	-gape	agape
	-wake	awake, as in "He is awake."
	-sunder	asunder
a- + adjective	-loud	aloud
	-fresh	afresh
	-weary	aweary
a- + bound form	-jar	ajar
	-gog	agog

These are UW's (uninflected words) because they take no inflectional endings. Although they do have the prefix *a-* in common, it seems unwise to label them formally as either adjectives or adverbs since positionally they appear in both adjectival and adverbial slots. Therefore we shall bin them as UW's. However, you meet them later in two positional classes.

Exercise 12–9

Classify the italicized words as N (noun), V (verb), Aj (adjective), Av (adverb), or UW (uninflected word).

1. Sue likes to play *golf* on Sunday mornings.
2. Only the *dregs* are left.
3. There will be a *meeting* at four tomorrow afternoon.
4. Which nation *colonized* Tierra del Fuego?
5. Every social class has its own *snobbery*.
6. May you be healthy and *prosperous*.
7. Be careful not to run *aground*.
8. She smiled *cheerfully*.
9. The *quickest* way is to use your pocket calculator.
10. We counted the tickets in *haste*.

13

Parts of Speech: Structure Classes

A structure class is a part-of-speech class. Examples of the members of some structure classes are these: *the, could, unless, him, of, very, every,* A structure class has three characteristics:

1. Members of a given structure class are recognized mainly by position, as they have no characteristics of form in common and, excepting a few, do not change form.
2. A structure class is small, the largest one (prepositions) having only about fifty members.
3. A structure class has a stable membership and is a closed class, that is, it rarely admits new members.

Because structure classes are small, stable, and closed, we get to know their member words individually, like Uncle Elmer. For example, we are never in doubt about *could*. We know that it is an auxiliary and that its fellows are words like *would, should, will,* and *can.* Thus, instead of defining these classes, it will be enough to describe their position and list the membership.

A. Qualifiers

The qualifier occurs in the position just before an adjectival or an adverbial as shown by the empty slots in these sentences:

The dinner was _____ good.
She performed _____ skillfully.

Thus it is evident that words like *very* and *rather* are qualifiers. The function of a qualifier is to modify; and the word following the qualifier, like *good* and *skillfully* (that is, the word modified), is called the head.

Exercise 13–1

Underline the qualifiers. In each blank indicate whether the qualifier modifies an Aj (adjective) or an Av (adverb).

1. That is very kind of you. _____
2. It is too hot in this classroom. _____
3. You played quite acceptably in the second half. _____
4. Marion was somewhat unhappy. _____
5. A rather shy boy was trying to dance. _____

Most qualifiers are uninflected words, like those in the preceding exercise. However, the qualifier position can accept any form-class, as these examples show:

Noun: The table was only *inches* wide.
Verb: The water is *boiling* hot.
Adjective: My dress seems *lighter* blue than yours.
Adverb: You did *fairly* well.

Each of the italicized terms above is a qualifier by position. Its function is to modify.

Exercise 13–2

Indicate the form-class of the italicized qualifiers, using the abbreviations N, V, Aj, Av, and UW.

1. You are *too* kind. _____
2. Are you *completely* happy with your courses? _____
3. This water is *freezing* cold. _____
4. The bottle is *bone* dry. _____
5. He is *fighting* mad. _____
6. The novel proved *extremely* distasteful. _____
7. I feel *quite* fine, thank you. _____
8. Dorothy was *rather* gracious in her response. _____
9. I prefer a *brighter* red tie. _____
10. Monty appears *enormously* wealthy. _____
11. The baby is a *month* old. _____

A few qualifiers have the same form as adjectives—for instance, *pretty* good, *mighty* fine, *jolly* hot, *great* big, *full* well, *dead* right. In the qualifier position, however, these do not take -*er* and -*est,* so we shall consider them as uninflected qualifiers that are homophones of adjectives.

Some qualifiers are not used before all adjectivals and adverbials but have a limited distribution. We shall not take time to investigate the vagaries of such distributions, but a glance at a few examples might prove instructive.

stark naked	*much* alive	*about* exhausted
clean out	*just* under	*brand* new
fresh out	*almost* ready	*plumb* crazy
right along	*precious* little	*real* good
beastly cold	*that* good	

Sometimes noun phrases and idiomatic expressions are used in the position before adjectivals and adverbials and must therefore be regarded as qualifiers. Among the common ones are

a lot	kind of
a great deal	sort of
a little	a bit (of)

With qualifiers of adjectivals and adverbials in the comparative degree, the list is somewhat different. For example, look at these sentences:

*I feel *much* good.
*I feel *very* better.

As a native speaker you know at once that these are un-English. Now switch the qualifiers and the sentences will feel comfortable, like a well-tailored suit. The point is that the qualifiers used before a comparative are not quite the same ones as those before the positive degree. The last question of the following exercise will enable you to identify those qualifiers that are used with the comparative.

Exercise 13-3

You are given below a list of words and phrases that are qualifiers when in the qualifier slot. Following the list are questions to answer.

a bit	kind of	a whole lot
a good deal	least	enough
a great deal	less	even
almost	any	indeed
a lot	awful	just
lots	pretty	some
mighty	quite	somewhat
more	rather	sort of
most	real	still
much	right	too
no	so	very
plenty		

You must not forget that you are dealing with a positional class. So don't worry about words on this list that have homophones in other positional classes, e.g.,

Adjectival: It was the *most* fun.
 What a *pretty* girl.
Adverbial: She is coming *too*.
 They are *still* swimming.
Nominal: I've had *plenty*.
 He ate *a whole lot* of potatoes.

Questions

1. Which qualifier has a position after, not before, its head?   ————

2. Which two qualifiers can occur either before or after the head?   ———— ————

3. Which qualifiers can occur in the slot below?

 She is coming ———— now?   ———— ———— ————

4. Which qualifiers can occur in the slot before comparatives, as in one of these sentences?
 She is ———— happier today.   ———— ———— ————
 Is she ———— happier today?   ———— ———— ————

B. Prepositions

Prepositions are words like *of, in,* and *to* which are usually followed by a noun, noun phrase, personal pronoun, or noun-substitute called the object of the preposition. The unit of preposition-plus-object of preposition is called a prepositional phrase.

Examples: George sat *between* the two deans.
 George jumped *on* it.
 George went *from* this *to* that.

English has a small group of prepositions, of which the most frequently used ones are *at, by, for, from, in, of, on, to,* and *with.* Those in greatest use are, in order of frequency, *of, in,* and *to.* These one-syllable prepositions usually have weak or third stress in their common uses.

Examples: He came with the girl.
 That is the girl with whom he came.
 That is the girl whom he came with.
 That is the girl he came with.

Monosyllabic prepositions now and then take a primary stress instead of a weak or third stress. Compare

I came with hér.   I came with hĕr.

There was no cóurage ĭn hĭm.   There was no courage ín hìm.
Where is he fróm?

Such changes of stress are not completely predictable.

Exercise 13–4

Underline the preposition and show by a stress mark how you pronounce
it. Underline the object twice. If there is no object, write *no* in the blank
after the sentence.

1. The car stopped at the station. _____
2. He came from the farm. _____
3. This is the farm he came from. _____
4. These roses are for you. _____
5. The chimpanzee in the cage was yawning. _____
6. The lad stood on a barrel. _____
7. The plumber washed in the basin. _____
8. The rose by the window was wilted. _____
9. He objected to the last paragraph. _____
10. What is it for? _____

Among our prepositions are a number of two-syllable ones, such as
*about, above, after, against, among, before, behind, below, beneath, be-
tween, beyond, despite, except, inside, into, outside, under, upon.* These
are different from the one-syllable prepositions in their stress behavior.
You will find this out for yourself in the next exercise.

Exercise 13–5

You are given here a series of sentences containing two-syllable prepositions. The stresses are supplied. Using these sentences as your data, make
a generalization explaining the operation of stresses in dissyllabic prepositions. It would be advisable to test your generalization by composing more
sentences in the pattern given, to see if your conclusion is sound.

1. The sheriff came bĕhìnd Clarence.
2. The sheriff came behínd him.
3. We walked ùndĕr the tree.
4. We walked únder it.
5. The party advanced ìnto the jungle grass.
6. The party advanced ínto it.
7. Henderson stood bĕfòre the judge.
8. Henderson stood befóre him.
9. She knew everything ăbòut Einar.
10. She knew everything abóut him.

Generalization: _____

_____

_____

Some of these words we have been dealing with can be either prepositions or adverbials. Compare

Preposition: She looked *up* the stairs.
Adverbial: She looked *up*.
Preposition: They went *inside* the house.
Adverbial: They went *inside*.

Exercise 13–6
Underline the prepositions once and the adverbials twice. Put the proper primary stress marks on these words.

1. The swimmers waited below.
2. The swimmers waited below the dam.
3. She liked to sit near.
4. She sat near the window.
5. The paint bucket fell off the porch.
6. The paint bucket fell off.
7. The refreshments came after.
8. The refreshments came after the program.
9. I haven't seen him since.
10. I haven't seen him since yesterday.

In addition to the prepositions already mentioned, there is in English a group of *-ing* prepositions that all have a verb as a stem. Here are some of the more common: *assuming, beginning, barring, concerning, considering, during, following, including, involving, pending, regarding, succeeding.*[1]

Examples: *Considering* your loss, the bill will not be sent.
Assuming the accuracy of the report, action must be taken at once.
We will delay the papers, *pending* arrival of the contract.

Exercise 13–7
Underline the *-ing* prepositions once and the *-ing* verbs twice.

1. Barring accidents, the picnic will begin at eleven.
2. There will be a smoker following dinner.

[1] The stem of *during is dure,* an obsolete English verb meaning "to last." The stem of *pending* is *pend-,* which comes from a French base meaning "to hang, suspend."

3. She is only following her orders after all.
4. May I have a conference regarding my examination?
5. He was regarding the newcomer with curiosity.
6. Considering the time, we had better stop now.
7. The entire squad, including the water boy, will make the trip.
8. I am including damage to my window in the bill.
9. The store will be closed weekends, beginning Saturday.
10. He was vague concerning the details.

The final group is composed of compound prepositions. These are relatively numerous and of various types. Often it is difficult to say whether a word group should be considered a preposition or not. Here is a short list of two types.

Two-Part	*With Noun*
together with	on account of
contrary to	in spite of
ahead of	with regard to
due to	in advance of
apart from	in front of
up to	on behalf of
out of	in place of
away from	in lieu of
up at	in addition to
as for	by way of
inside of	in comparison with
because of	by dint of
owing to	in case of
instead of	by means of
	by way of

Those in the first column it is simplest to call compound prepositions. In the second column we seem to have either a compound preposition or two successive prepositional phrases (when an object is added after the last word). One argument for calling them compound prepositions is that we normally do not place modifiers before the noun following the first preposition, as we can do with ordinary prepositional phrases. For example, in *on account of* the word *account* is not modified.

Exercise 13–8
Underline the compound prepositions.

1. We arrived ahead of time.
2. The game was called off on account of rain.
3. The oldest daughter is up at the camp.
4. Contrary to our expectations, the movie was a delightful spoof.
5. We came by way of Brookline.

6. I want to thank you on behalf of these refugees.
7. They served rice instead of potatoes.
8. They served rice in lieu of potatoes.
9. In spite of her protestations, Harriet was persuaded to join the guild.
10. In case of accident, call your insurance agent.

Finally, here is a little afterthought on prepositions. The name *preposition* implies that this structure word occupies a *pre-* position, that is, one before its object. Such is usually the case. But you will also find it at the end of a few structures:

1. Relative clause: The job (that) he worked *at.*
2. Passive: The lock had been tampered *with.*
3. Infinitive: Clay is fun to play *with.*
4. Exclamation: What a hedge of thorns we stumbled *into!*
5. QW question: Which room did you find it *in?*
6. Set expressions: The world *over,*
                 your objection *notwithstanding.*

So you can forget the schoolroom superstition that a preposition is an improper word to end a sentence with. In some cases, such as "Where are you from?", any other word order would sound silly or artificial. In other cases you may have a stylistic choice. For instance, "The doctor with whom I was conferring" is formal, whereas "The doctor I was conferring with" is informal. Both are standard acceptable English.

C. Determiners

A determiner is a word that patterns with a noun. It precedes the noun and serves as a signal that a noun is soon to follow.

Example: *The* gymnasium

If the noun is preceded by adjectives and nouns, the determiner precedes these modifiers.

Examples: *The* new gymnasium
       The brick gymnasium
       The new brick gymnasium

The absence of a determiner to signal a following noun will sometimes produce ambiguity. Here is a case from a newspaper headline:

Union demands increase.

We do not know how to interpret *increase* because a signal is absent. A *will* would show that it is a verb:

Union demands will increase.

A determiner would indicate that it is a noun:

Union demands *an* increase.

The following is a partial list of determiners:

a/an	my	this
the	your	that
	his	these
	her	those
	its	
	our	
	their	
	John's (any possessive of name)	

Those in the middle column are, in form, the prenominal possessive personal pronouns (pages 129–135).

Six of these determiners—his, John's, this, that, these, those—may also be used in place of a noun—that is, as noun substitutes.

Examples: *That* will be enough.
I prefer *Elizabeth's*.
What can one do with old cars like *these?*
I can't tell Jim's tennis shoes from *his*.

Exercise 13-9

In the blanks write a D (determiner) or NS (noun-substitute) to show the category of the italicized word.

1. Do you like *my* new hat? _____
2. Do you like *this?* _____
3. Have you *a* match? _____
4. *These* fellows are my new teammates. _____
5. *These* are my new teammates. _____
6. We did not disturb *George's* room. _____
7. *Its* roots grew under the pavement. _____
8. Have you seen *our* formals? _____
9. *This* cold is invigorating. _____
10. *Smith's* house is for sale. _____
11. *His* is the best plan. _____
12. Where are *the* red phlox you planted? _____
13. *That* deep pool is a good place for trout. _____
14. Jack has *an* interest in grinding rocks. _____
15. *Your* slip is showing. _____

Exercise 13-10

Each of these newspaper headlines is ambiguous, that is, can be read in two ways. Add a determiner to each in such a way that a noun will be identified and the meaning reduced to a single one.

1. Police raid gathering   _____
2. Complete faculty at State   _____
3. Rule book not obscene   _____
4. Clean model house   _____
5. Girl shows top baby beef[2]   _____

D. Auxiliaries

Auxiliaries are closely associated with the verb and are of three kinds. The first kind is called modal auxiliaries:

There are ten modal auxiliaries:

can	could
may	might
shall	should
will	would
	must
	ought (to)[3]

The modal auxiliaries are bound together as a group by two characteristics of form: (1) The present-tense form does not take an -*s* in the third person singular; for example, we say "She may," not "She mays." (2) They do not have participle forms, present or past.

These modal auxiliaries precede verb stems and give them special shades of meaning like futurity, volition, possibility, probability, permission, and necessity. They are sometimes called verb markers because they signal that a verb is about to follow. The majority of the modals are said to have tense. In the first four pairs—*can, could; may, might; shall, should; will, would*—the second member is the past tense of the first member. This is apparent in indirect discourse:

I think I *can* help you.
I thought I *could* help you.

Must and *ought (to)* do not have parallel forms, like the others. To express the past tense of *must,* in the sense of necessity, one says *had to,* e.g.,

This morning I *must* trim the hedge.
Yesterday I *had to* trim the hedge.

And for the past tense of *ought (to),* one uses *ought (to)/should* plus *have* plus a past participle, e.g.,

You *ought to* see those strawberries.
You *ought to have/should have* seen those strawberries.

---

[2] *Baby beef* means calves, which farm boys and girls exhibit at fairs.

[3] This account omits the uses of *dare* and *need* as auxiliaries. You might like to investigate their uses in questions and negative sentences.

The negatives of *must* and *ought to* are not regular. If *must* means "is necessary," then its negative means "is not necessary." This negative meaning is expressed by *do not have to* or *need not,* and not by *must not,* which is a forbiddance of the action of the following verb. Thus:

Affirm. You must return tomorrow.
Neg. You don't have to return tomorrow.

or

You need not return tomorrow.

but not

You must not return tomorrow.

The negative of *ought to* is expressed by *ought not to* or *hadn't ought to* (Northern form) or *should not.* Thus:

Affirm.: You ought to carry that log away.
Neg.: You ought not to carry that log away.

or

You hadn't ought to carry that log away.

or

You shouldn't carry that log away.

The form *hadn't ought to* is used in speech only, not in writing, and of the three, *shouldn't* is perhaps the most commonly employed.

Often the ideas that modal auxiliaries express do not include an element of time. Here are all ten expressing delicate nuances of meaning exclusive of time, save that a notion of futurity is implicit in all of them.

May I help you?	You ought to be careful.
Might I help you?	Will you come again?
Can I help you?	Would you come again?
Could I help you?	Shall I return it?
You must be careful.	Should I return it?

On the whole the meanings expressed are many and subtly shaded, and you are lucky that, as a native speaker, you already have a command of them.

The second kind of auxiliary is the two primary auxiliaries, *have* and *be.* Their forms are:

Stem	have	be
Present tense	has/have	am/is/are
Present participle	having	being
Past tense	had	was/were
Past participle	had	been

When immediately preceding a main verb, *have* is followed by a past participle, as in "He has *eaten,*" and *be* is followed by either a past participle, as in "The white cat was *found*," or a present participle, as in "They are *studying*."

When auxiliaries are employed in groups of two or three, an obligatory sequence is followed: modal + *have* + *be*.

Examples:	*modal*	*have*	*be*	{-ING vb}/{-D pp}
I	might	have	been	fishing/shot
George	may		be	reading/startled
They		had	been	sleeping/seen
She	must	have		quit

In main-verb sequences only one modal auxiliary is used. With *have* only one form is used in main-verb sequences. But *be* may be doubled, as in "He *was being* punished."

The third kind of auxiliary is the periphrastic auxiliary *do,* and it is a special case. *Do* is a "dummy" form that has these uses:

1. In questions it carries the tense and provides the inversion that signals a question.

> **Examples:** Does John study?
> Did John study?
> When does John study?
> Where did John study?

This inversion parallels the pattern for modal auxiliaries.

> Will John study?
> When will John study?

2. In negative sentences it carries the tense and positions the negative word *not* between an auxiliary and the verb, following the pattern of modal auxiliaries.

> **Example:** John didn't study.
> (Cf. John couldn't study.)

3. In declarative affirmative sentences it provides emphasis and requires a primary or a secondary stress.

> **Examples:** John díd study.
> John dîd study very hárd.

4. In tag questions it replaces a main verb in the simple present or in the past tense.[4]

> **Examples:** She likes ice cream, *does*n't she?
> He sold the house, *did*n't he?

5. In sentences beginning with a negative adverbial like *seldom, never, not only,* it expresses, in an inverted structure, the tense.

[4] For tag questions see pages 300–302.

Examples: Never *did* I dream of such a thing.
Not only *does* he dream, he has nightmares.

Exercise 13–11

Give the number of auxiliaries, from 0 through 3, in each sentence.

1. I shall be waiting for you.   _____
2. You ought to have done better.   _____
3. Helen should have been working. _____
4. Mr. Owens has your car.   _____
5. The elephant has been injured.   _____

Exercise 13–12

Label the italicized auxiliaries as **MA** (modal auxiliaries), **PA** (primary auxiliary), or **P** (periphrastic auxiliary).

1. Joyce was *being* attacked by the critics.   _____
2. *Could* you hold this turkey for me?   _____
3. *Did* he find the right address?   _____
4. The butler *may* have committed the crime.   _____
5. The net *was* lying in a heap.   _____

Exercise 13–13

A verb may be preceded by one, two, or three auxiliaries. Underline the auxiliaries. Then write above each one MA (for modal auxiliary), *have,* or *be.* Which sequence, if any, differs from that given on page 177?

1. Those words must be justified.

2. She ought to have written her mother.

3. They could be coming by plane.

4. The car could have been wrecked by that.

5. You might have mowed it shorter.

The behavior and patterning of auxiliaries differ from those of verbs in three respects.

1. A sentence with a verb can begin a conversation and be satisfactorily understood by the listener. Upon meeting a friend you might say, "I worked like a dog yesterday," and receive a nod of comprehension and sympathy. But if you used only a modal auxiliary in such an introductory sentence, "I could yesterday," your friend might look at you with concern and reply, "Could what?"

The point here is that an auxiliary is not used as a full verb. It may be used, however, as a substitute verb for a verb already mentioned, as in

He ate an orange and so *did* I.
I can drive and so *can* he.

Or it may be used in reference to a previously stated verb. For example, in reply to the question, "Are you going to the play?" you might say, "Yes, I am."

2. The negative of a verb phrase containing an auxiliary or auxiliaries is made by putting *not* after a single auxiliary or after the first auxiliary in a sequence.

They will *not* tell.
They have *not* been reporting the right figures.

This {not} may take the form of *n't* /-ɪnt/, /-ənt/, or /-nt/. A negatived verb, on the contrary, requires a form of *do* plus *not* preceding the verb stem.

I told him.
I *did not* tell him.

3. To make a question with an auxiliary, the subject and the auxiliary, or first auxiliary in a sequence, are reversed:

She can do a good job.
Can she do a good job?
The chairman has been told.
Has the chairman been told?

But with a verb, unless the verb is a form of *be,* we formulate a question by following the pattern do {do} + subject + verb stem:

They studied the constitution carefully.
Did they study the constitution carefully?

Exercise 13–14
Rewrite each sentence in two ways—as a negative and as a question. Then decide whether the italicized word is an auxiliary or a verb, using the criteria in paragraphs 2 and 3 immediately preceding this exercise. Indicate your decision by writing Aux or V in the blank at the right.

Example: She *began* working.   Neg. *She did not begin working.*
                                        Q. *Did she begin working?*   **V**

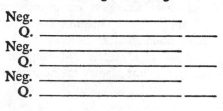

1. He *was* eating.   Neg. _____
                             Q. _____

2. He *quit* eating.   Neg. _____
                             Q. _____

3. The worker *was* killed. Neg. _____
                             Q. _____

4. The worker *has* gone. Neg. _____
   Q. _____

5. We *should* hurry. Neg. _____
   Q. _____

6. We *can* hurry Neg. _____
   Q. _____

7. They *are* going Neg. _____
   Q. _____

8. They *kept* going. Neg. _____
   Q. _____

9. He *might* have been sleeping. Neg. _____
   Q. _____

10. He *will* play. Neg. _____
    Q. _____

E. Pronouns: Personal, Interrogative, Relative

1. PERSONAL PRONOUNS

The personal pronouns might be presented like the paradigms of the noun, the verb, and the comparable, showing stems and inflectional suffixes. But this is a highly complicated procedure, and since the group is small and closed, it will suffice to deal with its members as a set of related forms, like the other structure classes.

Singular

	Subject	Object	Prenominal Possessive	Substitutional Possessive
1st	I	me	my	mine
2nd	you	you	your	yours
3rd M	he	him	his	his
F	she	her	her	hers
N	it	it	its	its

Plural

1st	we	us	our	ours
2nd	you	you	your	yours
3rd	they	them	their	theirs
Interr. Relative	who	whom	whose	whose

Let us look at them through the framework terms.

1. Number. You are already acquainted with the terms *singular* and *plural,* with their meanings of "one" and "more than one." One difference from noun number here is that *we* does not mean more than one *I* but *I* and somebody else. The singular and plural have the same *you* forms. Earlier in our history the singular forms were *thou, thee, thy, thine.* These were in everyday use by the English who settled our country in the early 1600s, and you meet them in Shakespeare's plays and the King James Bible, both of the same period. They survive today in liturgical language and, partially, in the speech of the Friends.

2. Function Terms

a. The pronouns in the *subject* column are those used in the functions of subject of the verb and subjective complement.

Examples: The Smiths and *we* are going to the ballet.

It was *she* who missed the test.

b. The pronouns in the *object* column are those which function mainly as objects of the verb and of the preposition.

Examples: I gave *her* the letter yesterday.

We saw *her* in the car.

A package came from George and *him*.

c. The prenominal possessives occur before nouns.

Example: With *my* brains and *your* industry we could make a fortune.

d. The substitutional possessives occur as substitutes for nouns. The form *its* is rarely used.

Examples: That lawn mower is *ours* (= our lawn mower).

Yours (= your term paper) was the best.

3. Person

a. The first person in the singular denotes the speaker. In the plural it denotes the speaker plus anybody else, one or more.

b. The second person denotes the person or persons spoken to.

c. The third person denotes those other than the speaker or those spoken to.

4. Sex Reference. Only three of the horizontal rows of pronouns have sex reference—the *he, she,* and *it* rows. The *it* can refer to certain creatures of either sex—*infant, dog, pig*—and to sexless things—*story, stone, justice.*

2. INTERROGATIVE PRONOUNS: *WHO, WHOM, WHOSE*

As the first word in a question, the subject form *who* is normally used in cultivated speech, regardless of its function.

Examples: *Who* borrowed my tie? (subject of verb)

Who did you take to the theater? (object of verb)

Who are you referring to? (object of preposition)

In cases like the last two examples *whom* is occasionally used by the ultra-fastidious, but it sounds stiff and bookish. The object form *whom* is used directly after prepositions, as in "To whom?" and "With whom did you go?" But in easy conversational style the latter is likely to be "Who did you go with?"

Whose book is this? (prenominal possessive)
Whose is this book? (substitutional possessive)

3. RELATIVE PRONOUNS: *WHO, WHOM, WHOSE*

With the relative pronouns *who* is used as the subject of the verb, and *whom* as object of the verb and object of the preposition.

Examples: The girl *who* received a West Point appointment was welcomed by the cadets. (subject of verb)

The girl *whom* I voted for won by a close margin. (object of preposition)

The girl *whom* I admired most was Jack's sister. (object of verb)

The teacher *whose* book I borrowed had an extra copy. (possessive relative)

We had a beautiful maple *whose* leaves turned scarlet in September. (This use of *whose* with nonhuman reference is not uncommon in reputable English.)

As you doubtless noticed from the examples above, *who* and *whom* (interrogative and relative) have human reference, whereas *whose* (interrogative) has human and *whose* (relative) both human and nonhuman reference.

There are two more relative pronouns, *which* and *that*.

Which has nonhuman reference and in its uses parallels those of *who, whom, whose.*

Examples: The tree *which* fell was a large oak. (subject of verb)

The tree *which* I prefer is an oak. (object of verb)

The tree *which* we sat under was an oak. (object of preposition)

The tree under *which* we sat was an oak. (object of preposition)

That has both human and nonhuman reference. Its uses are the same as those of *which*, except that it does not directly follow a preposition.

Examples: The flavor *that* pleases me most is chocolate. (subject of verb)

The teacher *that* I like best is Mrs. Lopez. (object of verb)

The author *that* I am writing about is Camus. (object of preposition)

But

*The author about *that* I am writing is Camus (ungrammatical)

One more observation about relative pronouns is relevant: When a relative pronoun functions as an object of the verb or object of the preposition, it may be omitted.

Examples: The pet [*which, that*] he wanted to buy was a French poodle.

The carpenter [*whom*] we hired was Mr. Cutter.
The doctor [*whom*] I am waiting for is Dr. Harris.

Exercise 13–15

Assume you are writing a term paper in a formal style. Fill in the blanks with the relative *who* or *whom*.

1. The candidate _____ the convention chose had always voted for civil rights legislation.
2. She interviewed a well-known scientist with _____ she had previously corresponded.
3. The doctor _____ developed the vaccine warned against possible side effects.
4. The psychiatrist with _____ Carlson conferred was optimistic about the case.
5. All the persons _____ they arrested protested their innocence.

Exercise 13–16

Fill in the blanks with *who* or *which* or both. After the sentence indicate whether the reference is Hum (human) or Nhum (nonhuman).

1. That's the girl _____ won all the honors.   _____
2. The council listened to the citizens _____ presented the petition.   _____
3. It was the spotted kitten _____ ran under the porch. _____
4. We feared the enemy _____ was across the hill.   _____
5. The coffee _____ you bought is stale.   _____

Exercise 13–17

Place in each blank within the sentence either a prenominal or a substitutional possessive. In the blank after the sentence classify the one you used by PP or SbP.

1. This is _____ seat.   _____
2. This seat is _____.   _____
3. Have you seen _____ canary?   _____
4. I compared it to _____.   _____
5. _____ is a poor bathing suit.   _____
6. I'd prefer one like _____.   _____
7. Where is _____ friend today?   _____
8. _____ bucket is leaking.   _____
9. He found it with _____.   _____
10. She bought _____ sister a compact.   _____

PART III
THE
SYNTAX
OF
ENGLISH

14
Noun and Verb Phrases

A. Noun Phrases

Up to this point we have examined systematically the phonemic and morphemic structure of English. Now we shall see how words are combined into larger structures—phrases, clauses, and sentences. This is the domain of syntax. The syntactic architecture of the English sentence is extraordinarily complex and can be blueprinted by various methods, none of them perfect. In the presentation that follows you will be shown the main outlines only, with the admonition that there are different ways of interpreting the same syntactic facts and that English syntax contains territories as yet uncharted.

A noun phrase consists of a noun and all the words and word groups that belong with the noun and cluster around it. The noun itself is called the *headword* or *head,* and the other words and word groups are modifiers of the noun.

Examples: The yellow *tulips*
The yellow *tulips* in the garden
The yellow *tulips* in the garden which were gaily blooming

In these examples *tulips* is the head. Of the rest of the words, the modifiers, we observe that the single-word modifiers, like *the* and *yellow,* precede the head and that the word-group modifiers, like *in the garden* and *which were blooming,* follow the head.

Exercise 14–1

Underline the head of the following noun phrases.

1. The fence
2. The old fence
3. That new aluminum fence
4. The fence between the houses
5. The old fence which was painted green
6. The old fence between the houses which was painted green
7. A worn-out putter
8. My worn-out putter lying in the attic
9. A used car, broken down by abusive driving
10. The children's swings in the park which were in use all day long

Exercise 14–2

Make each list of words into a noun phrase and underline the headword.

1. Table, the, small, study
2. European, any, opera, great
3. Somber, evening, that, sky
4. My, shoes, roommate's, tennis
5. Linen, white, handkerchiefs, the, other, all
6. Soft, a, on the head, pat
7. Hard, a, which staggered him, blow
8. Ski, that, lying in the basement, broken
9. With a lame leg, a, who was walking on crutches, junior
10. The, in the front row, whose books he was carrying, girl

Most sentence positions that are occupied by nouns can also be occupied by noun phrases:

Examples: *Boys* often build dams in the spring.
Small boys who are not in school often build dams in the spring.
Jim wanted a *car.*
Jim wanted a *new sports car with wire wheels which would have a fast getaway.*

Exercise 14–3

Expand the italicized nouns by adding modifiers before, after, or both before and after. Then underline these noun phrases.

Example: The *lock* was broken.
Expanded: The rusty lock on the front door was broken.

1. *Sailboats* are beautiful to watch.
2. They sailed under the *bridge.*
3. He makes *jewelry.*

4. The player under the basket is my *brother*.
5. I gave the *cat* a dish of milk.
6. Her mother buys *chairs* at auctions and refinishes them.
7. *Camping* is not always fun.
8. She makes *pottery* on her wheel at home.
9. It is good exercise to do long cross-countries on *skis*.
10. The doctor remains in his *office* till five.

B. Verb Phrases

A verb phrase consists of a verb and all the words and word groups that belong with the verb and cluster around it. The verb itself is called the *headword* or *head,* and the other words and word groups are the auxiliaries, modifiers, and complements of the verb. *Complements* is the generic term for the completers of the verb, which we shall later learn to know as direct object, indirect object, objective complement, and subjective complement.

Examples: soon *arrived*
    arrived late
    soon *arrived* at the station
    arrived just as the plane came in
    was *waiting* at the door
    may have been *stolen* by the cashier

Exercise 14–4
Underline the head in these verb phrases.

1. Stepped lightly
2. Stepped into the room
3. Quickly stepped in
4. Stepped where he was told
5. At once shouted to the crowd to stand back
6. Without hesitation shouted for help
7. Were watching for the signal
8. Had been eaten by the cat
9. Would have driven to the fair
10. Spoke loudly

Here are some verb phrases containing complements. Never mind the details now, for you will study them later; just notice that the words in each phrase are connected with the verb.

Examples: *built* a scooter
    built his son a scooter
    seemed gloomy and dejected
    elected George a member of the fraternity
    became president of his class

Exercise 14-5

Underline the head of these verb phrases.

1. Sold his last semester's books
2. Sold me his last semester's books
3. Appeared happy in his new job
4. Always chose Jim chairman of the dishwashing committee
5. Still remained the best candidate
6. Cheerfully gave a handsome contribution
7. Never paid his bills on time
8. At once called his uncle a brick
9. Often was weary after his workout
10. Soon returned the book she had borrowed

Many English sentences can be divided into two parts, one consisting of a noun phrase, the other a verb phrase.

Exercise 14-6

Draw a vertical line separating these sentences into a noun phrase and a verb phrase. Underline the noun head and the verb head.

1. The red pony in the pasture galloped along the fence.
2. Many students attended the Christmas party.
3. The senior who sells the most tickets will be honored at the prom.
4. The pipes in the classroom pounded noisily.
5. The choir in the loft sang the last hymn softly.

In sentences like these the headword of the noun phrase is the subject of the verb; you will hear more about this shortly. The entire phrase may be called the modified or the complete subject. The verb phrase is called the predicate.

Exercise 14-7

Add a verb phrase to each of these noun phrases, making complete sentences.

1. The tiny leak in the hose _____
2. The canoe that he wanted _____
3. The pie _____
4. The steaming apple pie _____
5. The passenger in the front seat who
   was watching the speedometer _____

Exercise 14–8

Add a noun phrase to introduce each of the following verb phrases making complete sentences.

1. ... later regretted his decision. _____
2. ... came after his dog when school was over. _____
3. ... will soon return to college. _____
4. ... always seemed to have a complaint to make. _____
5. ... merrily swung the heavy pack on his back
   to begin the long hike. _____

When the complete subject begins a statement, it can be easily located by what is called the front-shift test. To apply this test you simply change the statement into a yes-or-no question, as in these sentences:

1. Statement: [That tall man with the yellow checked shirt] is her teacher.
   Yes-or-no question: *Is* [that tall man with the yellow checked shirt] her teacher?
2. Statement: [The student who told me] could have been wrong.
   Yes-or-no question: *Could* [the student who told me] have been wrong?
3. Statement: [The cowboy who was leading the parade] rode a brown horse.
   Yes-or-no question: *Did* [the cowboy who was leading the parade] ride a brown horse?

Now note what happened in these sentences. In the first statement the verb *be* was front-shifted to the beginning of the yes-or-no question. In the second statement the first auxiliary was front-shifted. In the third statement, which has no auxiliary, the auxiliary *did* was supplied and placed in the front-shift position at the beginning of the yes-or-no question. The part of the statement around which the front-shift occurs is the complete subject.

Exercise 14–9

Change each statement into a yes-or-no question. Then underline the complete subject.

1. The boy who mows the lawn was ill.

   _____

2. Her youngest brother broke his bicycle.

   _____

3. The students on the debate squad should be excused.

   _____

4. The monkeys playing on the swings are from India.

5. The old gymnasium which was built in 1907 will be replaced.

C. Subject and Verb

At this point it is advisable to take up the subject-verb relationship. Let us begin with this simple sentence:

The teacher holds class every day.

If we change the word *teacher* to the plural form *teachers,* we must change the verb to *hold.* We describe this noun-verb relationship by saying that the noun "is tied to" or "agrees with" the verb. And the noun in the sentence that is tied to the verb is the subject of the verb. Thus the tie or agreement shows that *teacher* is the subject. This "tie" test is the most generally useful way to identify the subject in various kinds of sentences, regardless of the position of the subject.

Also, you can usually locate the subject by applying this simple rule of thumb: Ask who? or what? of the verb. Who holds? The teacher holds. Hence *teacher* is the subject.

Here are two absurdly simple exercises just to fix the subject-verb relationship in your mind. It will be enough to do them orally.

Exercise 14–10

Change the plural subjects to singular ones and make the necessary changes in the verbs. If you write out this exercise, use a double-pointed arrow to connect the subject and the verb: e.g., Children play.

1. Cats purr.
2. Students study.
3. Houses deteriorate.
4. Vases break.
5. Visitors depart.

Exercise 14–11

Now reverse the process, changing the subject from singular to plural.

1. The cat prowls.
2. The musician plays.
3. The professor teaches.
4. The bus waits.
5. The comedian laughs.

When a noun phrase is in the subject position, it is the headword of the phrase that is tied to the verb and is therefore the subject.

Examples: The duties of the center depend on the kind of offensive employed.

The height of the bushes varies.

Exercise 14–12

Below each sentence write the headword subject and the verb to which it is tied.

1. The purposes of the training make me eager to begin.
   _____   _____

2. The leader of the trainees selects a deputy.
   _____   _____

3. One among the flock of swans maintains guard.
   _____   _____

4. The difference between the two men appears when they are at a game.
   _____   _____

5. The troublemakers on the squad were hard to locate.
   _____   _____

If a verb is preceded by auxiliaries, the subject is tied to the first auxiliary.

Example: The visitor has gone.

The visitors have gone.

Exercise 14–13

Rewrite these sentences, changing the singular subjects to plural. Underline the auxiliary that is tied to the subject.

1. The patient is being watched.
   _____

2. The janitor has waxed the floor.
   _____

3. The wrestler does not smoke.
   _____

4. The car has been stolen.
   _____

5. The ship was disappearing beyond the horizon.
   _____

Thus we see that subject and verb, and subject and auxiliary, are tied together by reciprocal changes in form. But there is a difficulty here. Of all the auxiliaries only *be, have,* and *do* have an inflectional -s ending for the third-person singular. The others—*can, could, may, might, shall, should, will, would, must, ought*—have the same form throughout the singular and plural.

Examples: Singular: He *will* go.
Plural: They *will* go.
Singular: The neighbor *may* help.
Plural: The neighbors *may* help.

Likewise, the forms of the past tense have no singular-plural change of form that can show a subject-verb tie.

Examples: Singular: I *sang.*
Plural: We *sang.*
Singular: The thief *ran.*
Plural: The thieves *ran.*

How, then, can we find the subject where no tie is perceptible in the form of the verb or auxiliary? It is done this way: Change the verb or auxiliary to another form that is capable of agreement. This form will be a present *he-she-it* or *they* form of the verb or auxiliary. For example, to find the subject of

The sopranos in the choir *sang* well.

change *sang* to *sings* and *sing:*

The sopranos in the choir *sing* well.
The soprano in the choir *sings* well.

Sopranos sing are the tied forms, or those that are in agreement; hence *sopranos* is also the subject in *sopranos sang.*

Exercise 14–14

Below each sentence write the singular and plural noun and verb forms that enable you to find the subject.

1. The cat slept under the table.
   _____ _____   _____ _____

2. Under the table slept the cat.
   _____ _____   _____ _____

3. One junior among the students refused to sign.
   _____ _____   _____ _____

4. The milkman delivered on Tuesdays and Fridays.
   _____ _____   _____ _____

5. There went my papers.
   _____ _____   _____ _____

With auxiliaries the process is the same. If the auxiliary is accompanied by *not,* then substitute *do* and *does:*

The men in room 217 *can* not play handball.

The substitutions

The *men* in room 217 *do* not play handball
The *man* in room 217 *does* not play handball

show that *men* is the subject of the sentence in question. Or you can test for subject by substituting the verb itself for the auxiliary:

One of my brothers *could* play golf.

The substitutions are

One of my brothers *plays* golf.
Two of my brothers *play* golf.

Thus *one* is the subject of the original sentence.

A special problem occurs in QW questions beginning with *who, what,* and *which,* as in cases like these:

Who is your friend?
What was that explosion?

We can, of course, show putative agreement with *friend* and *explosion* by these changes:

Who are your friends?
What were those explosions?

But since *who* and *what* do not have singular-plural forms, they still might be considered the subjects, especially as they occupy the normal subject position before the verb. Compare, for example,

The dean is your friend.
The deans are your friends.

So let's try a transformation test and see what happens. We know that in a noun-object clause the subject immediately precedes the verb, e.g.,

Sentence:	The soldiers occupied the fort.
Noun-object clause:	We know [what fort *the soldiers* occupied].
	We know [what *soldiers* occupied the fort].
Question:	What color is her dress?
	What color are her dresses?
Noun-object clause:	We know [what color *her dress* is].
	We know [what color *her dresses* are].

Now, when we put the questions "Who is your friend?" and "What was that explosion?" into noun-object clauses, we get

We know [who *your friend* is].
We know [what *that explosion* was].

Therefore, since *friend* and *explosion* immediately precede the verb of the noun-object clause, we say that they are the subjects of the verb in the original sentences.

Exercise 14–15

Put each question into a noun-object clause as indicated below. Then write the subject of the verb in the last blank.

1. Who am I?
   They found out _____.   _____
2. Who is he?
   We are eager to know _____.   _____
3. Who are they?
   The police could not discover _____.   _____
4. What was the amount?
   The auditor asked _____.   _____
5. Which one is yours?
   Can you tell _____.   _____

15
Basic Sentence Patterns

We do not speak English by merely stringing words together in some random fashion. Instead, we carefully arrange our words, for the most part unconsciously, into patterns. In English we use nine basic sentence patterns and a multitude of subpatterns. It will now be our purpose to examine these basic sentence patterns of English. Any sentence you speak will probably be based on one of them.

Included in these nine basic sentence patterns are specific sentence positions. Each position in each pattern is the home-slot of a particular grammatical meaning. Let us pause here to see what is meant by grammatical meaning. One pattern you will soon meet is illustrated by this sentence:

The *girl* bought a dress.

The noun *girl,* in isolation, would mean simply "young female human being." But by dint of occupying the first position in this pattern it acquires the additional meaning of the performer of the action, in this case, *bought.* In another pattern, as shown by

The *girl* is happy,

girl is not the performer of any action but, in this position in this pattern, has an added grammatical meaning of "that which is described."

Similarly, the verb, which occupies the second slot in each pattern, has the grammatical meaning of predication, assertion. It predicates or asserts the occurrence of an action or the existence of a condition, as in

Dick *broke* a branch.
She *seemed* alarmed.

197

It is the grammatical motor of the sentence. When attention is focused on the grammatical meaning, the verb is called predicator. In general practice, however, the term *verb* is commonly used for both aspects of the verb, its form as part of speech and its meaning as predicator.

Thus grammatical meaning is a meaning that is added to the sentence by virtue of a particular position in a particular pattern.[1] Now let us look at the patterns.

The first three patterns have only *be* as their verb. It is necessary to give *be* this special treatment because it behaves somewhat differently from other verbs.[2] And it is to be remembered that *be* has eight different forms: *am, is, are, was, were, be, being, been.*

Pattern 1: N *be* Aj[3]

Food   is   good.

In the nine basic patterns the subject always occurs in the first N position. In Pattern 1 the grammatical meaning of the subject is "that which is described."

In each of the first three patterns the verb *be* has a different meaning. Here the meaning is "may be described as."

In Pattern 1 the third term must be an adjective or adjectival:

That food is *poisonous.*

You can test for Pattern 1 in a simple way. It is capable of this expansion:

That food is good > That good food is very good.
That food is poisonous > That poisonous food is very poisonous.

If a sentence will not undergo this expansion, it belongs to some pattern other than Pattern 1. For example, the sentence

My mother is outside

[1] Grammatical meanings are also carried by morphological forms. For example, the italicized morphemes that follow have grammatical meanings: boy*s*, dream*ed*, sweet*ness*. The concept of grammatical meaning is a convenient one even though a sharp line between grammatical and lexical or dictionary meanings cannot always be drawn.

[2] For example, let us compare the verb *be* in Pattern 1 with the linking verb in Pattern 8 with respect to their behavior in the yes-or-no question, the tag question, and the negative statement.

Be in Pattern 1

Affirmative statement: Jane is happy.
Yes-or-no question: Is Jane happy? (inversion of subject and verb)
Tag question: Jane is happy, isn't she? (repetition of *is* in tag)
Negative statement: Jane is not (or isn't) happy. (placement of negative after *is*)

Linking verb in Pattern 4

Affirmative statement: Jane appears happy.
Yes-or-no question: Does Jane appear happy? (insertion of *does* before subject to

cannot be expanded to

*My outside mother is very outside.

So this sentence does not belong to the Pattern 1 type. The adjective in Pattern 1 is, in grammatical meaning, a modifier of the subject.

Sometimes a prepositional phrase will, as a modifier of the N, occupy the Adj position, as in

The teacher was in a bad mood. (= irritable)
His explanation was over my head. (= incomprehensible)

Exercise 15–1

Apply the expansion test to see which of these sentences belong to Pattern 1. Write 1 after such sentences.

1. The box is large. _____
2. The box is here. _____
3. My mother is kind. _____
4. My mother is out. _____
5. The boys were busy. _____
6. The boys were below. _____
7. The dahlias have been lovely. _____
8. The party must have been enjoyable. _____
9. The party was afterward. _____
10. Her brother was hungry. _____

The foregoing test for Pattern 1 does not work in all cases. Nor, for that matter, does any grammatical rule or test, unless it is accompanied by exceptions and qualifications. There is a limited number of adjectives that

signal question; if this followed the *be* model above, it would read *"Appears Jane happy?")

Tag question: Jane appears happy, doesn't she? (no repetition of verb in tag but replacement of verb with *does*)

Negative statement: Jane does not appear happy. (placement of negative not after but before verb *appear;* insertion of *does* right after subject)

You will find the same differences between the behavior of *be* in Pattern 3 and that of the linking verb in Pattern 9, as in "My sister was an outstanding student" versus "My sister remained an outstanding student."

[3] The symbol N often means more than a bare noun like *food.* It can also mean a noun phrase, as in "that food," "the food in the cafeteria," or "the delicious food in the cafeteria which we have every day at noon." Or it can mean a phrase or clause in the N position, as in "studying for exams," "on the riverbank," or "what you brought." Similarly, the symbols Aj, Av, and V may have a broader meaning than adjective, adverb, and verb. All this will be taken up in the next chapter. Until then you can get along satisfactorily on your present knowledge of these parts of speech.

can occur in either the first or the second slot, but not in both, in a Pattern 1 sentence like

The _____ food (= any noun) is very _____.

For example, some adjectives are used only before a noun, like *main* and *utter*. Some others appear, in this pattern, after *be + very,* like *afraid* and *content,* but not before the noun. Still others are restricted in various ways.[4] Furthermore, not all adjectives can be modified by *very.* We do not say, for instance, *"the very main speaker." But, apart from such aberrations, the test for Pattern 1 is useful.

Pattern 2: N *be* Av

The girl   is   here.

Pattern 2 differs from Pattern 1 in these respects:

1. The verb *be* in this pattern usually has the meaning of "be located" or "occur."

2. Pattern 2 is not capable of taking the Pattern 1 expansion.

3. The third position is occupied by a type of uninflected word that you will later learn is called an "adverbial." Words of this type include *here, there, up, down, in, out, inside, outside, upstairs, downstairs, on, off, now, then, tomorrow, yesterday, over, through, above, below, before, after. Up, in,* and *out* are partially and/or irregularly inflected with the forms *upper, uppermost, inner, inmost, innermost, outer, outermost, utmost, outmost.* For most words in the third position one can substitute *there* or *then.*

Examples: The pingpong table is downstairs.
The game was yesterday.
The balls are outdoors.

Often a prepositional phrase with a *there* or *then* meaning will occupy the third position.

Examples: The wolf is at the door.
The game will be at three o'clock.

---

[4] For example, *faint* and *ready* go in the first slot when the noun modified is inanimate, as in "a faint breeze" and "a ready answer." But they do not go in the first slot when the noun is animate, that is, in cases like *"a faint player" and *"a ready coach." The last two both sound un-English. Again, consider *due.* We can say "The train is due" but not *"The train is very *due." We ordinarily do not use *due* before a noun, as in *"the due train" but we do use it before a noun in a few set phrases like "with due respect" and "in due time."

The grammatical meaning of the subject (N position) in Pattern 2 is "that about which as assertion is made," and that of the Av is "modifier of the verb."

Exercise 15–2

After each sentence place a number 1 or 2 to identify the pattern it conforms to.

1. The picnic was outside. _____
2. The picnickers were happy. _____
3. The batter is tall. _____
4. The batter is inside. _____
5. They are on the lawn. _____
6. Our appointment is now. _____
7. The meeting will be in an hour. _____
8. The dean is in. _____
9. The dean is benevolent. _____
10. The bunks are below. _____

Pattern 3: N^1 *be* N^1

My brother   is   a doctor.

The superscript after the second N (noun) means that this noun has the same referent as N^1; that is, both *brother* and *doctor* refer to the same person. The meaning of *be* in Pattern 3 is "be identified or classified as." The first N^1 (subject) has the grammatical meaning of "that which is identified." The second N^1 means grammatically "that which identifies the subject" and is called the subjective complement. Personal pronouns also occupy this position. Such pronouns in the subjective complement position take primary stress, e.g.,

This is *shé.*
It's *mé.*
It was *théy.*
That is *míne.*

The following sentences are examples of Pattern 3:

Those coeds must be roommates.
They are my friends.
He had never been an honor student.
Harry is my favorite uncle.[5]

---

[5] Do not be deceived by a sentence like "These shoes are the wrong size." The grammatical meanings of its parts are those of Pattern 1, to which it belongs. "The wrong size" is a phrase modifying *shoes.*

Exercise 15–3

Indicate the pattern of each sentence by the numbers 1, 2, or 3.

1. Sandy must have been the culprit. _____
2. The dinner was over. _____
3. The dinner was tasty. _____
4. The dinner was a feast. _____
5. The Indians were the winners. _____
6. My cousin is a fool. _____
7. My cousin is proud. _____
8. The policeman may be wise. _____
9. The policeman may be there. _____
10. Policemen are the guardians of the law. _____

Pattern 4: N   LV   Aj

The   acrobat   seems   young

In Pattern 4 the verb is called a linking verb (LV), as it links the adjective with the subject. Any verb except *be* that may be substituted for *seems* in this frame is a linking verb.

Examples: The cyclist *appears* weary.
The physicist *grew* sleepy.

Some of the common linking verbs are *seem, appear, become, grow, remain, taste, look, feel, smell, sound, get, continue, go.* If verbs like these, however, are followed by an adverb or adverbial, then the pattern is not number 4 but number 6, which is coming soon.

Examples: The cyclist appeared *quickly* on the scene.
The physicist grew *rapidly* in knowledge.

Here, as in Pattern 1, the adjective is in grammatical meaning a modifier of the subject.

Exercise 15–4

Write the pattern number 4 or *other* after each sentence.

1. The milk remained sweet for a week. _____
2. The newcomer remained quietly in her room. _____
3. The dog smelled hungrily at the package. _____
4. The dog smells bad. _____
5. You look sharp today. _____
6. He looked sharply to the right. _____
7. The detective felt cautiously in the box. _____

8. He feels cautious about taking the risk.   _____
9. That apprentice looks careful.   _____
10. The apprentice looked carefully at the new machine.   _____

Linking verbs may of course be preceded by auxiliaries.

Examples: The party *may become* lively.
Your sister *must have seemed* friendly.

In addition to the limited number of common linking verbs, other verbs not usually thought of as linking may on occasion be followed by an adjective and therefore conform to Pattern 4.

Examples: The screw *worked* loose.
The defendant *stood* firm.
His face *went* pale.
The well *ran* dry.
He *proved* true to his cause.

For verbs like these one can substitute *be, become,* or *remain* with no substantial change of meaning.

Exercise 15–5

Write the pattern number 4 or *other* after each sentence.

1. The table stood near the desk.   _____
2. Jameson stood loyal to his firm.   _____
3. The students in the back row look sleepy.   _____
4. The investigator looked outside.   _____
5. Penelope turned red at the thought.   _____
6. She lay motionless on the hospital bed.   _____
7. Jim fell sick during the night.   _____
8. The wind blew strongly through the tall pines.   _____
9. The beer may stay cold until evening.   _____
10. You will never keep slender that way.   _____

Pattern 5: N^1 LV N^1

My sister   remained   an outstanding student.

The two superscripts show that both nouns have the same referent. The verb, which links *student* and *sister,* is a linking verb. The number of linking verbs that may occupy the verbal position in this pattern is very small. Among them are *remain, become, appear, seem, continue, stay, make.*

Sentences that follow Pattern 5 should not be confused with those in which the noun after the verb does not have the same referent as the first noun.

Examples: 5   Donald *continued* my friend, despite our differences.
       other Donald *met* my friend in the barber shop.
       5   My brother *became* a doctor.
       other My brother was *seeking* a doctor.

In Pattern 5, as in Pattern 3, the second noun means "that which identifies the subject," and is called the subjective complement.

Exercise 15–6

Write the pattern number 5 or *other* after each sentence.

1. Alma became the class president.   ——
2. After two years of faithful service the corporal became a sergeant.   ——
3. The military police restrained the sergeant from entering the hall.   ——
4. The chief seemed a good fellow.   ——
5. We saw the fellow.   ——
6. We stayed boon companions for years.   ——
7. The governor stayed the execution.   ——
8. They appeared friends to all of us.   ——
9. We shall continue the discussion tomorrow.   ——
10. Johannes had remained a bachelor for reasons of his own.   ——
11. My sister makes a delicious fruitcake.   ——
12. A fruitcake makes a fine gift.   ——

Pattern 6:N   InV (= intransitive verb)

Girls   smile.

The verb in Pattern 6 is of the kind called intransitive. An intransitive verb is self-sufficient; it can stand alone with its subject.

1. The sportsman *fished.*
2. The sportsmen *were fishing.*

It can be modified by words and word groups known as adverbs and adverbials.

Examples: The sportsmen fished *early.*
          The sportsmen were fishing *in the stream.*
          The sportsmen were fishing *when we drove up.*

But an intransitive verb is usually not completed by a noun or pronoun. For example, in

   They finished late

finished is intransitive, but in

   They finished the game

and

   They finished it

finished is not intransitive because it is completed by a noun or pronoun. If you are in doubt whether a word following the verb is a modifier that goes with an intransitive verb or a completer of a transitive verb, a substitution can settle the matter. If you can substitute *him, her, it,* or *them,* the word is a completer and the verb is not intransitive.

Examples: 1. He hammered fast.
2. He hammered the nail.

In the first sentence you cannot substitute *it* without spoiling the structural meaning. But in the second *He hammered it* is a suitable equivalent for *He hammered the nail.* Therefore the first *hammered* is intransitive and the second one transitive.

The subject of the verb in Pattern 6, and also in Patterns 7, 8, and 9 to follow, has the grammatical meaning of "performer of the action."

Some intransitive verbs characteristically do not occur alone but take an adverbial modifier. Examples: *lurk, sneak, lurch, sally, sidle, tamper, lie, live.* The last one, *live,* takes an adverbial modifier in three meanings: "reside" as in "He lives in Mexico"; "stay alive" as in "He lives on soy bean products"; "be alive" as in "He lived in the first half of the twentieth century." Also, intransitive verbs with a passive sense based on transitive verbs take an adverbial modifier, as in "Your car rides comfortably," and "Her book is selling well."

Exercise 15–7

Write InV after each sentence that contains an intransitive verb. All such InV sentences will be examples of Pattern 6.

 1. The audience clapped.   _____
 2. The audience clapped loudly.   _____
 3. The audience clapped loudly after the main act.   _____
 4. The audience clapped their hands.   _____
 5. They were drinking quietly at the table.   _____
 6. They were drinking their morning coffee.   _____
 7. She always paid promptly.   _____
 8. He paid his bills on the first of the month.   _____
 9. Jack left early.   _____
10. Jack left his clothes in the closet.   _____
11. This bed sleeps comfortably.   _____
12. A strange man is lurking behind the garage.   _____
13. Some textbooks read very slowly.   _____
14. Who tampered with my fishing tackle?   _____
15. They live in a small apartment.   _____

Pattern 7: N¹ TrV (= transitive verb) N²

The girl   bought   a   dress.

In Pattern 7 the verb is completed by a noun (or pronoun), for which one can substitute *him, her, it* or *them*. This noun, as shown by the superscript 2, does not have the same referent as the subject. It is called the direct object of the verb and has the grammatical meaning of "undergoer of the action" or "that affected by the verb."[6]

With two kinds of pronouns, however, the direct object does have the same referent as the subject. One is the set of *-self/-selves* pronouns, generally known as the reflexive pronouns. These occur as direct object in sentences like

She saw *herself.*
The lifeguards splashed *themselves.*

The other set consists of the reciprocal pronouns *each other* and *one another,* which function as direct objects in such sentences as

They found *each other.*
They fought *one another.*

Exercise 15–8

After each sentence write the pronoun that you can substitute for the italicized direct object.

   1. The salesman sold *the car.*   ————————————
   2. Both soldiers saluted *the colonel.*   ————————————

[6] The terms "undergoer of the action" and "that affected by the verb" seem roughly adequate to describe the grammatical meaning in many cases, as in

The waitress covered the table.

However, compare this with

A beautiful linen cloth covered the table.

Here *table* is really not an undergoer, in terms of any action. In fact, the semantic and logical relations between verb and object are so many and various that no general statement of grammatical meaning suffices to cover them all. For details on this problem see Otto Jespersen, *A Modern English Grammar on Historical Principles,* Part III, "Object," pp. 229–252. Jespersen does offer a useful rule of thumb for finding the subject and the object: "After we have found the subject by asking the question Who, or What, with the form of the verb actually used in the sentence, we may proceed by asking Whom, or What with the subject and the verb of the sentence." For an example take "The car struck the bicycle." What struck? The car. Hence *the car* is the subject. The car struck what? The bicycle. So *the bicycle* is the object.

In practice, the direct object is easily identified by three criteria:

   1. It consists of a noun or word group that is a noun equivalent.
   2. It follows the subject + verb phrase.
   3. It can normally be made the subject of a passive verb, as you will see after exercise 15–9.

3. Mrs. Grundy grew *roses* every year. _____
4. At the desk we met *the nurse.*   _____
5. The chauffeur repaired *the tire.*   _____
6. Mrs. Hooper injured *her ankle.*   _____
7. The collision broke *the wheel.*   _____
8. I met *your sister.*   _____
9. The veterinarian carried *the dog.*   _____
10. We trimmed *the bushes.*   _____

A verb like those above that is completed by a direct object is called a transitive verb. A transitive verb contrasts with the intransitive verb of Pattern 6, which does not take a direct object.

Examples: InV She sang beautifully.
TrV She sang a beautiful folk song.

As shown in the pair of examples above, most English verbs are both transitive and intransitive, and relatively few are transitive only or intransitive only.

Examples: InV only: The ship had vanished.
TrV only: We enjoyed the party.

Exercise 15–9

In this exercise you are to distinguish, as a review, between the verb *be,* linking verbs, intransitive verbs, and transitive verbs. After each sentence place a *be,* LV, InT, and TV to label the verb. In the second blank write the number of the sentence pattern.

1. The center *passed* the ball to the quarterback. ____ ____
2. I'll *pass.* ____ ____
3. Chris *became* a skillful tennis player. ____ ____
4. The sheriff *was* the leader of the posse. ____ ____
5. The sheriff *was leading* the posse. ____ ____
6. Your doughnuts *smell* delicious. ____ ____
7. Who *is leading* now? ____ ____
8. Harris *remained* the assistant coach. ____ ____
9. The dean *made* an important announcement. ____ ____
10. Your violin tone *sounds* rather squeaky. ____ ____
11. The announcement *may be* helpful to you. ____ ____
12. The firm *sent* a form letter to all its customers. ____ ____
13. A French poodle *makes* an affectionate pet. ____ ____
14. The driver *turned* sharply. ____ ____
15. The driver *turned* the car around. ____ ____
16. She *is* inside. ____ ____
17. Emily Walton *was* the judge in the case. ____ ____

A transitive verb has two forms, which we call active and passive. The active form is the one that is followed by the direct object, which we have seen in Pattern 7. From this active form we can make the passive form. Here is an illustration:

Active: The waiter poured the coffee.

Passive: The coffee was poured (by the waiter).

In this process there are four things to notice:

1. The object of the active form becomes the subject of the passive form. This is shown above in the shift of *coffee.*

2. The passive is made up of a form of the verb *be* plus a past participle, as in *was poured.*

3. The subject of the active verb may be made the object of the preposition *by,* or it may be suppressed.

4. In the passive, two grammatical meanings are shifted around. The performer of the action, *waiter,* is now the object of the preposition, and the undergoer, *coffee,* is the subject.

Exercise 15-10

These sentences contain transitive verbs in the active form. Change the sentences to the passive form.

1. The servant opened the window. _____
2. He rolled the dice. _____
3. Most adolescents like dancing. _____
4. We chose the mountains for our vacation.

    _____
5. Jim has never read *King Lear.* _____
6. The tourists burned wood in the fireplace.

    _____
7. The shepherd counted his sheep. _____
8. We began the game at four o'clock.

    _____
9. The Smiths built a new house on the river.

    _____
10. The nature club spotted a pileated woodpecker.

    _____

Exercise 15-11

These sentences contain transitive verbs in the passive form. For each verb underline the *be* auxiliary once and the past participle twice. Then change the sentences to the active form. In cases where there is no *by* phrase, you will have to supply a subject.

1. The rat was killed by the terrier.

    _____

2. The pancakes were turned by the cook.

3. Much corn is raised in Iowa.

4. An early folk tune was heard.

5. The dishes have been washed.

6. A good time was had by all.

7. Jane was teased by her boy friend.

8. The flag had been lowered.

9. The motorcycles were stopped by the traffic officer.

10. A carillon concert is played at 7:45 in the morning.

English also has a passive in which *be* is replaced by *get*, e.g.,

Active: The teacher excused Bill.
Passive: Bill got excused by the teacher.
Active: Helen rewarded him.
Passive: He got rewarded.

This *get* passive is useful in avoiding the occasional ambiguity of the *be* passive, as in

The gate was closed at ten o'clock.

This can mean either "Someone closed the gate at ten" or "The gate was not open at ten." With *got* only the first meaning is possible:

The gate got closed at ten.

Not all verbs accept the *get* passive, e.g.,

*The fiesta got enjoyed by the guests.

There is in English a tiny group of transitive verbs called middle verbs that do not form the passive. These are illustrated in the sentences below. Try turning each sentence into the passive and see if the result sounds English to your ears.

The box contains a pair of shoes.
She lacks the necessary money.
A wondrous adventure befell our hero.
Your humor eludes me.
He can afford a new car.
My mother has a new car.

The apples cost fifty cents.
They parted company.

Verbs with reflexive pronouns are not made passive, e.g.,

He scratched himself.

Pattern 8: N^1 TrV N^2 N^3

The mother   bought   the girl   a dress.

In Pattern 8 there are seven matters to be observed:

1. The superscripts 1, 2, and 3 indicate that each noun has a different referent; *mother, girl,* and *dress* are three separate entities.

2. We see two grammatical objects after the verb *bought*. These two objects are called, in order, the indirect and the direct object. If we omit the first one, the pattern becomes number 7 and *dress* is seen to be the direct object.

3. The indirect object may often be replaced by a prepositional phrase beginning with *to* or *for,* or occasionally with a different preposition.

Examples: He sold *the student* a ticket.
He sold a ticket *to the student.*

He built *them* a playpen.
He built a playpen *for them.*

He played *me* a game of chess.
He played a game of chess *with me.*

He asked *her* a question.
He asked a question *of her.*

4. The verbs that can be used in Pattern 8 are in a restricted group. Some of the common ones are *give, make, find, tell, buy, write, send, ask, play, build, teach, assign, feed, offer, throw, hand, pass, sell, pay.*

5. A Pattern 8 sentence may be transformed into the passive by making either the direct or the indirect object the subject of the passive verb:

A dress was bought the girl by her mother.
The girl was bought a dress by her mother.

In some cases, however, the passive transform does not sound fully natural and seems to demand a preposition, as in

The sergeant found the recruit a rifle.
A rifle was found *(for)* the recruit.

6. The grammatical meaning of the indirect object is "beneficiary of the action of the verb-plus-direct-object."

7. If a pronoun is used in the position of the direct object (N^3), it must be the first of the two objects:

The mother bought *it* for the girl
Not *The mother bought the girl *it.*

Similarly, if N² and N³ are both pronouns, again the direct object must occur first:

The mother bought *it* for her.
Not *The mother bought her *it.*

Exercise 15–12

The following sentences follow Pattern 8. Replace the indirect object by a prepositional phrase. Put the latter where it sounds most natural.

1. The librarian found me the pamphlet.

2. He assigned Jack the toughest job.

3. The spaniel brought his master the stick.

4. Susie fed the baby robins some juicy worms.

5. Her mother sent her a new sweater.

Exercise 15–13

These sentences also follow Pattern 8. Transform each one into two sentences by making first the indirect and second the direct object the subject of a passive verb.[7]

1. She gave him a dirty look.

2. The company made the manager a fine offer.

3. The dealer dealt me a bad hand.

[7] When a Pattern 8 sentence is made passive, one object becomes the subject and the other is retained after the verb. The latter is called a retained object. Examples:

Bill gave George a tennis racket.
                    RO
George was given a tennis racket.
                         RO
A tennis racket was given George.

4. He offered his roommate the car.

_____

_____

_____

5. The instructor asked her a question.

_____

_____

_____

Pattern 9: N¹ TrV N² plus one:
a. N² b. Aj c. Pronoun d. Av (of place), uninflected
e. Verb, present participle f. Verb, past participle
g. Prep phrase h. Inf phrase with *to be*

Pattern 9 contains a choice of eight different forms in the final position. These are illustrated as follows:

 a. The basketball team chose Charlotte *captain*.
 b. He considered her *brilliant*.
 c. I thought the caller *you*.
 d. We supposed him *upstairs*.
 e. I imagined her *eating*.
 f. I believed him *seated*.
 g. We considered her in the way. (= bothersome)
 h. We thought Chico to be a fine player.

In this pattern the words in the last two positions imply an underlying sentence with *be* as its verb or auxiliary. This is suggested by the way the illustrative sentences above can be changed in form while preserving the same meaning:

 a. The basketball team chose Charlotte to be captain.[8]
 b. He considered her to be brilliant.
    He considered that she was brilliant.
 c. I thought the caller to be you.
    I thought that the caller was you.
 d. We supposed him to be upstairs.
    We supposed that he was upstairs.
 e. I imagined her to be eating.
    I imagined that she was eating.
 f. I believed him to be seated.
    I believed that he was seated.
 g. We considered her to be in the way.
    We considered that she was in the way.
 h. We thought Chico to be a fine player.
    We thought that Chico was a fine player.

---

[8] The underlying sentence is "Charlotte is captain."

Exercise 15–14

Translate each Pattern 9 sentence into one of the two forms shown directly above.

1. The committee declared Isabelle the winner.
2. She believed George honest.
3. I imagined them outside.
4. We thought her overworked.
5. I supposed him working.
6. We thought her above reproach.

As Pattern 9 is most commonly exemplified by N^2 in the final position, we shall restrict our attention to this form of the pattern. Pattern 9, like its predecessor Pattern 8, has two objects following the verb. But it differs from Pattern 8 in three respects:

1. In the order of objects the direct object comes first. In some sentences, if we eliminate the second object, we are left with Pattern 7, which contains only the direct object after the verb:

The basketball team chose Charlotte.

The second object is called the objective complement, because it completes the direct object.

2. In Pattern 9 both objects have the same referent; that is, both *Charlotte* and *captain* refer to the same person.

3. In Pattern 9, only the first object, the direct object, can be made the subject of a passive verb. We can transform the pattern sentence into

Charlotte was chosen captain

but we cannot make the objective complement such a subject, for

*Captain was chosen Charlotte

makes no sense.

In the passive of Pattern 9 the subject comes from the direct object of the active.

                        DO   OC

Example: Active: He appointed Ruth secretary.

                  Subj.   **SC**

       Passive: Ruth was appointed secretary

                           DO   OC

Since the sentence underlying "Ruth secretary" is "Ruth is secretary," we should retain the same relationship in the passive by calling *secretary* **the** subjective complement.

Only a very small group of verbs can be used for Pattern 9. Among them are *name, choose, elect, appoint, designate, select, vote, make, declare, nominate, call, fancy, consider, imagine, think, believe, feel, keep, suppose, find, prove, label, judge.* A different but overlapping set of these verbs is used for each of the eight forms in the final position.

The grammatical meaning of the objective complement is "completer of the direct object."

Exercise 15–15

In each sentence strike out the indirect object or the objective complement. Then write the pattern number, 8 or 9, after the sentence.

1. She played him a trick.   _____
2. We appointed Evelyn the committee chairman.   _____
3. You threw us a curve.   _____
4. The student body selected Arabella their representative. _____
5. The faculty chose Sieverson the head counselor.   _____
6. We found her a sandwich.   _____
7. The dealer sold me an air mattress.   _____
8. She fed him the baby food.   _____
9. The city elected Mouchy mayor.   _____
10. He named his new boat Belle.   _____

With Pattern 9 we complete the list of the nine basic sentence patterns in English.

Exercise 15–16

After each sentence write the number of the pattern it represents.

1. Your recital was wonderful.
2. Mabel was here a moment ago.
3. The rancher told his guests a tall tale.
4. The archers were not successful hunters.
5. The frogs croaked in the marsh.
6. Jerry thought the proposal a mistake.
7. She had been secretary a long time.
8. The Romans won the first battle.
9. The judges believed Lightning the best horse in the show.
10. The director found him a new costume.
11. My uncle remains the worst bridge player in town.
12. The coach designated Jan the new manager of the team.
13. Migrant workers pick the strawberries in early June.
14. The pickles are near the wieners.
15. We considered his offer a fine gesture.

16. Your cigar smells so aromatic!   L Adj
17. He has always seemed a serious boy.   L N
18. Who is at the cottage this week?   ___
19. They stayed roommates for three years.   L N
20. The board elected Mr. Stoopnagel the president.   N²

Exercise 15–17

Unless we recognize the pattern of a sentence, we do not know what the sentence means. The following sentences illustrate this thought. Each one is ambiguous because we do not know which of two patterns it represents. After each sentence write the numbers of the patterns that it represents.

1. He found her a pig.   ___ ___
2. The bouncer turned out a drunkard.   ___ ___
3. The girl in the back seat looked forward.   ___ ___
4. They are discouraging transfers.   ___ ___
5. I'm getting her socks.   ___ ___
6. The man gave the library books.   ___ ___
7. It was a little pasty.   ___ ___
8. He accepted Wednesday.   ___ ___
9. Thorne taught himself during his young manhood.   ___ ___
10. The doctor made them well.   ___ ___
11. She taught the group singing.   ___ ___
12. He found the mechanic a helper.   ___ ___
13. Our spaniel made a good friend.   ___ ___
14. The judges designated the girl winner.   ___ ___
15. The detective looked hard.   ___ ___
16. Mary called her mother.   ___ ___

Functions

It is tremendously important that you understand what is to follow here, for upon your understanding of this will depend your weal or woe in the chapter ahead.

Each of the positions in the pattern sentences has a dual role.

1. Each position is the habitat of a particular part of speech—noun, verb, adjective, or adverb—as was shown by the abbreviations N, V, Aj, and Av. For example, consider Pattern 7:

N¹ Tr V   N²
The boy gobbled the hamburger.

Here the N¹ and N² positions are characteristically inhabited by nouns. You could replace *boy* and *hamburger* by hundreds of other nouns. And the TrV position is characteristically inhabited by verbs of the kind that are followed by noun-objects. In short, each position is a part-of-speech hang-out.

2. The second role of each position is to signal the grammatical meaning of its occupant. This grammatical meaning is known as FUNCTION. In the sentence above, for example, the occupant of the N¹ position has the FUNCTION of performer of the action of the verb. It is the *boy* who gobbled the hamburger. This FUNCTION, that of performer, is labeled SV, subject of the verb.

In the same sentence N² is another home for nouns, but the occupant here has a different FUNCTION, that of undergoer of the action of the verb. It is the *hamburger* that underwent the gobbling. This FUNCTION, that of undergoing, is labeled DO, direct object of the verb.

As another example let us look at Pattern 1:

    N   be Aj
The candy is sweet.

The first role of the Aj position is to house adjectives, such as *good, hard, soft, chewy, nutty,* and so on. The second role of this Aj position is to signal the FUNCTION of its occupant. This FUNCTION is to modify. *Sweet* modifies *candy.* And any adjective in this third position will modify any noun in the first position.

Function, then, is the grammatical job that any word (or word group) does in its particular position. It is the grammatical meaning. Here now are the labels for all the functions you will meet in this book, together with a condensed, rough-and-ready note on the job of each. This is a reference list only, so don't try to master it here and now.

Label of Function	*Grammatical Meaning*
1. Subject of verb	That which performs action of verb (Patterns 6, 7, 8, 9)
	That which is described (Patterns 1, 4)
	That which is identified (Patterns 3, 5)
	That about which an assertion is made (Pattern 2)
2. Verb or predicator	That which asserts an action or state (Patterns 2, 6, 7, 8, 9)
	"May be described as" (Patterns 1, 4)
	"May be identified as" (Patterns 3, 5)
3. Subjective complement	That which follows *be* or a verb like *become* and identifies the subject.
4. Direct object	That which undergoes the action of the verb. (See note on page 206.)
5. Indirect object	That person or thing to or for whom an action is performed.
6. Objective complement	That which completes the direct object and describes or identifies it.
7. Object of preposition	That which is related to another word by a preposition.
8. Complement of noun	A word group that behaves like a direct object of the verb corresponding to

the noun. **Example:** His hope *that she would win* was strong.

9. Complement of adjective   A word group that directly follows and completes an adjective. **Example:** I am glad *that you came.*

10. Modifier   That which modifies, limits, or adds to the meaning of a word or word group. A modifier can be a word or word group.

11. Connector   That which connects words and/or word groups. The connectors (by function) are the coordinating conjunctions, subordinating conjunctions, prepositions, and relatives.

In the chapter to follow we shall distinguish the different noun positions by using the FUNCTION label of the occupant of each position. Thus we shall refer to these noun positions by the labels of SV, SC, DO, IO, and OC. And to these will be added one that you have not yet had, OP, object of the preposition.

Three Modes of Classification

As a preliminary to the next chapter it will be useful to examine briefly the three major modes of classification that you must keep clearly in mind.

1. Classification by Function. In classification by function, you will recall, specific positions in specific patterns signal grammatical meanings. In

The boy gobbled the hamburger

the position of *hamburger* signals that its grammatical meaning, or FUNCTION, is that of undergoer of the action, and this FUNCTION is labeled direct object of the verb.

2. Classification by Form. In Chapter 12, "Parts of Speech: Form-Classes," you classified words by word-form alone, using inflectional and derivational suffixes to determine the individual classes. The result was five form-classes: nouns, verbs, adjectives, adverbs, and uninflected words. But this was not satisfactory as a complete part-of-speech catalog because an embarrassingly large number of words were unclassifiable as noun, verb, adjective, or adverb and had to be put in a miscellaneous file called uninflected words. This unsatisfactory situation will be remedied in Chapter 16, where you will encounter parts of speech as distinguished by position.

3. Classification by Position. In classification by position it is the part of speech, not the function, that is associated with positions. Certain groups of positions are normally occupied by particular parts of speech. For instance, the positions that bear the functions of SV, SC, DO, IO, OC, and OP (object of preposition) are frequently occupied by nouns. Thus we think of these six positions as noun positions, and any word or word group occupying them, whether a noun or not, we label a *nominal* by position, regardless of its function or form-class. A few cases will make this clear. In the illustrative sentences that follow, the items in brackets are all **nominals.** The function of each is given in parentheses.

1. [The prettiest] sat in the center. (Subject)
2. [Whoever desired] sat in the center. (Subject)
3. [Now] is the time to study. (Subject)
4. [Under the pines] is the place to study. (Subject)
5. That is [she]. (Subjective complement)
6. That is [whom I saw]. (Subjective complement)
7. He chose [the prettiest]. (Direct object)
8. He chose [whatever he wanted]. (Direct object)
9. She gave [whomever she met] a cheery smile. (Indirect object)
10. Hard practice made Evelyn [a good swimmer]. (Objective complement)
11. Hard practice made me [what I am]. (Objective complement)
12. Can you see from [where you sit]? (Object of preposition)

Note that you can readily put a noun in each of these positions because each is the customary abode of a noun.

Similarly, any word or word group occupying slots normally filled by a verb, adjective, or adverb is by POSITIONAL classification a verbal, adjectival, or adverbial. The *-al* is the suffixal signal that tells you that you are dealing with a major positional class.

In addition the small closed parts of speech—like determiner and auxiliary—are known as structure classes. You studied them in Chapter 13.

Here are three examples to illustrate this threefold classification, although they will become fully meaningful to you only after you have completed the next chapter. Take the sentence

The *shouting boys* will play *tennis.*

1. *Shouting* is a modifier by function, a verb by form, and an adjectival by position.
2. *Boys* is the subject of the verb by function, a noun by form, and a nominal by position.
3. *Tennis* is the object of the verb by function, an uninflected word by form, and a nominal by position.

16
Parts of Speech: Positional Classes

An English sentence is an arrangement of words, not as words but in their capacity as parts of speech. If we do not, as listeners or readers, grasp the identity of these parts of speech, we cannot understand with certainty the message being communicated. Consider, for example,

They are encouraging reports.

Here the word *encouraging* is the stumbling block. It may be a verb, so that the sentence means

They encourage reports

or it may be an adjectival, giving the meaning of

These reports are encouraging.

Not knowing the part of speech of this one word, we find the sentence ambiguous. In a carefully controlled context, of course, this sentence might not be ambiguous.

As native speakers we already have an operational command of the parts of speech. Now we shall continue to approach them analytically and study the specific ways by which we identify them.

But first here is a schematic overview of the parts of speech. If you will refer to it occasionally, it may keep you from getting lost in a thicket of details.

I. Form-classes. These are large and open classes, admitting new members. They are based in changes in form that a word can undergo.

    A. Noun
    B. Verb
    C. Adjective
    D. Adverb
    E. Uninflected word

II. Structure-classes. These are small and closed classes, rarely admitting new members. Members of these classes are normally uninflected, and we recognize them by position alone. You have already studied the first five below.

    1. Determiner
    2. Personal pronouns
    3. Auxiliary
    4. Qualifier
    5. Preposition
    6. Restricter
    7. Predeterminer

    8. Postdeterminer
    9. Subordinating conjunction
    10. Coordinating conjunction
    11. Relative
    12. Expletive

III. Positional-classes. These are based on the positions occupied by the form-classes. The members of these classes are both words and word groups.

    1. nominal
    2. verbal
    3. adjectival
    4. adverbial

A. Nominals

Certain sentence positions are characteristically the habitation of nouns. You already know that these positions are those occupied by items having these functions:

    SV Subject of verb
    SC Subjective complement
    DO Direct object of verb
    IO Indirect object of verb
    OC Objective complement
    OP Object of preposition
    RO Retained object

But occupancy of these positions does not positively identify nouns because words of other form-classes can occupy them as well. Here are a few illustrative cases involving the SV position.

Pattern 6. The *rich* live on the bay.

Here the SV slot is occupied by an adjective, recognizable as such because it can be inflected with *-er* and *-est,* e.g.,

The *richest* live on the bay.

Pattern 3: *Steadily* is the best way to work.

Here an adverb, formed of the adjective *steady* plus the adverbial derivational suffix *-ly,* sits comfortably at home in the SV slot.

Pattern 7: *Swimming* develops the lungs.

We recognize *swimming* as a verb in form, a verb stem *swim* plus the verbal {-ING vb}. You may be tempted to call it a noun, but observe: (1) It cannot take a noun inflection, either the {-s pl}, as in "Your paintings are beautiful," or the {-s ps}, as in "the meeting's end." (2) It does not contain a noun-forming derivational suffix. So in form it cannot be a noun.

Pattern 7: The *pathos* of the novel moved her.

Pathos is not a noun because in form it cannot take either the noun plural or the noun possessive and it contains no noun-forming derivational suffix. Since it takes no inflection of any kind, it is an uninflected word.

In the four illustrative sentences above we have seen an adjective (*rich*), and adverb (*steadily*), a verb (*swimming*), and an uninflected word (*pathos*) each occupying a noun position. What we shall do is to set up a positional class called nominal. Any word, whatever its form-class (noun, verb, adjective, adverb, or uninflected word), will be tabbed a nominal if it occupies one of the seven noun positions listed above. This gives us a double-track classification for parts of speech, one by form and the other by position. Such a procedure is perfectly sound, for any given entity may be classified in various ways by using different bases of classification. You yourself, for example, might be classified "female" by sex, "junior" by class, "brunette" by hair pigmentation, "Unitarian" by church affiliation, and so on. A few more examples may be pertinent.

1. We enjoyed the *game.*

Game is a noun by form, since it can be pluralized in its context, and a nominal by position, since it occupies the DO slot.

2. What can one expect from the *young?*

Young is an adjective by form because it is inflected by *-er* and *-est.* One could say "from the younger" but not "from the youngs." It is a nominal by position because it is in the OP slot.

3. *Now* is the best time.

Now is an uninflected word by form and a nominal by position, occurring in the SV position.

Exercise 16-1

The italicized words are nominals because they occupy the sentence positions that are the home territory of nouns. The occupants of these positions perform the FUNCTIONS of SV, SC, DO, IO, OC, and OP, but BY POSITION they are NOMINALS.

In the first blank give the form-class of the italicized nominal, using N (noun), V (verb), Aj (adjective), Av (adverb), and UW (uninflected word).

In the second blank indicate the particular function of the position the nominal occupies, the function of: SV, SC, DO, IO, OC, or OP.

	Form	Function of position
Example: The *poor* grew troubled.	Aj	SV
1. The *cheapest* are on that counter.	———	———
2. The *seniors* held a class meeting.	———	———
3. The *hearings* were postponed.	———	———
4. He hated *starving*.	———	———
5. Can you see the game from *here?*	———	———
6. The winners were the *men* from Homburg Hall.	———	———
7. That car is a *gas-gulper*.	———	———
8. We believed the letter a *hoax*.	———	———
9. The safest way to drive is *carefully*.	———	———
10. We gave the *upstairs* a good scrubbing.	———	———
11. *Below* was dangerous.	———	———
12. Her roommate disliked the *chaos* in Jo's room.	———	———

Word groups as well as individual words can be nominals, and they occupy the usual noun positions. In the sentence

About a plateful is my limit.

the opening word group *about a plateful* is a prepositional phrase occupying the SV position and is a nominal because the SV is the position of a noun. In the next sentence

A chipmunk emerged from under the porch.

the prepositional phrase *under the porch* is the object of the preposition *from*. Because it occupies an OP position it is a nominal by position.

Exercise 16-2

The italicized word groups are nominals. In each blank indicate the function of the group by SV, SC, DO, IO, OC, OP.

1. Jerry knows *that history is never completely true.* ———
2. His greatest ambition is *to win the match.*

3. You made me *what I am.* _____

4. He assigned *whoever was late* an extra problem. _____

5. Do you object to *what I wrote?* _____

6. *Petty gossiping* makes one unpopular. _____

7. *Under seventeen* requires an accompanying parent. _____

Whether or not a word group is a nominal can be tested by substitution. A word group is a nominal if it can be replaced by one of these: a noun or noun phrase, *this, that, these, those, he/him, she/her, it, they/them.*

Exercise 16–3

The italicized word groups are nominals. Write in the first blank one of the substitutes mentioned above. In the second blank indicate the function of the group.

1. *To win the match* was his greatest ambition.

 _____ _____

2. Can you see from *where you sit?* (Try a noun.)

 _____ _____

3. I brought a scarf for *my favorite aunt from Peoria.*

 _____ _____

4. He did not give *finding the cat* a second thought.

 _____ _____

5. *Where we are going* has not been decided.

 _____ _____

6. She became *what she had hoped.*

 _____ _____

7. He hated *arriving late.*

 _____ _____

8. We found *what we wanted.*

 _____ _____

9. *That she is beautiful* is evident to all.

 _____ _____

10. They made him *what he had always wanted to be.* Fyupia

 _____ _____

Exercise 16–4

Underline the nominal word groups. In the blank give the function of the word group.

1. They heard what we said. _____

2. What you do is legal. _____

3. That was what I thought too. _____

4. You must do the best with what you have. _____

5. Jack made whoever came there the same offer. _____

6. We will name the baby whatever his grandfather wishes. _____

7. We thought of paying cash. _____

8. I'll take whichever is the most durable.   _____
9. Betty forgot to bring the coffee.   _____
10. George postponed mailing the letter.   _____

B. Verbals

Verbals are those forms that occupy verb positions. The kingpin verbal position is that of the main verb. It comes after the opening N slot. The verb by form is a verbal by position.

Examples: The golf team may *play* tomorrow.
They have been *loitering* near the bank.
The victim must have been *shot* from the side.

Exercise 16–5

Underline the verbal in each sentence.

1. The activity clubs had been making floats.
2. A survey is being made of TV watchers.
3. He has left for the summer.
4. Your tennis racket may have been stolen.
5. Gertrude had sung a solo.

In order to identify the other verbal positions, we must first make a distinction between two kinds of verb forms. Certain verb forms and verb phrases have complete assertive power; they are needed to make a sentence go. Here are some examples:

a. I *choose* carefully.
   She *chooses* carefully.   } Contrastive inflection for person

b. She *chooses* carefully.
   They *choose* carefully.   } Contrastive inflection for number

c. They *choose* carefully.
   They *chose* carefully.   } Contrastive inflection for tense

d. She *has* been chosen carefully.   } Contrastive inflection
   They *have* been chosen carefully.   } for person and number

e. I *am* being chosen.   } Contrastive inflection for
   They *were* being chosen.   } person, number, and tense

Two characteristics are noteworthy about these utterances:

1. You can comfortably place a period after each one; each has sentence-completeness because each contains a fully assertive verb or verb phrase.

2. Each pair contains one inflected form, except the last pair, which contains two inflected forms, *am* and *were*. Here are the explanatory details:

In *a,* the verb form *chooses,* inflected for third person, contrasts with the uninflected form in *I choose.*

In *b*, the verb form *chooses*, inflected for singular number, contrasts with the uninflected form in *They choose*.

In *c*, the verb form *chose*, inflected for past tense, contrasts with the uninflected form in *They choose*.

In *d*, the primary auxiliary *has*, inflected for person and number in one form, contrasts with the uninflected forms in *I have* and *They have*.

In *e*, the irregular primary auxiliary *am* contrasts with the verb form in *He is* for first person, with the verb form in *We are* for singular number, and with the verb form in *I was* for present tense. And the irregular primary auxiliary *were* contrasts with the verb form in *He was* for plural number and with the verb form in *They are* for past tense.

Verb forms that are capable of full assertion in a sentence and of being inflected for person, number, and tense are called **finite verbs** and by position they are finite verbals.

The second sort of verb forms is the **nonfinite.** These do not assert fully and are not inflected for person, number, or tense. There are three nonfinite verb forms: the present participle {-ING vb}, the past participle {-D pp}, and the infinitive (to) + verb stem. These frequently appear in sentence portions, like the following:

1a. *Shaking* his fist
1b. *Being* angry
1c. The willow *bending* in the wind
1d. *Remaining* sad

2a. *Having crushed* the invaders
2b. *Having been* uneasy
2c. The guide *having disappeared*
2d. *Having stayed* calm

3a. *To stop* this nonsense
3b. *To be* sensible
3c. His cousin *to come*
3d. *To become* rich

Oral Exercise 16–A
Add something to each of the twelve foregoing sentence portions in order to make a sentence of each. Do not change the wording of the sentence portion.

You may have observed that each sentence portion above conforms in part to one of the nine basic sentence patterns. In 1a, 2a, and 3a there is a direct object, respectively *fist, invaders,* and *nonsense*. This is a partial Pattern 7. In 1b, 2b, and 3b there is the verb *be* + an adjective, *angry, uneasy,* and *sensible*. This is a partial Pattern 1. In 1c, 2c, and 3c there is a subject, namely, *willow, guide,* and *cousin,* used with an intransitive verb. This is characteristic of Pattern 6. And in 1d, 2d, and 3d we find a linking verb + an adjective, *sad, calm,* and *rich.* This is a partial Pattern 4.

All of the verb forms above are nonfinite and participate in one of the nine partial sentence patterns, but do not have the full assertive power of the main verb. These forms we call **nonfinite verbals.**

Exercise 16–6

Indicate the number of the sentence pattern that each of the italicized nonfinite verbals participates in.

1. *Picking* strawberries was her favorite occupation. _____
2. Perkins did not approve of *assigning* students long papers. _____
3. *To give* generously is a Christian virtue. _____
4. *Being* a minister, Prentiss spoke gently. _____
5. We regretted the warblers *leaving* for the South. _____
6. *Remaining* a conscientious objector, Harkness did not return to his native country. _____
7. Seeing the photos is not *being* there. _____
8. *Having been* competent in camp activities, Juanita was invited to return as a counselor. _____
9. He wanted *to call* the lawyer a fraud. _____
10. Heinrich congratulated Gretchen for *becoming* slender. _____
11. We watched George *throw* the discus. _____
12. We watched George *throwing* the discus. _____
13. We wanted George *to throw* the discus. _____

Exercise 16–7

Underline the nonfinite verbals. Indicate in the blanks the basic sentence pattern each verbal or verbal group participates in.

1. Having sprinkled the lawn, he turned off the water. _____
2. She remembered seeing the play before. _____
3. Do you like to be there? _____
4. We urged the guests to remain for dinner. _____
5. She was proud of being a member of the band. _____
6. He wanted the teacher to give him an A. _____
7. After having been cheerful for weeks, Chuck was now depressed. _____
8. Keeping quiet, she peered through the window. _____
9. Harris made his brother repay the loan. _____
10. Calling Josephine an artist was a compliment. _____
11. Jim's father did not object to his becoming a Marine. _____

When a nonfinite verb form—present participle {*-ing* vb}, past participle {*-d* pp}, and (*to*) + verb stem—appears alone in a noun position, it is labeled a nominal, as in

To err is human. (SV position)
She enjoys *skiing.* (DO position)
Her hobby is *gardening.* (SC position)

Likewise, the whole sentence portion containing a verbal and occurring in a noun position is labeled a nominal, as in

Playing field hockey is her favorite pastime. (SV position)
He liked *to play the piano.* (DO position)
Their business is *raising turkeys* (SC position)
Jim got paid for *mowing the lawn.* (OP position)

Exercise 16–8

The italicized parts of the sentences below are nominals by position. Indicate the function of each, using these abbreviations:

SV subject of verb   DO direct object of verb
SC subjective complement   OP object of preposition

1a. *Motorcycling* always gives Genevieve a thrill.   _____
 b. *Riding a roller coaster* always gives Genevieve a thrill.   _____
2a. Fred earned money by *delivering.*   _____
 b. Fred earned money by *delivering papers.*   _____
3a. Charlotte likes *to swim.*   _____
 b. Charlotte likes *to play volleyball.*   _____
4a. What can he do besides *complain?*   _____
 b. What can he do besides *play the drums?*   _____
5a. Jerry enjoys *fishing.*   _____
 b. Jerry enjoys *playing bridge.*   _____
6a. Its only purpose was *swindling.*   _____
 b. Its only purpose was *soaking the rich.*   _____

Complements of the verbal. The main verb, as we saw in the basic sentence patterns, can be complemented by nominals functioning as subjective complement, direct object, indirect object, and objective complement. These same kinds of complements can follow not only the main verb but other verbals in the sentence as well. A few examples will make this clear.

Her hobby was *making prints.*

Here the main verb *was* has as its subjective complement the nominal *making prints.* Within this nominal *prints* is the direct object of the verbal *making.*

He enjoys *playing golf.*

In this case the main verb *enjoys* has as its direct object the nominal *playing golf,* and within this nominal the verbal *playing* has *golf* as its direct object. Here is another:

We wanted *to teach her a lesson.*

In this example, the main verb *wanted* has as its direct object the nominal *to teach her a lesson.* And within this nominal the verbal *to teach* has an indirect object *her* and a direct object *lesson.* In the next sentence,

George asked *her to drive the car*

we say that the main verb *asked* has the direct object *her to drive the car* and that, within this nominal, *her* is the subject of the verbal *to drive* and *car* the direct object.[1] This analysis is supported by the possibility of substituting a nominal clause like this:

George asked *that she drive the car.*

Exercise 16–9

In the preceding exercise you investigated the function of nominals (embodying a verbal) in the sentence. Now we shall look inside such nominals to ascertain the functions of their parts relative to the embodied verbal. Each nominal embodying a verbal is italicized, and after each such nominal, its function in the sentence is given in parentheses. Within the nominal one or two words are printed in small capitals. Indicate the function within the nominal of each word printed in small caps.

Example: *Eating* CHOCOLATES made her sick. (SV)   DO

This tells you that *eating chocolates* is a nominal embodying a verbal (*eating*), that it is the subject of the main verb *made,* and that you are to indicate the function of *chocolates* within the nominal. *Chocolates* is, of course, the direct object of the verbal *eating.* You will probably also notice that *eating chocolates* is a partial Pattern 7.

For your answers, use these abbreviations:

SV subject of the verb	IO indirect object
SC subjective complement	OC objective complement
MD adjectival modifier	OP object of preposition
DO direct object	

  1. She hated *to miss the* PARTY. (DO)   ____
  2. Dimitri tried *to remain* CALM. (DO)   ____
  3. *Shooting* QUAIL takes a great deal of skill. (SV)   ____
  4. I expect YOU *to be* TRUTHFUL. (DO)   ____ ____
  5. *Finding the* TRAIL *again* was no easy matter. (SV)   ____
  6. Thank you for *washing* DISHES. (OP)   ____
  7. *Being a golf* CHAMPION was exhilarating to Olga. (SV)   ____
  8. I saw THEM *break the* WINDOW. (DO)   ____ ____
  9. The doctor advised HIM *to stop* SMOKING. (DO)   ____ ____
 10. *Electing* BETTY PRESIDENT required a lot of
      campaigning. (SV)   ____ ____

---

[1]An alternate analysis is to consider the slot before the verbal (i.e., _____ to drive the car) an indirect object and the rest, the direct object. This is supported by the passive form of the sentence: She was asked to drive the car by George.

11. He wished *to give* HAROLD *a* BICYCLE. (DO) ___ ___
12. Fleming thought *visiting* MUSEUMS an exciting excursion
    into the past. (DO) ___

Verbals and sentence portions containing verbals occur not only as nominals but also as adjectivals and adverbials, functioning as modifiers. These will be dealt with at the end of the next chapter, after you have studied the following material there:

1. Sentence modifier (p. 249)
2. Participial phrase, *-ing,* adjectival (p. 262)
3. Participial phrase ,*-ed*, adjectival (p. 262)
4. Infinitive phrase, adjectival, to ——— (p. 262)
5. Infinitive phrase adverbials (p. 273)
6. Participial phrases in *-ing* and *-ed* as adverbials (p. 273–274)[2]

C. Adjectivals

Adjectivals, like nominals and verbals, occupy certain characteristic sentence positions.

1. The first position is that between the determiner (that is, words like *a, the, this, that, these, those, his, her, our, their, Johnny's*) and the noun, for example,

That *joyful* freshman[3]

In this noun phrase *joyful* is an adjective by form—the source noun *joy* plus the derivational suffix *-ful*—and an adjectival by position. This position may be occupied by two other form-classes and by uninflected forms. The noun is shown in

That *college* freshman

The verb appears in

That *laughing* freshman
That *recommended* freshman

And here are uninflected words in this adjectival slot:

An *inside* job
Her *inmost* thoughts

A series of adjectivals may occur between the determiner and the noun, as in

The mâny êarnest univêrsity séniors

---

[2] Note to instructor: You may wish to assign these parts, together with the relevant exercises, now, to wrap up the verbals.
[3] The determiner is also an adjectival by position, and it is a modifier by function.

Here there are three successive adjectivals in a fixed and unchangeable order. Because these are not interchangeable—that is, not mutually substitutable—we shall set up subclasses of adjectivals, which will be discussed in the next chapter under "Prenominal Modifiers."

Exercise 16-10

The italicized words are adjectivals. Indicate the form-class of each with the symbols N (noun), V (verb), Aj (adjective), and UW (uninflected word). Mark the stresses on the adjectival and the noun.

1. A *clean* apron ____
2. An *evening* party ____
3. The *college* dormitory ____
4. The *class* dance ____
5. A *hopeful* sign ____
6. Their *back* yard ____
7. Those *neighborhood* cats ____
8. Sally's *new* radio ____
9. That *paper* book ____
10. A *fighting* rooster ____
11. These *broken* boxes ____
12. An *upstairs* room ____
13. Their *garage* door ____
14. The *office* typewriter ____
15. Our *school* principal ____
16. The *above* statement ____
17. That *funny* hat ____
18. A *scenic* drive ____
19. Those *chattering* girls ____
20. His *glass* eye ____

The preceding exercise illustrates the first and most common adjectival position.

2. The second adjectival position is the third slot in Pattern 1:

N   *be*   Aj
Those boys are young

3. The third adjectival position is the third slot in Pattern 4:

N	LV	Aj
The boat	remained	*wet, shiny.*
The man	appeared	*aghast, aware.*
The man	seemed	*in the money* (= rich).

Exercise 16-11

Underline the adjectivals that occupy position 3 in Patterns 4 and 1. In the blanks indicate the pattern number.

1. The baby's cheeks are pink. _____
2. In the late afternoon the forest seemed dark. _____
3. The visitor became afraid. _____
4. The scouts seemed asleep. _____
5. This frog appears alive. _____
6. The privet hedge grew tall. _____
7. The privet hedge is green. _____
8. The grass was dewy this morning.

   9. The catamaran remained dirty.   _____

10. The villagers looked hostile.   _____

---

   4. The fourth adjectival position is the one after the noun. It accepts adjectives, adverbs, verbs (participles), uninflected words, and word groups.

Examples: adjectivals: The waitress, *old* and *weary,* sat heavily down.
                       The blondes *especially* → wore blue.
                       That girl *jogging* is my sister.
                       The floor *below* is rented.

   When an adjective is in this postnoun position, it usually does not occur alone but with another adjectival, as in

   A fire, *red* and *yellow,* threw shadows around the room.

or with a modifier, as in

   The plumber, rather *angry,* threw down his wrench.

There are occasional instances, however, in which the adjective does appear alone after the head noun. Examples: *money necessary, resources available, court martial, God Almighty, time immemorial, consul general, sum due.*

Exercise 16–12

Underline the adjectivals, and in the blanks indicate the form-class by using the symbols: Aj (adjective), Av (adverb), V (participle), and UW (uninflected word).

   1. One person alone heard the message.   _____
   2. Those coeds there are sophomores.   _____
   3. The surface, black and smooth, reflected   _____   _____
       the sunshine.
   4. The weather today suggests a thunderstorm.   _____
   5. We started our trip homeward.   _____
   6. The woman speaking became our vice-president.   _____
   7. His demeanor, excessively grim, annoyed the
       guests.   _____
   8. Selmer canceled his trip abroad.   _____
   9. The coach particularly ate in silence.   _____
  10. The door ajar worried the janitor.   _____

   In this postnominal position we find word-group adjectivals of different structures:

   It is time *to go.* (Infinitive)
   Andy watched his dog, *which was swimming after a stick.* (Relative clause)[4]

   [4] The relative clause adjectival is presented on pages 262 *ff.*

Andy watched his dog, [which was] *swimming after a stick.* (Reduced relative clause)

He was a man *who was disturbed by many phantasies.* (Relative clause)

He was a man [who was] *disturbed by many phantasies.* (Reduced relative clause)

The sweater *that I prefer* is the striped one. (Relative clause)

The sweater *I prefer* is the striped one. (Reduced relative clause)

Mount Washington is the place *where we spent a strenuous week.* (Relative clause)

The second chapter *of the book* presented the problem. (Prepositional phrase)

This is a medicine *good for gastritis.* (Modified adjective)

Exercise 16–13

Underline the word-group adjectival and encircle the word it modifies.

1. This will be a day to remember.
2. The chap sitting in that cubicle is Marge's friend.
3. This is not the size I ordered.
4. The drugstore on the corner sells the *Times.*
5. Our guests came on the week when I was housecleaning.
6. A girl spoiled by her mother is not a good roommate.
7. Just choose a time convenient to yourself.
8. Who is the head of this club?
9. Have you finished the book I lent you?
10. He was a sight to behold.

---

5. A fifth position for adjectivals occurs in written English. This is the slot at the beginning of a sentence before the subject:

Angry and upset, the applicant slammed the door.

But this presubject position is also an adverbial position:

Angrily, the applicant slammed the door.

In the former sentence we consider *angry* and *upset* to be adjectivals, not adverbials, because they can be used in other positions that are clearly the territory of adjectivals:

The applicant was angry and upset.
The applicant appeared angry and upset.
The angry and upset applicant . . .

In a nominal position they would of course be nominals:

The angry make few friends.
The upset sometimes need treatment.

6. "Something" adjectival. Words composed of *any-, every-, no-,* or *some-* plus *-body, -one, -place,* or *-thing* can be followed by an adjectival.

Nothing *good* was on the table.

Exercise 16–14

Underline the postnominal adjectivals.

1. Would you like something sweet?
2. We cannot find anyplace desirable.
3. Nothing exciting happened.
4. Everybody interested is invited to appear.
5. An invitation was extended to everyone concerned.

D. Adverbials

The positional class, adverbials, cannot be delimited with precision and is difficult to describe without enormous complications. One difficulty is that there are numerous subclasses of one-word adverbials, and each subclass has its own positions in the various sentence patterns. To illustrate, let us look at the traditional adverbial subclasses of time, place, and manner. We'll choose two examples of each class:

Time: a. soon   b. tomorrow
Place: a. here   b. outside
Manner: a. well   b. skillfully

Now we'll take a simple sentence of Pattern 7 and see how these adverbials assume their positions in this pattern. We'll begin with the *a* group.

	1	2	3	4	5
	He	will	play		tennis.
Time:	Soon	soon	soon	_____	soon
Place:	Here	_____	_____	_____	here
Manner:	_____	_____	_____	_____	well

Next let's look at the *b* group of the same three adverbial subclasses—time, place, and manner.

	1	2	3	4	5
	He	will	play	tennis.	
Time:	Tomorrow	_____	_____	_____	tomorrow
Place:	_____	_____	_____	_____	outside
Manner:	_____	_____	skillfully	_____	skillfully

Here it is evident that each member of the group *a* adverbials of time, place, and manner has a distribution unlike that of its mate in group *b*. In other words we have positional sub-subclasses.

Exercise 16–15

Here is a simple Pattern 4 sentence, with adverbial positions numbered above it. Below the sentence are three adverbials. In the blanks write the numbers of the positions in which each adverbial sounds natural in spoken English. Compare these positions with those in the preceding example. The point is that each pattern dictates its own adverbial positions.

               1   2   3   4
Pattern 4:   N   LV Aj
               The leaves turned brown.

Time: recently   _____
Place: everywhere   _____
Manner: gradually   _____

Next we divide adverbials of time into three subclasses.

Adverbials of definite time, answering the question "When?":
    yesterday, last week, at three o'clock, tomorrow, early, late, soon, then, now.

Adverbials of frequency, answering the question "How often?":
    always, never, seldom, rarely, frequently, often, sometimes, generally.

Adverbials of duration, answering the question "How long?":
    hours, for hours, a week, the whole night, until dawn, since yesterday.

Each of these subgroups of time adverbials has its favored or admissible positions, as the next exercise will show.

Exercise 16–16

A. In these two sentences which one of the three subclasses of time adverbials normally occupies the empty slot?

  1. Pattern 2:   The game was _____.   _____
  2. Any pattern, preverb
       position: We _____ played ball. _____

B. In the next sentence which position seems to be the most natural one for adverbials of duration, such as *all afternoon?*

          1   2   3   4
  3. Pattern 7: Jim studied chemistry.   _____

With this brief discussion you may begin to suspect the complexity of the problem of describing adverbial positions. In addition there are further complicating circumstances that we cannot pursue here. So we shall limit this description to a general statement of five common adverbial positions, moving position by position from the first one (at the beginning of the sentence) to the last one (at the end).

1. Before the pattern, with or without juncture:

Really, you should know better.
Now it's time to go.

2. After the subject and before the auxiliary or verb:

She *often* would forget her keys.
He *actually* expects to marry her.

3. After the auxiliary or the first auxiliary:

He would *seldom* make the effort.
They could *easily* have made another touchdown.

4. After the verb in Pattern 6 and after *be* in Patterns 1, 2, and 3:

He drove *recklessly*.
She is *seldom* late.
She is *outside*.
Her brother is *always* a gentleman.

5. After the complement of the verb (SC, DO, OC):

Hoskins will be quarterback *tomorrow*.
Hoskins will play football *tomorrow*.
They may choose Hoskins captain *tomorrow*.

But this postcomplement position is also position 4 in Pattern 9:

They elected Monty *captain*.
We considered her *reasonable*.

There need be no trouble here. Since *captain* is a noun and *reasonable* an adjective, we obviously have in these sentences a nominal and an adjectival, not adverbials. This positional overlap, however, can produce ambiguity, as in

He considered the applicant *hard*.

Here *hard* can be looked at two ways. It is an adverbial at the end of Pattern 7, as you can substitute for it an adverb, like *carefully*. But it is also an adjectival in Pattern 9, as it permits a substitute like *unsuitable*. Hence the ambiguity.

In any of these five positions we can label a word an adverbial, unless we have an instance of positional overlap. In such cases the form-class that occupies a slot or that can be substituted will determine the positional classification. Here is an illustration of each case.

He eats *doughnuts*.

The postverb position admits nominals, adjectivals, and adverbials. In this example the postverb slot is occupied by the form-class of noun *(doughnuts)* so that the word is positionally nominal. In the second illustration,

He eats *fast*,

we can substitute the adverb *quickly* for *fast*. Thus *fast* is called an adverbial.

The passive transformation offers another test to distinguish nominals from adverbials in this postverbal position. If we compare

He ate Wednesday
He ate sandwiches

we see that the first cannot be made passive, for no one would say

*Wednesday was eaten by him.

Hence *Wednesday* is not a nominal but an adverbial. But we can say

Sandwiches were eaten by him.

Therefore, in "He ate sandwiches," the word *sandwiches* is a nominal.

Another way to spot adverbials is by their mobility. Most adverbials can be moved to one or more positions in the sentence without disturbing the sentence pattern or sounding un-English. In the illustrative "tennis" sentences, for instance, five of the six adverbials were movable.

As a last resort for identifying adverbials, try elimination. If the term in question is not a nominal, verbal, or adjectival—and not a structure word —then it is by elimination an adverbial.

It must never be forgotten that we are dealing with a positional class and that any form-class can be an adverbial, e.g.,

Noun:	He will come *Sunday*.
Verb:	They stood *eating*. (= thus)
Adjective:	They played *dirty*.
	Come *quick*.
Adverb:	Come *quickly*.
Uninflected word:	Come *back*.

In the word-stock of English there are many uninflected words often employed in adverbial positions, and it may be useful to you to inspect a sample of them before proceeding with the next exercise. Here they are:

1. Uninflected words used both as adverbials and prepositions:
   above, about, after, around, before, behind, below, down in, inside, on, out, outside, since, to, under, up.

2. "-ward" series, with optional -s:
   afterward, backward, downward, forward, inward, outward, upward.

3. "Here" series:
   here, herein, hereby, heretofore, hereafter.

4. "There" series:
   there, therein, thereby, therefore, thereafter.

5. "-where" series:
   anywhere, everywhere, somewhere, nowhere.

6. "-way(s)" series:
   crossways, sideways, anyway.

7. "-time(s)" series:
   meantime, sometime, anytime, sometimes.

8. Miscellaneous

today, tonight, tomorrow, yesterday,[4] now, then, seldom, still, yet, already, meanwhile, also, too, never, not, forth, thus, sidelong, headlong, maybe, perhaps, instead, indeed, henceforth, piecemeal, nevertheless, downstairs, indoors, outdoors, offhand, overseas, unawares, besides, furthermore, always.

Exercise 16–17

Underline each one-word adverbial. In each blank of the first column write the number that shows which of the five numbered adverbial positions it occupies:

1. before the pattern, with or without juncture
2. after the subject and before the auxiliary or verb
3. after the auxiliary or the first auxiliary
4. after the verb in Pattern 6 and after *be* in Patterns 1, 2, and 3
5. after the complement of the verb (SC, DO, OC).

In each second blank identify the form-class of the adverbial by N (noun), V (verb), Aj (adjective), Av (adverb), or UW (uninflected word).

1. Bob should talk loud.
2. Indeed, bring him with you.
3. He drove the car madly around the track.
4. I certainly will.
5. They entered singing.
6. He frequently reads in bed.
7. The deer was standing below.
8. I'll see you inside.
9. I will eventually make a report.
10. We usually stopped for tea.
11. They stood around for ten minutes.
12. Will you set the plant here?
13. It is still a long distance to Albany.
14. The vice-president had already signed the contract.
15. The bus approached rapidly.
16. We had seldom walked to the park.
17. Meanwhile Giovanni started the fire.
18. The ride was also tiresome.
19. They rode Saturday.
20. The ants were everywhere.

Word groups as well as single words can occupy adverbial positions and thereby be classified as adverbials. Here are some illustrative groups in the five positions.

---

[4] A few of these words have noun homophones, e.g., "And all our *yesterdays* have lighted fools / The way to dusty death."

1. Before the pattern, with or without juncture:

With a sharp ax you can do wonders.
By using a little red here, you can balance your colors.
Unless you follow the printed directions, the set will not fit properly together.

2. After the subject and before the auxiliary or verb:

Angelina *in her own way* was a darling.

3. After the auxiliary or first auxiliary:

You may *in this way* be of great assistance.

4. After the verb in Pattern 6 and after *be* in Patterns 1, 2, and 3:

He drove *with abandon.*
She is *at any event* happy.
The wolf is *at the door.*
He is *without doubt* an expert.

When an infinitive (*to* + verb) follows the verb, it may be in one of two positions:

Adverbial, after verb in Pattern 6, as in

They waited *to escape.*

Nominal, position 3 in Pattern 7, as in

They expected *to escape.*

If *in order to* can be substituted for *to,* the infinitive is in the adverbial position: "They waited *in order to* escape." If *that* or *it* can be substituted for the infinitive, it is in the nominal position: "They expected *that/it.*"

5. After the complement of the verb (SC, DO, OC):

My brother was a doctor *for twenty years.*
Tom put his watch *where he could find it in the dark.*
They believed the man crazy *after questioning him.*

A prepositional phrase after the object of the verb may be ambiguous:

They watched the hunter *with the binoculars.*
She spied the dog *on the corner.*

In these two sentences the prepositional phrase is either adjectival or adverbial.

Exercise 16–18

The adverbial word groups are italicized. In the blank indicate by number the adverbial position of each.

1. I'll dress *while you shave.* _____
2. *When the coffee is ready,* blow the whistle. _____

3. He might *under the circumstances* agree to the job. _____
4. Our guide split the log *with ease*. _____
5. *Chewing his tobacco meditatively,* White Foot studied the blackening sky. _____
6. A hungry trout rose *to the surface*. _____
7. *By that time* the fish were no longer biting. _____
8. *To find the camp,* just follow the creek downstream. _____
9. *From the hilltop* you can see the sawmill. _____
10. Jake hunts *to make a living*. _____
11. You must hold the knife *this way*. _____

Exercise 16–19

This is a review of the four positional parts of speech. In the blanks identify each italicized element by N-al (nominal), V-al (verbal), Aj-al (adjectival), or Av-al (adverbial).

1. Last *Monday* was a holiday. _____ Av-al N
2. The *Monday* washing is on the line. Aj
3. Mrs. Reed always jogs *Mondays.* Av
4. Won't you come *in?* Av
5. The outs were angry with the *ins.* N
6. They stomped *upstairs.* Av
7. They slept in the *upstairs* room. Aj
8. One can see the airport from *upstairs.* N
9. Jake was *wrestling* with his math. V
10. The *wrestling* roommates were exhausted. Aj
11. Juniper found *wrestling* exciting. N
12. They came in *wrestling.* Av
13. The student movie is presented *weekly.* Av
14. The student movie is a *weekly* occurrence. Aj
15. His *way* is the best. N
16. He did it *his way.* Av
17. The mechanic ran the engine *full speed.* Av
18. *By this means* he burned out the carbon. Av
19. He raised the hood *because the engine was hot.* Av
20. They found the cabin *just what they wanted.* N

Exercise 16–20

This is a review of the four form-class parts of speech. Classify the italicized words by writing in the blanks N (noun), V (verb), Aj (adjective), Av (adverb), or UW (uninflected word). Remember to use derivational as well as inflectional criteria.

1. Minnie is fond of Siamese *cats.* _____
2. The island was *colonized* by the Northmen. _____
3. One of her *stockings* is torn. _____
4. What *punishment* do you think should be administered? _____
5. Fritz *always* says the wrong thing. _____

6. Her room was in a state of *chaos*. ———
7. We'll *gladly* refund your money. ———
8. The nurse puts a *disinfectant* on the cut. ———
9. Carl sleeps late *mornings*. ———
10. How *peaceful* the house seems today! ———
11. You should *shorten* that dress. ———
12. The salesman quietly turned *away*. ———
13. Our ladder is not *tall* enough. ———
14. The class listened to a *reading* from Shakespeare. ———
15. I don't know *offhand*. ———

E. A Maverick: Verb-Adverbial Composites[5]

The form we are about to examine is extraordinarily intricate in its behavior. As you progress through the explanations, all may appear clear-cut and simple. But if you stray from this carefully laid-out path to inquire into instances of your own finding, you may meet with variations, exceptions, and impasses. So be warned that beneath the specious simplicity of what is to follow lies a tangle of complication.

A verb-adverbial composite consists of two words, a verb followed by an adverbial like *up, down, in, out, over*. There are two kinds, intransitive and transitive, each with partially different structural and transformational characteristics.

INTRANSITIVE VERB-ADVERBIAL COMPOSITE (VAC)

We shall begin with an example that illustrates the characteristics of the intransitive verb-adverbial composite.

He *turned up* (= appeared) at seven o'clock.

There are three characteristics to be noted here which tend to be common to intransitive VAC's and which can be used as VAC tests.

Test A—Meaning. The meaning of *turned up* as a unit is different from that of the individual meanings of the two parts added together. Other examples:

We *took off* (= departed) for Memphis.
The violence of the storm may *let up* (= lessen) soon.

Test B—Immovability. The adverbial element of an intransitive VAC is not movable, for you would be unlikely to say

---

[5] This structure has various names: "verb-adverb combination" (A. G. Kennedy), "phrasal verb" (Dwight Bolinger), "verb-particle combination" (Bruce Fraser), "two-word verb" (G. A. Meyer).

*Up he turned.
*Off we took.
*Up the storm let.

Test C—Inseparability. The two parts of an intransitive VAC are inseparable. A modifier separating them results in a strange or non-English locution, as in

*He turned suddenly up at seven o'clock.
*We took immediately off for Memphis.
*The violence of the storm may let soon up.

All three of these traits are not necessarily characteristic of every intransitive VAC, and the meaning test in particular may result in uncertain decisions. Let us say, therefore, that if the expression in question shows ONE of the three characteristics, we can label it an intransitive VAC.

In contrast to the intransitive VAC there is the simple verb plus adverbial, as in

He climbed up.

This does not have any of the three characteristics noted above for the intransitive VAC:

A. The meaning is that of *climbed* plus that of *up,* as shown by the question "Where did he climb?" "Up."

B. The *up* can be moved, as in

Up he climbed with the agility of a squirrel.

C. The two parts can be separated by a modifier, as in

He climbed nimbly up the tree.

Exercise 16–21

Classify the italicized words as VAC (intransitive verb-adverbial composite) or V + A (verb plus adverbial).

1. The two friends *fell out.* (= quarreled) _____
2. The two friends *walked out.* _____
3. England will always *carry on.* _____
4. Willard *went in.* _____
5. After drinking heavily, he suddenly *passed out.* (lost consciousness) _____
6. You should *keep on* with your investigation. (= continue) _____
7. The dean *gave in* to the request of the committee. (= acceded) _____
8. He *fell down* unexpectedly. _____
9. The shop may *close down.* _____
10. Betsy likes to *show off.* _____

TRANSITIVE VERB-ADVERBIAL COMPOSITE (VAC + O)

The transitive verb-adverbial composite has an object, as you would expect, and is symbolized by VAC + O. Here is an example:

He *turned down* (= rejected) the offer.

A distinction must be made here between the VAC + O and the verb plus prepositional phrase, V + PP. The latter is illustrated in

He *turned down* the driveway.

There are three useful tests that enable us to make this distinction; and, as was the case with the intransitive VAC, we shall label a verb a VAC + O if it passes ONE of these tests.

Test A—Adverbial Postpositioning. In a VAC + O sentence the adverbial can be placed after the object of the verb:

He *turned* the offer *down.*

This change is impossible with the preposition:

*He turned the driveway down.

Furthermore, when the object of the VAC + O is a personal pronoun, the adverbial MUST be placed after the pronoun object and only there:

He *turned* it *down.*

If one said

He turned down it

the last two words would be a preposition and its object.

Exercise 16–22

Using Test A, classify the italicized words as VAC + O (verb-adverbial composite and object) or V + PP (verb and prepositional phrase).

1. I will *turn in the requisition.*   _____
2. I will *turn in the street.*   _____
3. We *called up the plumber.*   _____
4. Mother *called up the stairs.*   _____
5. He *broke in his new car.*   _____
6. The windshield *broke in his new car.*   _____

Test B—Inseparability. The verb-adverbial in the VAC + O cannot be separated by a modifier, but a modifier can occur between a verb and a prepositional phrase. For example,

VAC + O: He *turned up* (= discovered) a new manuscript.
V + PP: He *turned* (sharply) *up* the country road.

Exercise 16–23

Insert a modifier wherever you can after the verb. Then classify the italicized words as VAC + O or V + PP.

1. The wind *blew down* the valley.   _____
2. The wind *blew down* the tree.   _____
3. Jean *ran up* a bill.   _____
4. Jean *ran up* a hill.   _____
5. Will you *turn on* the light in that room? _____
6. My car can *turn on* a dime.   _____

Test C—Relative Transformation. The V + PP sentence can be transformed into a relative structure in which the preposition is followed by a *which* or *whom*, thus:

V + PP: She ran *down* the hill

can be transformed into

The hill *down which* she ran.

In this relative structure, note that the preposition *down* is separated from the verb *ran*.

In the VAC + O sentence, this form of the transformation is not possible. For instance,

VAC + O: She *ran down* (= criticized adversely) her roommate

cannot become

*Her roommate *down* whom she *ran*.

Instead, the two parts of the VAC + O must remain together:

Her roommate whom she *ran down*.

Exercise 16–24

For each sentence that permits it make a relative transformation, following the first example under Test C above as a model. Then label the italicized parts of each sentence as VAC + O or V + PP.

1. The police *ran in the criminal.*   _____
   _____

2. The horses *ran in the pasture.*   _____
   _____

3. The teacher stood *drînking în the móonlight.*   _____
   (= observing with pleasure)
   _____

4. The teacher stood *drînking ĭn the móonlight.*   _____
   _____

5. Alice *pricked up her ears.*   _____
   _____

6. Keith *looked over her bare shoulder.* ———

7. We prevailed on the dean. ———

8. He knocked over the chair. ———

9. He stepped over the chair. ———

10. Jake closed down his shop. ———

Exercise 16–25

Apply all three tests to each pair of italicized words. Indicate by letter (A, B, C) which tests show the item to be a VAC + O.

1. The butler *carried in* the tray. ———
2. Marge *made up* her mind. ———
3. Marge *made up* the story. ———
4. She *turned over* the pancake. ———
5. Father *looked over* the evening paper. (= scrutinized) ———
6. The Senate *brought about* a change. ———
7. Ed always *turns out* a long term paper. ———
8. The clerk *wrapped up* the meat. ———
9. Will you *take over* the job? ———
10. Willie soon *wore out* his shoes. ———

Some sentences similar to those we have been discussing may seem to have two adverbials, as in

He can't *get along with* them. (= tolerate)

Such expressions are most simply analyzed as being composed of an intransitive VAC (or a verb plus adverbial) followed by a prepositional phrase. It may seem to you that *with* should belong with the verb and adverbial in a three-part verb because no other preposition can replace it. But remember that many verbs are linked to one specific preposition; for instance, we object *to,* flirt *with,* exclude *from,* and compensate *for.*

That the preposition is not a part of the verb is suggested when we make questions with such forms, as in

With whom can't he get along?

Exercise 16–26

Make a question of each sentence, following the model just above.

1. She *looked down on* her former friends. (= scorned)

2. McBride *made off with* the child. (= stole, kidnapped)

_____

3. We *made up with* the girls.

_____

4. They won't *put up with* that spoiled child. (= endure)

_____

5. We should *look in on* the Smiths. (= visit)

_____

17
Modification

The nine basic sentence patterns that we studied in Chapter 15 were exemplified by somewhat skeletal sentences in order to reveal the structure without interference from unneeded parts. But in our actual speaking and writing we seldom use sentences so spare and bony. Instead we flesh out our sentences with many kinds of modifiers.

A modifier is a subordinate element in an endocentric structure.[1] It is a word or word group that affects the meaning of a headword in that it

---

[1] An endocentric structure has the same function as one of its parts or is replaceable by one of its parts.

Endocentric Structure	Replacement
those dirty dogs	dogs
extremely dirty	dirty
dog across the street	dog
dog which was howling	dog
reads rapidly	reads
reads to relax his mind	reads
often reads	reads
quite often	often

The replacing part is the head. The other words and word groups are the modifiers. The replacing part may retain a determiner from the endocentric structure because a certain class of nouns (count nouns) require a determiner in the singular:

> Elmer bought *a shiny new bicycle.*
> **Replacement:** Elmer bought *a bicycle.*

describes, limits, intensifies, and/or adds to the meaning of the head. In the noun phrase *the blue shirt,* for example, the word *blue* describes the shirt; it limits by excluding other colors; and it adds to the plain meaning of *shirt.*

Modifiers may appear before or after the heads they modify, and sometimes they are separated from the head by intervening words. Here are some examples of modifiers with heads.

Modifier	*Head*	*Modifier*
dirty	dog	
that	dog	
	dog	there
	dog	across the street
	dog	barking angrily
	dog	to be feared
	dog	which was howling
extremely	dirty	
	reads	rapidly
	reads	standing
	reads	when he wants to relax
	reads	nights
	reads	to calm his mind
often	reads	
quite	often	

The position of a modifier sometimes shows the head that it modifies:

The _____ flower

This slot, which we call adjectival, is the position of a modifier of the following noun, whether the slot is filled by an adjective (*lovely*), noun (*garden*), or a verb (*blossoming*). At times there is no positional cue to show what is modified:

A butterfly in the garden *which was fluttering among the flowers.*

In this sentence it is the meaning that reveals that the *which* group modifies *butterfly* and not *garden.* At other times we rely upon formal cues, not position or meaning, to keep the modification clear:

The flowers in the garden which *were* blossoming beautifully.
The flowers in the garden which *was* blossoming profusely.

When neither position nor formal signals reveal the modification, and when the meaning does not make it clear, we have an ambiguity, as in

A flower in the garden which was blossoming beautifully.

Exercise 17-1

Rewrite these sentences, replacing each italicized endocentric structure by its head. Retain the determiner when necessary.

1. His laughter was *extremely loud.*

2. *The jar on the shelf* is filled with dates.

3. McPherson was *a dour man who seldom smiled.*

4. The two *strolled through the park after they had finished work.*

5. The constable *laughed nastily.*

6. We heard *the loud rattling clank of the chain.*

7. *The angry squirrel in the pine* scolded the blue jays.

8. *The contract that he signed* had paragraphs of fine print.

9. The searchers found *the car lying on its side.*

10. Claribel *jumped into the deep pool.*

In the above exercise the parts that you left out were modifiers, both single-word and word-group modifiers. Take another look at these modifiers before going on to the next exercise.

Exercise 17–2
Write down the one-word heads that are modified by the italicized words.

1. A *noisy* motorcycle sputtered there. _____
2. A noisy motorcycle sputtered *there.* _____
3. The motorcycle *in the yard* had not been recently used. _____
4. He stopped *for a second.* _____
5. She stopped *to pick up the agate.* _____
6. It was *very* nice of you. _____
7. Lisa came to the coffee shop *rather* often. _____
8. He stopped *when the clock struck twelve.* _____
9. That fellow *making his bed* is the supervisor. _____
10. Gerald owned a long black whip, *which he could snap expertly.* _____

The two exercises above illustrate modification. Modification is a function, and a word or word group that performs this function is a modifier. A modifier belongs not with the form-classes or the position-classes but with the function-classes, such as the subject of verb, direct object, indirect object, object complement, and object of preposition. Words, you remember, have a threefold classification—by form, by position, and by function. Here is an example by way of reminder:

The *jolly* minstrel sang a ballad *lustily.*

In this sentence *jolly* is classified as an adjective by form, an adjectival by position, and a modifier by function; and *lustily* is called an adverb by form, an adverbial by position, and a modifier by function.

Now we are ready to look at modification systematically.

A. Sentence Modifiers

A sentence modifier is an adverbial that modifies, as its head, all the rest of the sentence, and is often set apart by terminals—rising, sustained, or falling.

Example: Naturally, he behaved at the party.

Here *naturally* modifies *he behaved at the party.* Compare this

He behaved naturally at the party.

In this sentence *naturally* modifies the verb *behaved,* and the meaning is different from that of the former sentence. Here are examples of seven structures in which sentence modifiers are commonly found.

1. Single-word adverbial:
   Luckily, I knew how to swim.

2. Clause adverbial:
   Since the door was closed, we climbed in the back window.

3. Prepositional phrase:
   In fact, the contract is invalid.

4. Absolute structure:[2]
   The guests having departed, we resumed the normal household routine.

5. Infinitive phrase:
   To keep dry in a tent, you should be provided with a fly.

6. Participial phrase in *-ing*:
   Considering the circumstances, he was lucky to escape alive.

7. Relative in *-ever*:
   Wherever she is, I will find her.

Each of these, we note, is in initial sentence position, the most common one for sentence modifiers. However, sentence modifiers may appear in medial and final positions as well.

---

[2] A noun plus a present or past participle or both. This structure is a sentence portion but never a complete sentence.

Exercise 17–3

Rewrite the seven sentences above, placing the sentence modifiers in positions other than initial.

1. _____
2. _____
3. _____
4. _____
5. _____
6. _____
7. _____

Exercise 17–4

Place above each juncture position separating the sentence modifier from the rest of the sentence an **R, S,** or **F** to show whether the juncture is rising, sustained, or fading. There will be considerable variation among different speakers at these points, so do not be disturbed if your answers do not accord with the key.

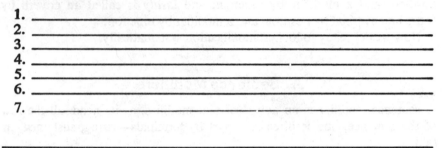

                  R

Example: In fact, he knew how to swim.

1. Apparently, the iron lung had been malfunctioning.

2. The iron lung, apparently, had been malfunctioning.

3. The iron lung had been malfunctioning, apparently.

4. Before frying the trout, the Indian guide greased the pan with raw bacon.

5. He spends his money, most of the time, on repairs for his car.

6. To be sure, the orchestra is not the best in the world.

7. The orchestra, to be sure, is not the best in the world.

8. The orchestra is not the best in the world, to be sure.

9. Unfortunately, he did not keep up his grades.

10. He did not keep up his grades, unfortunately.

It is not always possible to distinguish a sentence modifier from one which modifies a part of the sentence. But often there is a difference between the meaning of a sentence modifier and that of an identical expression which does not seem to be a sentence modifier. The next exercise will illustrate.

Exercise 17–5

Underline the sentence modifiers.

1. Oliver did not die happily.
2. Happily, Oliver did not die.
3. He was anxious to tell the truth.
4. He was anxious, to tell the truth.
5. Hopefully, we are going to London.
6. We are going to London hopefully.
7. Honestly, he is going to sell his car.
8. He is going to sell his car honestly.
9. Frankly, I do not wish to speak.
10. I do not wish to speak frankly.

B. The Noun Phrase: Prenominal Modifiers

The noun phrase, you will recall, consists of a noun head together with all the modifiers that accompany it, before and after.

$$NH$$

Example: All my many old school friends of other days who have passed
away

We shall take up first those modifiers that precede the head. These are known as prenominal modifiers and constitute subclasses of the adjectival. Let us begin with the simple modification structure of determiner plus noun head, e.g.,

D   NH
the fence

In case your memory has misted over here are the determiners again:

Article	Poss. Aj.	Poss. of Names	Demonstrative
the	her	John's	this
a/an	his		that
	its		these
	my		those
	our		
	their		
	your		

Between the determiner and the noun is the position for adjectives:

D	AJ	NH
that	low	fence
your	sturdy	fence

The same position is also occupied by nouns that modify the noun head, e.g.,

D	N	NH
our	garden	fence
their	wire	fence

When an adjective and a noun both precede the noun head, the adjective precedes the modifying noun, thus:

D	AJ	N	NH
our	sturdy	garden	fence
that	low	wire	fence

Exercise 17–6

Make each list of words into a noun phrase following the pattern of *D Aj N NH*.

1. a, street, village, narrow _____
2. large, dormitory, college, this _____
3. players, tall, those, sophomore _____
4. photogenic, swimmer, that, girl _____
5. this, counselor, enthusiastic, senior _____
6. wool, blue, necktie, George's _____
7. leather, her, shoes, old _____
8. desk, hardwood, large, his _____
9. cheap, ballpoint, these, pens _____
10. typewriter, student, my, portable _____

This pattern of *D Aj N NH* is often ambiguous, as the adjective may modify either the first noun or the second noun. Consider

a decent college graduate.

This phrase may mean either "graduate of a decent college" or "decent graduate of a college." The overlapping of stress patterns may play a part in such ambiguities, as in

Those hôt cár dèals.

Here the modifier-plus-noun stress pattern of ˆ ′ (hôt cár) overlaps with that of the compound-noun ′ ˋ (cár dèals). Thus the meaning can be either "hot car-deals" (car deals that are hot) or "hot-car deals" (deals in hot cars).

Exercise 17–7

Give two meanings for each of these ambiguous noun phrases.

1. A smâll árms fàctory   a. _____

                                                            b. _____

2. That grêasy kíd stùff   a. _____
                                b. _____
3. The bâsic bóok sèrvice   a. _____
                                b. _____
4. A fôreign lánguage tèacher   a. _____
                                b. _____
5. An ôld cár enthùsiast   a. _____
                                b. _____

We can now add to the prenominal modifiers another group, one that precedes the determiners and whose members are called predeterminers. This group consists of *all, both, half, double,* and a few others, as in

PRE/D	D	AJ	N	NH
all	my	old	school	friends

Exercise 17–8
Make each list into a noun phrase, beginning with a predeterminer.

1. blocks, your, cement, half, new   _____
2. long, copper, wires, all, the   _____
3. engagement, both, lovely, her, rings   _____
4. fresh, those, flowers, prairie, all   _____
5. recalcitrant, both, coons, baby, my   _____

The possessive of common nouns (not personal or geographical) appears between the determiner and the noun head. Let us examine its possible positions, using the pattern

D	AJ	N	NH
the	red	garden	roses

We will use the noun possessive *summer's* and see where it fits.

D		AJ	NH
the	summer's	red	roses

D	AJ		NH
the	red	summer's	roses

D		N	NH
the	summer's	garden	roses

D		AJ	N	NH
the	summer's	red	garden	roses

All these sound like normal English. But we would not say

D	N		NH
the	garden	summer's	roses

So it appears that the possessive of common nouns occurs anywhere between the determiner and the noun head, except between N and NH. Yet what about

D	N		NH
a	cotton	man's	shirt?

This too sounds English. It is likely that different subclasses of the noun or the noun possessive permit different positioning patterns. This is a matter that requires investigation. With this limitation in mind we can say here that the possessive of common nouns can occur anywhere between the determiner and the noun head.

These noun possessives at times make for ambiguity in the noun phrase. For example, we can interpret *the late summer's roses* as "the roses of late summer" or "the late roses of summer." Such ambiguities in the written words sometimes disappear in the spoken form because of the ability of the suprasegmentals to distinguish meanings. The noun phrase *her new doll's house* is ambiguous to the eye, but the ear will distinguish between *hèr nêw dôll's hóuse* and *hèr nêw dóll's hòuse*.

Exercise 17–9

Give two meanings for each of these noun phrases in their written form.

1. An old girl's bicycle   a. _____
   b. _____

2. The world women's congress   a. _____
   b. _____

3. A nice woman's fur coat   a. _____
   b. _____

4. A large woman's garment   a. _____
   b. _____

5. An advanced learner's dictionary   a. _____
   b. _____

The next step is to enlarge the class of determiners. The fourteen determiners you have learned can all be preceded by the predeterminers *all, both,* and *half.* But besides these fourteen there is a second set of determiners, and these are not preceded by predeterminers. There are twelve of the latter:

another	either	neither	what (a)
any	enough	no	which
each	much	some	whose

These belong in the determiner class because they precede adjectives and are mutually exclusive both with one another and with the members of the first set.[3] The first set we shall label the *the* determiners, subset A; the others are the *another* determiners, subset B.

---

[3] Don't be misled by cases like *this much cider.* Here *this* is not a prenominal modifier. It does not modify *much cider* or *cider;* it is a qualifier like *very* and merely modifies *much.*

The order of the prenominal modifiers we have examined so far may be shown thus:

V	IV	III	II	I	NH
Pre D	*Det*	(Class yet	*Aj*	*Noun*	
	A. *the*	to come.)			
	B. *another*				

Exercise 17–10

Place above each modifier the number of the class to which it belongs. In this and the following exercises be careful about two successive nouns. They may be either a noun modifying a following noun, as in *côllege déan,* or a single compound noun, as in *cláss pìn.*

	IVB	II	I	NH
Example:	any	small	cloth	rag

1. Another huge glass ornament

2. Each happy farm duck

3. Some long winter vacations

4. All our friendly neighborhood dogs

5. Either short cotton dress

6. Enough college friends

7. Both my studious roommates

8. No cold cheese sandwich

9. Much evening enjoyment

10. Neither tired economics student

Above you noticed a blank Class III. This contains words that follow determiners and precede adjectives and are called postdeterminers. The list is as follows:

ordinal numbers: first, second . . . last
cardinal numbers: one, two, three . . .

every	most
few	other
less	same
little (quantity)	several
many (a)	single
more	such (a)

This is an untidy class. Not all postdeterminers can follow all determiners, but each one can follow at least one determiner. And within the group there are complicated orders of precedence. For example, *other* usually follows, not precedes, another postdeterminer, as in *many other boys, several other boys, most other boys, few other boys;* but when *other* is combined with a cardinal number, either order is allowed: *the three other boys, the other three boys.* If you try to plot the precedences of these postdeterminers, you will end with about six columns. This whole jungle of determiners and postdeterminers is a *terra incognita* that has not yet been mapped out with complete success. For our purpose it will suffice to recognize the class as a whole without exploring its internal complications.

Exercise 17–11
Place the class number—V, IV, III, II, or I—above each modifier.

1. The last three pickles
2. His every wish
3. Many fine university seniors
4. Some other bad newspaper reports
5. Much more white sand
6. Those same hungry ants
7. Both those two aimless fellows
8. Any such childish pranks
9. Harry's few acquaintances
10. What other foolish ideas

Exercise 17–12
Make each list of words into a noun phrase. Above each modifier write the number of the class to which it belongs.

1. summer, several, flowers, pink   _____
2. garden, both, old, his, hoes   _____
3. junctures, three, these, all, terminal   _____
4. bad, schedule, another, examination   _____
5. two, silk, my, dresses, pretty   _____

Exercise 17–13
Make each list into two noun phrases, and write above each modifier the number of the class to which it belongs.

1. truck, delivery, any, large   _____

2. that, steel, heavy, construction _____

3. excellent, some, factory, parts _____

4. vacation, summer, long, student's, the _____

5. dog, first, good, her, house _____

One final class of prenominals remains, the restricters. This is a very small set of words like *just, only, even, especially, merely.* Like the other prenominals these can modify the noun head alone—

just girls
even water
especially candy

or the noun head with its modifiers—

just college girls
just romantic college girls
just another romantic college girl.

These precede the predeterminers and are therefore in Column VI (see page 258) to the left of the noun head.

Exercise 17–14

Make a noun phrase of each list and write above each modifier its class number.

1. guests, all, our, especially _____
2. kitten, spotted, particularly, her _____
3. the, empty, even, box _____
4. white, socks, athletic, some, just _____
5. only, ten, minutes, short _____

A summary of the prenominal modifiers is given in the chart on page 258.

This brief look at the six subclasses of prenominal adjectivals is perhaps enough to give you an inkling of the complexity of the modifications that we practice in our daily speech. We have left numerous questions of prenominal order unexplored, and we might take just a quick look to see what they are like. Here are a few:

1. What is the position of these classes?

a. uninflected adjectivals: an *inside* look
b. {-ING vb} verbs: an *approaching* stranger
c. {-D pp} verbs: the *fallen* snow

PRENOMINAL MODIFIERS

VI	V	IV	III	II	I	Noun Head
Restricter	*Predeterminer*	*Determiner*	*Postdeterminer*	*Adjective*	*Noun*	

VI Restricter	V Predeterminer	IV Determiner	III Postdeterminer	II Adjective	I Noun
EXAMPLES: especially even just merely only particularly almost nearly	EXAMPLES: all both half double	A. ARTICLES a/an the POSSESSIVE ADJS. her his its my our their your POSS. OF NAMES John's DEMONSTRATIVES: this that these those B. another any each either enough much neither no some what (a) which whose	CARDINAL NUMBERS: 1, 2, 3 . . . ORDINAL NUMBERS: first, second . . . last every few less little (quantity) many (a) more most other same several single such (a) POSS. OF COMMON NOUN	EXAMPLES: red blue green old new young big little (size) large small high low tall short thick thin intellectual dogmatic thoughtful commendable excellent prevalent Japanese Chinese American silken woolen wooden POSS. OF COMMON NOUN	EXAMPLES: school college dormitory house garden fence garage gate summer rock wool silk steel iron clay plastic cloth brass copper leather nylon brick cement paper shoe coat skirt

2. In Class I which nouns precede which other nouns? For example, you would probably say "an iron garden gate" but not "a garden iron gate." What principle of precedence is operative here?

3. In Class II which adjectives precede which other adjectives? Would you say "a pink Chinese flower" or "a Chinese pink flower"? "A wonderful little book" or "a little wonderful book"? There are subclasses of adjectives in terms of precedence, e.g., those of color, nationality, and shape-size—and those inflected with -er and -est as opposed to those taking *more* and *most*. What orders of precedence do we as native speakers follow in using these different subclasses?

C. The Noun Phrase: Postnominal Modifiers

Modifiers of the noun headword may be placed after the headword as well as before it.

Examples:
1. The apartment, spotlessly *clean*
2. The apartment, *large* and *empty*
3. The apartment *downstairs*
4. The freshmen *especially*
5. The weather *this morning*
6. The apartment *in front*
7. The apartment *standing empty*
8. The apartment *located in the rear*
9. The apartment *to rent*
10. The apartment *which is empty*
11. The apartment, *the home of the Snopeses*

After the next exercise these postnominal modifiers will be described in the order of the examples above.

Exercise 17–15

Each of the italicized expressions above has the function of modifying the headword, but each is different in form. In the following sentences similar noun modifiers are italicized. After each sentence place the number of the modifier above to which it corresponds.

1. We watched the brown river, *swollen with rain*. _____
2. I want to rent the bicycle *outside*. _____
3. It was a large outdoor swing, *the property of our neighbor*. _____
4. The fireworks were a sight *to behold*. _____
5. The hoe *leaning against the house* is dull. _____
6. The mountaintop, *high* and *craggy*, was hidden in a cloud. _____
7. The building *which is near the library* is new. _____
8. The fan *in the corner* has only one speed. _____
9. I'll see you the day *before you go*. _____
10. The skiing *last winter* was good. _____

11. That car *in front* is mine. _____
12. There stood Jane, *miserably tired.* _____
13. The seniors *especially* arrived early. _____

FORMS OF POSTNOMINAL MODIFIERS

1. Modified Adjective. A bare adjective modifying a noun often occurs in the prenominal position. But an adjective in the postnominal position is usually modified by a qualifier.

The mailman, exuberantly *happy,* whistled merrily.
He had never seen a woman more *lovely.*

2. Compounded Adjectives. When two or more adjectives modify a noun, they can occur after the noun.

The mailman, *weary* and *wet,* trudged along in the rain.
A woman *old* and *gaunt* stood at the door.

Exercise 17–16

Underline the postnominal adjectivals.

1. A new blossom, scarlet and exotic, excited his attention.
2. The emerald ring, inordinately expensive, was beyond his means.
3. There stood the quivering horse, stalwart and proud.
4. He tossed the bag, new and glossy, into the luggage compartment.
5. The problem, extremely complicated, would not yield to his operations.

---

3. Uninflected Word. Nouns may be modified by some of the uninflected words that are often adverbial. (See p. 231.)

The people *upstairs*
The poker game *now*

The uninflected word in this position usually has a place or time meaning.

Exercise 17–17

Underline each postnominal modifier and put a wavy line under the noun it modifies. Insert primary stresses and juncture arrows.

Example: The river belów → wound through the górge.

1. The paragraph above is too long.
2. The students here are a courteous group.
3. This matter too must be discussed.
4. The party yesterday had a large attendance.
5. The weather outside is foul.

4. Adverb. An adverb may modify a noun that precedes it.

My meaning exactly
The blue dress particularly

Structures like 3 (uninflected word) and 4 (adverb) above will now and then be ambiguous in writing, as in

The poker game now is exciting.
The blue dress particularly interested her.

This happens because the postnominal position coincides with the preverbal position. In such cases the suprasegmentals usually show whether the word in the ambiguous position modifies the preceding noun or the following verb; thus in speech the ambiguity is eliminated.

The poker game nów → is excíting.
The póker game → now is excíting.
The blue dress partícularly → ínterested her.
The blue dréss → partícularly interested her.

Exercise 17–18

The sentences below are ambiguous. For each put in the primary stress and the sustained juncture arrow that will indicate that the word in the ambiguous position goes with what follows it.

Example: The méetings → thereafter took place in the Georgian Lóunge.

1. My older brother especially likes to go fishing.
2. The discussion later was heated.
3. Her fiancé then was Elmer Jukes. (*then* = at that time)
4. The rabbits also enjoyed our lettuce.
5. The members only were allowed to buy beer.

Oral Exercise 17–A

Read aloud each sentence in the preceding exercise as you have marked it. Then read each one aloud in a different way to show a sustained juncture AFTER the modifier instead of before it.

---

5. Noun Phrase Adjectival. A noun phrase may modify a preceding noun.

The party *last night*
Our vacation *next summer*

Exercise 17–19

Underline each noun phrase that modifies a noun.

1. The decision that time was correct.
2. The lecture this morning was sparkling.

3. Your dinner the next time had better be good.
4. My course last fall converted me.
5. Your class the third hour always begins late.

---

6. Prepositional Phrase Adjectival

The bend *in the river*

7. Participle or Participial Phrase, *-ing*, Adjectival [4]

The woman *weeping* was escorted to the door.
The hawk, *spotting his prey*, swooped to the meadow.

8. Participle or Participial Phrase, *-ed*, Adjectival

They refused to pay the money *demanded*.
The snow, *driven by the wind*, sifted through the cracks.

9. Infinitive Phrase Adjectival, *to* ——

I have a lesson *to study*.

Exercise 17–20

Underline the words or phrases of the preceding four types (6–9) that modify nouns. In the blanks indicate by number the type of phrase.

1. The majority of the voters appeared satisfied.   ———
2. There was Al, licking his ice-cream cone.   ———
3. She gave him a sandwich to eat.   ———
4. Johnny wanted the red scooter with the white trim.   ———
5. We watched the fullback, urged on by the crowd, fight his way forward.   ———
6. Do you have something to do?   ———
7. The sailboat gliding across the bay looked majestic.   ———
8. On the river bank sat little Robert, covered with mud.   ———
9. The roof of the garage was beginning to leak.   ———
10. The puppies tugging at the rope soon gave up.   ———
11. No man living has seen this tomb chamber.   ———
12. She was disappointed in the results obtained.   ———

---

10. Relative Clause Adjectival. A noun may be modified by a relative clause. In the examples that follow the relative clauses are italicized.

1. The trees *that had mistletoe* were half dead.
2. The old carpenter, *who had been laying the floor,* stood up and straightened his back.

---

[4] In 7·and 8 the entire participial phrase is an adjectival modifying the preceding noun—*hawk* and *snow*. Within these phrases, *spotting,* and *driven* are verbals. Other analyses are possible.

3. The partner *whom she selected* was a bashful, red-headed boy.
4. In the bargain basement he found his sister, *whom he had been look-ing for.*
5. It was the vice-president *to whom I sent the letter.*
6. The client *whose stock he was handling* died.
7. The boat *he wants* is a catamaran.
8. The success *that you become* depends on your initiative.

With the help of these examples we can easily learn to identify relative clauses, which have these characteristics:

   a. A relative clause is introduced by a relative: *that, who, whom, whose, which,* and *ø* (= zero or omitted).
   b. The relative has a function in its own clause. For instance, in sentences 1 and 2 *that* and *who* are subjects of the verb. In sentence 3 *whom* is the direct object. In sentences 4 and 5 *whom* is the object of a preposition. In sentence 6 *whose* is a modifier. In sentence 7 the relative is omitted. Such a zero relative can always be replaced by a *that* functioning as the direct object or subjective complement. In sentence 8 *that* is a subjective complement.

Exercise 17–21

Underline each relative clause, double-underline the relative, and tell in the blank the function of the relative, using these abbreviations:

SV = subject of verb   SC = subjective complement
DO = direct object   Md = modifier
OP = object of preposition   ø = relative omitted

1. The composer whom he studied with was Hindemith him-self. _____
2. The doctor who performed the operation was Bernard Diamond. _____
3. That is the book I ordered. _____
4. The bait that Jack used was an old-fashioned spinner. _____
5. This is Roger Stuffy, whose mother is president of the PTA. _____
6. The old battered boathouse, which had long been our meeting place, was torn down. _____
7. She is not the woman that her mother was. _____
8. He was a young, blue-eyed pilot, who immediately won our hearts. _____
9. Another boy who helps me is Skunky Hooper. _____
10. The girl whom I met at the play disappeared during the intermission. _____

We shall next divide relative clauses into two kinds, a division that is useful for punctuation and for control of meaning. The two kinds are traditionally called restrictive and nonrestrictive clauses.[5] Let's begin with examples:

Restrictive: He walked to the garage *which he liked best.*
Nonrestrictive: He walked to the garage, *which was a mile away.*

Do you sense the difference in the structural meaning of the two relative clauses? The first clause points out one garage among many. Of all the garages, he walked to the particular one that he preferred. This can be called a defining clause. In the second sentence, however, there is only one garage, and as additional information we learn that it is a mile away. This can be called a commenting clause. In short, the restrictive clause restricts the meaning to part of the total, but the nonrestrictive clause makes no such limitation. This is the semantic way of distinguishing the two kinds of relative clauses.

Now we shall distinguish them structurally by means of terminal junctures. Look at these two cases:

$$\text{2 \quad 3 \ 2 \ 2 \qquad 3 \quad 2 \ 2 \qquad 3 \qquad\qquad 1}$$
Nonrestrictive: The bóy → who often úshers → has been rúshing me ↓
$$\text{2 \qquad\qquad 3 \quad 2 \ 2 \qquad 3 \quad 1}$$
Restrictive: The boy who úshers → is my latest stéady ↓

The key is in the **word that precedes the relative**—in these examples, the word *boy.* If this preceding word is lengthened (i.e., if it is followed by a terminal juncture), the relative clause is nonrestrictive, as in the first example above. But if no terminal juncture is present at this point, the relative clause is restrictive, as in the second example. Here are two more examples:

$$\text{3 \qquad 1}$$
Nonrestrictive: Billie whistled to Rágs, ↓ who thumped his tail on the floor. ("Rags" is lengthened, i.e., is followed by a terminal.)
$$\text{3 \qquad 2}$$
Restrictive: They didn't like the hédge that I planted. ("Hedge" is not lengthened, i.e., is not followed by a terminal.)

Exercise 17–22
Read each sentence aloud in a natural manner, using the punctuation as a guide. If you lengthen the **word preceding the relative,** insert the appropriate terminal juncture after the word.

At the end of the sentence place an R or NR to indicate whether the relative clause is restrictive or nonrestrictive.

[5] Note: The restrictive-nonrestrictive distinction is characteristic of all postnominal-phrase modifiers: prepositional phrases, participial phrases in *-ing* and *-ed*, infinitive phrases, appositives, and noun phrases. This is not surprising, as all of these can be considered as elliptical forms of relative clauses.

Examples: 1. The daughter who was eighteen won the pretzel-
baking contest.[6]   R

       2. Chris married the youngest daughter, ↓ who was
a winsome lass of eighteen.   NR

1. The blouse that she preferred was made of sea island cotton. ____
2. She wore an old blue blouse, which had always been her favorite.   ____
3. The house, which he had long admired, was built of bricks. ____
4. The house that he built was of steel.   ____
5. Jane, who is fond of dictionaries, bought the new *Webster's
Third.*   ____
6. The man whom I marry must have curly hair.   ____
7. I'll take a man who respects me.   ____
8. The car I want is an MG.   ____
9. The student whose purse he returned offered Dick a generous
reward.   ____
10. Thomas bought a silk, red-and-gray-striped necktie, which his
roommate admired.   ____

By this time you have probably noticed the relation between the type of relative clause and its punctuation: a nonrestrictive clause is set off. And now you should have no trouble in punctuating them. But as a lagniappe here are a few practical hints:

1. A *that* clause is always restrictive.
2. A clause with a zero relative is restrictive.
3. If you can substitute *that* for *who, whom,* or *which,* the clause is restrictive.
5. After a personal or geographical name, like Elmer Perkins or Brandy Branch, the clause is usually nonrestrictive.

Relative clauses may also begin with *when, where, why, after, before,* and similar words, e.g.,

The hour *when we leave* has not been decided.

These relatives function as adverbials within the relative clause.

---

[6] Here you may lengthen *eightéen,* producing a juncture, but this has nothing to do with the R/NR distinction, for in speaking we normally place a juncture between the complete subject and the verb, when the subject is long. It is what happens at *daughter who* that counts. Here nothing happens, so the clause is restrictive. But in 2, you have ... *dáughter ↓ who;* hence the clause is non-restrictive.

Exercise 17–23

Underline the relative clause and write the relative in the blank at the right.

1. Do you know the reason why she deserted him? _____
2. The woods where we camp are filled with mushrooms. _____
3. The year after he enlisted was a momentous one. _____
4. Let me know the minute when he comes in. _____
5. I cannot find the place where I lost it. _____

The relative *that* belongs in the **structure class** of **relatives.** It should not be confused with the *that* which is a member of the **structure class** of **subordinating conjunctions.** These will be taken up very soon. The subordinating conjunction *that* stands outside the sentence pattern of its clause and performs no function in it. Example: I know *that* he is sick.

Exercise 17–24

Encircle each relative and indicate its function. Underline each subordinating conjunction.

1. The lawyer said that the will must be filed. _____
2. The lawyer that he chose was a shyster. _____
3. It cannot be doubted that he is competent. _____
4. Are you sure that you returned the book? _____
5. The book that cost me a fine was *The Castle.* _____

Similarly, the relatives *when, where, why, after,* and *before* should not be confused with their homophones, which are subordinating conjunctions connecting nominal or adverbial clauses with the rest of the sentence. Here are five illustrative sentences with the nominal or adverbial clauses italicized.

Exercise 17–25

Underline the subordinating conjunction in each sentence, noting that it stands outside the clause and serves the function of connector.

1. Phone me *when you are about to leave.* (adverbial clause)
2. Did you find out *where she lives*? (nominal clause in DO slot)
3. We always pick up the litter *after we have picknicked in a public park.* (adverbial clause)
4. You must mow the lawn *before you leave to play tennis.* (adverbial clause)
5. I know *why he bought the car.* (nominal clause in DO slot)

11. Appositive Adjectival. The final postnominal modifier that we shall study is the appositive. The two examples following show what an appositive is.

2   3   2 2   3   2 2   3   1

The *Bailey Búgle* → a college néwspaper → appears wéekly ↓

2   3   1 2   3   1

The top awards were won by two sísters ↓ horsewomen in the riding set ↓

In these sentences the expressions *a college newspaper* and *horsewomen in the riding set* are the appositives. From these sentences we observe that:

1. An appositive is a noun phrase (frequently a noun):

a college newspaper
horsewomen in the riding set

2. An appositive follows a noun phrase or noun:

The *Bailey Bugle,* a college newspaper
two sisters, horsewomen in the riding set

Occasionally an appositive occurs in a position other than after a noun or noun phrase, e.g.,

That was what he wanted, *a riding horse.*

A promising lad of eighteen, Harry was soon a favorite among his class-mates.

3. An appositive and the noun phrase or noun it follows have the same referent—that is, they refer to the same entity. In our examples the *Bugle* and *a college newspaper* are the same thing, the *sisters* and *horsewomen* are the same persons.

Exercise 17–26

Underline each appositive.

1. His heart was set on Alpha Gamma Beta, the debating club.
2. Mary Evans, a graduate in journalism, became a feature writer for *The Saturday Review.*
3. The three puppies, offspring of registered parents, were taken to the veterinarian's office.
4. A Republican from Vodka Valley, Ivanovitch sat at the speaker's table.
5. We pushed off with the boat into the river, a sluggish, slowly winding stream.

Appositives may be divided into two kinds, restrictive and nonrestrictive, distinguished by the suprasegmentals that accompany them. Here they are:

2   3   1

Restrictive: Richard visited his friend the dóctor. ↓

<pre>
          2   3   1 2   3   1
</pre>
Nonrestrictive: Richard visited the dóctor, ↓ a friend from cóllege days. ↓

With the restrictive appositive there is no juncture between the noun phrase and its following appositive—in the first example above, between *friend* and *the doctor.* But with the nonrestrictive appositive there is a terminal juncture at this point, shown in writing by a comma. This terminal is usually a sustained → or a rising ↑ juncture. However, it is likely to be the fading juncture ↓ if at this point the sentence pattern may be considered complete. For example,

<pre>
  2 3   2 2   3   2 2   3   1
The mótorcycle, → a secondhand contráption, → was in good shápe ↓
  2   3   1 2   3   1
They stopped before the hóuse, ↓ a decorated Victorian mánsion ↓
</pre>

Exercise 17–27

Underline each appositive. Supply the marks of stress, pitch, and juncture on the word before each nonrestrictive appositive. In each blank indicate, by R and NR, whether the appositive is restrictive or nonrestrictive.

1. We saw *Hamlet,* a play by Shakespeare. _____
2. Next week they will present the play *Hamlet.* _____
3. My brother Keith is a good tennis player. _____
4. Keith, my oldest brother, is a good tennis player. _____
5. The poet Shelley wrote "Adonais." _____
6. The river Severn is wide at the mouth. _____
7. William the Conqueror crossed the English Channel. _____
8. The class was studying Byron, a fiery, Romantic poet. _____

In writing, two postnominal modifiers are often placed in succession after the noun head. This practice causes structural ambiguity when it is not clear what the second modifier refers to. For example:

> Many institutions are now offering plans other than straight savings accounts that offer premium interest.

Here the second modifiers, *that offer premium interest,* can modify either *plans* or *accounts.* The next case contains an ambiguity that had to be settled by the courts:

> The law requires that the applicant be "conscientiously opposed to participation in war in any form."

The question was whether *in any form* modifies *war* or *participation.*

Oral Exercise 17–B

Point out the ambiguities caused by two successive postnominal modifiers. These modifiers are set off by brackets.

1. The poem was about the land [next to the poet's own] [which Mr. Edwards uses in the summer].
2. There were two stairways [leading to each floor] [which could accommodate all the people in case of emergency].
3. Prominent people who have been robbed include Lord Peel, [a descendant of Sir Robert Peel,] [who lost $19,200 worth of antiques].
4. Few couples [with children] [that are not rich] can afford to live in Manhattan.
5. We enjoyed the party [after the game] [yesterday].

D. The Verb Phrase: One-Word Adverbials

A verb phrase, as you have already seen, consists of a verb and all the modifiers and complements that cluster around it. The one-word modifiers are the adverbials, which you have already studied in some of their characteristic positions. All adverbials in these positions are part of the verb phrase, except those that serve the function of sentence modifiers. We classified the three common kinds of adverbials as expressing time, place, and manner. Then we subdivided the time adverbials into three subclasses —adverbials of definite time, frequency, and duration. Although these five categories account for the majority of one-word adverbials, there are also others that are outside these classes, e.g.,

... will *perhaps* drive.
... should do it *anyway*.
... may dance *instead*.

Here a short review exercise may be salutary.

Exercise 17–28

Underline the one-word adverbials in these verb phrases. After each sentence classify them as P (place), M (manner), DT (definite time), F (frequency), D (duration), and O (other).

1. ... shouted angrily.   _____
2. ... often drove without her license.   _____
3. ... rarely drove carelessly.   _____   _____
4. ... felt fearfully in the drawer.   _____
5. ... never work long.   _____   _____
6. ... was walking ahead.   _____
7. ... could even smell him.   _____
8. ... had always lived there.   _____   _____
9. ... was sewing inside.   _____
10. ... may still snow.   _____
11. ... were happily chatting in the patio.   _____
12. ... put it anywhere.   _____
13. ... cautiously looked sidewise.   _____   _____
14. ... read the story aloud.   _____

15. ... tasted the ginger timidly.   ———
16. ... studies nights.   ———
17. ... gnashes his teeth sleeping.   ———
18. ... ate seated.   ———
19. ... played cleaner than the others.   ———
20. ... came prepared.   ———

E. The Verb Phrase: Word-Group Adverbials

In the verb phrase we find various kinds of word groups operating to modify the verb headword. They are the following:

1. Prepositional phrase adverbials: eats *in the kitchen*
2. Noun phrase adverbials: eats *every hour*
3. Clause adverbials: eats *when he is hungry*
4. Infinitive phrase adverbials: eats *to satisfy his appetite*
5. Participial phrases in -ing as adverbials: came *running to the table*
6. Participial phrases in -ed as adverbials: returned *wounded in the leg*

1. Prepositional Phrase Adverbials. Prepositional phrases that modify the verb headword often come right after the verb, in adverbial position 4:

The car slid *into the garage.*

Two such modifying phrases may appear in succession, each modifying the verb:

The car slid *into the garage with its headlights on.*

Positions before the verb (position 2) and within the auxiliary-verb combination (position 3) are also possible:

Harry *at that time* was studying Akkadian.
Harry was *at that time* studying Akkadian.

And after the direct object one may often find a prepositional phrase modifying the verb head (position 5):

He put the chair *on the lawn.*

Two of the positions mentioned above are subject to ambiguity. You can guess which ones if you remember that in the noun phrase a prepositional phrase modifies an immediately preceding noun, e.g.,

The chair *on the lawn*
The garage *with the lights on*

They are the postnominal positions, of course—the one after the object of the preposition and the one after the direct object. Here is what can happen:

The car coasted into the garage with the lights on.
He found the chair on the lawn.

Each sentence is here structurally ambiguous.

Exercise 17–29

After each sentence write N if the italicized prepositional phrase modifies a noun headword, V if it modifies a verb headword, and Amb if it is structurally ambiguous.

1. He greeted the girl *with a smile.* _____
2. The child *in the blue rompers* ran *into the kitchen.* _____ _____
3. Jake was fishing *from the bridge* *for the first time.* _____ _____
4. He looked at the girl *with the binoculars.* _____
5. We watched the game *on the front porch.* _____
6. We had never *until that time* visited the tomb. _____
7. She hurried *to the auditorium* *for her interview.* _____ _____
8. The flower *between the pages* was flat and dried. _____
9. She pressed the flower *between the pages.* _____
10. Georgia waited *in her room* *for the news.* _____ _____

2. Noun Phrase Adverbials. Noun phrases are used as modifiers in the verb phrase to modify the verb head or the head with auxiliaries, as in

... held the hammer *that way.*
... will pay *the next time.*

Exercise 17–30

Underline the modifying noun phrases in these verb phrases.

1. ... will see you this Friday.
2. ... sold the cat the following day.
3. ... had come the whole way.
4. ... work a little while.
5. ... return another time.

3. Clause Adverbials.[7] Clause adverbials in this context are those word groups that have a subject and predicate and begin with such words as *after, although, as, as if, as soon as, because, before, if, once, since, that, unless, until, when, where, in case (that), in order that.* These words are called **subordinating conjunctions.** Unlike the relatives they have no function within the clause they introduce. They state a relationship, e.g., cause, time, condition, and, in the function of connectors, make the clause a part of a larger grammatical structure. When such clauses are separated from the rest of the sentence by juncture, they are sentence modifiers, as we have learned. But when they occur in the verb phrase with no junctural separation, they are modifiers of the verb or modified verb.

[7] Also called adverbial clauses.

Examples: The terrified lad ran *until he was exhausted.*
Call *when you need me.*
I'll scream *unless you let go.*
She telephoned *as soon as she could.*
He looked at the toad *as if it were poisonous.*

Subordinating conjunctions constitute another part of speech, not a form-class but a structure-class. The structure-classes, you recall, are small and closed classes that we identify by position. So far you have met the structure-classes of determiner, auxiliary, personal pronoun, qualifier, relative, and preposition, each occupying its characteristic position.

Subordinating conjunctions perform the grammatical job of connecting, and so, in function, are connectors. Some words in those other structure-classes are also connectors by function: prepositions and relatives, which you have already met, and coordinating conjunctions, which will appear shortly.[8]

Exercise 17–31

Identify the structure-class of the italicized words, using Aux (auxiliary), D (determiner), P (preposition), Q (qualifier) and SCj (subordinating conjunction).

1. *Each* student *can* have one ticket.　　　＿＿＿＿　＿＿＿＿
2. Please shut *the* door *when* you leave.　　　＿＿＿＿　＿＿＿＿
3. She has been very happy *since* he asked her *to* the prom.　　　＿＿＿＿　＿＿＿＿
4. It looks *as if* it *may* rain.　　　＿＿＿＿　＿＿＿＿
5. The job will be *quite* easy *after* you have started.　　　＿＿＿＿　＿＿＿＿

Exercise 17–32

Identify the function-class of the italicized words, using Md (modifier) and C (connector)

1. They ran *around* the track.　　　＿＿＿＿
2. Jake bought *a* motorbike.　　　＿＿＿＿
3. Come early *if* you can.　　　＿＿＿＿
4. Georgie seems *rather* gloomy today　　　＿＿＿＿
5. I'll wait *until* class is over.　　　＿＿＿＿
6. They walked *to* the pool.　　　＿＿＿＿
7. We'll be late *unless* you hurry.　　　＿＿＿＿
8. The door *of* the room was open.　　　＿＿＿＿
9. *Those* planes are easy to fly.　　　＿＿＿＿
10. Jim lost the race *because* he stumbled.　　　＿＿＿＿

[8] Relatives have a double function: that of connector and that of the relative's function in its clause, that is, SV, DO, etc.

Exercise 17–33

The modifying word groups in each verb phrase are italicized. Identify each one as PpP (prepositional phrase), NP (noun phrase), or CAv (clause adverbial).

1. Come *as you are.* _____
2. Gerald has been working on his paper *the whole afternoon.* _____
3. I'll wait for you *where the road forks.* _____
4. I'll just sit *a while.* _____
5. The blue jay perched *on the eaves.* _____
6. Ellen has not written *since she left.* _____
7. Don't touch that wire *with your bare hands.* _____
8. Please mail this *before the post office closes.* _____
9. Bernie walks *two miles* to school *every day.* _____ _____
10. Let me know *if you need assistance.* _____
11. Why don't you come over *this evening?* _____
12. We must get home *before the sun rises.* _____
13. I'll write that letter *the first thing* in the morning. _____
14. You can't stop *once you have started.* _____
15. He will be at the office *until it closes.* _____

4. Infinitive Phrase Adverbials. It is necessary to distinguish between the infinitive phrase as adverbial modifier and as a direct object of the verb. The distinction can easily be made by substitution, as you learned in the section on adverbials. These sentences will remind you:

Adverbial Modifier: He works *to (= in order to) succeed.* (Sentence pattern 6)
Object: He wants *to succeed (= it/that).* (Sentence pattern 7)

Exercise 17–34

In each blank label the italicized infinitive phrase as AM (adverbial modifier) or DO (direct object of verb).

1. The children like *to gather hazelnuts.* _____
2. They waited *to see the result.* _____
3. O'Brian wanted *to be relieved of the office.* _____
4. O'Brian dieted *to reduce his weight.* _____
5. She studied long hours *to make an A in the course.* _____

5. Participial Phrases in *-ing* and in *-ed* as Adverbials. You have previously met participial phrases in *-ing* and *-ed* as modifiers of the noun.

Their function as modifiers in the verb phrase is similar, as these sentences will show:

Modifier of noun: The girl *eating the sundae* is a freshman.
Modifier of verb: The girl sat *eating a sundae.*
Modifier of noun: The sonata *played at the recital* was Beethoven's *32nd.*
Modifier of verb: He returned *defeated by the weather.*

Exercise 17–35

The participial phrases are italicized. Point out what they modify by NM (modifier of noun) and VM (modifier of verb).

1. He gulped his coffee *standing up.*   ———
2. She sat *fascinated by the music.*   ———
3. He left *encouraged by the interview.*   ———
4. The girl *laughing at his sally* is a flatterer.   ———
5. Hal spends every evening *drinking beer.*   ———
6. Professor Doolittle had a good time *arguing with his students.*   ———
7. He lay *drowned by the high tide.*   ———
8. The bicycle *smashed by the truck* was a total loss.   ———
9. He stood *addressing the crowd.*   ———
10. She entered *singing a gay tune.*   ———

Exercise 17–36

Using numbers 1 to 6 classify the italicized word-group adverbials in the verb phrase as

1. Prepositional phrase   4. Infinitive phrase
2. Noun phrase   5. Participial phrase in *-ing*
3. Clause adverbial   6. Participial phrase in *-ed*

1. The patient lay *on the operating table.*   ——
2. She labored *to improve her flower garden.*   ——
3. We must send them a card *this Christmas.*   ——
4. He fell *wounded by the arrow.*   ——
5. Open your eyes *when you hear the bell.*   ——
6. She danced *keeping her eyes closed.*   ——
7. Bring a chair *if you can.*   ——
8. Jim's work had much improved *by that time.*   ——
9. You can do the problem *either way.*   ——
10. She sat *splashing the water.*   ——

Oral Exercise 17–C

Adverbial modifiers in the verb phrase, both single and successive modifiers, can be a source of ambiguity. In the sentences below, such modifiers are enclosed in brackets. Explain the ambiguity in each sentence.

1. She washed the chair [on the porch].
2. I want a copy of the picture [in the paper].
3. He searched among the ruins I had sifted [for artifacts].
4. Cuba called [for planes] [to aid its radar].
5. Carl had been found guilty [of gambling] [in the municipal court].
6. He promised to call [at ten o'clock].
7. Take the big bag [upstairs].
8. It was a plot to sell industrial secrets worth millions [to the Dupont Company].
9. His work was drawn on [largely] by later dictionary makers.
10. Harriman, who headed the negotiating team in Moscow, Russia, invited the congressmen [to explain the situation].

Verbals Again. In the previous chapter, exercise 16–8, we dealt with sentence portions that contained verbals and were nominals by position. In this chapter, we have observed sentence portions that contain verbals (infinitive phrase, participial phrase in -*ing* and -*ed*) and that are not nominals, but adjectivals and adverbials. Now, let us solidify your grasp of verbals by an exercise which contains sentence portions that are nominal, adjectival, or adverbial. It may pay you to review Section A, near the beginning of this chapter, to refresh your mind on sentence modifiers.

Exercise 17–37

In each sentence below, a sentence portion containing a verbal is italicized. Indicate whether it is a nominal, adjectival, or adverbial by using the abbreviations Nom, Aj, or Av.

1. Jim wants *to become a physical therapist.* _____
2. *To become a physical therapist,* one must have five years of college training. _____
3. His ambition *to become a physical therapist* was strong. _____
4. That is a movie *to see.* _____
5. *The weather having cleared up,* we continued our game. _____
6. The player, *dispirited and protesting,* strode to the dressing room. _____
7. *Having been picking strawberries all morning,* we were quite tired. _____
8. The text *chosen by the instructor* was up to date. _____
9. Jenny admired the chip shot *performed by Nicklaus.* _____
10. Sue objected to *taking the test over.* _____
11. The girl *taking the test over* was Sue. _____
12. Karl opened his book bag *to look for his term paper.* _____
13. The desire *to finish his term paper* kept nagging at Karl. _____
14. His desire was *to finish his term paper early.* _____
15. The coach, *having diagramed the play,* waited for questions. _____

18
Levels of
Modification

A. Immediate Constituents

In our treatment of modification up to now we have dealt with only first-level modifiers and their heads. For example, in a noun phrase like

The man who stood on the corner of the street

we have pointed out that

who stood on the corner of the street

is a relative clause modifying its head, *man,* but we have ignored the modifiers of modifiers and the modifiers of modifiers of modifiers, ad infinitum. Let us illustrate these by means of the noun phrase above. Within the modifying clause

who stood on the corner of the street

we see that

on the corner of the street

is an adverbial modifying its head, *stood.* And within

on the corner of the street

it is apparent that

of the street

is an adjectival modifying its head, *corner*. We might show these internal modifications in terms of levels, like this:

	The man who stood on the corner of the street
M level 1:	*who stood on the corner of the street*
M level 2:	*on the corner of the street*
M level 3:	*of the street*

Or we might use concentric boxes or circles to diagram this nesting characteristic of modifiers:

H	H	H
The man ←	who stood ←	on the corner ← of the street

It is expedient, however, to deal with such levels or boxes of modification as part of a broader view of sentence structure known as immediate constituent analysis.

Grammatical structures in English, large and small, tend to be binary. This means that most structures can be divided into two parts and that native speakers of English show considerable agreement on the point of division. For example, where would you divide these structures into two parts?

1. The house on the hill was wrecked by the tornado.
2. Standing near the tomb
3. All my college friends

It is likely that most of your class will divide after *hill, standing,* and *all.*

Each of the two parts into which any structure is divided is called an immediate constituent, abbreviated IC. In the complete IC analysis of a sentence we cut the sentence into two parts, or IC's, then cut each of these two again into two, and so on until we have only individual words remaining as parts. Here is how such an analysis looks:

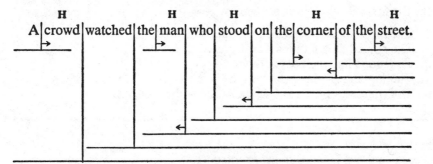

In this analysis an arrow points from each modifier to its head, and you can see in graphic form the levels of modification amid the total pattern.

Now we shall see how various English structures are cut into IC's, recognizing, however, that not all sentences are amenable to this kind of analysis and that there is an element of arbitrariness in our procedure.

1. Sentences Containing a Sentence Modifier. The first IC cut separates a sentence modifier from the rest of the sentence. Examples:

Of course, | the money must be paid.
→

Unless you learn to swim, | you cannot go on this trip.
→

To earn money, | they organized a car wash.
→

Speaking earnestly, | the lad convinced the dean.
→

I was sleeping, | to tell the truth.
←

Exercise 18–1

Make the first IC cut in these sentences:

1. In fact, both tires are flat.
2. When the game is over, let's meet for a bite to eat.
3. I'll give you a hand, certainly.
4. To attract birds, one must provide shelter and food.
5. Smiling slightly, she gently rebuked him.

---

2. Sentence. In a sentence without a sentence modifier the first cut is made between the noun phrase functioning as subject and the verb phrase functioning as predicate. Examples:

The canoe in the boathouse | had dried out during the winter.

The low-flying plane that roared above the trees | frightened the children.

Exercise 18–2

Make the first IC cut in these sentences.

1. The tulips in the flower bed drooped and died.
2. The striped Dutch tulips were gorgeous.
3. They soon had the boat in the water.
4. The lapping of the waves upon the shore lulled them to sleep.
5. The wine steward uncorked the bottle with a flourish.

Exercise 18–3

Make the first two IC cuts in these sentences.

Example: Unless you hurry, | we | shall be late.
→

1. Indeed, your first bullfight may not delight you.
2. Smoking a briar pipe, Thurston remained pensive.
3. If I weren't afraid, I would pet him.
4. We will build the float tomorrow, notwithstanding their objections.
5. At long last the letter of acceptance arrived.

---

3. Clause adverbials. In a clause adverbial the first IC cut is made after the subordinating conjunction, leaving as the two IC's the conjunction and a sentence.

Example: Although|it is growing late . . .

Exercise 18–4

Make your first IC cut in these clause adverbials.

1. When Hubert plays his guitar
2. Unless you bring a bottle opener
3. Since the paddle is broken
4. If the motor begins to cough
5. Once this rain is over

---

4. Relative Clause. If the relative is a subject *who, which,* or *that,* the first IC cut is made after this relative.[1]

Example: . . . who|plays in the band.

Exercise 18–5

Make the first IC cut in these relative clauses.

1. . . . who was late for dinner.
2. . . . that inspired him.
3. . . . which cost too much.
4. . . . which was chasing a rabbit.
5. . . . that caused my spine to tingle.

---

5. Prepositional Phrase. The first cut is right after the preposition.

Example: in|the box

---

[1] We shall bypass the relatives that function as object of the verb, object of the preposition, and subjective complement, but here is how they might be handled:

DO   which|they|found

OP   which|she|paid for

SC   that|your mother|was

Exercise 18–6

Make the first IC cut in these prepositional phrases.

1. under the fence
2. from the greenhouse
3. between the blue flowers
4. across the wide, sluggish river
5. to the flower-starred meadow

6. Infinitive Phrase. The first IC cut is made after the *to.*

Example: to|raise the most luscious sweet corn

This is a reasonable though arbitrary cut. Some speakers may feel with justice that the division is after *raise.*

Exercise 18–7

Make the first IC cut in these infinitive phrases.

1. to lessen the tension
2. to depend on that rope
3. to repair the parachute
4. to haul in the sail
5. to avoid the black flies

7. Noun Phrase. (a) Beginning at the end, cut off successively each postnominal modifier until you reach the noun head.

Example:

NH
The students|in the dormitory|who chatter all evening

Be careful about what goes with what in these postnominal modifiers.

NH   VH
Example: The students| who |chatter all evening| in the dormitory

In this example you will note that *in the dormitory* does not modify *students,* but, as the arrow shows, modifies *chatter all evening.*

Ambiguous postnominal modifiers offer more than one possibility of cutting.

NH   NH
Examples: The boy| in |the car| that wouldn't work

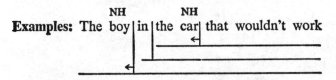

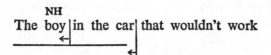

NH

The boy | in the car | that wouldn't work

(b) After you have cut off the postnominal modifiers, begin at the front and cut off successively the prenominal modifiers until you reach the noun head.

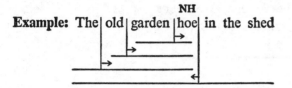

NH

Example: The | old | garden | hoe | in the shed

Exercise 18–8

Make all the IC cuts for the modifiers of the noun head in these noun phrases. Use arrows to show what modifies what. You will have to copy these sentences on other sheets of paper.

1. The boy on the corner who sells papers
2. A small ragged boy
3. A small boy on the corner who sells papers
4. The rabbits in the nest that was hidden
5. The rabbits in the nest that were hidden
6. The driver of the bus who was tired
7. The driver of the bus that was late
8. The bottle on the table there

---

8. Verb Phrase

a. Preverbal modifiers of the verb are cut off from the front, back to the verb head. There is seldom more than one before the verb.

VH

Example: happily | jumped on the table

b. Auxiliaries are cut off successively up to the verb head.

VH

Example: may | have | been | eating

Adverbials embedded in the auxiliaries are taken in order.

VH

Example: could | never | have | survived

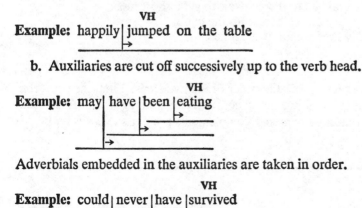

c. After the preverbal modifiers have been cut off, one begins at the back and cuts off successive modifiers and/or complements up to the verb head.

Examples:

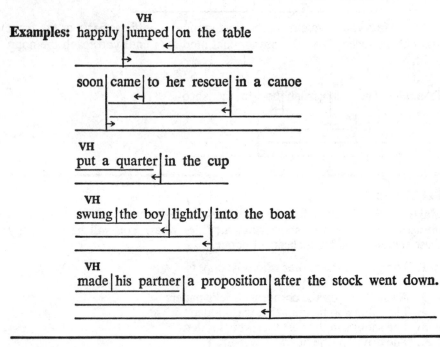

Exercise 18–9

Make the successive IC cuts for modifiers of the verb. Use arrows to show modification. Use other paper for this exercise.

1. ... reluctantly came to his mother when he heard the whistle
2. ... never swam in cold water after a heavy meal
3. ... at once ran to the coach upon seeing the hand signal
4. ... often walked to the pool in his bathing suit
5. ... eagerly grabbed at the gunwale to get a short rest
6. ... quickly pushed the boat onto the bank
7. ... carefully fired a shot at the target

In verb phrases remember the order of the two steps: First, the preverbal modifiers and auxiliaries are cut successively, beginning at the front. Second, the postverbal modifiers and complements are cut successively, beginning at the back.

Exercise 18–10

Make all the IC cuts required for the auxiliaries, adverbials, and complements in these verb clusters. Do not cut further into the phrases and clauses. Use arrows to show modification. Use other paper for this exercise.

1. . . . often had come to practice before the appointed time
2. . . . drove his car rapidly to the doctor's office
3. . . . should not have anchored the boat so close to the shore
4. . . . quickly made her way to the post office
5. . . . became a captain in the spring when promotions were announced

---

Now we are ready to try some IC analyses of entire sentences. Remember the order of cutting:

1. Cut off any sentence modifiers.
2. Cut between the subject noun phrase and the predicate verb phrase.
3. Cut these phrases into successive IC's, down to the individual words.

Exercise 18–11

Make an IC analysis of these sentences down to the individual words. For this purpose copy the sentences on another sheet of paper.

1. If everyone is ready, we can begin to load the car.
2. Balancing on the edge of the board, he poised for the dive.
3. All of the members had already paid their dues.
4. In those exciting pages we followed the adventures of the swimmer who battled the waves.
5. After unloading the supplies, we hoisted the canoe on our shoulders for the long portage.

In doing IC analyses of complicated sentences, you may discover some knotty problems. These can be avoided if you confine such analysis to the basic sentences. By way of review let us put the nine basic sentences through their IC cuts. Here they are, padded out with a few modifiers.

Exercise 18–12

Make a complete IC analysis of each sentence. Use other paper for this exercise.

1. Your food is exceedingly good.
2. The salesman from Skunk Hollow is here.
3. My oldest sister is the doctor in residence.
4. Many younger girls giggle outrageously.
5. The girl in the next house bought a silk dress at the auction.
6. The doting mother bought the girl a dress from the Smart Shop.
7. The basketball players chose Harry their captain for next year.
8. That muscular acrobat seems quite young.
9. My cousin Ruth remained an outstanding student.

B. Coordination

In the chapter about modifiers we were dealing with the phenomenon of subordination, for a modifier is always subordinate to its head. Now we turn to a related matter, coordination.

In English we have a small structure-class consisting of eight structure words called **coordinating conjunctions.** These are *and, but, for, nor, not, or, so, yet*. These conjunctions connect grammatical equivalents—form-classes or position-classes or structure-words or grammatical structures or sentences. A few cases will illustrate this connection of equivalents.

Connection of equivalent form-classes

Nouns	1. The library *and* the gymnasium are nearby.
Adjectives	2. George is powerful *but* clumsy.
Verbs	3. He studied hard, *yet* failed.
Adverbs	4. Arabella dances lightly *and* gracefully.

Connection of equivalent position-classes

Adjectivals	1. My business *and* academic friends . . .
	2. He was popular *and* in good health.
Adverbials	3. Is it upstairs *or* in the garage?
Nominals	4. He did what he pleased, *not* what was expected.
Verbals	5. We watched him rowing hard *but* getting nowhere.

Connection of equivalent structure-words

Auxiliaries	1. You can *and* should help your brother.
Prepositions	2. Was the witness walking to *or* from the scene of the accident?

Connection of equivalent grammatical structures

Prepositional phrases	1. You can sleep on the beach *or* in the woods.
Relative clauses	2. Bess was a girl who could swim *but* who was afraid to dive.

Connection of sentences

Ned began nodding, *for* the room was hot.

Since coordinating conjunctions fulfill the grammatical function of connecting, they belong to the function-class of connectors, as do prepositions, relatives, and subordinating conjunctions.

All the coordinating conjunctions except *not* can occur between two sentences, changing them into a single sentence, but in other positions their distribution is limited. In other words, not all of them can be used to connect the same equivalents. For example, we do not use *for, nor,* or *so* to connect two adjectives.

In writing, these coordinating conjunctions are sometimes used to begin a sentence, as in

Jane was never on time. But that made no difference to Bob.

This would be uttered with a fading terminal juncture after *time* whether the punctuation mark were a comma, semicolon, or a period. Hence this way of beginning sentences can be considered simply as a writing convention that in no manner changes the classification of the coordinating conjunction.

Exercise 18–13

Underline each coordinating conjunction, and below each sentence identify the grammatical items that it connects.

Example: Samuel was equally happy hunting ducks or playing chess.
  participial phrases

1. You and I ought to play them.

2. Winterbottom ran swiftly yet gracefully.

3. I don't know who you are or what you want.

4. We worked fast, for darkness was approaching.

5. These flowers are for Helen, not for you.

6. Bill wanted to study late, so he drank another cup of coffee.

7. She smiled but remained silent.

8. I have not cleaned the fish, nor do I intend to.
  (*Nor* produces an inversion.)

9. Do you want to play now or wait till evening?

10. Rising and stretching, Harry yawned and began to dress.

These conjunctions are sometimes doubled up, as in *and yet, and so, but yet,* and *but not.* Compare, for instance, these two sentences:

1. He was tired *but yet* he couldn't sleep.
2. He was tired *but* he couldn't sleep *yet.*

The first *yet* is a coordinating conjunction; the second is an adverbial with a different meaning.

In addition to the set of eight coordinating conjunctions there is a second set that occurs in pairs:

either ... or
both ... and
neither ... nor
not (only) ... but (also)
whether ... or

These are a subclass of coordinating conjunctions known as correlative conjunctions.

Exercise 18–14

Underline the correlative conjunctions, and below each sentence identify the grammatical items that are connected.

1. Either you leave or I will call the police.

2. They stood both in the aisles and on the platforms.

3. Jenkins had neither the time nor the energy to finish the job.

4. Our navigator was not only knowledgeable but careful not to make errors.

5. The main requirement for this position is not specialized knowledge but the ability to handle people tactfully.

6. The question is whether to stay or go.

C. Multiple Constituents

We are now in a position to account for coordinate items in an IC analysis. An illustration will show the procedure:

enjoy | drama | and | opera

This verb phrase contains after the cut a multiple IC, the coordinate nouns *drama* and *opera*, but *and* is set off as a separate element and does not belong to either IC. Here are more examples:

... bought | an | old car | and | set | off | for | the hills.

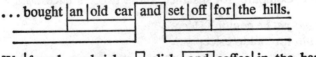

We | found sandwiches, | relish, | and | coffee | in the hamper.

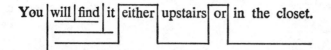

You | will | find | it | either | upstairs | or | in the closet.

(Note here that though *upstairs* and *in the closet* are different in form, they are equivalent in that both are adverbials.)

Exercise 18–15

Make a complete IC analysis of each of these sentences. Use other paper for this exercise.

1. His favorite snack was fish and chips.
2. Both men and women may join the club.
3. The third problem is challenging but baffling.
4. You look attractive in either the blue sweater or the yellow.
   (After *yellow,* the word *sweater* can be said to be understood, since it has already been mentioned in the sentence. Thus the items following *either* and *or* may be considered grammatical equivalents.)
5. I will give you directions, but the rest is your responsibility.

19
Some
Syntactic
Details

In the foregoing pages of this section we have dealt chiefly with those matters that are central to an understanding of English syntax. Now we shall go back to examine a few concepts that were bypassed in the interest of a fast forward progression.

A. Complements

1. Complement of the Adjective/Adjectival. The term *complement* has been used thus far to mean any nominal completer of the verb, such as subjective complement and direct object. Now we shall broaden the term to include two more kinds of completers. Let us begin by examining two sentences:

I fear *that they are lost.*
I am fearful *that they are lost.*

In the first sentence "that they are lost" is obviously a complement of the DO type; that is, it is a nominal functioning as the direct object of the verb. Since the second sentence closely parallels the first in meaning and form, it seems reasonable in this sentence to call "that they are lost" a nominal functioning as a complement of the adjective *fearful*. The next trio is similar and illustrates in addition the prepositional phrase as complement of the adjective.

He hoped *that a change would occur.*
He was hopeful *that a change would occur.*
He was hopeful *of a change.*

Likewise, an infinitive phrase can be a complement of an adjective:

He hesitated *to see her.*
He was hesitant *to see her.*

Many adjectives that do not have a related verb, as those above do, also take complements of the adjectives, for example:

I want *to see her.*
I am eager *to see her.*

Patterns 1 and 4, both of which contain adjectivals in the third position, can be extended by means of this particular complement, as these examples show:

I am happy *that you are here.*
Her roommate became tired *of studying.*
She is indifferent *whether you come or not.*
Jim is certain *to succeed.*

It is not always easy to make a clear-cut distinction between an adverbial and a complement of an adjectival. One can perhaps say that in natural speech the complement of the adjectival is not transposable but retains its position after the adjectival, whereas the adverbial is movable, e.g.;
Complement of the adjectival:

She was glad *that he was safe,*

but not

*That he was safe she was glad.

Adverbial:

She was glad *when he arrived.*

and also

When he arrived she was glad.

Exercise 19–1

Indicate whether the italicized word groups are

DO   direct object of verb
CAj   complement of the adjective/adjectival
Av-al adverbial

1. Jim doubts *that he can pass the course.*   _____
2. Jim is doubtful *that he can pass the course.* _____

3. Jim is doubtful *of passing the course.*   _____
4. We were reluctant *to leave.*   _____
5. Jane learned *that something unpleasant had happened.*   _____
6. Jane was conscious *that something unpleasant had happened.*   _____
7. Juliet forgot *that she had a job to finish.*   _____
8. Juliet became forgetful *of her duties.*   _____
9. Jerry was sick *when the game began.*   _____
10. Jerry was sick *of watching.*   _____
11. Penelope was anxious *to be sure.*   _____
12. Penelope was anxious, *to be sure.*   _____
13. The lad was afraid *of venturing into the deep water.*   _____
14. Are you sure *of it?*   _____
15. Mrs. Hawkins is devoted *to her daughter.*   _____

---

2. Complement of the Noun. Turning from the complement of the adjective to the complement of the noun, let us again begin with a comparison of two sentences:

I fear that they are lost.
My fear that they are lost ...

Here, if the *that* clause in the first sentence is a complement of the verb (DO), it seems reasonable to assume that the *that* clause in the second sentence is a complement of the noun. Observe that the word *that* is not a relative because it has no function within the clause. Thus the clause is not a relative clause. Here *that* is a subordinating conjunction. It stands outside the clause and connects it with the noun *fear.* The clause is a nominal that functions as a complement of the noun. Likewise, in

He contended that war is evil.
His contention that war is evil ...

we seem to have a complement of the verb (DO) and a complement of the noun. Note that in each pair above the noun has a corresponding verb that is either homophonous with (*fear*) or morphologically related to (*contend*) the noun.

Next, let us look at a sequence of illustrative sentences:

I believe that Henry is lazy.
My belief that Henry is lazy ...
My idea that Henry is lazy ...
The fact that Henry is lazy ...

Here again the first two sentences appear to contain a complement of the verb (DO) and a complement of the noun, respectively. But the third, which means substantially the same as the second, has a noun *idea,* for which the English language happens to have no generally used corresponding verb, that is, a verb meaning "to possess or form an idea." In the fourth *fact* is still further removed from any verb in English, and the "that" clause begins to look like a modifier of the noun, such as an appositive. Shall we call all four of these *that* clauses, and all similar clauses, complements of the noun, or should we make a distinction between complements and modifiers of the noun? Here, as often in grammatical analysis, we must make a hard and somewhat arbitrary decision. In this book it will prove more workable to apply the concept of the complement of the noun to any *that* clause like those above, regardless of whether or not the noun has a related verb.

Exercise 19–2

Underline complements of the noun once and relative clauses twice.

1. The assertion that women are poor drivers does not hold up under investigation.
2. We entertained a suspicion that Mink had been cheating.
3. The principle that water runs only downhill seems sometimes to be contradicted by our senses.
4. The canoe that leaked badly was an old wooden one.
5. His conviction that the stars influence our lives could not be shaken.
6. His notion that the stars influence our lives could not be shaken.

Next we turn to the infinitive phrase as a complement of the noun. In these two sentences,

She decided to tell the truth.
Her decision to tell the truth . . .

it looks again as if we have a complement of the verb (DO) and a complement of the noun. And again the noun (*decision*) has a corresponding verb (*decide*). But with this structure we shall say that only nouns with related verbs can take a complement of the noun in infinitive form. This means nouns like *refusal, desire, intention, promise, hope.* If the noun is not of this kind, the infinitive following it will not be a complement of the noun but probably a postnominal modifier. Compare:

Complement of the noun: His refusal *to submit without a fight* was courageous.
Postnominal modifier: He was not a man *to submit without a fight.*
Complement of the noun: His desire *to consider the motion* was thwarted.
Postnominal modifier: The next thing *to consider* is the stage set.

Infinitive structures are many and varied and complex, and this procedure will work best with the system you are studying here.

Exercise 19–3

Underline complements of the noun once and postnominal modifiers twice.

1. His offer to buy the whole lot was accepted.
2. We heard of Tom's attempt to raise money for the needy.

3. Agatha needed somebody to love.
4. They did not approve of Harry's intention to register late.
5. It was a thrilling game to watch.
6. Their hope to win was strong.
7. Robert's resolution to practice daily soon faded away.
8. There is a man to admire.
9. Father's order to stay away from the telephone was sullenly obeyed.
10. We approved Josephine's determination to live within her budget.

---

3. Complements in *-ing* **and** *to* _____. English verbs may be divided into three classes according to the form of the verbal complement that immediately follows them. The first class contains those followed by the *-ing* form of the verb but not by *to* plus a verb stem:

He enjoyed eating.

not

*He enjoyed to eat.

Those of the second class are followed by *to* plus a verb stem but not by the *-ing* form:

He agreed to come.

not

*He agreed coming.

Those of the third class are followed by either the *to* or the *-ing* form:

He preferred sleeping.

and

He preferred to sleep.

There is no general principle that dictates which form to use immediately after a verb. As a native speaker you know from long experience with our language which forms are permitted with which verbs. But a non-native speaker must go through the arduous task of learning them one by one.

Verbs taking complements in *-ing* and *to* _____ are called *catenatives* because they can co-occur in chains, such as

He wanted to stop trying to postpone working.

Exercise 19–4
Give the form of the verbal complement that immediately follows each verb by writing in the blank *-ing* or *to* or *both*.

1. refuse _____ 4. offer _____
2. miss _____ 5. postpone _____
3. start _____ 6. continue _____

7. promise _____
8. avoid _____
9. hate _____
10. try _____

11. decide _____
12. risk _____
13. cease _____
14. mention _____

B. Subjunctive Forms of the Verb

English has two verb forms, *were* and the stem of any verb, which have special uses.

1. The verb stem, instead of the inflected form of the verb, is used in certain nominal clauses, as is shown by these sentences:

It is necessary that she *go* at once.
It is imperative that you *be* on time.
The boss insisted that Willard *arrive* at eight sharp.
She suggested that I *be* the cook.

2. The form *were* is used in subordinate contrary-to-fact clauses beginning with *if, as if,* and *as though* and in nominal clauses after the verb *wish,* as in

If he *were* really my friend, he would get me a ticket.
Betty looks as if she *were* exhausted.
I wish I *were* in Italy.

In extremely formal English one sometimes hears *be* in *if* clauses, e.g.,

If that *be* the case . . .

When these forms are used in the positions described, the verb is called subjunctive. Often these subjunctive forms are replaced by other forms or structures, as in

It is necessary *for her to go* at once.
It is necessary that she *should go* at once.
If he *was* really my friend, he would get me a ticket. (informal usage)
I wish I *was* in Italy. (informal usage)

Exercise 19–5

Underline the subjunctive forms of the verb in these sentences.

1. If she (was   were) home, she would answer the phone.
2. I wish he (was   were) with me now.
3. If that (is   be) true, make the most of it.
4. The director asked that Elizabeth (stands   stand) in the front row.
5. It is traditional that the table (is   be) decorated.
6. It is advisable that a lawyer (writes   write) the contract.
7. Rubenstein plays Chopin as though he (was   were) inspired.
8. The rules required that they (are   be) in uniform.

9. If I (was   were) the pilot, I'd avoid that thunderstorm.
10. The invitation requested that she (answers   answer) promptly.

C. Noun Subgroups

Nouns can be divided into different subclasses according to the grammatical purpose one has in mind. We have already met two such classes. The collective-noun class was used to decide questions of number, and the animate-inanimate class was related to the choice between the {-s ps} possessive and the *of* structure.

Now we shall take a look at three more noun subclasses, which are based on the ways nouns behave with determiners in conjunction with the singular and the plural. These three classes are the count noun, the mass noun, and the proper noun.

1. COUNT AND MASS NOUNS

The count-noun class includes everything that is readily countable, like *beetles, books, sounds, concepts, minutes.* Count nouns have both singular and plural forms. In the singular they must always be preceded by a determiner, e.g.,

A car drove by
The car drove by

but not

*Car drove by.

In the plural they may occur either with or without a determiner:

Cars are dangerous on slippery roads.
Those cars are dangerous on slippery roads.

The mass-noun class includes everything that is not readily countable, like *steam, music, justice, advice, water, bread, Latin, silk.* Mass nouns have no plural; they occur in the singular under these conditions:

Without a determiner: *Information* is useful.
With *the*:   *The* information is useful.
But not with *a*:   **An* information is useful.

Many words may be mass nouns in one context and count nouns in a different context, e.g.,

Mass: *Beer* is refreshing in summer.
Count: They had *two beers.* (Remember that mass nouns have no
       plural.)
Mass: *Virtue* is its own reward.
Count: Her *virtues* were well known.

Mass: You have *egg* on your chin.
Count: *Eggs* were served for breakfast.

As a rule of thumb it is worth remembering that count nouns can be modified by *many* and mass nouns by *much*.

Exercise 19–6

In the blanks write *count* or *mass* to classify the italicized words.

1. The *wines* of France are world-famous.   _____
2. The Thibaults drink *wine* with their meals.   _____
3. Hobson enjoys his *leisure*.   _____
4. There is *truth* in what he says.   _____
5. These *truths* you must never forget.   _____
6. Mrs. Lopez buys *coffee* every day at the market.   _____
7. Please bring me a *coffee*.   _____
8. Charles studied *Russian* in college.   _____
9. Today's world puts a high value on *knowledge*.   _____
10. We heard a *Russian* at the United Nations.   _____

Note of Qualification: The eminent Canadian linguist Edward Sapir once wrote a three-word sentence so wise and true that it has been widely quoted: "All grammars leak." And right here is a leak that you may have already noticed. Mass nouns are sometimes nouns because they may have a derivational or a possessive suffix, though never a plural: *information, enjoyment, honesty, electricity, ignorance, water* (the water's edge), *weather* (the weather's fickleness). But other mass nouns, not having formal indications of nounness, should, strictly speaking, be labeled mass nominals: *fun, peace, heat, sunshine, toast, luggage, furniture, dust.* At times the question of noun versus nominal hinges on whether or not a given "mass noun" takes the possessive morpheme {-s ps}. For example, do you, or does anyone, say *the mail's lateness, the dust's moisture, the sunshine's brilliance, the hair's color, his luck's continuance, the bread's flavor, the milk's taste, the lightning's flash?* In this chapter the term *mass noun* is used both for "mass nominals" and for dubious cases like those in the preceding sentence.

2. PROPER NOUNS

The proper-noun class consists of the names of particular, often unique, persons, places, and things, e.g., Charlotte Brook, the *Mona Lisa,* the *Queen Mary* (ship), Maine, the Rocky Mountains, Mount Washington. They are considered a subclass of nouns because most of them conform in part to the noun paradigm, and they appear in noun positions. Syntactically, they behave like count nouns, with a few restrictions that are worth noting:

1. In the singular proper nouns usually appear without a determiner.

Examples: *June* is a month for weddings.
We talked with *Margaret.*
The inside of *Chartres Cathedral* is beautiful in the sunshine.

However, a determiner is used with singular proper nouns when such nouns are restrictively modified, as in these cases:

The June in which she was married was warm.
It was *a June* to remember.
The Margaret whom I remember had red hair.

2. Proper nouns that are always plural are normally accompanied by *the,* occasionally by a different determiner of the *A* group.

Examples: *The Appalachians* are an old mountain chain.
I don't like *your Bahamas; they* are too commercialized.
We are going to visit *the Hebrides.*

3. Certain proper nouns are usually singular and take *the.*

Examples: We took *the Maasdam* (ship) to Rotterdam.
The Museum of Modern Art has a new show.
He waded across *the Rio Grande.*
We stayed at *the Americana.*
The Atlantic Ocean is rough in winter.

These proper nouns, however, can also be used in the plural:

Several Americanas have been built on the Eastern coast.
There are *two Atlantic Oceans* in the Northern Hemisphere, the warm one of the tropics and the cold one toward the Pole.

Exercise 19–7

The proper names have been left uncapitalized. Classify the italicized nouns by *count, mass,* or *proper.*

1. Aunt Tilda's favorite *month* is *may.* _____ _____
2. There is *dust* on the *mantelpiece.* _____ _____
3. The class had a *picnic* at *riverview park.* _____ _____
4. *Cotton* is more absorbent than *linen.* _____ _____
5. In the *alps* are many lovely *valleys.* _____ _____
6. Do you like *cream* in *coffee?* _____ _____
7. Numerous *injustices* were perpetrated by the *invaders.* _____ _____
8. Can one expect *justice* in this *court?* _____ _____
9. The *aliens* are visiting us next *week.* _____ _____
10. They sailed on the *statendam* for the *canary islands.* _____ _____

D. The Expletive *There*

One widely used kind of sentence not yet mentioned deserves consideration. It is the kind that begins with *there + be,* as in

There is a man under my bed.

Here *there* is an expletive, that is, a meaningless slot-filler occupying the normal position of the subject. The subject itself comes after the *be.* Sentences beginning with the expletive *there* are rearrangements of basic pattern sentences, and most of them conform to one of three types.

The first type, illustrated both above and below, follows the pattern of *there + be +* subject + adverbial of place or time, as in

There are two men under my bed.

This type is a rearranged form of Pattern 2:

A man is under my bed.
Two men are under my bed.

The second type is illustrated by this sentence:

There was a policeman looking for you.

This second type follows the pattern of *there + be +* subject + -ing participle + ∅ or remainder. It is usually derived from Patterns 6, 7, or 8 employing an *ing* verb.

Examples:
  a. Pattern 6:   A politician was speaking.
     There + be: There was a politician speaking.
  b. Pattern 7:   Some boys were eating apples.
     There + be: There were some boys eating apples.
  c. Pattern 8:   Several jockeys were giving their horses water.
     There + be: There were several jockeys giving their horses water.

The third type comes from the passives of Patterns 7, 8, or 9, with Pattern 9 being the most frequent.

Examples:
  a. Pattern 9:   The police found a shotgun.
     Passive: A shotgun was found by the police.
     There + be: There was a shotgun found by the police.
  b. Pattern 8:   The company made him an offer.
     Passive: An offer was made him by the company.
     There + be: There was an offer made him by the company.
  c. Pattern 9:   They elected a Swede captain.
     Passive: A Swede was elected captain.
     There + be: There was a Swede elected captain.

The pattern of the preceding sentences is *there + be +* subject + *-ed* participle + remainder or ∅.

In all of these cases the expletive *there* was followed by *be*. Now and then a few other verbs appear in this structure, for example:

There remained only three doughnuts.
There stood a handsome lad in the doorway.

The expletive *there* should not confused with the adverbial *there*. The expletive bears weak or third stress whereas the adverbial has secondary or primary stress.

Examples:
Thĕre (expletive) are sóldiers in town.
Thêre (adverbial) go to the sóldiers.
They are thére (adverbial).
Thêre (adverbial) they áre.

Exercise 19-8
Change each sentence into one beginning with the expletive *there*.

1. A rabbit is in your garden.

2. Some squirrels were cracking nuts.

3. A moon craft was pictured by *Life*.

4. Some boob was chosen commissioner.

5. Five men have been working on the rules.

Exercise 19-9
Over each italicized *there* place a stress mark showing how you stress the word. Then indicate in the blank whether the *there* is an (1) expletive or (2) adverbial.

1. *There* are some girls swimming in the lake.   _____
2. *There* come the girls.   _____
3. *There* are weeds in this water.   _____
4. The weeds are over *there*.   _____
5. *There* was a woman's purse lost at the concert.   _____

E. The Expletive *It*

Another expletive is *it*, which occurs as a "dummy" in the subject position before the verb. It takes the place of the real subject, which follows later in the sentence, as in

It is nice that you could come.

If you apply here the subject-finding rule of thumb—Who or what is nice?
—the answer will give you the subject "... that you could come." The subject is always a word group.

Exercise 19–10

Underline the subject in these sentences.

1. It is odd that the tree fell in that direction.
2. It occurred to me that the road might be impassable.
3. It is hard to see the difference.
4. It doesn't matter whether she wears the green or the yellow suit.
5. It is necessary that you write a tactful letter.

The expletive *it* may also represent a following direct object, as in

I think it a shame that she lost the match.

Here "... that she lost the match" is the direct object.

Exercise 19–11

Underline the direct object represented by a preceding expletive *it*.

1. She makes it a practice to revise all her papers.
2. I believe it unwise to set out in this storm.
3. He felt it unnecessary that we postpone the game.
4. The dean found it difficult to deny their petition.
5. I thought it strange his leaving so suddenly.

The expletive *it* should not be confused with the impersonal *it*, which also occurs at the sentence beginning as a "dummy" subject. This *it* is usually found in short sentences referring to weather, time, or space.

It is raining.
It seems cold.
It is seven-thirty.
It is a long way to London.

There are also idiomatic uses of *it* that are neither expletives nor impersonals.

He is baching it.
Beat it.
We hoofed it to the fair.
You'll catch it when father returns.
Beat it. (= go away)
Let's get it over.
I'll have it out with you.
You'll catch it when father comes home.

How goes it?
It looks bad for the White Sox.
We hoofed it to the fair.

Exercise 19–12

Indicate whether the *it* in each sentence is an Exp (expletive) or an Imp (impersonal)

1. It is too bad that you can't attend.
2. It is bad outside.
3. She considered it incomprehensible that he should fail.
4. It is warming up.
5. It is ten after three.

F. The Tag Question

A tag question is a word or phrase placed at the end of a sentence, thereby making that sentence into a yes-or-no question, as in

You have eaten lunch, *haven't you?*

In many languages the tag question is invariable in form, like Chinese *ma,* Spanish *verdad,* Dutch *niet waar,* and Italian *non è vero.* English too has invariable single-word forms in *huh* and *eh,* as in

You're leaving, eh?

But for the most part we use a set of phrases that are complex in structure.

Let us begin by looking at the use of the affirmative and the negative in tag questions, illustrated by these two sentences:

$$\begin{matrix} & 2 & 3\uparrow \\ \text{She is a junior,} & \text{isn't she} \end{matrix}$$
$$\begin{matrix} & 2 & 3\uparrow \\ \text{She isn't a junior,} & \text{is she} \end{matrix}$$

The point to note here is this: If the statement is affirmative, the tag must be negative; if the statement is negative, the tag must be affirmative. Furthermore, the tags convey certain expectations. A tag in the negative with a 2 3 ↑ intonation contour, as in the first example, conveys the mild expectation of an affirmative response; whereas a tag in the affirmative with a 2 3 ↑ contour, as in the second example, conveys the mild expectation of a negative response. However, if the 2 3 ↑ contour of the tag is changed to 3 1 ↓, the expectation is greatly strengthened in each case. Here are four illustrative sentences:

```
2     3      1↓2     3↑
```
She's coming   isn't she   (Mild expectation of an affirmative response)

```
2     3      1↓3      1↓
```
She's coming   isn't she   (Strong expectation of an affirmative response)

```
2        3      1↓2     3↑
```
She isn't coming   is she   (Mild expectation of a negative response)

```
2       3       1↓3      1↓
```
She isn't coming   is she   (Strong expectation of a negative response)

The verb in the tag question follows four patterns:

1. When the verb of the statement is *be,* the same form of *be* is used in the tag.

Examples: The Smiths are your friends, aren't they?
He was late for his appointment, wasn't he?
There is a new student on your floor, isn't there?

2. When the verb of the statement is preceded by one or more auxiliaries, the first auxiliary is repeated in the tag.

Examples: They were playing bridge, weren't they?
George could have paid, couldn't he?
She has gone, hasn't she?
Mabel doesn't play golf, does she?

3. When the verb is a single-word present or past form (except for *be*), the verb in the tag is the equivalent form of *do.*

Examples: Evelyn plays the piano, doesn't she?
Eve ate the apple, didn't she?
His sons both go to college, don't they?

4. When the verb of the statement is an imperative, the tag verb is *will,* in either the affirmative or the negative, and the pronoun is *you.*

Examples: Write me a letter, will you?
Write me a letter, won't you?

The tag question never contains a noun as subject. Instead, the subject is always a personal pronoun in the subject form, or the expletive *there* is used instead of the subject. (On rare occasions you may hear *one:* "One arrives on time, doesn't one?") For examples of the tag subject see all the illustrative sentences above.

Exercise 19–13

Indicate the kind of response expected, using these numbers:

1. mild expectation of affirmative response
2. strong expectation of affirmative response
3. mild expectation of negative response
4. strong expectation of negative response

   2   3   1↓2   3↑
1. You invited Elizabeth   didn't you   _____
   2   3   1↓3   1↓
2. She watched the program   didn't she   _____
   2   3   1↓3   1↓
3. He should have told her   shouldn't he   _____
   2   3   1↓2   3↑
4. They weren't driving fast   were they   _____
   2   3   1↓3   1↓
5. Adolph likes beans   doesn't he   _____
   2   3   1↓3   1↓
6. She isn't in her room   is she   _____

Answers to Exercises

IMPORTANT: At times your answer may be correct and yet not agree with the answer given here. In the phonology this will happen because there are many variations of pronunciation, both dialectal and idiolectal, in American English, and your pronunciation may be one of these. In other parts of the grammar your "wrong" answer may represent a variant usage or a different but legitimate way of viewing a particular form or structure. Therefore, whenever you are in doubt about an answer, do not hesitate to bring up the matter in class.

Also, you should use these answers intelligently. Suppose, for example, that you are asked to find an English word that begins with the sounds /gw-/. If your own mental resources, aided by a desk dictionary, do not yield the answer in a reasonable time, don't spend further effort on it; simply look at the answer and then go on with the assignment.*

EXERCISE 1-1

The nasals are the final sound in *rim, bin, sing, trim, pain, wrong.* The other final sounds are orals.

EXERCISE 1-2

The voiced sounds are the final sound in *hum, pin, among, fin,* and *song.* The other final sounds are voiceless.

---

* Despite painstaking care by several persons during the writing, copyreading, and two proofreading stages, there may still be errors in the answers. So the author will be most grateful to anyone who finds and takes the trouble to report wrong answers to him at 1710 Tremont Street, Cedar Falls, Iowa 50613. Such errors do not have to stand until there is a new edition but can be corrected in a later printing of this edition.

EXERCISE 1–3

The first sound in each of these words is voiced: *vine, then, zeal, late,* and *rate.* The other initial sounds are voiceless.

EXERCISE 1–4

The first sound in each of these words is voiced: *bin, dime,* and *goon.* The initial sound in each of the other three words is voiceless.

EXERCISE 1–5

1. p b	6. r t	11. d t
2. b d	7. f v	12. d k
3. l r	8. z t	13. l m
4. p k	9. h g	14. t n
5. g s	10. s w	15. n ŋ

EXERCISE 1–6

1. pæk	8. kip	15. kɪk	22. get
2. kep	9. kɪd	16. kæp	23. gæt
3. pit	10. kæt	17. pɛk	24. bæk
4. pɪt	11. bik	18. pɪk	25. bek
5. pet	12. bɪg	19. pik	26. tæp
6. pɛt	13. det	20. gæd	27. tep
7. pæt	14. dɛt	21. get	28. tɪp

EXERCISE 1–7

1. fud	6. šo	11. vudu	16. zu
2. fʊt	7. ðo	12. šʊk	17. θɔt
3. fo	8. θɔ	13. hu	18. ðoz
4. fɔt	9. sup	14. ho	19. oθ
5. šu	10. ɔt	15. zon	20. vɪžən

EXERCISE 1–8

1. pər	4. fɪr	7. startəd	10. hərd
2. mərdər	5. čərčəz	8. foldəd	11. hərt
3. čɪldrən or čɪldərn	6. rəbz	9. rɪgard	12. hət

EXERCISE 1–9

1. ərj	6. əbəv	11. ližər	16. pakət
2. stap	7. bərd	12. ərbən	17. təde
3. kət	8. rəst	13. ad	18. kəbərd
4. sofə	9. rən	14. əfɛkt	19. jərni
5. rəg	10. bərč	15. əfɛkt	20. hat

EXERCISE 1–10

1. sit	1
2. ɪnfɛkt	2
3. pepər	2
4. dɪsɪnčænt	3
5. ənɔstəntešəs	5

EXERCISE 1–11

1. may	6. jɔy	11. hay	16. tray
2. tɔy	7. čayvz	12. awč	17. strayp
3. haw	8. ðaw	13. mayti	18. rawdi
4. tay	9. šay	14. rɔyl	19. kɪlrɔy
5. kaw	10. ray	15. kɔy	20. dɪstrɔy

EXERCISE 1–12

(Numerous variations are possible here.)

1. wɪr	10. mornɪŋ	19. pɛr	28. krawd
2. bɪr	11. mornɪŋ	20. pe-ər	29. pər
3. ðɛr	12. norθ	21. stɛr	30. prawd
4. ðɛr	13. norðərn	22. ste-ər	31. bər
5. kɛr	14. flor	23. mɛr	32. brɛd
6. mɛri	15. hɪr	24. me-ər	
7. mɛri	16. tur	25. spərɪŋ	
8. mɛri	17. hors	26. sprɪŋ	
9. barj	18. hors	27. kər	

In exercise 1–12 these groups are especially likely to show dialectal variation: 6, 7, 8; 10, 11; 17, 18. Also, pronunciation may vary according to the position in the sentence. Compare, for example:

1. The stair /stɛr/ is crowded.
2. He ran up the stair /ste-ər/.

For some of the /-or/ words some speakers will have /-ɔr/, e.g., *north, morning, floor, horse.*

EXERCISE 1–13

1. pɪp	6. gæg	11. fæst	16. lɪkər
2. bɪb	7. stapt	12. fæsən	17. sɪks
3. tat	8. stapgæp	13. uzd	18. gɛst
4. did	9. hɪkəp	14. hænd	19. kip
5. kok	10. səbpɔynt	15. hænz	20. kup

EXERCISE 1–14

The /k/ of *coop* is far back and is rounded because of the influence of the following /u/, which is back and rounded. The /k/ of *keep* is further front and is unrounded because of the influence of /i/, which is front and unrounded.

EXERCISE 1–15

1. inəf	7. wɪð, wɪθ	13. haws	19. anəst
2. wayf	8. sɛnt	14. həzbənd	20. aməj
3. wayvz	9. klos	15. ləkšəri	haməj
4. fɪfθ	10. kloz *or* kloðz	16. ləgžʊriəs	
5. sawθ	11. nuz	17. mɛžər	
6. səðərn	12. nuspepər	18. həmbəl	

EXERCISE 1–16

Examples:

1. baynd	4. məs	6. jæm	8. ædər
2. bes	5. dim	7. lərk	9. sæŋ
3. bol			

EXERCISE 1–17

1. fud	7. ič	11. strɔŋgər	16. əpɪnyən
2. fyud	8. sɪŋər	12. ɪlužən	17. tray
3. i-an	sɪŋgər	13. fok	18. wɛr
4. yan	9. lɪŋgər	14. mɪlk	19. hwɛr, wɛr
5. jəj	10. strɔŋ	15. yuz	20. birɛt
6. saləm			

[Exercise 1–18 omitted]

EXERCISE 1–19

1. frog	9. chiefs	15. affect	20. horse
2. sorry	10. lives	effect	hoarse
3. why	11. sends	16. wash	21. something
4. room	12. sense	17. wash	22. language
5. room	cents	18. wash	23. contact
6. pretty	scents	19. horse	24. contact
7. woman	13. pounds	hoarse	25. Tuesday
8. women	14. across		

1. Let me go.
2. I'm going to cry.
3. Who asked you?
4. I told him.
5. We told them.

6. I should think he would.
7. She's pretty cheeky.
8. They could have bought them.
9. I'll miss you.
10. I'll treat you.

EXERCISE 2–1

1. lɛdɛr
 =
 badəl
 =
 fordi
 =
2. sawθ
 səðərn
 =
3. ɪt
 ɪdɪz
 =
4. wərθ
 wərði
 =
5. gat
 ayv gadɪt
 =
6. kəp
 kəbərd
 =

7. gus
 guzbəri
 =
8. šət
 šədəp
 =
9. hæv
 ay hæftə fíš
 =
 ay hæv tû fíš[1]
10. haw mɛni gɛs wɪl yə hæftə fid
 =
 haw mɛni gɛs wɪl yə hæv tə fid
11. yuzd
 hi yustə dæns
 =
 hi yuzd tú ɛgz

[1] Your /hæv/ may sound like this: [hævf].

EXERCISE 2–2

Singular	Plural		Singular	Plural
1. stap	staps		11. sən	sənz
2. rayt	rayts		12. sɔŋ	sɔŋz
3. kek	keks		13. dal	dalz
4. məf	məfs		14. fɪr	fɪrz
5. brɛθ	brɛθs		15. glæs	glæsəz
6. mab	mabz		16. roz	rozəz
7. rayd	raydz		17. dɪš	dɪšəz
8. frɔg	frɔgz		18. mɪraž	mɪražəz
9. wev	wevz		19. dɪč	dɪčəz
10. səm	səmz		20. ɛj	ɛjəz

Answer to question 1: The three forms of the plural are /-s/, /-z/, and /-əz/.

Answer to question 2: A singular form ending in an s-like sound—/s/, /z/, /š/, /ž/, /č/, /j/—is followed by /-əz/. As for the remaining, /s/ follows a voiceless sound and /z/ follows a voiced sound.

EXERCISE 2–3

Present	Past		Present	Past
1. pæs	pæst		11. həg	həgd
2. læf	læft		12. rev	revd
3. map	mapt		13. mɪl	mɪld
4. bæk	bækt		14. stər	stərd
5. rəš	rəšt		15. rat	ratəd or radəd
6. rɛnč	rɛnčt		16. lod	lodəd
7. rab	rabd		17. sit	sitəd or sidəd
8. sim	simd		18. sad	sadəd
9. lon	lond		19. nid	nidəd
10. rɔŋ	rɔŋd		20. ripit	ripitəd or ripidəd

The answers are just what you expected:
1. The -ed suffix has three forms: /-t/, /-d/, and /-əd/.
2. The /-əd/ follows a /t/ or /d/. The /t/ follows other voiceless sounds, and /d/ follows other voiced sounds.

EXERCISE 2–4

1. strɛnθ   /ŋ/ becomes /n/ because of /θ/. Both /n/ and /θ/ are dentals or interdentals. This pronunciation is an occasional variant.
2. ðɪšUgər   /s/ becomes identical with /š/. They are adjacent sounds.
3. græmpə   /nd/ becomes /m/ because of /p/. Both /m/ and /p/ are bilabials.
4. græmə   /nd/ becomes /m/ because of /m/. Both /m/ and /m/ are bilabials.
5. hæŋkərčɪf   /nd/ becomes /ŋ/ because of /k/. Both /ŋ/ and /k/ are velars.
6. kaŋkər   /n/ becomes /ŋ/ because of /k/. Both /ŋ/ and /k/ are velars.
7. wəžər   /z/ + /y/ move together in position, becoming /ž/.
8. hi lɛfθə tawn   /t/ is lost because of difficulty of articulation. /ð/ becomes /θ/ because of /f/. Both /f/ and /θ/ are voiceless.
9. jəsθɪŋk   /t/ lost because of difficulty of articulation.
10. dɪjə   /d/ + /y/ move together in position. becoming /ǰ/.

EXERCISE 2–5

1. The assimilated /mp/, with two bilabials juxtaposed, is easier to say.
2. *Emplane* is more likely to become the standard form, for reason given in answer above.
3. *Condemn* contains the alveolar /n/ because the next sound, /d/, is also alveolar. *Congress* contains the velar /ŋ/, because the next sound, /g/, is also velar.
4. The intervocalic /t/ of *writing* is often voiced, becoming /d/.
5. The /n/, which is alveolar, is assimilated to the /p/, bilabial, becoming /m/, also bilabial.
6. a. The /t/ of *patre* is between two voiced sounds and thus becomes voiced as /d/.
   b. In *donna* the VL /m/ of *domna* has become identical with the following /n/. In *damme* the VL /n/ has become identical with the preceding /m/.
   c. In VL *debta* the /b/ has assimilated to the /t/, becoming identical with it, producing OF *dette*.
   d. The /t/ in VL *armata* is surrounded by vowels and therefore becomes voiced, resulting in *armada*.
   e. In VL *amta* we have a bilabial /m/ next to an alveolar /t/. The /m/ becomes more like its neighbor by changing to the alveolar /n/.
   f. Same as d. The voiceless /t/ between two vowels in *salata* becomes voiced, or /d/, because its neighbors are voiced.

g. The letter "c" in VL *securo* represents the sound /k/, which is voiceless. But because it is between two voiced sounds, vowels, it too becomes voiced as /g/.

h. The OE *hæfde* was probably pronounced /hævdə/. The /v/ then assimilated to the /d/, becoming identical with it.

All these assimilated forms, you will note, require less effort to say than their progenitors.

EXERCISE 2-6

1. Old English *brid*, young bird
2. Old English *thridda*, third
3. Old English *gærs* and *græs*, grass
4. Middle English *clapsen*, clasp. Middle English already had the metathesized form *claspen*.
5. Middle English *drit*

EXERCISE 2-7

1. Yes. The Middle English original of *glimpse* was *glimsen;* and the Old English original of *empty* was *æmtig*, which in Middle English became *emti* and *empti*. Old English and especially Middle English spellings were variable, so do not be disturbed at differences in etymologies in different dictionaries.
2. *Sampson* and *Thompson*. Both *p*'s are epenthetic.
3. These words are sometimes heard with an excrescent /p/: *comfort, warmth, Tomkins, dreamt.*

EXERCISE 2-8

1. *Lend.* Epithetic /d/. Middle English *lenen*, to lend.
2. *Bound.* Epithetic /d/. Middle English *boun*, ready, prepared.
3. *Against.* Epithetic /t/. Middle English *agenes* and *ageinst.*
4. *Midst.* Epithetic /t/. Middle English *middes.*
5. *Amongst.* Epithetic /t/. Middle English *amonges.*

EXERCISE 3-1

a.
1. /s/
2. /z/
3. /š/
4. /ž/
5. /ø/ = none

b.
6. /s/
7. /k/
8. /š/
9. /č/

c.
10. /i/
11. /ɛ/
12. /ɪ/
13. /ə/
14. /a/

EXERCISE 3-2

a.
1. shame
2. machine
3. ocean
4. suspicious
5. schist
6. conscience
7. sure
8. nausea
9. tension
10. attention
11. issue
12. mission
13. anxious
14. luxury

b.
1. dote
2. oh
3. coat
4. foe
5. soul
6. mow
7. yeoman
8. hautboy
9. sew
10. beau
11. dough

EXERCISE 3–3

a. 1. /lit/
   2. /vek/
   3. /zayt/
   4. /nok/
   5. /fub, fyub/

   6. /θit/
   7. /nut/
   8. /dit/
   9. /pot/
   10. /bo/ (cf. foe, doe, woe)

b. 1. dit
   2. tet
   3. jat
   4. zot
   5. chut
   6. zale, zail

   7. omect, omeked
   8. bamthum,
        bamthem
   9. sile
   10. /thoot/

EXERCISE 3–4

/ɪn/		/æt/		/at/	
pɪn	pin	pæt	pat	pat	pot
bɪn	bin	bæt	bat	bat	bot
tɪn	tin	tæt	tat	tat	tot
dɪn	din	kæt	cat	dat	dot
kɪn	kin	gæt	gat	kat	cot
gɪn	gin	fæt	fat	gat	got
fɪn	fin	væt	vat	šat	shot
θɪn	thin	ðæt	that	hat	hot
sɪn	sin	sæt	sat	jat	jot
šɪn	shin	hæt	hat	nat	not
čɪn	chin	čæt	chat	lat	lot
jɪn	gin	mæt	mat	rat	rot
mɪn	min	næt	gnat	yat	yacht
lɪn	lin	læt	lat	wat	watt
rɪn	rin	ræt	rat		
wɪn	win				

In comparing the three lists of spelled words we find a high degree of correspondence between the consonant phonemes and the letters that represent them.

EXERCISE 3–5

a. In subset *a* a one-syllable word ending in a silent *e* drops the *e* before a suffix beginning with a vowel.

b. In subset *b* a one-syllable word ending in a single consonant preceded by a single vowel doubles the consonant before a suffix beginning with a vowel.

EXERCISE 3–6

When a suffix is added to words ending in a silent *e*, the *e* is retained before a suffix beginning with a consonant but is dropped before a suffix beginning with a vowel.

EXERCISE 3–7

1. ænθəni	Tony	toni		
2. θiədɔr	Ted	tɛd		
3. dɔrθi	Dot	dat		
4. arθər	Art	art		
5. ilɪzəbɛθ	Betty	bɛti	or	bɛdi
6. mæθyu	Matt	mæt		
7. nəθæniəl	Nate	net		

The /t/ of the nicknames has come down by oral tradition from the time when the *th* was pronounced /t/. The /θ/ of the full names is a spelling pronunciation. *Thomas* and *Esther* have resisted spelling pronunciation.

EXERCISE 3–8

Answers cannot be given for this exercise because it is *your* pronunciation that you are investigating. But frequent spelling pronunciations are:

1. bričɪz
2. blækgard
3. kəmptrolər
4. ælmənd
5. nɛfyu
6. kakswen
7. grinwɪč
8. fælkən
9. pɔl mɔl
10. arktɪk

EXERCISE 3–9

1. kəm
   hom
2. muv
   šəv
3. frɛnd
   find
   sɪv
4. swɔr
   sɔrd
5. hɔrnɛt
   awr
6. haws
   kərawz
   feməs
7. kɔr, kor
   aylənd
   dɛt
   savərn, savrən
   numædɪk
8. kərnəl

EXERCISE 4–1

1. defér
2. díffer
3. pervért (verb)
4. pérvert (noun)
5. conflíct (verb)
6. cónflict (noun)
7. évil
8. supérb
9. románce, or rómance
10. detáil, or détail
11. reséarch, or résearch
12. defénse, or défense

EXERCISE 4–2

1. díctionàry
2. sécretàry
3. sèparátion
4. íntellèct
5 fùndaméntal
6. àviátion
7. pèrpendícular
8. àcadémic
9. ùnivérsity
10. àbsolútely

EXERCISE 4–3

1. áccènt
2. aùstére
3. ámbùsh
4. hùmáne
5. bláckbìrd
6. fòrgíve
7. ìráte
8. páthòs
9. díphthòng
10. phónème

EXERCISE 4–4

1. ìntĕlléctŭăl
2. désĭgnàte
3. èdŭcátĭon
4. búsўbòdў
5. ìntĕrrúptĭon
6. hùmànĭtárĭăn
7. sócĭalìzed
8. cérĕmònў
9. mílĭtàrў
10. ùnĭnspíred

EXERCISE 4–5

1. remárkable
2. remârkable invéntion
3. tíresome
4. tîresome jób
5. cóntract (noun)
6. côntract brídge

7. práiseworthy
8. prâiseworthy remárk
9. académic
10. acadêmic procéssion
11. blóoming
12. blôoming plánt

EXERCISE 4–6

1. a wooden gáte
2. a gate of wóod
3. completely góne
4. gone complétely
5. run for the práctice
6. practice for the rún

7. Jack and Jíll
8. tea or cóffee
9. not at áll
10. all at ónce
11. call the thief a líar
12. call the liar a thíef

EXERCISE 4–7

1. insíde
2. însìde jób
3. ôvernìght gúests
4. cût-glàss bówl
5. înlaìd tíles
6. âlmòst kílled
7. òverséas
8. Chìnése
9. foùrtéen
10. lêft-hànded pítcher

   òverníght
   cùt-gláss
   ìnlaíd
   àlmóst
   ôversèas jób
   Chînèse ármy
   fôurtèen yéars
   lèft-hánded

EXERCISE 4–8

1. bláckbòard
2. hótbèd
3. pá",lefàce
4. máilmàn
5. shórtcàke

6. róundhoùse
7. páperbàck
8. rócking chàir
9. spínning whèel
10. flýing tèacher

EXERCISE 4–9

1. hôt hóuse
2. dârk róom
3. blâck bírd
4. tênder fóot
5. hândy mán

6. rêd skín
7. fûnny bóne
8. dâncing téacher
9. môwing máchine
10. môving ván

EXERCISE 4–10

1a. a chair that is high
2a. a fish that is game, plucky
3a. a book that is blue
4a. a house that is green

5a. two u's
6a. a horse which is racing
7a. a room that is smoking
8a. any man who is traveling

9a. any girl who is dancing
10a. a lotion that feels cool

1b. a special chair for babies
2b. a fish that may be taken as game
3b. an examination booklet
4b. a glass-covered building where green things are raised

5b. the 23rd letter in the alphabet
6b. a horse for purposes of racing
7b. a room that is for smoking
8b. a commercial salesman who travels in his business

9b. a girl whose profession is dancing
10b. a lotion for cooling

11a. a teacher who is French   11b. a teacher who teaches French

12a. a hand that is not short   12b. writing by hand as opposed to typing

EXERCISE 4-11

1. Someone is running horses against one another.
2. They are horses for racing.
3. He likes to run or race greyhounds.
4. He raises greyhounds for racing.
5. On the stove they have apples which are being cooked.
6. These apples are for cooking.
7. Sally has a compulsive ambition to become a doctor.
8. Sally's ambition is to drive, so that she can use the family car.

EXERCISE 4-12

1. She abhors dogs that are scratching.
   She doesn't like to scratch dogs.
2. Books that are emotionally stirring always disturbed him.
   When anyone moved books, he was always disturbed.
3. We enjoy visitors who provide us entertainment.
   We like to entertain visitors.
4. Those reports encourage us.
   They encourage reports.
5. Oil that was burning frightened him.
   Whenever anyone burned oil, he became frightened.

EXERCISE 4-13

1. júmp ròpes
2. jùmp rópes
3. wâsh rágs
4. wáshràgs
5. mâp róutes
6. máp ròutes
7. flâsh líghts
8. fláshlìghts
9. wâtch dógs
10. wátchdògs

EXERCISE 4-14

1. cûtting úp
2. cútùp
3. hânded óut
4: hándòuts
5. hêld óver
6. hóldòver
7. côme dówn
8. cómedòwn
9. cómeòn
   câme ón

EXERCISE 4-15

1. ɪnstɔ́l
2. ɪnstɔ̌léšən
3. ár
4. ðe ɔ̌r gɔn
5. dipóz
6. dɛpɔ̌zíšən
7. hǽv
8. hi məstɔ̌v lɛft
9. ɔ́r
10. wɪl ɪt bi wɪnd ɔ̌r ren
11. hi kǽn bədi wont
12. hi kɔ̌n du ɪt
13. ðí
14. ðɔ̌ bɛst wən
15. ǽz yu sí, ǽžu sí
16. jəst ɔ̌z gʊd
17. mǽn.
18. pósmɔ̌n

EXERCISE 5-1

    2   3 1
1. He walked to the láb ↓
    2   3   1
2. Get out of my síght ↓

    2   **3**   **1**
3. Where is my néektie ↓
    2   **3**   **3**
4. She won't be home till twélve ↑
    2   **3** **3**
5. Are you going to the game eárly ↑
    2   **3** **3** **2**   **3**   **1**
6. To tell the trúth, ↑ I haven't learned to dánce ↓
    2   **3** **3** **2**   **3** **1**
7. Unless you take the cár, ↑ I won't gó ↓

EXERCISE 5–2

    2   **3** **1**
1. When do we éat ↓
    2   **3** **2**
2. If you'll cóme, → (or ↑)
    2   **3**   **2**
3. For the móst part, → (or ↑)
    2   **3**   **2**
4. He's very hándsome, → (or ↑) (but)
    3   **2**
5. Géorge, → (come home at once.)
    2   **3** **1** **2** **3**
6. We're going to eat in Chicágo ↓ Whére ↑ (= In what city did you say?)
    2   **3** **1** **3** **1**
7. We're going to eat in Chicágo ↓ Whére ↓ (= In which restaurant?)

EXERCISE 5–3

    2   **3**   **3 23** **1**
1. Will you have hot chócolate ↑ or mílk ↓ (one or the other)
    2   **3**   **3 23** **3**
2. Will you have hot chócolate ↑ or mílk ↑ (or something different)
    2   **2**   **3 2**   **3 2**   **3 2**   **3** **1**
3. I'm taking phýsics, ↑ chémistry, ↑ Gérman, ↑ and American hístory ↓
    2   **3**   **1**   **1 1**   **1**
4. "When are you driving hóme?" ↓ she ásked ↓
    2   **3** **1** **1**   **2**
5. Give me a líft, ↓ Gertrude ↑

EXERCISE 5–4

    2   **3** **3**
1a. Did his sister make him a *cáke* ↑
    2   **3**   **3**
  b. Did his *síster* make him a cake ↑
    2   **3**   **3**
  c. Did his sister *máke* him a caĸe ↑
    2   **3**   **3**
  d. Did his sister make *hím* a cake ↑
    2   **3** **3**
2a. Is the library in your college quite *lárge* ↑
    2 **3**   **3**
  b. Is the *líbrary* in your college quite large ↑
    2   **3**   **3**
  c. Is the library in *yóur* college quite large ↑

EXERCISE 5–5

1a. Students of cooking who belong to the Salvation Army.
  b. The Salvation Army is cooking up some nice juicy students for a mission supper.
2a. I said that Bill was an amateur, not a professional.
  b. I called Bill, who was an amateur.
  c. I called an amateur to get some help from Bill.
3a. Haven't you anything better to do than to go around scratching girls?
  b. Bess, why are you scratching yourself?
4a. Have some honey (on your waffle).
  b. Have some, honey.
5a. Ham, what are we going to have for supper?
  b. Are we having ham for supper?
6a. I am to leave instructions.
  b. I have been instructed to leave.
7a. I suspect that you were there on the spot.
  b. I suspect that you were right in that matter.
8a. People who drink Old Stump do so out of ignorance.
  b. People who drink Old Stump don't know any better whiskey.
9a. I believe man is idealistic.
  b. I believe that that particular man is idealistic.
10a. All of it is here in the book.
  b. It's OK, here in the book.

EXERCISE 5–6

1a. fâir crówd
  b. fáir cròwd
2a. wét sùit
  b. wêt súit
3a. a récord sàle
  b. a rêcord sále
4a. a sécondary ròad prògram
  b. a sêcondary róad prògram
5a. They're wáding pòols
  b. They're wâding póols.

EXERCISE 5–7

1a. Every dáy → passengers enjoy a meal like thís.
  b. Everyday pássengers → enjoy a meal like thís.
2a. The blue dréss → particularly interested her.
  b. The blue dress particularly → ínterested her.
3a. Franch pláne → with twenty-four cráshes.
  b. French plane with twenty-fóur → cráshes.
4a. I consider thése → érrors.
  b. I consider these érrors.
5a. The sóns → raise méat.
  b. The sun's ráys → méet.

EXERCISE 5–8

    2
1. ...lake that...
   2 3   1 2
2. ...Láke ↓ which...
  2
3. ...freshmen who...
   2 3   2 2
4. ...fréshmèn → who...

2
5. ...canoe that...
   2 3   1 2   2 3   3 2
6. ...Smíth ↓ who...or...Smíth ↑ who...
   2
7. ...students who...
   2 3
8. ...shrúbs which...
   2 3   1 2
9. ...lílacs ↓ which...
   2 3   2   2
10. ...Blóom → who...

EXERCISE 5–9

   2 3   1 2   3   1
1. ...Bóulder ↓ a promising júnior ↓
   3   2 2   3   2⟶
2. Hóskins → a first-string quárterback....
   2 3 2 2   3   2⟶
3. *Typhóon* → a well-known nóvel...
   2   3 1
4. ...novel *Typhóon* ↓
   2 3   1 2   3   1
5. ...nécktie ↓ a hand-painted béauty ↓
   2   3   2⟶
6. ...sister Káren....
   2 3   2 2   3   2⟶
7. ...Káren → my younger síster...
   2 3   1 2   3 1
8. ...Válley ↓ a county séat ↓
   2 3   1 2   3 1 ↓
9. ...*Cármen* ↓ a work by Bizét ↓
   2   3   2
10. ...opera *Cármen*... →

EXERCISE 5–10

1a. A strip artist who is funny dies.
 b. An artist who produces comic strips dies.
2a. He accidentally drowns a man who is wanted.
 b. He, a wanted man, accidentally drowns.
3a. Automatic collectors of the bridge toll. (That is, machines)
 b. Toll collectors for the automatic bridge.
4a. Teachers of the mentally retarded.
 b. Teachers who are mentally retarded.
5a. Wow!
 b. Come here, kid.
6a. The body works that belong to George.
 b. George's body engages in work.
7a. I love the out-of-doors.
 b. I do my loving outdoors.
8a. A certain amount of work in the library.
 b. Some people work in the library.
9a. He gave the books belonging to the library.
 b. He gave books to the library.
10a. More doctors and still more doctors are specializing.
  b. Doctors are specializing more and more.

EXERCISE 6–1

1a. ay + skrim
b. ays + krim

In *a* the /ay/ and the /s/ are both longer than in *b*, indicating that they are respectively prejunctural and postjunctural. In *a* the /k/ has only slight aspiration, indicating that it is a post-/s/ /k/. In *b* the /k/ has strong aspiration, showing that it is a postjunctural /k/.

2a. nayt + ret
b. nay + tret

In *a* the /r/ is voiced, showing it is postjunctural. In *b* the /t/ has strong aspiration, showing that it is postjunctural. In *b* the /r/ may be devoiced, showing that it follows /t/ directly without an intervening juncture.

3a. ðæt + stəf
b. ðæts + təf

In *a* the /s/ has the greater length of a postjunctural /s/, and the /t/ has the lack of aspiration of a post-/s/ /t/. The final /t/ of *a* is longer than the medial /t/ of *b*. In *b* the /s/ has the shortness of a prejunctural /s/, and the /t/ has the strong aspiration of a postjunctural /t/.

4a. sim + ebəl
b. si + mebəl

The greater length of /m/ in *b* tells our ears that it is postjunctural. (We should expect the prejunctural /i/ of *see* to be longer than the /i/ of *seem,* but laboratory experiment seems to show that the difference is not within the limits of human perception. Perhaps the /m/ following the /i/ serves to lengthen it. Compare for example the length of /i/ in *seat* and *seam.*)

5a. ɪts + lɪd
b. ɪt + slɪd

In *b* the greater length of /s/ shows that it is postjunctural, and the /l/ may be partly or wholly voiceless, showing that it directly follows /s/ without intervening juncture. In *a* the /l/ with normal voicing indicates that it is postjunctural.

6a. nu + dart
b. nud + art

In *a* the longer /u/ of /nu/ shows that it is prejunctural, and the longer /d/ of /dart/ shows that it is postjunctural.

7a. ɪt + sprez
b. ɪts + prez

In *a* /sprez/ has the longer /s/ characteristic of postjunctural /s/ and also the unaspirated /p/ of the /sp/ combination. In *b* the /s/ is shorter and the /p/ is aspirated, indicating a prejunctural /s/ and a postjunctural /p/.

EXERCISE 6–2

ME form	Process
1. a naddre	became "an adder"
2. a napron	became "an apron"
3. a nauger	became "an auger"
4. an ekename	became "a nickname"
5. a noumpere	became "an umpire"

EXERCISE 6–3

1. fîne + jób
2. mòst ŏf thĕ tíme
3. thĕ párty
4. thât + párty
5. tâlk + wísely
6. sòme ŏf thĕ + inspîred + ártìsts
7. Jâne + lôves + cándy
8. stône + fénce
9. bîrd ĭn thĕ búsh
10. óut + lòok

EXERCISE 7–1

The answers are in the text.

EXERCISE 7–2

1. splash	4. string	7. screech
2. spread	5. stupid	8. skewer
3. spew	6. sclerosis	9. squeak

EXERCISE 7–3

a. 1. spider	3. pew	8. quiet	c. 1. slam
2. stuff	4. trash	9. tree	2. sweet
3. skate	5. clean	10. twig	3. suit
b. 1. please	6. crazy	11. Tuesday	d. 1. lute (Cf. loot)
2. prey	7. cute		

EXERCISE 7–4

1. snow	8. dwell	15. flame	22. view
2. smoke	9. gleam	16. fresh	23. whinny
3. bleed	10. grass	17. feud	24. huge
4. breeze	11. gules	18. thread	25. chew
5. beauty	12. sphere	19. thews	26. juice
6. dream	13. music	20. thwack	
7. dew	14. news	21. shred	

EXERCISE 7–5

OSV
1. t r ee

OSV
2. c l ass

OSV
3. s w ig

O S V
4. c [y] ute

OSV
5. s mell

OSV
6. s n eeze

EXERCISE 7–6

VSO
1. clump

VSO
2. hi n t

VSO
3. he l p

VSO
4. ha r d

VSO
5. si n k
VSS (glide before nasal)
6. ba r n
VOO (fricative before stop)
7. ta s k

EXERCISE 7–7

1. pueblo	6. svelte	11. Schmidt	16. Vries
2. Buena Vista	7. spitz	12. Schneider	17. voyageur
3. guava	8. shtetl	13. schwa	18. zloty
4. moire	9. shkotzim	14. tsetse	19. Zwingli
5. noir	10. Schlitz	15. Vladivostok	20. joie

EXERCISE 7–8

1. /ŋ/   2. /ž/

EXERCISE 7–9

1. s 1	5. tθ 2	9. ŋkθ 3	13. lftθ 4
2. sk 2	6. mpt 3	10. kst 3	14. ksts 4
3. skt 3	7. nts 3	11. -rst 3	15. kstθs 5
4. ltθ 3	8. nts 3	12. kstθ 4	16. lftθs 5

In 12, 13, 15, and 16 the /t/ is questionable.

EXERCISE 7–10

1. it	4. ɛvri	7. əbəv	10. ʊmlaut
2. ɪt	5. æt	8. ar	11. ozon
3. et	6. ərǰ	9. uz	12. ɔfəl

The final unstressed vowel in words like *every, ready, forty* is usually pronounced with a tongue position between /i/ and /ɪ/. In this book we have arbitrarily assigned it to the /i/ phoneme.

EXERCISE 7–11

/u/	/ʊ/
uz	ʊmpf
udəlz	ʊrdu
ups	
ulɔŋ	

EXERCISE 7–12

1. sit	5. sæt	9. sup
2. sɪt	6. sərf	10. sʊt
3. set	7. səf (sough)	11. sop
4. sɛt	8. sab	12. sɔt

EXERCISE 7–13

4. /həra/, /ala/, /ša/, /pa/, /ma/, /aha/ = hurrah, Allah, shah, pa, ma, aha

EXERCISE 7–14

1. /mi/	5. /glu/
2. /me/	6. /mo/
3. /mər/ = myrrh	7. /sɔ/
4. /sofə/	

EXERCISE 8–1

1. 1	4. 2	7. 2	10. 1	13. 2	16. 2	19. 2
2. 2	5. 1	8. 1	11. 2	14. 2	17. 1	20. 1
3. 1	6. 1	9. 2	12 1	15. 1	18. 2	

EXERCISE 8–2

1. before
2. again
3. like
4. one who
5. not

6. marked by
7. most
8. not
9. not
10. bad

EXERCISE 8–3

1. speak*er*
2. king*dom*
3. *petro*dollar
4. idol*ize*
5. selec*tive*

6. *bio*mass
7. *inter vene*
8. *re*make
9. dream*ed*
10. *un*do

EXERCISE 8–4

1. *woman*ly
2. en*dear*
3. *fail*ure
4. *fam*ous
5. in*fam*ous

6. *light*en
7. en*light*en
8. *friend*ship
9. be*friend*
10. *Boston*ian

11. un*likely*
12. pre*war*
13. sub*way*
14. *fals*ify
15. unen*liven*ed

EXERCISE 8–5

1. hear
2. kill
3. mouth, speak
4. water

5. writing
6. body
7. hold
8. hang

9. hand
10. throw

EXERCISE 8–6

1. earth writing   geology
                    oceanography
2. life study   biochemistry
                    mythology
3. book lover   bibliography
                    Francophile
4. come   convene
5. seize   apprehend
6. run   current
7. look   spectacles
8. place, put   depose

9. breathe   respire
10. gnaw   erode
11. carry   report
12. break   erupt
13. year   annuity
14. flesh   carnage
15. marriage   polygamy

OPTIONAL EXERCISE 8–7

1. day's eye
2. little mouse
3. eyebrow
4. wind eye
5. little donkey

6. the die (sg. of dice)
7. pebble
8. kick
9. goad
10. pond

EXERCISE 8–8

1. against
2. around
3. with

antimissile
circumferènce
cocurricular
collide
comply
convoke
correlate

4. against	contravene
5. do the opposite of	deactivate
6. not	dishonest
7. not	incompetent
	impossible
	illegal
	irreplaceable
8. in, on	inscribe
	impale
9. between	intercede
10. within	intravenous
11. against, opposite	obstacle
	oppress
12. before	preconceive
13. after	postmortem
14. forward	progress
15. backward	retrogress
16. half	semisoft
17. under	substandard
18. over	superhuman
19. not	unattractive
20. do the opposite of	unfold

EXERCISE 8–9

1. feet
2. mice
3. took, taken
4. grew, grown
5. spun, spun
6. shook, shaken
7. rang, rung
8. tore, torn
9. rode, ridden
10. found, found

EXERCISE 8–10

1. 2	6. 3
2. 3	7. 2
3. 2	8. 2
4. 3	9. 2
5. 2	10. 3

EXERCISE 8–11

1. livened
2. terminating
3. moralizers
4. provincialisms
5. gruesomely
6. workability
7. innermost
8. marriageability
9. gangsterdom
10. affectionately

EXERCISE 8–12

1.	{-D pt}	past tense
2.	{-s pl}	noun plural
3.	{-s 3d}	present third-person singular
4.	{-s sg ps}	noun singular possessive
5.	{-s pl ps}	noun plural possessive
6.	{-ING vb}	present participle
7.	{-ER cp}	comparative

8. {-D pt}   past tense
9. {-EST sp}   superlative
10. {-D pp}   past participle
11. {-D pt}   past tense
12. {-D pt}   past tense
13. {-ING vb}   present participle
14. {-s pl}   noun plural
15. {-s 3d}   present third-person singular

EXERCISE 8–13

1. happiness
2. friendship
3. girlhood
4. composure
5. shrinkage
6. activity
   activism
   activation
   activeness
7. supremacy
   supremeness
8. trueness
   truth
   truism
9. paganism
10. discovery

EXERCISE 8–14

1. V (N)	N		14. N (V)	Aj
2. V (N)	Aj		15. N (V)	N
3. V	N		16. N (Aj)	N
4. V	N		17. N	A (N)
5. Aj (N)	V		18. V	Aj
6. Aj	V		19. V	Aj
7. Aj	Av		20. V	Aj
8. N (V)	Aj		21. N	Aj (N)
9. N (V)	N		22. N (V)	Aj
10. V (N)	N		23. Aj	V
11. V	N		24. Aj	N
12. N	Aj		25. V	N
13. N (V)	N			

EXERCISE 8–15

1. reasonableness
2. formality
3. organization
4. purification
5. puristic

EXERCISE 8–16

1. kindnesses
2. beautified
3. quarterlies
4. popularized
5. depths
6. pressures
7. arrivals
8. orientated
9. friendlier
10. funniest

No words can be formed by adding another inflectional suffix to the above words.

EXERCISE 8–17

You may have more than those given below.

1. sinful, sinfulness, sinless, sinlessness, sinner
2. kindly, kindliness, kindless, kindness, unkind, unkindly, unkindliness, unkindness

3. alive, aliveness, lively, liveliness, livelihood, liven, enliven, unenliven, unlively, un-liveliness
4. transportable, transportability, transporter, transportation, transportational
5. audibility, auditory, auditive, audile, audio, audit, auditor, auditorium, audience, audition, audiophile

EXERCISE 8-18

1. {-ER cp}
2. {-ER rp}
3. {-ER n}
4. {-ER cp}
5. {-ER rp}

EXERCISE 8-19

1. Aj-al	6. V-al	11. Aj-al
2. N-al	7. V-al	12. Aj-al
3. V-al	8. Aj-al	13. V-al
4. Aj-al	9. V-al	14. Aj-al
5. N-al	10. N-al	15. Aj-al

EXERCISE 8-20

1. V-al	6. V-al
2. Aj-al	7. V-al
3. Aj-al	8. Aj-al
4. V-al	9. Aj-al
5. V-al	10. Aj-al

EXERCISE 8-21

1. a. It was a completed job.
   b. It was an artistic (perfected, polished) job.
2. a. Our new surgeon is quiet, reticent.
   b. Our new surgeon is kept in reserve, set aside to practice his specialty.

EXERCISE 8-22

1. 1	5. 2	9. 2
2. 2	6. 2	10. 2
3. 2	7. 1	
4. 1	8. 2	

EXERCISE 8-23

1. IS	6. DS	11. DS	16. Amb
2. DS	7. Amb	12. DS	17. Amb
3. DS	8. DS	13. DS	18. DS
4. IS	9. DS	14. DS	19. DS
5. IS	10. DS	15. IS	20. DS

EXERCISE 8-24

1. Pauline	9. Caroline, Carolina
2. chanteuse	10. empress
3. protégée	11. laundress
4. czarina	12. proprietress
5. songstress	13. waitress
6 majorette	14. trickster
7. heiress	15. executrix
8. equestrienne	

EXERCISE 8–25

1. Bobby
2. gosling
3. statuette
4. locket
5. dearie
6. babykins
7. packet
8. puppy
9. tablet
10. Annie
11. lordling
12. droplet
13. laddie
14. manikin
15. cigarette

EXERCISE 8–26

1. fillette
   sonnette
2. casita
   maquinilla
3. stanzina
4. fetita
5. puliki (the word iki means "small" in Hawaiian)
6. Hündchen
7. casinha
8. huisje

The three vowels used as diminutive suffixes are /i/, /ɛ/, and /ə/. The diminutive vowel /ɪ/ is frequent in English but infrequent in some other languages.

EXERCISE 8–27

Unlawful is wrongly cut because the first cut leaves *unlaw,* which is not a free form.

EXERCISE 8–28

1. item | ize | d

2. pre | pro | fess | ion | al

3. news | paper | dom

4. counter | de | clar | ation

5. mal | con | struc | tion

6. contra | dict | ory

7. dis | en | throne

8. mid | after | noon

9. Ice | land | ic

10. super | natur | al

11. un | com | fort | able

12. fest | iv | al

13. en | gag | ing

14. ex | press | ion | ism

15. mis | judg | ment

or mis | judg | ment

EXERCISE 8-29

Morpheme	Free allomorph	Bound allomorph
1. {strong}	/strɔŋ/	/streŋ-/
2. {chaste}	/čest/	/čæst-/
3. {courage}	/kərəj/	/kərej-/
4. {Bible}	/baybəl/	/bɪbl-/
5. {wife}	/wayf/	/wayv-/

EXERCISE 8-30

The two forms *a/an* have the same meaning and are in complementary distribution, *a* occurring before consonants and *an* before vowels.

EXERCISE 8-31

1. {wide} = /wayd/ ~ /wɪd-/
2. {broad} = /brɔd/ ~ /brɛd-/
3. {wolf} = /wulf/ ~ /wulv-/
4. {able} = /ébel/ ~ /əbíl-/
5. {supreme} = /səprím/ ~ /səprɛm-/
6. {divine} = /dəváyn/ ~ /dəvɪn-/
7. {fame} = /fem/ ~ /-fəm-/
8. {vise} = /vɪž-/ ~ /vayz/
9. {sun} = /sən/
10. {atom} = /ǽtəm/ ~ /ətám-/

EXERCISE 8-32

1. sənz
2. næps
3. pæsəz
4. hɔgz
5. sæks
6. fɪzəz
7. dɪšəz
8. gəražəz
9. hoz
10. stæfs
11. čərčəz
12. gɔrjəz
13. səmz
14. hiθs
15. gɔŋz

{-s pl} = /-s/   /-z/   /-əz/

CD: /-əz/ after /s/, /z/, /š/, /ž/, /č/, and /j/
/-s/ after other voiceless sounds
/-z/ after other voiced sounds

EXERCISE 8-33

{be} + {-D pt} = /wəz/ ∞ /wər/

EXERCISE 8-34

1. /sɔ/ = /si/ + /i > ɔ/
2. /bigæn/ = /bigɪn/ + /ɪ > æ/
3. /bɪt/ = /bayt/ + /ay > ɪ/
4. /gev/ = /gɪv/ + /ɪ > e/
5. /gru/ = /gro/ + /o > u/
6. /rod/ = /rayd/ + /ay > o/
7. /grawnd/ = /graynd/ + /ay > aw/

8. /tʊk/ = /tek/ + /e > ʊ/
9. /tɔr/ = /tɛr/ + /ɛ > ɔ/
10. /spok/ = /spik/ + /i > o/

EXERCISE 8–35

1. meat
   meet
   mete
2. might (noun)
   mite
   might (aux.)
3. you
   yew
   ewe

4. pear
   pare
   pair
5. its
   it's
6. to
   two
   too (= also)
   too (= more than should be)

EXERCISE 8–36

1. point
2. moving light; smallness; repetition
3. light, smallness, repetition
4. smallness, repetition
5. undesirable
6. undesirable
7. abrupt stoppage of movement
8. unabrupt stoppage of movement
9. smallness
10. smallness

11. light
12. repetition
13. smallness
14. repetition
15. undesirable
16. smallness
17. abrupt stoppage of movement
18. smallness; repetition
19. smallness
20. repetition

ORAL EXERCISE 8–A

The answer is: *small*.

EXERCISE 9–1

1. 0, 8
2. 7, 7
3. 3, 5

4. 6 7 8, 6
5. 0, 7
6. 6, 7

EXERCISE 9–2

1. knave	S	8. pur | ist	Cx	15. en | able	Cx
2. knav | ish	Cx	9. oyster	S	16. mete	S
3. graph	S	10. mis | anthrope	Cx	17. met | er	Cx
4. tele | graph	Cx	11. philo | sophy	Cx	18. hydro | meter	Cx
5. aqua | naut	Cx	12. cannibal	S	19. disco | graphy	Cx
6. bi | cycle	Cx	13. refus | al	Cx	20. ski | nik	Cx
7. pure	S	14. dent | al	Cx		

EXERCISE 9–3

1. 1
2. 7
3. 2
4. 4
5. 3
6. 8

7. 8
8. 3
9. 3
10. 5 or 1
11. 3
12. 9

EXERCISE 9–4

1. Cd
2. Gs
3. Cd
4. Gs
5. Cd, Gs
6. Cd
7. Gs

8. Cd
9. Cd
10. Gs
11. Cd
12. Gs
13. Cd
14. Gs

EXERCISE 9–5

1. shárp | shòoter   Cd
2. shârp shóoter   Gs
3. act   S
4. re | act   Cx
5. rattle | snake   Cd
6. pass | book   Cd
7. apparatus   S
8. glow | worm   Cd

9. im | port   Cx
10. rip | cord   Cd

11. un | earth   Cx
12. rat- | a- | tat   Cx
13. beauty   S
14. beauti | fy   Cx
15. geo | metry   Cx
16. búll's | èye
       (of target)   Cd
17. bùll's éye   Gs
       (of bull)
18. out | last   Cd
19. bio | chemical   Cx
20. in | accessible   Cx

EXERCISE 10–1

1. C
2. D
3. E
4. I
5. I

6. E
7. C
8. E
9. D
10. D

EXERCISE 10–2

1. pornographic
2. discothèque
3. taxicab
4. cabriolet
5. delicatessen
6. vibrations
7. geneva
8. hypodermic

9. curiosity
10. memorandum
11. Frederick
12. Albert, Alfred, Alvin
13. Thomas
14. Joseph
15. Philip, Philbert

EXERCISE 10–3

1. disport
2. turnpike
3. omnibus
4. caravan
5. parachute

6. periwig
7. acute
8. Eugene
9. Elizabeth
10. Anthony

EXERCISE 10–4

1. American Indian

2. maître d'hôtel
3. condensation trail
4. taximeter cab
5. motor + pedal
6. agitatsiya (= agitation) + propaganda. From Russian
7. communication satellite
8. agriculture business

EXERCISE 10–5

1. recreational vehicle
2. National Organization of Women, negotiable order of withdrawal (new bank term meaning check)
3. United Nations Educational, Scientific, and Cultural Organization
4. Old Kinderhook
5. self-contained underwater breathing apparatus
6. Organization of Petroleum Exporting Countries
7. white, Anglo-Saxon Protestant
8. Intercontinental Ballistic Missile
9. GP = general purpose
10. light amplification by stimulated emission of radiation

EXERCISE 10–6

1. flinch + funk
2. happen + circumstance
3. stagnation + inflation
4. simultaneous + broadcast
5. gelatin + Latin *ignis*, fire, + Eng. -ite
6. smoke + fog
7. dumb + confound
8. tele- + broadcast
9. dance + handle
10. splash + spatter

EXERCISE 10–7

1. transistor
2. autobus
3. escalator
4. blurt
5. squawk

EXERCISE 10–8

1. need   needy
   speed   speedy
   seed   seedy
   bead   beady
2. televise
3. donate
   orate

EXERCISE 10–9

1. housekeeper
2. typewriter
3. administrator
4. resurrection
5. baby-sitter
6. advance-registration
7. lazy
8. sideling
9. escalator
10. reminiscence
11. snap-judgment
12. deficit-spending
13. emotion
14. reluctance
15. party-pooper
16. back-seat driver
17. hang glider

EXERCISE 10–10

1. femel
2. Fr. carriole
3. Sp. cucaracha
4. agnail, angnail (*ag-, ang-* meant painful.)
5. Welsh rabbit (*Welsh rabbit* was probably a jocular term, like *prairie oysters* for eggs and *Cape Cod turkey* for codfish.)
6. Dutch *kool* (cabbage) + sla (salad) became English coleslaw.
7. bridegome (When *-gome* [man] became obsolete, the nearest similar term for a human male was *groom.*)
8. helpmeet (*Helpmeet* was formed by a misunderstanding of Genesis ii:18 and 20, "...an help meet [= fitting] for him."

EXERCISE 10–11

1. From the fourth Earl of Sandwich "who once spent twenty-four hours at the gaming table with no other refreshment than some slices of cold beef between slices of toast." OED
2. Hamburger (= of Hamburg, Germany)
3. Frankfurter (= of Frankfurt, Germany)
4. Wiener (= of Vienna) + wurst (= sausage)
5. Bologna, Italy
6. French, serge de Nîmes (= serge of Nîmes, France)
7. Kashmir, India
8. Short for *jean fustian,* a tough cloth. The *jean* is from French Gênes (Genoa, Italy), where it was made.
9. Jules Léotard, an aerial gymnast
10. Guy Fawkes, an English conspirator of the seventeenth century. In England on Guy Fawkes Day his effigy, clad in grotesque and ill-fitting garments, was carried about the streets and then burnt in the evening amid fireworks. It was accompanied by other effigies of unpopular persons which were called "guys."

EXERCISE 10–12

1. wiggle
2. patter
3. wit
4. super
5. none
6. both

EXERCISE 10–13

1. 3
2. 3
3. 3
4. 1
5. 2
6. 2
7. 2
8. 3
9. 2
10. 2

EXERCISE 11–1

	Plural	Possessive	Plural + Possessive
1.	carpenters	carpenter's	carpenters'
2.	women	woman's	women's
3.	brothers brethren	brother's	brothers'
4.	clouds	cloud's	clouds'
5.	cattle	————	cattle's
6.	ducks duck	duck's	ducks'

7. Japanese	_____	_____
8. means	_____	_____
9. athletics	athletics'	_____
10. scissors	scissors'	scissors

(There are differences of usage among the noun forms, particularly with the possessive.)

EXERCISE 11–2

1. them Pl		6. them Pl
2. it Sg		7. it Sg
3. it Sg		8. them Pl
4. them Pl		9. it Sg
5. them Pl		10. it Sg

EXERCISE 11–3

1. few
2. that
3. its
4. their
5. both

EXERCISE 11–4

1. was
2. were
3. is
4. are
5. has

EXERCISE 11–5

1. Sg	4. Sg	7. Pl
2. Pl	5. Sg	8. Sg
3. Pl	6. Pl	9. Sg
		10. Pl

EXERCISE 11–6

1. child, children
   /čɪldrən/ = /čayld/ + /ay > ɪ/ + /-rən/
2. herring, herring
   /herɪŋ/ = /herɪŋ/ + /ø/
3. foot, feet
   /fit/ = /fʊt/ + /ʊ > i/
4. leaf, leaves
   /livz/ = /lif/ + /f > v/ + /-z/
5. wolf, wolves
   /wʊlvz/ = /wʊlf/ + /f > v/ + /-z/

EXERCISE 11–7

One allomorph	*Two allomorphs*
grief	scarf
chief	truth
belief	wharf
waif	sheath
	wreath
	staff

EXERCISE 11-8

1. /a/ > /i/
2. /-z/ or /ə > i or ay/
3. /-əz/ or /s > rə/
4. /-əz/ or /ɪks > əsiz/
5. /əm > ə/
6. /ɪs > iz/
7. /-ɪm/
8. /∅/ or /-əz/
9. /-z/ or /əm > ə/
10. /əs > i or ay/
11. /-z/ or /əm > ə/
12. /o > i/
13 /-əz/ or /əs > ay/
14. /əs > iz/
15. /-n/

EXERCISE 11-9

1. 4	5. 5	9. 3, 1
2. 3, 5	6. 3	10. 5
3. 2	7. 5	
4. 6	8. 4	

EXERCISE 11-10

1. 5, 6
2. 1, 6
3. 1, 2
4. 1, 3, 5, 6
5. 5, 6

EXERCISE 11-11

There are no *right* answers, as this is an investigation of the usage of the class.

EXERCISE 11-12

1. N	6. N	11. —
2. —	7. N	12. N
3. N	8. N	13. N
4. —	9. —	14. N
5. —	10. —	15. —

EXERCISE 11-13

Pres. 3rd Sg.	Pres. P.	Past T.	Past Part.	
1. bids	bidding	bid, bade	bid, bidden	3, 4, or 5
2. bites	biting	bit	bit, bitten	4 or 5
3. keeps	keeping	kept	kept	4
4. freezes	freezing	froze	frozen	5
5. sets	setting	set	set	3
6. sells	selling	sold	sold	4
7. puts	putting	put	put	3
8. rises	rising	rose	risen	5
9. teases	teasing	teased	teased	4
10. sleeps	sleeping	slept	slept	4

EXERCISE 11–14

	Past T.	Past P.			Past T.	Past P.
1.	stəŋ	stəŋ		8.	ræŋ	rəŋ
2.	krɛpt	krɛpt		9.	kɛpt	kɛpt
3.	drov	drɪvən		10.	dɛlt	dɛlt
4.	sæŋ	səŋ		11.	swæm	swəm
5.	rod	rɪdən		12.	spən	spən
6.	rot	rɪtən		13.	wən	wən
7.	kləŋ	kləŋ		14.	spræŋ	sprəŋ

Class 1: sting, cling, spin, win $\{$-D pt $\} = /\text{ɪ} > \text{ə}/$
$\{$-D pp $\} = /\text{ɪ} > \text{ə}/$

Class 2: creep, keep, deal $\{$-D pt $\} = /\text{i} > \text{ɛ}/ + /\text{t}/$
$\{$-D pp $\} = /\text{i} > \text{ɛ}/ + /\text{t}/$

Class 3: drive, ride, write $\{$-Dpt $\} = /\text{ay} > \text{o}/$
$\{$-Dpp $\} = /\text{ay} > \text{ɪ}/$
$+ /\text{ən}/$

Class 4: sing, ring, swim, spring $\{$-Dpt$\} = /\text{ɪ} > \text{æ}/$
$\{$-Dpp$\} = /\text{ɪ} > \text{e}/$

EXERCISE 11–15

1. N	5. N	9. N	13. NV	17. N
2. NV	6. V	10. NV	14. N	18. NV
3. V	7. NV	11. N	15. N	19. NV
4. N	8. V	12. V	16. NV	20. V

EXERCISE 11–16

1. I have practiced my piano lesson <u>yesterday</u> afternoon.
2. I practiced my piano lesson yesterday afternoon.
3. Her roommate received an award last Wednesday.
4. Her roommate has received an award <u>last</u> <u>Wednesday</u>.
5. <u>Two</u> <u>years</u> <u>ago</u> I have visited Spain.
6. She stayed in the hospital fifteen days.
7. She has stayed in the hospital fifteen days.
8. It has rained since one o'clock.
9. She has played tennis last night.
10. I have worked in the <u>garden</u> <u>for</u> three days.

EXERCISE 11–17

1. I	5. I	9. C
2. P	6. P	10. I
3. C	7. CP	
4. CP	8. I	

EXERCISE 11–18

With some of these forms there is variation in usage both among different speakers and in the speech of a single individual. The answers here are the forms that the author would generally use, and yours may be different.

1. angrier   angriest
2. healthier   healthiest
3.   bitterest
4. commoner   commonest
5. crueler   cruelest

6.		foolishest
7.	handsomer	handsomest
8.		
9.	mellower	mellowest
10.	pleasanter	pleasantest
11.	quieter	quietest
12.	remoter	remotest
13.	severer	severest
14.		solidest
15.	stupider	stupidest
16.	nobler	noblest
17.	dustier	dustiest
18.	dirtier	dirtiest
19.	livelier	liveliest
20	gentler	gentlest

EXERCISE 11–19

1.	oftener	oftenest
2.	No	
3.	No	
4.	No (But cf. Tennyson's	

Music that gentlier on the spirit lies
Than tired eyelids upon tired eyes.)

5.	later	latest
6.	No	
7.	No	
8.	No	
9.	No	
10.	slower	slowest
11.	No	
12.	nearer	nearest
13.	No	
14.	farther	farthest
	further	furthest
15.	quicker	quickest
16.	No	
17.	louder	loudest
18.	No	
19.	higher	highest
20.	lower	lowest

EXERCISE 11–20

1.	better	best	4.	littler	littlest
2.	worse	worst		less	least
3.	older	oldest	5.	more	most
	elder	eldest	6.	fewer	fewest
				less	least

EXERCISE 11–21

1. Aj	6. NA
2. NA	7. Aj
3. Aj	8. Aj
4. NA	9. NA
5. NA	10. Aj

EXERCISE 12–1

1. president . . . plan.   3, 3
2. janitors . . . umbrella.   2, 3
3. counselor . . . approach.   3, 3
4. aunt . . . son.   3, 3
5. Mother's cake.   1, 3

[Exercise 12–2 omitted]

EXERCISE 12–3

1. failure	fail	-ure	11. sickness	sick	-ness
2. payment	pay	-ment	12. refusal	refuse	-al
3. assistant	assist	-ant	13. width	wide	-th
4. sailor	sail	-or	14. sincerity	sincere	-ity
5. catcher	catch	-er	15. freedom	free	-dom
6. collision	collide	-ion	16. Childhood	child	-hood
7. leakage	leak	-age	17. lawyer	law	-yer
8. Reformation	reform	-ation	18. scholarship	scholar	-ship
9. discovery	discover	-y	19. fragrance	fragrant	-ce
10. amusement	amuse	-ment	20. intimacy	intimate	-cy

EXERCISE 12–4

1. met	4	past tense	6. eats	5	pres. 3rd sg.
2. swept	4	past part.	7. set	3	past tense
3. leave	4	stem	8. lying	5	pres. part.
4. spreading	3	pres. part.	9. bought	4	past part.
5. eaten	5	past part.	10. sank	5	past tense

EXERCISE 12–5

1. amplified	ample	-ify
2. personifies	person	-ify
3. prove	proof	-ve
4. weaken	weak	-en
5. liberalized	liberal	-ize
6. strengthen	strength	-en
7. idolize	idol	-ize
8. terrorized	terror	-ize
9. soften	soft	-en
10. frightened	fright	-en

EXERCISE 12–6

	-er	*-est*	*-ly*	*-ness*
1.	closer	closest	closely	closeness
2.	icier	iciest	icily	iciness
3.	sweeter	sweetest	sweetly	sweetness

4. sadder	saddest	sadly	sadness
5. higher	highest	highly	highness
6. sunnier	sunniest	sunnily	sunniness
7. gentler	gentlest	gently	gentleness
8. smaller	smallest	—	smallness
9. littler	littlest	—	littleness
10. faster	fastest	—	fastness
11. holier	holiest	holily	holiness
12. longer	longest	—	longness
13. friendlier	friendliest	friendlily	friendliness
14. iller	illest	illy	illness
worse	worst		
15. —	—	naturally	naturalness

(Some of the words that fit the blanks above, like *illy* and *holily*, are listed in current dictionaries but are probably of low frequency. The use of some others, like *friendlily*, is a matter of dialect or idiolect.)

EXERCISE 12–7

1. gold — -en
2. help — -less
3. love — -ly
4. mess — -y
5. peace — -ful
6. insul- — -ar
7. nerve — -ous
8. fragment — -ary
9. repent — -ant
10. affection — -ate
11. fool — -ish
12. rhythm — -ic
13. region — -al
14. tire — -ed
15. separate /et/ — /ət/
16. recur — -ent
17. instruct — -ive
18. perish — -able
19. meddle — -some
20. congratulate — -ory
21. please — -ant
22. good — -ly
23. live — -ly

EXERCISE 12–8

1. Aj
2. Av
3. Av
4. Aj
5. Av
6. Av
7. Av
8. Av
9. Aj
10. Aj
11. Av
12. Av
13. Av
14. Av
15. Av

EXERCISE 12–9

1. UW

2. N

3. N
4. V
5. N
6. Aj

7. UW
8. Av
9. Aj
10. UW

EXERCISE 13-1

1. very   Aj
2. too   Aj
3. quite   Av
4. somewhat   Aj
5. rather   Aj

EXERCISE 13-2

1. UW
2. Av
3. V
4. N
5. V
6. Av

7. UW
8. UW
9. Aj
10. Av
11. N

EXERCISE 13-3

1. enough
2. indeed, still
3. just, right, even
4. a bit, a good deal, a great deal, a lot, almost, any (in questions and negatives), a whole lot, even, indeed, lots, much, no, some, somewhat, still

EXERCISE 13-4

1. The car stopped ăt the station.

2. He came frŏm the farm.

3. This is the farm he came fròm.   No

4. These roses are fŏr you.

5. The chimpanzee ĭn the cage was yawning.

6. The lad stood on a barrel.

7. The plumber washed ĭn the basin.

8. The rose bў the window was wilted.

9. He objected tŏ the last paragraph.

10. What is it fór?

EXERCISE 13-5

Dissyllabic prepositions have a primary stress when the object is a personal pronoun and weak and third stresses when the object is a noun.

EXERCISE 13-6

1. bĕlów

2. bĕlòw

3. néar

4. nèar

5. òff

6. óff

7. áfter

8. àftĕr

9. sínce

10. sìnce

(Prepositions usually take third and weak stresses.)

EXERCISE 13–7

1. Barring
2. following
3. following
4. regarding
5. regarding
6. Considering
7. including
8. including
9. beginning
10. concerning

EXERCISE 13–8

1. ahead of
2. on account of
3. up at
4. Contrary to
5. by way of
6. on behalf of
7. instead of
8. in lieu of
9. In spite of
10 In case of

EXERCISE 13–9

1. D	6. D	11. NS
2. NS	7. D	12. D
3. D	8. D	13. D
4. D	9. D	14. D
5. NS	10. D	15. D

EXERCISE 13–10

1. Police raid a gathering
2. Complete the faculty at State
   A complete faculty at State
3. Rule the book not obscene
   The rule book not obscene
4. A clean model house
   Clean the model house
5. A girl shows top baby beef
   Girl shows top the baby beef

EXERCISE 13–11

1. 2
2. 2
3. 3
4. 0
5. 2

EXERCISE 13–12

1. PA
2. MA
3. P
4. MA
5. PA

EXERCISE 13–13

1. <u>MA be</u>
   <u>must</u> <u>be</u>
2. <u>MA   have</u>
   <u>ought</u> to <u>have</u>
3. <u>MA be</u>
   <u>could</u> <u>be</u>
4. <u>MA have be</u>
   <u>could</u> <u>have</u> <u>been</u>
5. <u>MA have</u>
   <u>might</u> <u>have</u>

None differs from the sequence described.

EXERCISE 13–14

1. Neg. He was not eating.   Aux
   Q.   Was he eating?
2. Neg. He did not quit eating.   V
   Q.   Did he quit eating?
3. Neg. The worker was not killed.   Aux
   Q.   Was the worker killed?
4. Neg. The worker has not gone.   Aux
   Q.   Has the worker gone?
5. Neg. We should not hurry.   Aux
   Q.   Should we hurry?
6. Neg. We cannot hurry.   Aux
   Q.   Can we hurry?
7. Neg. They are not going.   Aux
   Q.   Are they going?
8. Neg. They did not keep going.   V
   Q.   Did they keep going?
9. Neg. He might not have been sleeping. Aux
   Q.   Might he have been sleeping?
10. Neg. He will not play.   Aux
    Q.   Will he play?

EXERCISE 13–15

1. whom
2. whom
3. who
4. whom
5. whom

EXERCISE 13–16

1. who   Hum
2. who   Hum
3. which   Nhum

4. who, which   Hum, Nhum
5. which   Nhum

EXERCISE 13–17

1. *my*   PP
2. *mine* SbP
3. *his*   PP
4. *ours* SbP
5. *hers* SbP

6. *yours* SbP
7. *your*   PP
8. *their* PP
9. *ours*   SbP
10. *her*   PP

EXERCISE 14–1

1. fence
2. fence
3. fence
4. fence
5. fence

6. fence
7. putter
8. putter
9. car
10. swings

EXERCISE 14–2

1. The small study table
2. Any great European opera
3. That somber evening sky
4. My roommate's tennis shoes
5. All the other white linen handkerchiefs
6. A soft pat on the head
7. A hard blow which staggered him
8. That broken ski lying in the basement
9. A junior with a lame leg who was walking on crutches
10. The girl in the front row whose books he was carrying

EXERCISE 14–3

Here are a few samples of the kinds of modifiers you might use.

1. The sailboats on the bay are beautiful to watch.
2. They sailed under the wooden bridge near the lighthouse.
3. He makes exquisite jewelry which is bought by collectors.

EXERCISE 14–4

1. Stepped
2. Stepped
3. stepped
4. Stepped
5. shouted

6. shouted
7. watching
8. eaten
9. driven
10. Spoke

EXERCISE 14–5

1. Sold
2 Sold

6. gave
7. paid

3. Appeared
4. chose
5. remained

8. called
9. was
10. returned

EXERCISE 14–6

1. pony ... | galloped
2. students | attended
3. senior ... | will be honored
4. pipes ... | pounded
5. choir ... | sang

EXERCISE 14–7

Here are samples of what you might do.

1. The tiny leak in the hose soon became enlarged.
2. The canoe that he wanted was a narrow, aluminum model.
3. The pie had a rich, flaky crust.
4. The steaming apple pie made her mouth water.
5. The passenger in the front seat who was watching the speedometer became nervous.

EXERCISE 14–8

Here are samples of what you might do.

1. Emil later regretted his decision.
2. The lad with the freckled nose came after his dog when school was over.
3. The summer vacationers will soon return to college.
4. That gloomy grind always seemed to have a complaint to make.
5. The mountaineer merrily swung the heavy pack on his back to begin the long hike.

EXERCISE 14–9

1. Was the boy who mows the lawn ill?
2. Did her youngest brother break his bicycle?
3. Should the students on the debate squad be excused?
4. Are the monkeys playing on the swings from India?
5. Will the old gymnasium which was built in 1907 be replaced?

EXERCISE 14–10

1. The cat purrs.
2. The student studies.
3. The house deteriorates.
4. The vase breaks.
5. The visitor departs.

EXERCISE 14–11

1. Cats prowl.
2. Musicians play.
3. Professors teach.
4. Buses wait.
5. Comedians laugh.

EXERCISE 14–12

1. purposes   make
2. leader   selects
3. one   maintains
4. difference   appears
5. troublemakers   were

EXERCISE 14–13

1. The patients are being watched.
2. The janitors have waxed the floor.
3. The wrestlers do not smoke.
4. The cars have been stolen.
5. The ships were disappearing beyond the horizon.

EXERCISE 14–14

1. cat sleeps   cats sleep
2. cat sleeps   cats sleep
3. junior refuses   juniors refuse
4. milkman delivers   milkmen deliver
5. paper goes   papers go

EXERCISE 14–15

1. They found out who I am.   I
2. We are eager to know who he is.   he
3. The police could not discover who they are. they
4. The auditor asked what the amount was.   amount
5. Can you tell which one is yours?   one
   Can you tell which one yours is?   yours

EXERCISE 15–1

1. 1		6. —
2. —		7. 1
3. 1		8. 1
4. —		9. —
5. 1		10. 1

EXERCISE 15–2

1. 2		6. 2
2. 1		7. 2
3. 1		8. 2
4. 2		9. 1
5. 2		10. 2

EXERCISE 15–3

1. 3		6. 3
2. 2		7. 1
3. 1		8. 1
4. 3		9. 2
5. 3		10. 3

EXERCISE 15–4

1. 4
2. other
3. other
4. 4
5. 4

6. other
7. other
8. 4
9. 4
10. other

EXERCISE 15–5

1. other
2. 4
3. 4
4. other
5. 4

6. 4
7. 4
8. other
9. 4
10. 4

EXERCISE 15–6

1. 5
2. 5
3. other
4. 5
5. other
6. 5

7. other
8. 5
9. other
10. 5
11. other
12. 5

EXERCISE 15–7

1. InV
2. InV
3. InV
4. —
5. InV
6. —
7. InV
8. —

9. InV
10. —
11. InV
12. InV
13. InV
14. InV
15. InV

EXERCISE 15–8

1. it
2. him
3. them
4. her, him
5. it

6. it
7. it
8. her
9. it, him, her
10. them

EXERCISE 15–9

1. TV 7
2. InT 6
3. LV 5
4. *be* 3
5. TV 7
6. LV 4
7. InT 6
8. LV 5
9. TV 7

10. LV 4
11. *be* 1
12. TV 7
13. LV 5
14. InT 6
15. TV 7
16. *be* 2
17. *be* 3

EXERCISE 15–10

1. The window was opened (by the servant).
2. The dice were rolled (by him).

3. Dancing is liked (by most adolescents).
4. The mountains were chosen (by us) for our vacation.
5. *King Lear* has never been read (by Jim).
6. Wood was burned in the fireplace (by the tourists).
7. His sheep were counted (by the shepherd).
8. The game was begun (by us) at four o'clock.
9. A new house on the river was built (by the Smiths).
10. A pileated woodpecker was spotted (by the nature club).

EXERCISE 15–11

1. was killed

   The terrier killed the rat.
2. were turned

   The cook turned the pancakes.
3. is raised

   Farmers raised much corn in Iowa.
4. was heard

   We heard an early folk tune.
5. been washed

   Mavis has washed the dishes.
6. was had

   All had a good time.
7. was teased

   Her boy friend teased Jane.
8. been lowered

   The sergeant had lowered the flag.
9. were stopped

   The traffic officer stopped the motorcycles.
10. is played

    A carillonneur plays a carillon concert at 7:45 in the morning.

EXERCISE 15–12

1. The librarian found the pamphlet for me.
2. He assigned the toughest job to Jack.
3. The spaniel brought the stick to his master.
4. Susie fed some juicy worms to the baby robins.
5. Her mother sent a new sweater to her.

EXERCISE 15–13

1. He was given a dirty look (by her).

   A dirty look was given him (by her).
2. The manager was made a fine offer (by the company).

   A fine offer was made the manager (by the company).
3. I was dealt a bad hand (by the dealer).

   A bad hand was dealt me (by the dealer).

4. His roommate was offered the <u>car</u> (by him).

The car was offered his <u>roommate</u> (by him).

5. She was asked a <u>question</u> (by the instructor).

A question was asked <u>her</u> (by the instructor).

EXERCISE 15–14

1. The committee declared that Isabelle was the winner.
The committee declared Isabelle to be the winner.

2. She believed that George was honest.
She believed George to be honest.

3. I imagined that they were outside.
I imagined them to be outside.

4. We thought that she was overworked.
We thought her to be overworked.

5. I supposed that he was working.
I supposed him to be working.

6. We thought that she was above reproach.
We thought her to be above reproach.

EXERCISE 15–15

1. She played a trick.	8	
2. We appointed Evelyn.	9	
3. You threw a curve.	8	
4. The student body elected Arabella.	9	
5. The faculty chose Sieverson.	9	
6. We found a sandwich.	8	
7. The dealer sold an air mattress.	8	
8. She fed the baby food.	8	
9. The city elected Mouchy.	9	
10. He named his new boat.	9	

EXERCISE 15–16

1. 1	**6.** 9	**11.** 5	**16.** 4
2. 2	**7.** 3	**12.** 9	**17.** 5
3. 8	**8.** 7	**13.** 7	**18.** 2
4. 3	**9.** 9	**14.** 2	**19.** 5
5. 6	**10.** 8	**15.** 9	**20.** 9

EXERCISE 15–17

1. 8, 9	**9.** 6, 7
2. 5, 7	**10.** 7, 9
3. 4, 6	**11.** 7, 8
4. 3, 7	**12.** 8, 9
5. 7, 8	**13.** 5, 7
6. 7, 8	**14.** 7, 9
7. 1, 3	**15.** 4, 6
8. 6, 7	**16.** 7, 9

EXERCISE 16–1

1. Aj	SV	**4.** V	DO
2. N	SV	**5.** UW	OP
3. N	SV	**6.** N	SC

7. N SC	10. UW IO
8. N OC	11. UW SV
9. Av SC	12. UW DO

EXERCISE 16–2

1. DO	5. OP
2. SC	6. SV
3. OC	7. SV
4. IO	

EXERCISE 16–3

1. that	SV
2. your seat	OP
3. her	OP
4. it	IO
5. that	SV
6. the girl	SC
7. that	DO
8. it	DO
9. it, her beauty	SV
10. that	OC

EXERCISE 16–4

1. what we said	DO
2. What you do	SV
3. what I thought too	SC
4. what you have	OP
5. whoever came there	IO
6. whatever his grandfather wishes	OC
7. paying cash	OP
8. whichever is the most durable	DO
9. to bring the coffee	DO
10. mailing the letter	DO

EXERCISE 16–5

1. making
2. made
3. left
4. stolen
5. sung

EXERCISE 16–6

1. 7	8. 1
2. 8	9. 9
3 6	10. 4
4. 3	11. 7
5. 6	12. 7
6. 5	13. 7
7. 2	

EXERCISE 16–7

1. having sprinkled the lawn	7
2. seeing the play before	7
3. to be there	2
4. the guests to remain for dinner	6
5. being a member of the band	3
6. the teacher to give him an **A**	8
7. After having been cheerful for weeks	1
8. Keeping quiet	4
9. his brother repay the loan	7
10. Calling Josephine an artist	9
11. his becoming a Marine	5

EXERCISE 16–8

1a. SV	4a. OP
b. SV	b. OP
2a. OP	5a. DO
b. OP	b. DO
3a. DO	6a. SC
b. DO	b. SC

EXERCISE 16–9

1. to miss the party		DO
2. to remain calm		Md
3. Shooting quail		DO
4. you to be truthful	SV	**MD**
5. Finding the trail again		DO
6. washing dishes		DO
7. Being a golf champion		SC
8. them break the window	SV	DO
9. him to stop smoking	SV	DO
10. Electing **Betty** president	DO	OC
11. to give Harold a bicycle	IO	DO
12. visiting museums		DO

EXERCISE 16–10

1. A *clêan* ápron	Aj
2. An *évening* párty, *or* an *évening* pàrty	N
3. The *côllege* dórmitory	N
4. The *clâss* dánce	N
5. A *hôpeful* sígn	Aj
6. Their *bâck* yárd	UW
7. Those *nêighborhood* cáts	N
8. Sally's *nêw* rádio	Aj
9. That *pâper* bóok	N
10. A *fîghting* róoster	V
11. These *brôken* bóxes	V
12. An *ûpstairs* róom	UW
13. Their *garâge* dóor	N
14. The *ôffice* týpewriter	N

15. Our *schôol* príncipal   N
16. The *abôve* státement   UW
17. That *fûnny* hát   Aj
18. A *scênic* dríve   Aj
19. Those *châttering.* gírls   V
20. His *glâss* éye   N

EXERCISE 16–11

1. <u>pink</u>	1		6. <u>tall</u>	4
2. <u>dark</u>	4		7. <u>green</u>	1
3. <u>afraid</u>	4		8. <u>dewy</u>	1
4. <u>asleep</u>	4		9. <u>dirty</u>	4
5. <u>alive</u>	4		10. <u>hostile</u>	4

EXERCISE 16–12

1. alone   UW
2. there   UW
3. black and smooth   Aj, Aj
4. today   UW
5. homeward   Av
6. speaking   V
7. grim   Aj
8. abroad   UW
9. particularly   Av
10. ajar   UW

EXERCISE 16–13

(Word-group adjectivals are set in regular type; words they modify are set in italics.)

1. *day* <u>to remember</u>
2. *chap* <u>sitting in that cubicle</u>
3. *size* <u>I ordered</u>
4. *drugstore* <u>on the corner</u>
5. *week* <u>when I was housecleaning</u>
6. *girl* <u>spoiled by her mother</u>
7. *time* <u>convenient to yourself</u>
8. *head* <u>of this club</u>
9. *book* <u>I lent you</u>
10. *sight* <u>to behold</u>

EXERCISE 16–14

1. <u>sweet</u>
2. <u>desirable</u>
3. <u>exciting</u>
4. <u>interested</u>
5. <u>concerned</u>

EXERCISE 16–15

recently	2, 4	
everywhere	4	[Possibly, position **1**
gradually	2, 3, 4	for all three]

EXERCISE 16–16

1. definite time
2. frequency
3. 4

EXERCISE 16–17

1. loud	4	Aj
2. Indeed	1	UW
3. madly	5	Av
4. certainly	2	Av
5. singing	4	V
6. frequently	2	Av
7. below	4	UW
8. inside	5	UW
9. eventually	3	Av
10. usually	2	Av
11. around	4	UW
12. here	5	UW
13. still	4	UW
14. already	3	UW
15. rapidly	4	Av
16. seldom	3	UW
17. Meanwhile	1	UW
18. also	4	UW
19. Saturday	4	N
20. everywhere	4	UW

EXERCISE 16–18

1. 4	5. 1	9. 1
2. 1	6. 4	10. 4
3. 3	7. 1	11. 5
4. 5	8. 1	

EXERCISE 16–19

1. N-al	8. N-al	15. N-al
2. Aj-al	9. V-al	16. Av-al
3. Av-al	10. Aj-al	17. Av-al
4. Av-al	11. N-al	18. Av-al
5. N-al	12. Av-al	19. Av-al
6. Av-al	13. Av-al	20. N-al or Aj-al
7. Aj-al	14. Aj-al	

EXERCISE 16–20

1. N	7. Av	13. Aj
2. V	8. N	14. N
3. N	9. N	15. UW
4. N	10. Aj	
5. UW	11. V	
6. UW	12. UW	

EXERCISE 16–21

1. VAC
2. V + A
3. VAC
4. V + A
5. VAC

6. VAC
7. VAC
8. V + A
9. VAC
10. VAC

EXERCISE 16–22

1. VAC + O
2. V + PP
3. VAC + O
4. V + PP
5. VAC + O
6. V + PP

EXERCISE 16–23

1. V + PP
2. VAC + O
3. VAC + O
4. V + PP
5. VAC + O
6. V + PP

EXERCISE 16–24

1. VAC + O
2. The pasture in which the horse ran. V + PP
3. VAC + O
4. The moonlight in which the teacher stood drinking. V + PP
5. VAC + O
6. Ambiguous.
    a. VAC + O Looked over = examined.
    b. Her bare shoulder over which Keith looked. V + PP
7. The dean on whom we prevailed. V + PP
8. VAC + O
9. The chair over which he stepped. V + PP
10. VAC + O

EXERCISE 16–25

1. A, B, C
2. A, B, C
3. A, B, C
4. A, B, C
5. A, B, C

6. A, B, C
7. A, B, C
8. A, B, C
9. A, B, C
10. A, B, C

EXERCISE 16–26

1. On whom did she look down?
2. With whom did McBride make off?
3. With whom did we make up?
4. With whom won't they put up?
5. On whom should we look in?

[The other form of these questions, e.g., "Whom did she look down òn," also suggests that the words in question, *on* and *with,* are prepositions because these words have weak or third stress, and this stress is characteristic of prepositions, not of the adverbials of VAC's.]

EXERCISE 17–1

1. His laughter was loud.
2. The jar is filled with dates.
3. McPherson was a man.
4. The two strolled.
5. The constable laughed.
6. We heard the clank.
7. The squirrel scolded the blue jays.
8. The contract had paragraphs of fine print.
9. The searchers found the car.
10. Claribel jumped.

EXERCISE 17–2

1. motorcycle
2. sputtered
3. motorcycle
4. stopped
5. stopped
6. nice
7. often
8. stopped
9. fellow
10. whip

EXERCISE 17–3

1. I knew how to swim, luckily.
2. We climbed in the back window, since the door was closed.
3. The contract is, in fact, invalid.
4. We resumed the normal household routine, the guests having departed.
5. You should be provided with a fly, to keep dry in a tent.
6. He was lucky, considering the circumstances, to escape alive.
7. I will find her, wherever she is.

EXERCISE 17–4

      R
1. Apparently
      R   R
2. The iron lung, apparently,
      F
3. malfunctioning, apparently.
      R
4. Before frying the trout,
      R   R
5. He spends his money, most of the time,
   R-F-S
6. To be sure,
      R   R
7. The orchestra, to be sure,
      F-R
8. not the best in the world,
      R
9. Unfortunately,
      F
10. He did not keep up his grades,

EXERCISE 17–5

1. _____
2. happily
3. _____
4. to tell the truth
5. hopefully
6. _____

7. honestly

8. _____

9. frankly

10. _____

EXERCISE 17–6

1. a narrow village street
2. this large college dormitory
3. those tall sophomore players
4. that photogenic girl swimmer
5. this enthusiastic senior counselor
6. George's blue wool necktie
7. her old leather shoes
8. his large hardwood desk
9. these cheap ballpoint pens
10. my portable student typewriter

EXERCISE 17–7

1. a. An arms factory that is small
   b. A factory for small arms
2. a. That stuff for greasy kids
   b. That kid stuff which is greasy
3. a. The service for basic books
   b. The book service that is basic
4. a. A language teacher who is foreign
   b. A teacher of a foreign language
5. a. A car enthusiast who is old
   b. An enthusiast about old cars

EXERCISE 17–8

1. Half your new cement blocks
2. All the long copper wires
3. Both her lovely engágement rìngs
4. All those fresh prairie flowers
5. Both my recalcitrant baby coons

EXERCISE 17–9

1. a. A girl's bicycle that is old
   b. A bicycle for an old girl
2. a. The congress of world women
   b. The women's congress of the world
3. a. A woman's fur coat that is nice
   b. A fur coat of a nice woman
4. a. A garment of a large woman
   b. A woman's garment that is large
5. a. A dictionary for advanced learners
   b. An advanced dictionary for learners

EXERCISE 17–10

    IVb   II   I
1. Another huge glass ornament
    IVb   II
2. Each happy fárm dùck
    IVb II   I
3. Some long winter vacations

V IVa   II   I
4. All our friendly neighborhood dogs
    IVb   II   I
5. Either short cotton dress
    IVb   I
6. Enough college friends
    V   IVa   II
7. Both my studious roommates
    IVb   II   I
8. No cold cheese sandwich
    IVb   I
9. Much evening enjoyment
    IVb   II
10. Neither tired económics stùdent

EXERCISE 17–11

IVa III   III
1. The last three pickles
IVa III
2. His every wish
III   II   I
3. Many fine university seniors
IVb   III   II
4. Some other bad néwspaper repòrts
IVb   III   II
5. Much more white sand

IVa   III   II
6. Those same hungry ants
    V   IVa III   II
7. Both those two aimless fellows
    IVb   III   II
8. Any such childish pranks
    IVa   III
9. Harry's few acquaintances
    IVb   III   II
10. What other foolish ideas

EXERCISE 17–12

III   II   I
1. Several pink summer flowers
    V   IVa II   I
2. Both his old garden hoes
    V   IVa   III   II
3. All these three terminal junctures

IVb   II
4. Another bad examinátion schèdule
IVa III   II   I
5. My two pretty silk dresses

EXERCISE 17–13

IVb   II
1. Any large delívery trùck
    IVb   II
    Any large trúck delìvery
    IVa   II   I
2. That heavy steel construction
    IVa   II
    That heavy constrúction stèel
    IVb   II
3. Some excellent párts fàctory
    IVb   II
    Some excellent fáctory pàrts

IVa   III   II   I
4. The student's long summer vacation
    IVa   III   II
    The student's long vacátion sùmmer
    IVa III   II
5. Her first good hóuse dòg
    IVa III   II
    Her first good dóg hòuse

EXERCISE 17–14

VI   V IVa
1. Especially all our guests
    VI   IVa   II
2. Particularly her spotted kitten

    VI IVa II
3. Even the empty box
    VI IVb   II
4. Just some white athlétic sòcks
    VI III II
5. Only ten short minutes

EXERCISE 17–15

1. 8
2. 3
3. 11
4. 9
5. 7
6. 2
7. 10
8. 6
9. 10
10. 5
11. 6
12. 1
13. 4

EXERCISE 17–16

1. scarlet ... exotic

2. expensive

3. stalwart ... proud

4. new ... glossy

5. complicated

EXERCISE 17–17

1. The *paragraph* abóve → is too lóng.

2. The *students* hére → are a cóurteous group.

3. This *matter* toó → must be discússed.

4. The *party* yésterday → had a large atténdance.

5. The *weather* outsíde → is fóul.

EXERCISE 17–18

1. My older bróther →
2. The discússion →
3. Her fiancé →
4. The rábbits →
5. The mémbers →

EXERCISE 17–19

1. that time

2. this morning

3. the next time

4. last fall

5. the third hour

EXERCISE 17–20

1. of the voters   **6**
2. licking his ice-cream cone   **7**
3. to eat   **9**
4. with the white trim   **6**

5. urged on by the crowd	8	9. of the garage	6
6. to do	9	10. tugging at the rope	7
7. gliding across the bay	7	11. living	7
8. covered with mud	8	12. obtained	8

EXERCISE 17–21

1. whom he studied with	OP
2. who performed the operation	SV
3. I ordered	∅
4. that Jack used	DO
5. whose mother is president of the PTA	Md
6. which had long been our meeting place	SV
7. that her mother was	SC
8. who immediately won our hearts	SV
9. who helps me	SV
10. whom I met at the play	DO

EXERCISE 17–22

1. The blouse that she preferred was made of sea island cotton.　　R
　　　　　　　3　　　1
2. She wore an old blue blóuse ↓ which has always been her favorite.　　NR
　　　3　　2
3. The hóuse → which he had long admired was built of bricks.　　NR
4. The house that he built was of steel.　　R
　　3　2
5. Jáne → who is fond of dictionaries bought the new *Webster's Third*.　　NR
6. The man whom I marry must have curly hair.　　R
7. I'll take a man who respects me.　　R
8. The car I want is an MG.　　R
9. The student whose purse he returned offered Dick a generous reward.　　R
　　　　　　　　　3　　　　1
10. Thomas bought a silk, red-and-gray nécktie ↓ which his roommate admired.　　NR

EXERCISE 17–23

1. why she deserted him	why
2. where we camp	where
3. after he enlisted	after
4. when he comes in	when
5. where I lost it	where

EXERCISE 17–24

(Relatives are set in regular type; subordinating conjunctions are set in italics)

1. *that*

2. that   **DO**
3. *that*
4. *that*
5. that   **SV**

EXERCISE 17–25

1. when
2. where
3. after
4. before
5. why

EXERCISE 17–26

1. the debating club

2. a graduate in journalism

3. offspring of registered parents

4. A Republican from Vodka Valley

5. a sluggish, slowly winding stream

EXERCISE 17–27

   3   1
1. Hámlet ↓ *a play by Shakespeare*   NR
2. *Hamlet*   R
3. *Keith*   R
   3   2
4. Kéith → *my oldest brother*   NR
5. *Shelley*   R
6. *Severn*   R
7. *The Conqueror*   R
   3   2
8. Býron → *a fiery, Romantic poet*   NR

EXERCISE 17–28

1. angrily	**M**	11. happily	**M**
2. often	**F**	12. anywhere	**P**
3. rarely	**F**	13. cautiously	**M**
carelessly	**M**	sidewise	**P, M**
4. fearfully	**M**	14. aloud	**M**
5. long	**D**	15. timidly	**M**
6. ahead	**P**	16. nights	**DT**
7. even	**O**	17. sleeping	**DT**
8. always	**F**	18. seated	**M**
there	**P**	19. cleaner	**M**
9. inside	**P**	20. prepared	**M**
10. still	**O**		

    You may have noticed how hard it is in some cases to fit an adverbial into a semantic pigeonhole. For example, do *ahead* (6) and *sidewise* (13) show place, or is it direction? Does *sleeping* (17) indicate time or manner or something else? Are *seated* (18) and *prepared* (20) really adverbials of manner; do they seem to belong in the same class with *angrily* and *carelessly?* Such difficulties often occur with semantic classifications.

EXERCISE 17-29

1. Amb
2. N V
3. V V
4. Amb
5. Amb

6. V
7. V V
8. N
9. Amb
10. V V

EXERCISE 17-30

1. ...this Friday
2. ...the following day
3. ...the whole way

4. ...a little while
5. ...another time

EXERCISE 17-31

1. D Aux
2. D SCj
3. SCj P

4. SCj Aux
5. Q SCj

EXERCISE 17-32

1. C
2. Md
3. C
4. Md
5. C

6. C
7. C
8. C
9. Md
10. C

EXERCISE 17-33

1. CAv
2. NP
3. CAv
4. NP
5. PpP
6. CAv
7. PpP
8. CAv

9. NP NP
10. CAv
11. NP
12. CAv
13. NP
14. CAv
15. CAv

EXERCISE 17-34

1. DO
2. AM
3. DO

4. AM
5. AM

EXERCISE 17-35

1. VM
2. VM
3. VM or NM
4. NM
5. VM

6. VM
7. VM or NM
8. NM
9. VM
10. VM or NM

EXERCISE 17-36

1. 1
2. 4
3. 2
4. 6
5. 3

6. 5
7. 3
8. 1
9. 2
10. 5

EXERCISE 17–37

1. Nom	9. Aj
2. Av	10. Nom
3. Aj	11. Aj
4. Aj	12. Av
5. Av	13. Aj
6. Aj	14. Nom
7. Aj	15. Aj
8. Aj	

EXERCISE 18–1

1. In fact, | both tires were flat.

2. When the game is over, | let's meet for a bite to eat.

3. I'll give you a hand, | certainly.

4. To attract birds, | one must provide shelter and food.

5. Smiling slightly, | she gently rebuked him.

EXERCISE 18–2

1. The tulips in the flower bed | drooped and died.

2. The striped Dutch tulips | were gorgeous.

3. They | soon had the boat in the water.

4. The lapping of the waves upon the shore | lulled them to sleep.

5. The wine steward | uncorked the bottle with a flourish.

EXERCISE 18–3

1. Indeed, | your first bullfight | may not delight you.

2. Smoking a briar pipe, | Thurston | remained pensive.

3. If I weren't afraid, | I | would pet him.

4. We | will build a float tomorrow, | notwithstanding their objections.

5. At long last, | the letter of acceptance | arrived.

EXERCISE 18–4

1. When | Hubert plays his guitar

2. Unless | you bring a bottle opener

3. Since | the paddle is broken

4. If | the motor begins to cough

5. Once | this rain is over

EXERCISE 18–5

1. ... who | was late for dinner.

2. ... that | inspired him.

3. ... which | cost too much.

4. ... which | was chasing a rabbit.

5. ... that caused my spine to tingle.

EXERCISE 18–6

1. under | the fence

2. from | the greenhouse

3. between | the blue flowers

4. across | the wide, sluggish river

5. to | the flower-starred meadow

EXERCISE 18–7

1. to | lessen the tension

2. to | depend on that rope

3. to | repair the parachute

4. to | haul in the sail

5. to | avoid the black flies

EXERCISE 18–8

1. The | boy | on the corner | who sells papers

2. A | small | ragged | boy

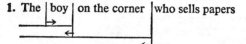

3. A | small | boy | on the corner | who sells papers

4. The | rabbits | in the nest that was hidden

5. The | rabbits | in the nest | that were hidden

6. The | driver | of the bus | who was tired

7. The | driver | of the bus that was late

8. The | bottle | on the table | there

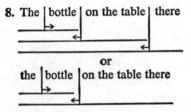

or

the | bottle | on the table there

EXERCISE 18-9

1. ...reluctantly | came | to his mother | when he heard the whistle.

2. ...never | swam | in cold water | after a heavy meal.

3. ...at once | ran | to the coach | upon seeing the hand signal.

4. ...often | walked | to the pool | in his bathing suit.

5. ...eagerly | grabbed | at the gunwale | to get a short rest.

6. ...quickly | pushed | the boat | into the water.

7. ...carefully | fired | a shot | at the target.

EXERCISE 18-10

1. ...often | had come | to practice | before the appointed time.

2. ...drove | his car | rapidly | to the doctor's office.

3. ...should | not | have | anchored | the boat | so close to the shore.

4. ...quickly | made | her way | to the post office.

5. ...became | a captain | in the spring | when promotions were announced.

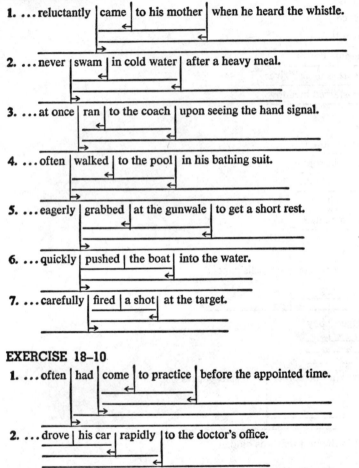

or

6. ... became | a captain | in the spring when promotions were announced.

EXERCISE 18–11

1. If | everyone | is | ready, | we | can | begin | to | load | the | car.

2. Balancing | on | the | edge | of | the | board, | he | poised | for | the | dive.

3. All | of | the | members | have | already | paid | their | dues.

4. In | those | exciting | pages, | we | followed | the | adventures | of | the | swimmer | who | battled | the | waves.

5. After | unloading | the | supplies, | we | hoisted | the | canoe | on | our | shoulders | for | the | long | portage.

EXERCISE 18–12

1. Your | food | is | exceedingly | good.

2. The | salesman | from | Skunk Hollow | is | here.

3. My | oldest | sister | is | the | doctor | in | residence.

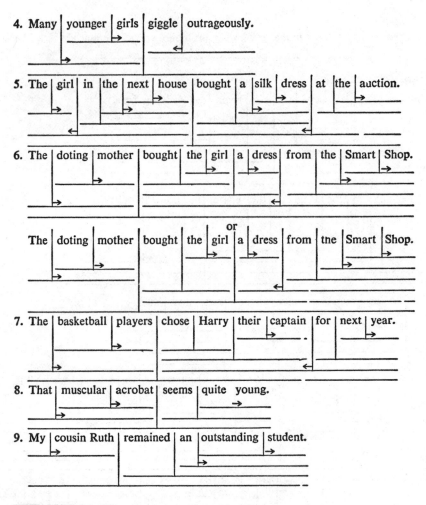

4. Many | younger | girls | giggle | outrageously.

5. The | girl | in | the | next | house | bought | a | silk | dress | at | the | auction.

6. The | doting | mother | bought | the | girl | a | dress | from | the | Smart | Shop.

or

The | doting | mother | bought | the | girl | a | dress | from | tne | Smart | Shop.

7. The | basketball | players | chose | Harry | their | captain | for | next | year.

8. That | muscular | acrobat | seems | quite | young.

9. My | cousin Ruth | remained | an | outstanding | student.

EXERCISE 18–13

1. and
personal pronouns
2. yet
adverbs
3. or
nominal clauses
4. for
sentences
5. not
prepositional phrases

6. so
sentences
7. but
verb phrases
8. nor
sentences
9. or
infinitives
10. and
present participles   verbs

EXERCISE 18–14

1. Either...or
sentences
2. both...and
prepositional phrases

3. neither...nor
noun phrases
4. not only...but
adjectives

5. not ... but

   noun phrases

6. whether ... or

   infinitives

EXERCISE 18–15

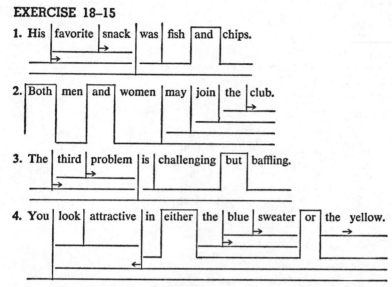

1. His | favorite | snack | was | fish | and | chips.

2. Both | men | and | women | may | join | the | club.

3. The | third | problem | is | challenging | but | baffling.

4. You | look | attractive | in | either | the | blue | sweater | or | the | yellow.

In sentences 3 and 4 above, modifiers like *challenging, baffling,* and *attractive* could be shown by an arrow looping over and to the left.

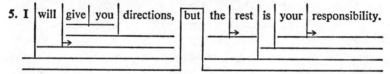

5. I | will | give | you | directions, | but | the | rest | is | your | responsibility.

EXERCISE 19–1

1. Do	6. CAj	11. CAj
2. CAj	7. DO	12. Av-al
3. CAj	8. CAj	13. CAj
4. CAj	9. Av-al	14. CAj
5. DO	10. CAj	15. CAj

EXERCISE 19–2

1. that women are poor drivers.

2. that Mink had been cheating

3. that water runs only downhill

4. that leaked badly

5. that the stars influence our lives

6. that the stars influence our lives.

EXERCISE 19–3

1. to buy the whole lot

2. to raise money for the needy

3. to love

4. to register late
5. to watch
6. to win
7. to practice daily
8. to admire
9. to stay away from the telephone
10. to live within her budget

EXERCISE 19-4

1. to
2. ing
3. both
4. to
5. -ing
6. both
7. to
8. -ing
9. both
10. both
11. to
12. -ing
13. both
14. -ing

EXERCISE 19-5

1. were
2. were
3. be
4. stand
5. be
6. write
7. were
8. be
9. were
10. answer

EXERCISE 19-6

1. count
2. mass
3. mass
4. mass
5. count
6. mass
7. count
8. mass
9. mass
10. count

EXERCISE 19-7

1. count proper
2. mass count
3. count proper
4. mass mass
5. proper count
6. mass mass
7. count count
8. mass count
9. proper count
10. proper proper

EXERCISE 19-8

1. There is a rabbit in your garden.
2. There were some squirrels cracking nuts.
3. There was a moon craft pictured by *Life*.
4. There was some boob chosen commissioner.
5. There have been five men working on the rules.

EXERCISE 19-9

1. Thĕre   1
2. Thêre   2
3. Thĕre   1
4. thére   2
5. Thĕre   1

EXERCISE 19-10

1. that the tree fell in that direction
2. that the road might be impassable
3. to see the difference
4. whether she wears the green or the yellow suit
5. that you write a tactful letter.

EXERCISE 19-11

1. to revise all her papers
2. to set out in this storm
3. that we postpone the game
4. to deny their petition
5. his leaving so suddenly

EXERCISE 19-12

1. Exp
2. Imp
3. Exp
4. Imp
5. Imp

EXERCISE 19-13

1. 1
2. 2
3. 2

4. 3
5. 2
6. 4

Index